40°   30°   20°   10°   0°

enland

ICELAND

60°

NORTH ATLANTIC OCEAN

UNITED KINGDOM

Belfast

IRELAND

Queenstown

London

Southampton

50

Cherbourg

FRANCE

PORTUGAL   SPAIN   40

Azores

"UNSINKABLE"

Daniel Allen Butler

"Unsinkable"

———◆———

The Full Story of RMS *Titanic*

STACKPOLE
BOOKS

Copyright © 1998 by Stackpole Books

Published by
STACKPOLE BOOKS
5067 Ritter Road
Mechanicsburg, PA 17055

Composition by Doric Lay Publishers

Printed in the United States of America

10 9 8 7 6 5 4 3

FIRST EDITION

Library of Congress Cataloging-in-Publication Data

Butler, Daniel Allen.
    Unsinkable : the full story of the RMS Titanic / Daniel Allen
Butler.
        p.   cm.
    Includes bibliographical references and index.
    ISBN 0-8117-1814-X
    1. Titanic (Steamship)   2. Shipwrecks—North Atlantic Ocean.
I. Title.
G530.T6B87   1998
363.12′3′091631—dc21   98-9294
                                                              CIP

To Eleanor,
who believed.

CONTENTS

	INTRODUCTION	*ix*
	PROLOGUE	1
Chapter 1	GENESIS	3
Chapter 2	SAILING DAY	23
Chapter 3	MAIDEN VOYAGE	43
Chapter 4	TEN SECONDS	63
Chapter 5	A SLOW COMPREHENSION	75
Chapter 6	PARTINGS AND FAREWELLS	95
Chapter 7	DESPERATE EXODUS	113
Chapter 8	"SHE'S GONE!"	125
Chapter 9	THE LONELY SEA	139
Chapter 10	WATCHING EIGHT WHITE ROCKETS	159
Chapter 11	HOMECOMING	167
Chapter 12	INQUESTS AND JUDGMENTS	179
Chapter 13	REQUIEM	199
Chapter 14	RESURRECTION	207
Chapter 15	REVELATION	221
	EPILOGUE	231
Appendix I	THE *TITANIC*: FACTS AND FIGURES	237
Appendix II	THE *TITANIC*, THE *CALIFORNIAN*, AND THE CULPABILITY OF CAPTAIN LORD	241
Appendix III	THE CONUNDRUM OF CAPTAIN SMITH	247
	AUTHOR'S NOTE	*253*
	GLOSSARY	*257*
	NOTES	*261*
	BIBLIOGRAPHY	*279*
	INDEX	*285*

INTRODUCTION

IT HAS BEEN SAID THAT "*TITANIC*" IS THE THIRD MOST WIDELY RECOGNIZED word in the world, following "God" and "Coca-cola." True or not, what is undeniable is that even though more than eighty-five years have passed since she went down, the *Titanic* still possesses a compelling power. Rarely does a tale so completely combine the elements of tragedy, drama, morality play, and social statement. Few events sum up their times as decisively as the loss of the *Titanic*, and it is a rare man or woman who is left unmoved in some way, great or small, by her story.

It is a story of heroism, self-sacrifice, and *noblesse-oblige*; nobility and prejudice; class and egalitarianism. No writer of fiction, no matter how gifted, would dare present the story of the *Titanic* as a product of the imagination: it would be too unbelievable. Even as fact it often stretches the bounds of credibility—yet it is all true.

No other disaster in history could have been more easily avoided or was more inevitable, and it is this apparent contradiction that runs through the entire story. A chain of events and decisions that began years before the *Titanic* was even built, and ending only seconds before she struck the iceberg, led to that deadly "convergence of the twain." And had any one of them been altered, the whole disaster, or at least the appalling loss of life, might have been averted. Nevertheless, each event, each decision relentlessly led to the next until the ship lay at the bottom of the ocean and had taken fifteen-hundred lives with it. The *Titanic*'s second officer, Charles Herbert Lightoller, would testify later how a once-in-a-lifetime combination of weather and sea conditions came together to make the iceberg nearly invisible to the ship's lookouts. Yet by the time she struck the berg, the *Titanic* was deep inside an icefield she had received no less than six warnings about that same day—the last one, which was rudely cut off, had come less than an hour before the collision. The ship complied with every safety regulation on the books, but carried enough lifeboats for only half the people on board her that night—only a third of her total capacity—and many of those left the ship only partially filled, due mainly to the belief held by so many passengers, even when the *Titanic* was already sinking, that she was unsinkable. The officers in charge of the lifeboats were instructed that women and children would have first priority in the boats, yet almost half of the survivors would be men.

Nor would the ironies and contradictions end in 1912. Forty-four years later, when the *Andrea Doria*, another ship widely regarded as "unsinkable," was rammed by the *Stockholm* on July 25, 1956, the Swedish ship dealt the Italian liner a mortal blow, breaching two adjacent watertight compartments. The list caused by the inrushing sea led to uncontrollable flooding, and the ship was pulled under as inexorably as the *Titanic* had been. In a grim twist of fate, had the *Andrea Doria*'s watertight construction been similar to the *Titanic*'s, she would have remained afloat, for the *Titanic* had been designed to survive that very type of accident.

Over the years, myths have sprung up around the story of the *Titanic*, myths about the ship itself—how and why she sank, and how certain individuals, classes, and nationalities conducted themselves the night she went down. Disturbingly, in the past decade a strong undercurrent of revisionism has swept into the telling of the tale, as motion pictures, novels, television productions, and even purported histories have adopted adversarial or confrontational attitudes toward entire classes or even the whole of the era in which the *Titanic* existed.

Among many of those who would tell us of the *Titanic*, it has become popular to color the story from unusual or unnatural perspectives. Social historians, engineers, psychologists, political writers, and garden-variety journalists have all attempted new recountings of the tragedy of that cold April night. Often they have much to say that is useful or intriguing, but usually one hears in the background some particular axe being ground—social, political, moral—as they deliver their judgments on the deeds done that night; at times, it seems that the *Titanic* is of almost secondary importance to whatever grievance they are airing.

Just as disturbing is a growing tendency among some of those same writers to present the story of the *Titanic* as if it were a wholly isolated incident that happened in a temporal vacuum, without foreshadowing or consequence, and as though the moral, ethical, and economic structure of society when the disaster occurred was fundamentally the same as that of the present day. To do so not only deceives the reader but distorts the actions and reactions of the builders, crew, and passengers of the *Titanic* by asking them to be held responsible by unreasonable standards.

But the most unsettling are those sensationalized accounts of the sinking, which from their beginnings are little more than thinly disguised witch hunts, hinting at dark conspiracies that range from insurance-fraud schemes by the *Titanic*'s owners to deliberately defective construction by her builders. An excellent example of this type of writing is the article that appeared in a popular scientific publication in late 1994, which reported that the quality of steel used in the *Titanic*'s hull plates did not meet the modern minimum standards for shipbuilding materials—standards not established until 1948—then inferred that the builders had knowingly used an inferior grade of steel.

This sort of revisionism has created the need for a new, straightforward telling of the *Titanic* story, one without the trappings and baggage of latter-day moralizing, social leveling, mythmaking, or finger pointing. The blame for a disaster of such magnitude cannot be placed on any one individual or group. If the builders, owners, and officers of the *Titanic* were complacent and overconfident, they were simply reflecting the attitude of every shipping line in the North Atlantic trade. If the passengers believed that the *Titanic* was indeed unsinkable, it wasn't because they had succumbed to the blandishments of the shipping line's advertisements or the pronouncements of the experts: in the forty years prior to the *Titanic*'s maiden voyage, only four lives had been lost on passenger ships on the North Atlantic trade. Imagine how blithely air travel would be regarded by present-day travelers, who usually seem to express little enough trepidation about the hazards of commercial flying, if the major airlines possessed a similar safety record. Never had any form of transportation been so safe and hazard free.

Fingerpointing apparently comes very easily to the society of the 1990s, and all too often those who take it upon themselves to record history indulge the public's passion for scapegoating. There is something horribly hypocritical about passing judgment on another human being's actions from the comfort and safety of an armchair. Even more hypocritical is making moral pronouncements on others' actions after having judged them by moral standards that they neither knew nor could conceive.

At the same time, there are some individuals, whose actions or inactions that night contributed decisively to the large loss of life, who have suddenly found legions of eloquent supporters determined to remove any onus of blame. Despite the evidence that has withstood eight decades of scrutiny, the verdict of guilt passed by his peers on the captain of the ship that stood still just ten miles from the sinking *Titanic* is for some historians no longer valid, if only for the reason that it was a verdict not reached by present-day, self-appointed experts and judges. Similarly, the owner of the *Titanic*, who managed to find a seat in a lifeboat and was ruined professionally and socially as a result, has lately been perceived as a victim in his own right, and an object of unfair persecution, at least in the eyes of modern critics, who have little or no understanding of the workings of the highly structured society of the Edwardian Era and its rigid standards of conduct.

It must be remembered that the *Titanic* was lost at a time when prejudices were an accepted fact of life, class distinctions were sharply drawn and sharply enforced, "egalitarianism" was just an obscure word in the dictionary, the "white man's burden" was still being shouldered, and the sun of the Pax Britannica hadn't yet set. Whether the beliefs, attitudes, and ideas of this era were ultimately right or wrong is immaterial: what is essential is to remember that at the time they were accepted as valid, and people's actions were determined by that validity.

Some things, though, never change. Courage, selflessness, meeting death with dignity are immutable. So are cowardice, arrogance, and stupidity. These qualities were all present in those aboard the *Titanic* the night she sank. It is true that the story of the *Titanic* contains its share of blunderers, incompetents, cowards, and even a villain or two. But more important is the story of the heroes, the men and women who rose above themselves by word or deed, who deserve to be remembered.

This is that story.

IT WAS A FORCE OF NATURE. FIVE THOUSAND YEARS IT HAD WAITED. IT WAS born in the midst of that vast sheet of ice that one day men would call the Greenland Glacier, when the Celts were migrating across Europe, the Babylonians were building their first cities in Mesopotamia, and tribes of Picts barely out of the Stone Age were populating Britain and Ireland. In three hundred years it had achieved its full stature and begun its slow migration to the arm of the Atlantic Ocean that would become known as the Labrador Sea. It was halfway there when the first Norse adventurers, setting out in their longboats, encountered its siblings. Huge and impregnable they seemed, like vast fortresses of the gods Odin and Thor. The Norsemen called them "mountains of ice"—icebergs.

Undisturbed by human affairs, the iceberg continued its slow procession to the sea, while empires were being created and plagues were sweeping across entire continents. Neither malevolent nor benevolent, it had no way of knowing that a ten-second encounter with another moving object would make it the most notorious iceberg in all the ages of the world.

Sometime in the early weeks of 1912, with a series of deafening cracks, it broke off from its parent glacier and thundered into the cold waters of the Labrador Sea, and began its slow drift southward toward the North Atlantic. . . .

CHAPTER 1

Genesis

There go the ships, and Leviathan. . . .
                                    —Psalm 104:26

IT WAS JUST A FEW MINUTES BEFORE NOON ON MAY 31, 1911. SHE STOOD proud in the bright late-spring sunshine, and she was ready. In a matter of moments she would become the largest moving man-made object in the world. The dignitaries, reporters, and workmen standing on the concrete apron that supported her gazed in awe at the wall of steel before them. Towering cliff-like over their heads for more than ten stories, she stretched away for almost a sixth of a mile. She was a ship unrivaled in size by any that had come before her, the epitome of the shipbuilder's art, the most luxurious ocean liner that would ever be built, destined to become the most famous ocean-going vessel in history. Today was her launching, and she was ready. She was the *Titanic.*

She was conceived, along with her two sisters, on a warm summer evening in 1907. A large Daimler-Benz towncar with elegant *Roi-de-Belge* coachwork stopped at the front entrance of 27 Chelsea Street in the fashionable Belgravia district of London. A gold-and-green liveried chauffeur ushered Mr. and Mrs. Joseph Bruce Ismay into the automobile, then drove them the short distance to Downshire House, Belgrave Square, home of Lord and Lady Pirrie. The Ismays were to be the dinner guests of Lord and Lady Pirrie that evening. Bruce Ismay was the managing director of the White Star Line; Lord Pirrie was the senior partner and chairman of the board of Harland and Wolff, a Belfast shipyard.

After dinner the ladies withdrew, as was the custom of the day, leaving Ismay and Lord Pirrie to their Napoleon and Havanas, the social occasion becoming an impromptu business meeting. A special relationship existed between the two firms these men represented, had done so for nearly forty years, and would continue for another quarter century. But the consequences of this informal meeting would be the high—and low—points of that relationship.[1]

Joseph Bruce Ismay was the eldest son of Thomas H. Ismay, one of the great shipping magnates of the last half of the nineteenth century and himself the son of a small Mayport boatbuilder. Thomas Ismay acquired the flag of the White Star Line in 1867, then promptly reorganized it as the Oceanic Steam Navigation Company, Ltd. The White Star Line was the successor to a line of wooden sailing ships that plied the profitable Australian emigrant trade in the middle of the nineteenth century, but Ismay was a perceptive businessman, and rewarding as the Australian trade was, he was shrewd enough to realize that there were far greater profits to be made on the transatlantic passenger run—the North Atlantic Ferry as it became known—bringing immigrants from the Old World to the New and shuttling wealthier passengers back and forth between the two. Almost immediately the White Star Line created a niche for itself by sailing liners that were fast and, by the standards of the day, luxurious. In 1870 Ismay formed a partnership with William Imrie and created a holding company called Ismay, Imrie and Company, one of the first business transactions of which was to contract with Harland and Wolff of Belfast to build a fleet of iron steamships for the White Star Line. It was to be a happy union.

The origins of Harland and Wolff dated back to the 1840s, when dredging of a deep-water passage in the section of the River Lagan known as the Victoria Channel created Queen's Island in the middle of the channel. Robert Hickson built a shipyard on the new island and began the construction of iron ships there in 1853. Edward J. Harland came to the yard, which was known as Hickson and Company, as a manager in 1854 and bought it outright from Hickson in 1859. Gustav Wolff was a silent partner when he first joined Harland in 1861, but by 1862 the yard was known as Harland and Wolff.

Gustav Wolff was the nephew of Gustavus Schwabe, a Hamburg financier who had relocated to Liverpool some years before. It was Schwabe who had loaned Harland the £5,000 he needed to buy Hickson's shipyard, and because Schwabe also owned a substantial interest in the Bibby Line, a small North Atlantic steamship company, he was in a position to assure himself that his investment in Harland paid off. It is a matter of record that of the more than 1,500 orders for ships on Harland and Wolff's books in the yard's 139-year history, the first three were for ships for the Bibby Line.

While it was true that being the nephew of Gustavus Schwabe had much to do with Harland's decision to take Wolff on as a partner, the yard itself bore the unmistakable stamp of one man only—Edward Harland. His talent for engineering, which bordered on genius, led Harland to make three lasting contributions to shipbuilding. One was purely aesthetic, but the other two were revolutionary. First he eliminated the unnecessary clutter of sailing ships from steamship design: bowsprits, jib booms, figureheads, and their associated rigging. This made the ships cleaner and more distinctive in appearance.

Next he squared off the bilges on the ships' hulls, at once making them more efficient in cutting through the water so that engine size would not need to be increased to increase speed, and also enlarging the carrying capacity of any given hull size. Finally, Harland replaced wooden upper decks with iron, which turned the hull into a giant box girder of immense strength, allowing far larger hulls than ever before to be built.

Harland and Wolff were shipbuilders in the most complete sense. Not only did the yard construct the hull and superstructure of the ships they designed, but the yard also produced the heavy machinery, engines, turbines, boilers, and most of the associated equipment as well. This not only made for a more efficient construction but also eliminated the costs of subcontracting, which saved the owners money. More importantly, it allowed Harland and Wolff to set and maintain the unusually high standards of quality that came to characterize their ships.

The first ship ever built for the White Star Line was the *Oceanic*, launched in 1870. She was constructed almost entirely of iron, as all-steel construction did not become standard in the shipbuilding industry until the mid-1880s. She was a large ship for her day, 420 feet long and displacing just over 3,700 tons. In many ways she would set the standard for all the White Star ships to follow. She lay long and low in the water, sporting a straight stem, a single low funnel, and four gracefully raked hollow cylindrical iron masts. Her staterooms were larger and brighter than any of her contemporaries: they had electric bells for summoning stewards; taps were available for hot and cold running water, fresh or salt, instead of the traditional pitcher and basin; lighting came from adjustable oil lamps instead of guttering candles; and each cabin was provided with steam heat. With her unparalleled accommodations and stunning appearance—"more like an imperial yacht than a passenger liner" wrote one observer—the *Oceanic* established the White Star Line as the arbiter of comfort on the North Atlantic.

Within a year she was joined by three identical sisters—the *Atlantic*, *Baltic*, and *Republic*—and followed a year after that by the slightly larger *Adriatic* and *Celtic* (all White Star ships had names ending in *-ic*). All were built by Harland and Wolff, and soon the Belfast shipyard found itself building ships almost exclusively for the White Star Line. The firm operated under an unusual "cost plus" basis with its client, building the finest ships possible, then billing White Star for the cost of construction plus a fixed percentage of the cost for a profit. By all accounts this was an eminently satisfactory arrangement all around, for it guaranteed the shipyard a reasonable return for its investment in time, labor, and material, while assuring White Star ships built by a yard whose reputation for quality and probity were already becoming legendary. It is a matter of record that each and every bill submitted to the White Star Line by Harland and Wolff was paid on time, without question.[2]

The shipyard at its peak employed more than 14,000 men, from marine architects and draftsmen, interior designers and decorators, electricians and

plumbers, carpenters and woodworkers, to a bewildering assortment of
caulkers, moulders, cloot men, heater boys, holder-ups, and shell platers. To
guarantee a steady supply of workmen trained to Harland and Wolff's exacting standards, an extensive apprenticeship program was introduced.

One of these apprentices came to the drafting department in 1862, a fifteen-year-old lad of Canadian birth and Scottish ancestry. His name was
William James Pirrie, and he was hardworking and ambitious. By the time he
was twenty-seven he had become a partner in the firm, and upon Harland's
death in 1894 he became chairman of the board. A year later he was created
a peer, so it was as Lord Pirrie that he sat down to dinner with Bruce Ismay
that summer night in 1907.[3]

J. Bruce Ismay's father, Thomas, had been able to buy the White Star
Line in 1867 with, curiously enough, the financial assistance of the same
Gustavus Schwabe who had backed Edward Harland. It was a calculated
business move by Ismay to abandon the Australian trade, which was making
the White Star Line a handsome profit, for the North Atlantic run, but Ismay
was perceptive enough to realize, a full quarter century before the passenger
trade on the Atlantic reached its flood tide, the vast money-making potential
that existed there. He was also clever enough to throw out conventional ideas
of shipboard accommodation and passenger comfort. Establishing a new
standard of luxury at sea—or more correctly, establishing a standard of luxury
at sea at all—by introducing the *Oceanic* and her sisters, Ismay not only
gained a head start in a race between British, German, and American shipping lines to build faster, more comfortable ships for the North Atlantic run,
but also laid the foundation for White Star's reputation for an unequaled elegance that the line would not relinquish for another half century.

In 1874 Ismay ordered a pair of new 5000-ton ships from Harland and
Wolff, the *Britannic* and *Germanic*, both capable of 19 knots and crossing
the Atlantic in seven and a half days. In 1889 the *Teutonic* and *Majestic*
appeared, nearly 10,000 tons each, with a designed speed of 20 knots, and
every bit as handsome and sleek as their forebears. But these ships represented a point of departure for the White Star Line. Ismay had been studying
the North Atlantic trade very closely, and came to some very definite conclusions about the line's future in it.

It was at this time that Ismay's son, J. Bruce, entered the family business.
Born in 1862, the younger Ismay was educated at Elstree and Harrow, two of
the most exclusive preparatory schools in England, and had spent a year as a
pupil at the fashionable finishing school of Dinard in Paris, France, though
he never acquired a university degree. After the year-long "world tour" that
was customary for young men of Ismay's station in that day, he went to work
for the White Star Line. His first day was to be an illuminating experience,
highlighting as it did the elder Ismay's character as well as the nature of the
relationship between father and son. Having left his hat and coat in his
father's office, the younger Ismay was startled to hear his father, in a voice
loud enough for everyone in the office to hear, tell a subordinate to instruct

the new office boy to leave his hat and coat elsewhere. Despite his imposing physical appearance—he stood six-feet-four and had grown up to be a handsome young man—and a carefully cultivated air of self assurance, Bruce Ismay found himself never quite able to move out of his father's shadow, to follow comfortably in his footsteps, or to escape his dominating presence altogether. It created a hidden defect in his character that would follow him aboard the *Titanic* and in one night shatter him.[4]

In the meantime, Thomas Ismay had decided that it was becoming too expensive to continue to pursue both unrivaled speed and unparalleled luxury in White Star ships. Instead, since luxury had made White Star's reputation, luxury would continue to be White Star's hallmark. The Line's ships would continue to be nearly as fast as its competitors', but the out-and-out race for the Blue Ribband would be run without the White Star Line.

The quest for the Blue Ribband, the mythical prize that went to the liner making the fastest Atlantic crossing, east- or west-bound, was by the end of the nineteenth century a competition filled with jingoistic overtones, becoming far more than a simple commercial rivalry between shipping firms. When the Cunard Line's *Campania* captured the Blue Ribband with an average speed of nearly 21 knots in 1896, the title had been in British hands for nearly two decades, usually being handed off between White Star and Cunard ships. Despite a slow start, however, two German shipping firms, Hamburg-Amerika and Norddeutscher-Lloyd, began gathering momentum and prospering from the burgeoning immigrant trade, and soon German ships began to establish a style all their own on the North Atlantic. Before long the directors of Norddeutscher-Lloyd decided that their ships should also set the pace. Approaching the Vulkan shipyard of Stettin, East Prussia, they had a simple proposal: "Build us the fastest ship in the world and we'll buy it; anything less and you can keep it."

The result was the mean-looking, imposing *Kaiser Wilhelm der Grosse*. She was the first in a series of German steamships notable not only for interiors where, as John Malcolm Brinnin put it, "the landscapes of Valhalla enscrolled on the walls and ceilings of grand saloons would all but collapse under their own weight," but also for a succession of increasingly more powerful engines that drove them at ever faster speeds across the Atlantic. Almost inevitably the pretensions of the ships' interior appointments were a reflection of the bombast and pomposity of Wilhelmine Germany, and they quickly became easy targets for the wits of the day, who referred to the decors as "hideously" or "divinely" "North German Lloyd," meaning, as one American contemporary put it, "two of everything but the kitchen range, then gilded."[5]

Her ostentation slowed her not a whit, for the *Kaiser Wilhelm der Grosse* romped across the North Atlantic on her maiden voyage in early 1897 at nearly 22 knots. Great Britain was aghast. "In that jubilee year [Queen Victoria's Diamond Jubilee], England was not feeling modest," wrote Humphrey Jordan.

She despised all foreigners without troubling to conceal the fact; she recognized herself, with complete assurance, as a great nation, the head of a mighty empire, the ruler of the seas. But with the jubilee mood still warming her citizens with a fine self-satisfaction in being Britons, England lost, and lost most decisively, the speed record of the Atlantic ferry to a German ship. The *Kaiser Wilhelm der Grosse* was a nasty blow to British shipping; her triumphant appearance on the North Atlantic came at a moment particularly unacceptable to the English public.[6]

Not content in merely besting the British, the Germans embarrassed them next by introducing the *Deutschland*, which belonged to the Hamburg-Amerika Line, and crossing the "Big Pond" at a speed of nearly 23 knots. Long, low, with a sleek four-funneled superstructure, the *Deutschland* looked the very part of the Atlantic greyhound. Yet her preeminence was to last less than a year when the new *Kronprinz Wilhelm* set a new record at 23 1/2 knots; the year after that the *Kaiser Wilhelm II* proved a shade faster still. This Teutonic monopoly on the Blue Ribband was more than Great Britain could stand: a head-to-head showdown was approaching between these upstart Germans and the established maritime power of the British. France and the United States, once serious contenders, were soon left in the wakes of these two great rivals.

A key to German success was that the German shipping lines were being heavily subsidized by their government, a course of action the British government was loathe to follow. Conversely, if the British hoped to overtake their German rivals, it would have to be done with government funding and naval design expertise. It was a race that Thomas Ismay had anticipated and refused to be drawn into.

What Ismay hadn't counted on, though, was the Americans, specifically one Junius Pierpont Morgan, who had the green gleam of money in his eye. Morgan, the greatest of a generation of trust builders, had conceived of a vast freighting monopoly that would control the shipping rates of goods and the fares of passengers being transported from Europe, from the moment they left the Old World until they arrived at their destination in the New. Since the American rail barons, and especially Morgan, had already monopolized U.S. railroads, all that remained for Morgan's dream to become reality was to gain control of the North Atlantic shipping lines.

Morgan's first move in that direction came in 1898, when he acquired the financially troubled Inman Line. The elder Ismay had attempted to form a consortium of British shipowners that would keep Inman out of Morgan's hands, but the attempt fell apart because too few of Ismay's colleagues believed Morgan was serious. It was one of the few failures in Ismay's career, and foreseeing a fierce rate war on the North Atlantic, he rued it until his death in 1899.

He was right. The same year Thomas Ismay died, Morgan purchased a controlling interest in both Hamburg-Amerika and Norddeutscher-Lloyd. A year later he gained either ownership or control of the Leyland Line, the Dominion Line, and the Red Star Line. Setting his sights on both White Star and Cunard, Morgan began cutting fares until his lines were offering a Third Class passage to America for as little as £2.[7]

J. Bruce Ismay, who succeeded to the directorship of the White Star Line after his father's death, was every bit as determined as his father to resist Morgan. Morgan, however, received help from an unexpected ally: Lord Pirrie. Realizing that a rate war would leave White Star with little capital for new ships, and having made Harland and Wolff dependent on White Star almost exclusively for new shipbuilding orders, Pirrie began to pressure the younger Ismay to accept Morgan's offer to buy the line. Thomas Ismay would have told Lord Pirrie to be damned and fought the "Yankee pirate" tooth and nail, but though Bruce Ismay was his father's son in many ways, he didn't possess the innate ruthlessness his father had. Rather than stand up to Pirrie, the younger Ismay eventually caved in, and in 1902 Morgan's shipping combine, now known as International Mercantile Marine (IMM), acquired control of the White Star Line.[8]

Cunard, meanwhile, had skillfully exploited Morgan's attempt to purchase White Star, and was ultimately able to wring considerable concessions from the British government to allow the company to remain in British hands. These included sizable annual operating subsidies, low-interest loans, and Admiralty assistance in designing two new superliners. Undoubtedly, had Ismay held out long enough, he would have gotten similar concessions from the government, but in a contest of wills with Lord Pirrie he was no match for the older man, and so Morgan gained the White Star Line.

The two new liners that Cunard was to build using Admiralty assistance were intended to outstrip any other vessel on the North Atlantic in sheer speed and outdo White Star's best in pure luxury. Launched in 1906, they were the *Lusitania* and the *Mauretania*. Immediately they presented a challenge to the White Star Line that could not go unanswered. Fast, luxurious, and imposing (it would be stretching the truth to call them beautiful), they became the most celebrated ships on the North Atlantic passage—and no one else had anything that even remotely compared to them.[9]

It was this stark reality that Ismay and Lord Pirrie confronted over cigars and brandy in the summer of 1907. Producing a sketch pad, Pirrie began outlining the dimensions and proportions of the ships that would become White Star's response to the *Lusitania* and *Mauretania*. The only concession that White Star would make, both men agreed, was in speed: the big Cunard ships had been designed using Admiralty expertise in the latest high-pressure turbine propulsion systems, an area where Harland and Wolff's experience was limited. As a result, the ships Lord Pirrie's yard would build would be a knot or two slower than Cunard's two speedsters. Beyond that, the *Lusitania* and *Mauretania* would have to be beaten at their own game. If Cunard wanted to build big, White Star would build bigger; if Cunard wanted to offer luxury, then White Star would offer luxury on a scale never before seen on the North Atlantic, nor, as circumstances would have it, would ever be seen again.

It was necessary, Ismay decided, to have three ships, all built to the same design, so that the White Star Line could offer weekly sailing east- and west-bound and maintain a cargo and passenger capacity that would nearly double that of the two Cunard ships. As the two men continued to talk, the doodles and sketches became more defined, and by the end of the evening Pirrie and Ismay had outlined the trio of ships that were to become the *Olympic*, *Titanic*, and *Gigantic*.[10]

In the remarkably short time of six months, ideas from that night became reality, and in December 1907 the keel of the *Olympic* was laid in the newly designated Slip No. 2 at Harland and Wolff. The new liners were so huge that the space previously used to build three hulls was devoted to two of the new giants. The construction of the trio was to be staggered: the *Olympic* being laid down first, followed a few months later by the *Titanic*. Once the *Olympic* was launched the *Gigantic*'s keel would be laid in her old slip. The new liners were projected to be ready to go into service in the spring of 1911, 1912, and 1913 respectively.

Simultaneously with the laying of the *Olympic*'s keel, construction began on an enormous gantry that would surround Slips No. 2 and 3. This huge latticework of timber and steel was to be the largest such gantry ever constructed, standing until 1973, when it was demolished for scrap. The gantry served as a cradle of sorts, allowing workmen access to all parts of the ships as they were being built.[11]

The size of the new ships was astonishing. Built in an age that was impressed by size, the shipping world recited their dimensions from memory: 882 1/2 feet in length, with a beam (width) of 98 feet, the ships stood 175 feet from the keel to the top of their four tall funnels. With a displacement of 45,000 tons, the three new sisters would be in every way the largest ships in the world, over 120 feet longer than the *Lusitania* and *Mauretania*, and more than 12,000 tons heavier. Within their hulls would be nine decks, accommodating 3,300 passengers and crew.

Despite their immense size, the ships were strikingly beautiful. The *Olympic*-class ships were the final expression of the traditional yacht-inspired shapes that had been the hallmark of Harland and Wolff ships for forty years. Elegant, unbroken lines flowed from a gently angled stem to a dignified counter stern, with a carefully proportioned superstructure topped by four gracefully raked, equally spaced funnels imparting a sense of power and balance to the appearance of the ships. Years later retired Harland and Wolff executives would regard the *Olympic* and the *Titanic*—especially the *Titanic*—as the yard's finest shipbuilding achievements.

The liners' aesthetic perfection—slim grace rather than mere ponderous bulk—was evenly matched by their technical sophistication, and the most remarkable and highly touted feature of their design was their watertight construction. Above the keel lay a double bottom, seven feet deep, which ended at the turn of the bilge, but the hull itself was designed to incorporate a carefully thought-out arrangement of watertight partitions. Rather than being built with the usual one or two "collision bulkheads" in the bow, the hull was divided into sixteen watertight compartments of roughly equal length, formed by fifteen watertight bulkheads built laterally across the ship. The arrangement of these bulkheads was far from arbitrary: several ships had been lost in the past half century to collisions with other vessels, most recently the White Star Line's own *Republic* in 1906, and the trio of new liners were designed to avoid a similar fate. These new ships were capable of floating with any two of their sixteen watertight compartments flooded, since a collision with another ship couldn't do worse than open up more than two adjacent compartments. In fact, they could float with any three compartments flooded, and under certain circumstances even float with four compartments open to the sea.

Oddly though, these bulkheads didn't carry up very high into the hull: after calculating how having two adjacent compartments flooded would affect the ships' trim, the designers determined that the first two and last five bulkheads need only go as high as D Deck, while the middle eight carried up only to E Deck, which at midships was barely fifteen feet above the waterline. The designers' research showed that even if one of the vessels were struck amidships and two compartments flooded, the weight of the seawater in the open compartments would be insufficient to pull the ship deep enough that the water would begin to overflow the top of the bulkheads into adjacent compartments.

Connecting these sixteen compartments were a series of immense watertight doors. Normally left open during the ship's operations, they could be rapidly closed by any of three different methods. There was a master switch on the bridge that closed most of the doors automatically, including all the doors on the bottom deck; or there were switches in each compartment so they could be closed individually by tripping a manual switch; and there was a float-triggered mechanism that automatically closed a door if there was six inches or more of water on the deck of the compartment. So comprehensive were these watertight arrangements that in a commemorative issue of the prestigious British journal *Shipbuilder*, published on the occasion of the *Olympic*'s launch, the authors of the piece labeled the ships "practically unsinkable." Before long, and perhaps inevitably, the qualifying adjective was forgotten by the general public.[12]

The *Titanic*'s keel was laid down on March 31, 1909. Designated Hull No. 401 (*Olympic* had been Hull No. 400), she was fully framed by April of the next year.[13] More than 3,000 workmen swarmed over her growing shape, as her shell plating was gradually laid over her frame and her internal structure was completed. There were a total of ten decks, starting with the uppermost, the Boat Deck, then lettered A through G, with two lower decks below that for the ship's machinery, the Orlop and Tank Top decks. A Deck was also called the Promenade Deck, and the two names were used interchangeably. The ships were framed entirely of mild steel, which was also used for the huge shell plates that formed the hull. These plates, some of which measured six feet high and thirty-four feet long, varied from three-quarters to seven-eighths of an inch thick.[14]

Overseeing the immense task of building such a huge ship was the yard's managing director, Thomas Andrews. Born in February 1873, he was the second son in his family, which had a long and honorable reputation in Ulster. His father, also named Thomas, had early on established himself as a local politician of some note, and in 1870 he had the good fortune to marry Eliza Pirrie, Lord Pirrie's daughter. The Thomas Andrews who would build the *Titanic* had from the earliest shown a marked fascination for ships, along with a remarkable gift for things mechanical. Consequently it came as no surprise—least of all to him—when at the age of sixteen he became a premium apprentice at the shipyard of Harland and Wolff.

Andrews's experience as an apprentice was typical of those of young men who were destined for supervisory and management positions at Harland and Wolff. The apprenticeship lasted for five years, beginning with three months in the joiner's shop, followed by a month in the cabinetmaker's shop, then two months actually working on ships. After that came two months in the main store (warehouse), then five months spent with the shipwrights, two in the moulding loft, two with the painters, eight months with the iron shipwrights, six months with the fitters, three with the patternmakers, and eight with the smiths. Andrews completed his term by spending a year and a half in the drawing office.

As in any apprenticeship there was a certain "gofer" element in Andrews's five years, but he was also expected to learn the tasks performed in the various shops, for a bright future had been projected for Andrews. An especially sharp aptitude for mechanical engineering and construction had marked him as a potential senior manager, a direction that was reinforced by the long stint in the drawing office. He learned not only the tasks required to build a ship, but came to know the men who performed them.[15]

Ships at the turn of the century were put together almost entirely with rivets, not welded as they are today, and while the keel and framing of the ships were riveted hydraulically, almost all the riveting of the shell plating was done by hand. Driving rivets was hard work, but the men who built the ships were equal to their task. They were strong, tough men, usually more wiry than big, and because of the physical demands of their job they would brook neither weakness nor slack. Their workday began at 6:00 A.M. and ended at 5:30 P.M. Working in teams of four, they were paid by the number of rivets each team drove each day—and if it rained they didn't work. First the "heater boy" (who could really be of any age) would work up a fire in a coke brazier, using a foot bellows to keep the heat up. Using long tongs he would heat a rivet until it was red hot. (For shell plating the rivets used were squat, nail-like slugs of iron three inches long and an inch thick.) Once a rivet was ready, the heater boy would toss it up to the "catch boy," who caught the rivet in a wooden bowl, then used a pair of tongs to place the rivet into the hole of two overlapping steel plates. The third man, the "holder-up," then placed a heavy hammer over the head of the rivet, while the fourth man, the "basher," working from the opposite side of the plate, would beat the rivet down until it filled the hole.

The shipyard workers were a close-knit bunch, and they extended their respect only to those who could bear up under the hard work. Clearly Andrews could sustain such labor: as his apprenticeship passed, he grew into early manhood, a six-foot, broad-shouldered, and handsome young man. But also his character grew, as he developed that indefinable something called "leadership," and he earned the admiration of the workmen and board members alike, in turn treating all with the dignity they deserved. The reputation for integrity that Andrews carried, were it not so well documented, would be hard to believe. In *Thomas Andrews, Shipbuilder*, author Shan Bullock paints a detailed if somewhat breathless portrait of the man in the Harland and Wolff yard:

> One sees him, big and strong, a paint smeared bowler hat on his crown, grease on his boots and the pockets of his blue jacket stuffed with plans, making his daily round of the Yards, now consulting with his Chief, now conferring with a foreman, now interviewing an owner, now poring over intricate calculations in the Drawing Office, now in company with his warm friend, old school-fellow and co-director Mr. George Cumming of the Engineering department, superintending the hoisting of a boiler by the two hundred ton crane into some newly launched ship by a wharf. Or he runs amok through a gang—to their admiration be it said—found heating their tea-cans before hornblow; or comes upon a party enjoying a stolen smoke below a tunnel shaft and, having spoken his mind forcibly, accepts with a smile the dismayed sentinel's excuse that "'twasn't fair to catch him by coming like that into the tunnel instead of by the way he was expected." Or he kicks a red-hot rivet, which has fallen fifty feet from an upper deck, missing his head by inches, and strides on, laughing at his escape. Or he calls some laggard to stern account, promising him the gate double quick next time without any talk. Or he lends a ready hand to one in difficulty; or just in time he saves another from falling down a hold; or saying that married

men's lives are precious, orders a third back from some dangerous
place and himself takes the risk. Or he runs into the Drawing
Office with a hospital note and a gift of flowers and fruit for the
sick wife of a draughtsman. Or at hornblow he stands by a gangway down which four thousand hungry men, with a ninety foot
drop below them, are rushing for home and supper and with
voice and eye controls them . . . a guard rope breaks . . . another
instant and there may be grim panic on the gangway . . . but his
great voice rings out, "Stand back, men," and he holds them as on
a leash until the rope is made good again.[16]

Andrews clearly loved his work, his men, and most of all his ships.
Sometime in the spring of 1910, Andrews brought his wife Helen to the
shipyard at night. They had been married in June of 1908, and Helen,
knowing full well the extent of her husband's responsibilities and ambitions,
described their life in terms Jane Eyre could have understood: "I am my husband's life as fully as he is mine." That night, as they stood together on the
half-finished decks of the *Titanic*, she was pregnant with their first and only
child, a daughter to be born in 1910, named Elizabeth. The earth at that
time was deep within the tail of Halley's Comet, and the nighttime sky that
spring seemed alive with fire, creating an awesome backdrop as Andrews,
nearly bursting with pride, showed his wife his newest creation.[17]

So the ship grew. By the end of October 1910, the shell plating was completed, and shortly thereafter the launching date was set for May 31, 1911.

That last day of May was to be one of the happiest days in the history of
the White Star Line. Not only was the *Titanic* to be launched, but the
Olympic was scheduled to be handed over to the Line that same afternoon.
The day dawned bright and clear—"a glorious day," as one writer described
it—and the crowds began to gather at the yard as early as 7:30 that morning.
Curiously enough, neither Harland and Wolff nor the White Star Line was
making much of a production out of the launch—certainly not the brass-
banded, bunting-behung, speechifying auspicious occasion the launch of the
Olympic had been the previous October. Of course, the *Olympic* was the first
of the three sisters to be launched, so a certain amount of celebration was to
have been expected. The *Titanic* needed no outside tub-thumping; she created her own. It was known that the *Titanic* was to be "the *Olympic* per-
fected," and that she would carry special amenities and modification that her
sister lacked. The news that J. Pierpont Morgan, chairman of International
Mercantile Marine, would be on hand created its own sensation, so it was
hardly surprising that by noon, nearly 100,000 people had lined the banks of
the River Lagan or clambered onto rooftops and or onto gantries scattered
about the shipyard to watch the *Titanic*'s launch.

Just before noon Lord Pirrie began to receive his guests at the shipyard's
offices on Queen's Road. They included of course Morgan, along with J. Bruce

Ismay, his wife and children, Thomas Andrews, and various local dignitaries. Promptly at noon Pirrie led his entourage down to a specially constructed grandstand before Slip No. 3, directly in front of the *Titanic*'s bow. The great gantry itself was hung with the Union Jack, the Stars and Stripes, and a string of signal flags spelling out "Good Luck." The press quickly filled the grandstand behind the official party. Looming before the grandstand, straight, sharp, almost knifelike, the great bow of the liner stood motionless. The upper hull gleamed from a fresh coat of black paint, and red lead antifoulant glowed below the waterline. Everything was set.

When his guests were seated, Lord Pirrie set out on a quick inspection of the launching gear. With him went Ismay. A picture of them walking together that day still exists. Both men are impeccably dressed in their suits, vests, and watch chains. Ismay has the inevitable bowler perched on his head, and in his right hand he carries a walking stick. Outwardly he is every inch the confident, self assured—one could almost say smug— shipowner, the very picture of the turn-of-the-century businessman. Lord Pirrie, fully a head shorter than Ismay, appears almost jaunty, with a yachting cap set squarely on his head. His gaze is directed just off to his right, as if something has just caught his attention. Both men appear highly pleased, especially Lord Pirrie: on top of everything else happening this day, he and Lady Pirrie are also celebrating their birthdays.

At 12:05 P.M. a red flag was raised at the *Titanic*'s sternpost, a signal for the tugs standing by, as well as any small craft belonging to spectators, to get well clear. At 12:10 a rocket was launched, signaling five minutes to go. The sound of hammers, saws, bellows, pistons, and engines began to fade, along with the noise of the assembled crowd. At 12:14 a second rocket was fired, the signal to launch. The valves on the hydraulic triggers were opened and restraining balks were knocked away, but for some seconds the *Titanic* seemed to remain motionless. Then came the first faint tremor of movement; the workers standing on her decks felt it and raised a cheer. Hearing this the crowds ashore looked closely—then they too could see the great hull beginning to move and their cheers joined in. Gathering momentum, the *Titanic* slid down the ways, her passage eased by twenty-one tons of tallow and soap, and into the water until, just sixty-two seconds after the launch signal was fired, she floated high and proud on the River Lagan.

Interestingly, there was no christening—that is, no bottle of champagne, wine, grape juice, or sea water was broken across the ship's bow as a signal to launch. Harland and Wolff didn't go for that sort of thing. As one of the shipyard's workers put it, "They just builds 'er and shoves 'er in."

The launch was not entirely without mishap, though. When the valves were opened, triggering the hydraulic rams that started the ship moving down the ways, a signal was sent to warn the workers who were in the slip. Some of them were to knock out shoring timbers holding the hull in place; others were there to watch for anything that might foul the ways and halt the launch or damage the hull. One of these men, James Dobbins, was pinned when a mass of shoring timbers were knocked away, crushing his left leg. Though he was rushed to a nearby hospital, the injury was so grave that he died the next day.

A special tender took Lord and Lady Pirrie, the Ismays, and Morgan out to the *Titanic*, where Morgan inspected the section of A Deck that would be devoted to a suite reserved for his exclusive use. They then ferried back to the shore for a luncheon at the yard offices. At 2:30 the entire party traveled down the River Lagan to Lough Swilly, where the *Olympic* lay waiting, having completed her sea trials. She would carry the party back to England, arriving at Liverpool on June 1, and once there she would be thrown open for public inspection.

Meanwhile, a flotilla of tugs had pushed the *Titanic* into the graving dock, where the long process of fitting out would be completed. There was machinery to install, the superstructure to finish, the four tall funnels to be stepped, and, of course, the interior to be completed. All in all the fitting out would take ten months, twice being interrupted by mishaps to the *Olympic*, which required pulling workers off the *Titanic* to make repairs to her sister. Also, experience gained with the *Olympic* would lead to modifications to the *Titanic*, most of them minor, but time consuming nonetheless.[18]

The heart of the ship was her engines. Cunard had drawn heavily on Admiralty experience with turbines in building the *Lusitania* and *Mauretania*, but Harland and Wolff wasn't able to utilize Admiralty design expertise, so the *Titanic* had to rely on "old-fashioned" reciprocating engines to drive her port and starboard wing screws, while her center screw was driven by a revolutionary low-pressure turbine. Though not necessarily as up-to-date as the turbines of the big Cunard liners, the design proved to be a near-perfect compromise, generating very little vibration and being quite economical. The three engines together produced about 55,000-shaft horse-power, sufficient to push the 45,000-ton *Titanic* to a designed top speed of 24 to 25 knots, which was two knots slower than the Cunard ships, but fast enough to make her competitive on the North Atlantic, and there would be compensations for the slower speed.

The two reciprocating engines were the largest such engines ever built. As *Shipbuilder* explained, they were of the four-cylinder, triple-expansion, direct-acting inverted type. Each engine stood nearly forty feet tall, with the largest of its cylinders nearly nine feet in diameter. It could turn at a top speed of eighty revolutions per minute, driving massive three-bladed propellers that were twenty feet in diameter.

Taking advantage of the exhaust venting from the two reciprocating engines, the steam was bled from the fourth cylinder of each engine and ducted to the low-pressure turbine, which drove the center shaft. Spinning at a much higher speed than the reciprocating engines, the turbine created almost no vibration itself, while the other two engines turned in opposite directions, effectively damping each other out and creating one of the smoothest powerplants in operation, which translated a very gentle movement to the structure of the ship. The center turbine did have one drawback: it could not be reversed, meaning that for the ship to go astern or if the other engines were reversed for an emergency stop, the turbine would be useless. However, this was considered to be no more than an inconvenience.

But for the turbine to spin and the reciprocating engines to turn, steam was needed in greater quantities than any ship had ever before generated. To create this giant head of steam, 29 boilers were installed: 25 double-ended (that is, with fireboxes at each end) and 4 single-ended. Each end had three fireboxes, making a total of 162 furnaces that had to be stoked with coal, a shovelful at a time. Nearly 600 tons of coal a day were needed to maintain a speed of 22 knots. Two hundred grimy, sweating stokers, firemen, and trimmers—who would move the coal from the bunkers, shovel it into the fireboxes, and keep the fires burning evenly across the firegrates—would be needed to feed the insatiable maws of these boilers, which stood fully two stories tall, twenty one feet in diameter.[19]

While it may seem that such figures and statistics of equipments and machinery amounts to little more than "rivet counting," they were the subjects of innumerable discourses and arguments over many a pint in the local pub, in the drawing rooms of middle-class families, and over cigars and brandy when the ladies withdrew after dinner in some of the finest houses in Britain and America. In many ways, the steamships of the late-nineteenth and early-twentieth centuries had become the secular equivalent of medieval cathedrals. They were the source of endless pride to the communities and nations that built them, and were just as much an expression of men's hopes and dreams of technical perfection as the great churches had once been of hopes for spiritual purity. And as in the days of the cathedrals, each level of society contributed to the great seagoing structures' creation and upkeep. The upper classes endowed them by paying for their most elaborate and expensive accommodations; the burgeoning middle class supplied their material needs by being purveyors of the foodstuffs and cellars, linens and cutlery, fuel and accouterments that each vessel required in prodigious amounts; and the working classes built them, investing a level of craftsmanship not seen since the raising of Salisbury or Winchester.

Every steamship line had its proponents, every vessel her partisans. Marine engineering had come to be regarded as the pinnacle of human achievement. Yet while the *Titanic* may have been a marine engineer's dream come true, the splendors of such details were lost on the general public. Instead, most people were more interested in the ship's accommodations. Here, as in every other aspect of her design, the results were breathtaking.

In an era when the comings and goings of titled or monied men and women on both sides of the Atlantic were followed by the lower classes with the same devotion that later generations would devote to professional athletes and popular entertainers, the style in which these rich and famous persons traveled had to be on a par with their station in society. Consequently, as far as First Class was concerned, the passenger accommodation was, again in the words of the magazine *Shipbuilder*, "of unrivaled extent and magnificence." The periodical continued:

> The First Class public rooms include the dining saloon, reception room, restaurant, lounge, reading and writing room, smoking room, and the verandah cafes and palm courts. Other novel features are the gymnasium, squash racquet court, Turkish and electric baths, and the swimming bath. Magnificent suites of rooms, and cabins of size and style sufficiently diverse to suit the likes and dislikes of any passengers are provided. There is also a barber shop, a darkroom for photographers, a clothes pressing room, a special dining room for maids and valets, a lending library, a telephone system, and a wireless telegraphy installation. Indeed everything has been done in regard to the furniture and fittings to make the first class accommodation more than equal to that provided by the finest hotels on shore.[20]

The centerpiece of the *Titanic*'s decor was the Grand Staircase. Beginning under an opulent, white-enameled, wrought-iron skylight on A Deck, it descended through four decks to the First Class entrance on D Deck, in an elaborate William and Mary style, surrounded by a Louis XIV balustrade. The landing on D Deck admitted directly to the First Class Dining Saloon. The largest such room yet seen in a ship, it was over 114 feet in length, and ran the full width of the hull. With a 500-seat capacity, it presented a vast sea of spotless white linen tablecloths, glittering crystal, and gleaming silver, with the chairs tastefully decorated in Scottish thistles, English roses, or French fleurs-de-lys.

The First Class Smoking Room, located on the Promenade, or A, Deck, perhaps best served to epitomize the care and expense lavished on the *Titanic*'s interior. A carefully orchestrated assembly of carved mahogany-paneled walls, inset with leaded glass panels and etched-patterned mirrors, enclosed the handsomely linoleumed floor, on which sat massive leather-covered armchairs beside lovingly carved, marble-topped tables. The First Class Smoking Room was an unbreachable bastion of masculinity and affluence carefully blended on a scale never seen before or since. The entire atmosphere immediately evoked images of silk waistcoats, gold watch chains, expensive cigars, and the deep baritones of rail barons, shipping magnates, international publishers, and millionaire businessmen. Nowhere else on the *Titanic* was the incredible investment of time and talent as evident—an investment no shipbuilder could ever afford to make again.

The staterooms and suites for the First Class passengers were, of course, on a scale in keeping with the other First Class amenities. Instead of the usual bunk or berth typical of the transatlantic liner of the day, each state-room had its own full-sized, wrought-iron bedstead, as well as a washstand with hot and cold running water. If a passenger was willing to spend the extra money, whole suites of three, four, or five rooms could be booked, in decors that included several Louis (XIV, XV, and XVI), Empire, Jacobean, Georgian, Queen Anne, Regence (as the British insisted on spelling "Regency" for years), and Old or Modern Dutch. The most exclusive of these suites were located on B Deck, and even featured a private promenade—at a cost of $4,350, that is, nearly £1,000—for a one-way passage: the equivalent of over $80,000 in 1997 dollars. At close to $40 a front foot, the *Titanic's* promenade suites, handsomely half-timbered in a mock-Tudor style, were the most expensive seagoing real estate ever.[21]

The craftsmanship and meticulous construction were carried over fully into Second and Third Classes as well. Indeed, Second Class rooms, public and private, could have been mistaken for First Class on almost any other ship on the North Atlantic, including the Dining Saloon, Smoking Room, and Library. The six decks that comprised Second Class were served by an electric elevator (First Class had three, but in 1911 any elevator was a novelty), and while the Second Class staircase may not have been as grand as that of First Class, it was still an exceedingly handsome structure. In what was certainly a bonus for Second Class, both First and Second Classes shared a common galley, one of the finest in existence afloat or ashore. (There are few four-star restaurants today that could duplicate the menu from First or Second Class for April 14, 1912.)

Third Class was a story unto itself. A great many myths have built up around the flood of immigrants that flowed to the shores of the New World at the end of the nineteenth century and the beginning of the twentieth, aided by a spate of romanticized reporting, photographs, and artwork from the period. All too often these steerage—as Third Class was commonly known—passengers are portrayed as "tired, poor . . . huddled masses," as babushka- and shawl-beclad mothers gripping the hands of small, wide-eyed children, or as young men in ill-fitting clothing clutching their few belongings in loosely tied bundles, all hoping to find their fortunes in such exotic locales as New York, Pittsburgh, or Chicago.

The truth, as with so many subjects of the journalism of that day, was a good deal more mundane. Despite the increasing numbers of central and southern Europeans emigrating to America, the majority of those leaving the Old World for the New were still Anglo-Saxon. Many were Germans, whose Fatherland was undergoing a rapid transformation from an agrarian society to an industrial juggernaut, with all the attendant social dislocations; many others were Britons, often skilled or semiskilled workers, forced to seek employment in America as Britain began her slow decline industrially and economically. To these people a ship was transportation, its sole purpose to take them from Southampton (or Cherbourg or Queenstown) to New York.

Passengers like these were not influenced by Grand Staircases, electric eleva-
tors, swimming baths, or Smoking Rooms. Their interests lay in clean quarters and decent food. In this respect the *Titanic* served them admirably.

Third Class berthing was divided between the fore and after ends of the
ship. Single men and married couples were berthed forward, while single
women and families were accommodated aft. (There was a Puritanical streak
in the White Star Line, apparently peculiar to the company, that did not
allow single men and women to have cabins anywhere near each other.) The
cabins were spacious, spotless, and if a bit austere, by all reports comfortable
enough. The unmarried men or women would share a room with three to
five other passengers of the same sex, while married couples and families had
rooms to themselves.

Third Class accommodations included a large number of permanent
cabins both fore and aft, as well as large sections of berths formed by movable wooden partitions, so that the numbers and sizes of the cabins could be
adjusted to the number of passengers, and the unused space given over to
open common areas. The days of the cramped, dark hold, reeking of
unwashed humanity and bilge, were long since a thing of the past in British
and German liners, but, as in so many other ways, the *Titanic* set new standards. The Third Class galley provided a fare that, though unspectacular,
offered good food and plenty of it; in some cases, especially those from the
more impoverished Irish counties, the steerage passengers ate better aboard
ship than they ever had at home. All in all, it was a good deal more than
most would be expecting when they paid for their passage.[22]

The *Titanic*'s maiden voyage had originally been scheduled for February
1912, but unforeseen events got in the way. On September 20, 1911, the
Olympic had collided with the Royal Navy cruiser HMS *Hawke*, and was
returned to Belfast for repairs. These took six weeks to effect, the workmen
being pulled off the *Titanic* workgangs. In February 1912 the *Olympic* lost a
propeller blade, again necessitating a return to Harland and Wolff, again causing work to be suspended on the *Titanic* for another three weeks. The time
was not wasted, though, since the decision had been made to incorporate a
number of modifications to the *Titanic* based on the in-service experience
with the *Olympic*, and the delays allowed the plans for these modifications to
be drawn up. Most of them were minor: the beds in some First Class cabins
seemed too springy; there should be cigar holders in the WC's; the crew's galley needed an automatic potato peeler, and so on.

One modification, though, was to permanently alter the *Titanic*'s appearance and instantly distinguish her from the *Olympic*: the forward two-fifths
of the Promenade Deck were enclosed by glass and steel windows because
First Class passengers on the *Olympic* had complained about spray thrown up
by the bow in rough or choppy weather being blown across the open deck.
This final modification was completed less than two weeks before the
Titanic's scheduled sailing day of April 10.

On the morning of April 2, 1912, the most magnificent sight Belfast would ever see presented itself as the *Titanic*, drawn by four tugboats, slowly made her way down the Victoria Channel to the Belfast Lough to begin her sea trials. One by one the boilers were lit until twenty had been fired. Just before noon Capt. Edward J. Smith ordered the blue and white signal flag "A" ("I am undergoing sea trials") hoisted from the bridge and three long blasts given from the *Titanic*'s siren. The next several hours were spent making a prolonged series of twists and turns, followed by a succession of runs straight across the Lough and back. The highest speed she was able to reach during these runs was 18 knots, and during one of these runs Captain Smith made a test to see how quickly she could stop. With both engines reversed and the turbine stopped the *Titanic* came to a halt in three minutes, fifteen seconds; the distance was 3,000 feet.

By dusk, both owners and builders seemed satisfied. The *Titanic* returned to Belfast to drop off most of the Harland and Wolff workers who had accompanied the ship on her sea trials. Eight remained on board, including Thomas Andrews, who would make the maiden voyage to assist in solving any technical problems that might come up during the crossing. That night the *Titanic* steamed down the Irish Channel and around the Lizard to Southampton, to begin coaling and provisioning. Sailing day would be April 10.[23]

CHAPTER 2

Sailing Day

*Prepare yourselves according to your fathers' houses, by
your divisions. . . .*

—II Chronicles 35:4

APRIL 10, 1912, DAWNED BRIGHT AND CLEAR, AS DID SO MANY DAYS THAT
spring. The sprawling docks, piers, and quays bustled with the seeming
chaos of a busy seaport. At the White Star Line's Ocean Dock lay the
Titanic, plumes of smoke gently rising from her funnels, her white upperworks gleaming in the sunshine, her enormous hull dwarfing every other
ship in the harbor. All morning long an endless stream of passengers and
crew strode up the gangways and vanished into the bowels of the ship. The
rush of people had begun a little after sunrise as the first of hundreds of firemen, greasers, trimmers, stokers, stewards, stewardesses, deckhands, and gal-
leyhands began to make their way up to the giant ship. Every now and then
a tremendous blast would issue forth from the *Titanic*'s great steam whistles,
rattling windows for miles around, the stentorian tones (the whistles were
pitched at C^3) letting one and all know that this was a sailing day.[1]

A maiden voyage was always cause for excitement in a seafaring town,
even one as seawise as Southampton. Friends and families of passengers and
crew, along with hundreds of sightseers, crowded down to the Ocean Dock.
The Rev. William G. Hurley recalled years later that "on the day it [the
Titanic] sailed, all England was merry in the celebration of a holiday for the
occasion. Flags were flying in the breeze in every city and hamlet. There was
the inevitable speech-making. That gloriously martial air, 'Britannia Rules
the Waves,' was the mighty theme-song of the day."[2]

It is a scene treasured by thousands to this day, as the great ship was
preparing to depart on what would most assuredly be an epic voyage, the
throngs cheering themselves patriotically hoarse, while brass bands played
and overhead flew the Union Jack, inspiring one and all with the greatness of
British maritime accomplishments.

Except it didn't happen that way. Like so many others have done on
other occasions, the Reverend Hurley was recalling those wonderful days

before the Great War "with advantages." Reflecting on the first years of the twentieth century from the perspective of its last, it is stunning to look upon the world of the Edwardian Era, a world that seems so far removed from the present that it is often difficult to believe that it is still a living memory for many. The values, beliefs, motives, the very pace of life seem nearly incomprehensible today. Barry Pitt, in his introduction to John Keegan's *August 1914*, caught the essence of this seeming unreality when he wrote:

> Dimly can be perceived a life which seems to bear no relation to the present one, conducted apparently to a different rhythm, by a different species of being, reacting to a totally different scheme of behavior. Bewhiskered monarchs write stiff family notes to each other before going out to shoot stag or bird, tiara'd queens whisper behind their fans, frock-coated statesmen hurry from capital to capital and debate in solemn enclave (occasionally one is shot), while the tight-collared and cloth-capped masses alternately riot or cheer, fortified the while on ale, wine, or porter, at a penny a pint. Away in a far corner a square of British infantry in blue and scarlet repels cavalry charges or hordes of fanatical natives. Perhaps the most astonishing aspect . . . is that the sun seems to have been shining all the time.[3]

Yet it was not a Golden Age or *Belle Epoque* except for the privileged minority of the upper classes. Class defined the Edwardian world. The method of making the distinctions between the classes varied from country to country—it was decided more by wealth than birth in the United States, just the reverse in Great Britain—but in any society the boundaries were usually quite clearly defined, never more so than when distinguishing between "we" and "they." Usually the classes fell into three categories—working, or lower class; the middle class; and the upper class, or aristocracy. Mobility, especially from the middle to the upper class, was discouraged and restricted, usually by tradition, occasionally by law, although the line between the lower and middle classes blurred occasionally.

It was not an era of unbridled confidence, innocence, comfort, stability, security, or peace, although it has often been portrayed as such. This is not to say that these qualities were not present; they were, but in an ongoing state of flux. People were more confident of their standards, believing in their values, secure in the ideas of progress. But equally present were doubts about the future, created by a complicated system of military alliances coupled with ever-growing expenditures for armaments; protests and demonstrations over appalling working conditions and hours as well as grossly inadequate wages for the working classes; violent confrontations between protesters and police, or strikers and strike-breakers, clashing in street brawls, while anarchists and nihilists carried out a haphazard rash of bombings and assassinations. A new form of hatred and fear manifested itself in bloody confrontations between

British police and the IRA, or Austro-Hungarian authorities and Serbian pan-nationalists, or Russian soldiers and Russian revolutionaries.

Yet it would be deceptive to depict the first decade of the twentieth century as too closely resembling the last, for through all the tension and upheaval, there was a constant note of confidence running though the times. Men and women everywhere, of all social classes, readily acknowledged that problems existed in society, though they might differ on how grave those problems were. But even the anarchist with his bomb believed that the problems had solutions; it was only a matter of how and when they would be found. It was that sense of confidence that made the Edwardian Era unique.

Perhaps most tellingly, these were the years of the music of Richard Strauss and Igor Stravinsky, the philosophy of Friederich Nietzsche and Henri Louis Bergson, the art of Cezanne and Seurat, the writings of Emil Zola and Bertrand Russell—all of them compelling, forceful, and dynamic, almost revolutionary. It was a remarkable expression of art imitating life, the artists and thinkers transforming the external expressions of their disciplines as thoroughly as the external trappings of Western society were being transformed.

This first decade of the twentieth century was the culmination of a hundred years of the most accelerated rate of change in society and technology that mankind had ever known. Between 1812 and 1912, humanity had gone from transportation, communication, production, and manufacturing methods powered by human or animal muscle, augmented by wind and water to a world of steam engines, steamships, and steam-powered machinery. The new century was one of electric lighting and communications (though as yet electricity was common only in the cities, and then only in the middle- and upper-class areas). By 1912 trucks, lorries, and motorcars powered by internal combustion engines were well on their way to supplanting horses as a means of transport.

In less than a century, mankind's rate of travel overland had more than trebled, while at sea it had more than quadrupled. Where in 1812 the best speed a traveler could hope for would be perhaps twenty miles an hour while riding in a horse-drawn coach, a railway passenger in 1912 would routinely reach speeds approaching seventy miles an hour on an express. A trip across the North Atlantic that once took more than a month was now accomplished in a week or less, and with a degree of safety and comfort unimaginable only a few generations before.

The accelerating rate of change was most marked in the last decade. In 1900 there had been fewer than 8,000 automobiles in the entire United States, but by 1910 there were close to a half-million. In 1903 the first flight of a heavier-than-air craft lasted twelve seconds and covered 852 feet; in 1909 Louis Bleriot had flown across the English Channel, a distance of twenty-six miles. The years between 1900 and 1910 had seen the introduction of the phonograph, wireless telegraphy, turbine-powered steamships, the electric light, the original Kodak "brownie" camera, heavier-than-air flying machines, motion pictures—all of them as reliable apparatus rather than mere technical novelties.

The Edwardian world would witness revelations in the physics of Roentgen's X-rays, Marie Curie's radium, and Einstein's $E=mc^2$; in the psychology of Jung, Freud, Pavlov, and Adler; and in medicine, where the secrets of vitamins, genes, and hormones would be unlocked. Science had been transformed from a dalliance for eccentrics into a systematic discipline, becoming the foundation of industry.

At the same time these changes unintentionally began an erosion in the nineteen-centuries-old faith in God as the source of all certainty and stability. The authority and infallibility of the Bible were no longer universally regarded as absolute, and the solid core of religious doctrines and dogmas that had bound Western civilization together was slowly crumbling. The industrial society that created and supported the multitude of innovations also built up new pressures in both prosperity and poverty, raising questions about the validity of the established order that churches could no longer answer convincingly, while growing populations and densely crowded cities created new antagonisms between classes, new problems for industry owners, and new opportunities for radicals and rabble rousers. Far from wallowing in its own decadence, as is all too often depicted, the Edwardian world was dynamic, even exciting, driven by the momentum of centuries of accumulated tensions and energies—industrial, economic, social—that created such contrasts of wealth and poverty, opulence and indigence such as no society had ever known before. It was this era that Mark Twain christened the "Gilded Age."

It was undeniably a time marked by money-grubbing and ostentation on the part of the upper classes, when "excess" and "success" became interchangeable. Just over one percent of the population of Great Britain controlled 67 percent of the nation's money, a proportion that held equally true for the United States. Of the two societies, the more ostentatious were the Americans, more than a handful of whom had accumulated fortunes greater than the world had ever seen. However, it was undeniable that these same Americans were better at making money than at spending it: like most *nouveau riche*, their hallmark was conspicuous consumption, with little discrimination or taste. They literally had more money than they knew what to do with, and the desire of American plutocrats to spend lavishly, coupled with a sense of insecurity due to the very rapidity that most of them had made their fortunes, drove them irresistibly to Europe, and ultimately to London.

It was inevitable that this upstart leisure class should be drawn to the greatest city in the world. Finding themselves among kindred people, these wealthy Americans discovered what they craved—and what America as a nation and the humility of their individual births could not hope to give them: the pomp and grandeur of a 1200-year-old monarchy, with all the stability, nobility, and grace that were its trappings; the company of men and women who carelessly and comfortably wore names and titles that were a part of history; and a society that was relaxed, mature, and secure in its own longevity.

"The Season" of 1911, perhaps the most wonderful in memory, had provided the Americans with the unforgettable splendor of the coronation of King George V and Queen Mary; the first performance in Great Britain of Diagilev's Russian Ballet, led by the legendary Anna Pavlova; long processions of motorcars down Park Lane in the evenings; and endless glittering balls and dinner parties in Belgravia. The stormy passage that summer of the Parliament Bill, which deprived the House of Lords of its veto power over the Commons, added yet another dimension of fascination for the visiting Americans. From Opening Night at the Royal Opera House Covent Gardens, in April, to the Cowes Regatta in July, the numbers of those from across the Atlantic attending threatened to equal or exceed those of their English friends and relatives—the latter the result of a spate of transatlantic marriages that was rapidly approaching epidemic proportions.[4]

The Boat Train that pulled out of Waterloo Station that Wednesday morning was laden with several such Americans. Leaving with traditional British punctuality at exactly 9:30 A.M., the train left behind the fussy Victorian muddle of smoke-streaked buildings, now covered by a new steel and glass roof, that had made Waterloo Station at once a national joke and a national treasure. Within its deep blue broadcloth-upholstered cars with gold-tasseled trim and mahogany woodwork, or in a similar train in France simultaneously bound from Paris to Cherbourg, were more than a dozen men whose total net worth exceeded £300,000,000—men like John J. Astor, Benjamin Guggenheim, Charles M. Hays, or even the occasional woman like Mrs. J. J. Brown of Denver, Colorado, better known as "Molly" Brown.

Perhaps the epitome of the American plutocrat, John Jacob Astor, he of the long, narrow face and aquiline nose above which sat dark, sad eyes, was once described, not unfairly, as "the world's greatest monument to unearned increment." He was the great-grandson of the first John Jacob Astor (the family repeated the name through several generations; the man who would be sailing on the *Titanic* was John Jacob Astor IV), a poor Schwabian who had emigrated to the United States in 1783 and amassed a fortune in the fur trade, in turn investing his money in property in and around New York. By the beginning of the twentieth century, the Astors held title to some of the most expensive real estate in the world, including the Astoria Hotel in New York, as well as some of the most deplorable slums on both sides of the Atlantic. Not surprisingly, since the Astors seemed to conduct their business with an attitude that stopped just short of divine right, this singular state of affairs neither alarmed nor embarrassed the family a whit.

Astor himself was certainly ambitious and, when need be, ruthless. Joseph Choate, one of the family's lawyers, once remarked of him, "He knew what he wanted and how to get it." He was also possessed of a great deal of vanity: during the Spanish-American War he had raised a regiment of volunteers (with himself as colonel of course) and though the unit saw only brief combat, ever afterward Astor enjoyed attending official functions in his uniform, and preferred to be addressed by his rank. Conspicuous consumption was nothing new to Astor: in his mansion at Newport, Astor had an eighteen car garage; and once, to satisfy a whim, he had even driven a locomotive on his private railway that drew a coach filled entirely with millionaires. His attitude toward money was suitably cavalier: he was once heard to remark that "a man who has a million dollars is almost as well off as if he were wealthy."

Yet there was a side to Astor that the public rarely saw. He was a bit of an eccentric, and something of a tinkerer and inventor who was intensely interested in turbines, and he held patents on a bicycle brake, road construction machinery, and a storage battery. He had even written a science fiction novel, *A Journey in Other Worlds*, whose hero, Colonel Bearwarden, was contracted by the Terrestrial Axis Straightening Company to make the Earth's axis perfectly vertical, creating perpetual springtime.

Astor was not invulnerable, though. In 1909 he had divorced his wife of eighteen years, Ava Willing Astor, in order to marry an eighteen-year-old girl, Madeline Force, who was actually younger than Astor's son Vincent. Divorce in the Edwardian era carried with it an almost ineradicable social stigma— something only the lower orders indulged in—and after being viciously cut by all his friends and fellow socialites, Astor decided that it would be best if he and his new bride wintered abroad. It wasn't until late 1911 that they had been married, as it had been nearly impossible to find a clergyman willing to perform the ceremony. To make the whole situation more scandalous, the new Mrs. Astor, who had now been married four months, was at least four months pregnant. The gossipmongers were having a field day with the colonel—the scandal, of course, being over why Astor would divorce his wife to marry Madeline rather than simply making her his mistress—and it seemed doubtful if he would ever regain his former social standing. Now he was returning to New York with his new bride, after spending four months in Egypt and Paris, hoping that some of his former stature could be salvaged.

In contrast, another passenger on board the Boat Train, Benjamin Guggenheim, would never have even considered such a socially hazardous idea as divorcing his wife for another woman. Not that he was any model of conservative respectability—after all, he had just finished an extended stay in Paris with his mistress, Madame Aubert, while Mrs. Guggenheim was in New York—but he knew how the game was played. The sexual hypocrisy of the upper classes in those days was astonishing: affairs and liaisons were almost commonplace, the only condition being that no matter how widespread the knowledge of the affair might be, it must never be publicly admitted, or as Vita Sackville-West put it, "Appearances must be respected, though morals might be neglected."

One of seven sons of Meyer Guggenheim, a Swiss who had moved to America before the Civil War, Benjamin and his brothers ran one of the most closely knit family enterprises in the United States, whose interests ranged from banking and finance to mining and smelting. Benjamin had taken a close interest in smelting, as new industries were demanding more specialized and refined metals than simple iron or steel. By investing heavily, Guggenheim had transformed the American smelting industry, with the result that all the other interests of the family became secondary. Whatever the details of his private life might be, Guggenheim was a gentle, soft-spoken man, whose quiet demeanor and pleasant appearance concealed a will of iron. Though neither harsh nor vindictive, Guggenheim was not a man to be crossed twice.

Neither was Charles Hays, president of the Grand Trunk Railway. By nature, railroadmen—and especially American railroadmen—were a ruthless lot, and to be able to hold his own with the likes of J. P. Morgan, E. H. Harriman, or James J. Hill, one had to have certain jugular instinct. A Canadian by birth, Charles Hays was as determined as any of them, building the Grand Trunk into the dominant railway around the Great Lakes, in the northern Midwest states, and in the Canadian provinces. He was looking to expand into the hotel business and had been studying firsthand management methods in Europe. Now he was returning to his native Canada to launch an entire chain of Grand Trunk–owned hotels.

Rarely do characters—in every sense of the word—like Molly Brown come along. Geoffrey Marcus's description of this remarkable woman is impossible to improve upon—he called her "the wife of the manager of a Leadville gold mine who had 'struck it rich' in 1894 and had thereafter prospered exceedingly. She was a middle-aged matron of Irish extraction, Amazonian proportions, and superabundant vitality." Her one desire in life was to be accepted by the social elite of Denver, Colorado, the descendants of the so-called "Sacred Thirty Six," but her rough-and-ready manner reminded the Denver socialites too much of their own origins, and they cut her mercilessly. (Admittedly, Molly's *faux pas* could be memorable, as in the time she referred to herself as "the Hand-Made of the Lord.") "The newly minted gentlemen had worked with pick and shovel on arrival," commented Richard O'Connor, "and their ladies had bent over their washboards; but all that was crammed into a forgotten attic of the past."[5]

Molly's husband, James Joseph Brown, didn't share his wife's social ambitions, preferring to hold onto his working-class roots; eventually a gulf opened between them and they separated. Molly went east, where she was a hit at Newport, her vitality like a breath of fresh air, and soon she was an accomplished world traveler. After becoming proficient in several foreign languages—although she could revert to basic Anglo-Saxon and "swear like a pit-boss" when provoked—she finally acquired the veneer of culture and civility that the left-behind Denver elite craved, and lacked, so badly. Her decision to return to the United States on the *Titanic* had been made at the last minute, after she had spent the winter in Egypt, part of it in the company of the Astors.

There were many others: Isidor Strauss, former Congressman and advisor to the President of the United States, part owner of Macy's and well-known philanthropist, returning with his wife Ida from a holiday on the French Riviera; George Widener, son of P. A. B. Widener, the tramway magnate from Philadelphia; and his son Harry, who already had a reputation as one of the eminent bibliophiles of the day, having just purchased from Sotheby's a very rare copy of Bacon's *Essaies*, remarking as he slipped it in his coat pocket, "If I am shipwrecked it will go down with me."

Philadelphia society was further represented by John B. Thayer, president of the Pennsylvania Railroad, traveling with his wife and teenage son Jack. Another Philadelphia family preparing to cross on the *Titanic* was that of steel magnate Arthur Ryerson, his wife Emily, and their three youngest children, Susan, Emily and John. They had embarked earlier that month on what was meant to be a rather lengthy tour of Europe; their luggage amounted to sixteen trunks, each carefully packed by Mrs. Ryerson's maid, Victorine, who had also come along. Their passage back to the States had been entirely unplanned, brought about because their eldest son, Arthur Jr., had been killed in an automobile accident near Philadelphia a few days previously. Mr. Ryerson cut their European trip short and booked passage for his family on the first available steamer to New York, which happened to be the *Titanic*.[6]

Col. Washington Augustus Roebling was also returning home, but this was at the end of what could best be described as a working vacation. Roebling had served in the U.S. Army Corps of Engineers during the American Civil War and was now the president and director of John A. Roebling's Sons, the engineering and steel firm founded by his father. Roebling was known the world over as the man who had completed the construction of the Brooklyn Bridge, a project begun by his father, and he had been in Europe studying the latest engineering developments in suspension bridge construction.

The American theater was represented by producer Henry B. Harris, who, along with his wife Renee, had been in England hoping to find new British productions that he could introduce on Broadway to maintain his string of successes. Harris owned a half dozen theaters in New York, Chicago, and Philadelphia, as well as part-interest in a number of others, and he was a brilliant theatrical agent as well. Over the years Harris had managed such international stars as Lily Langtree, Peter Dailey, and Robert Edeson, and he was always unusually mindful of the image his actors and actresses presented to the American public: he had been one of the handful of producers who had struggled to lift the American theater out of the pit of disrepute into which actor John Wilkes Booth had plunged it when he shot President Abraham Lincoln.

One of the better known Americans on board the Boat Train that morning was Maj. Archibald Butt, military aide to President William Howard Taft. A born adventurer, Butt in his time had been a soldier, a news correspondent, a novelist, and a diplomat. He possessed an easy charm and graciousness, equally at home with prince and peasant. An elderly black who worked at the White House once remarked of him, "There goes the man that's the highest with the mighty and the lowest with the lowly of any man in this city!"[7]

The Major was returning to Washington after an extended visit to Italy that had been ostensibly a diplomatic mission to the Vatican for the President, but had actually been a convalescence. For years Major Butt had been a close friend and confidant of Theodore Roosevelt, and had become close friends with William Taft while Taft had been Roosevelt's vice president. Once close political allies if not actually friends, Roosevelt and Taft began feuding almost as soon as Roosevelt left the presidency and Taft filled it. What this did to Archie Butt was put him in between the two men, and he found it nearly impossible to maintain his loyalty to Taft, his commander-in-chief, without turning his back on all the years he had spent as Roosevelt's friend. The situation had grown worse as Taft and Roosevelt, who had come to bitterly dislike each other, began vying for the Republican nomination for the Presidency in the upcoming election in November. In the end the strain had proven more than Butt could take, and he had asked Taft for a transfer to another posting. Taft instead gave him the assignment to the Vatican, hoping that the trouble with Roosevelt would die down in Butt's absence, and his jangled nerves would recover. Apparently Butt was unable to completely shake off his depression: in a last letter posted to his sister-in-law before the *Titanic* sailed, he wrote, "If the old ship goes down, you'll find my affairs in shipshape condition."

Accompanying Major Butt was his close friend Frank Millet. Like Butt, Millet had been many things in his time: one-time drummer-boy in the American Civil War and war correspondent in the Spanish-American War and several of the innumerable Russo-Turkish wars. His world travels had enabled him to become a well-known author and raconteur, but Millet was best known for his paintings. Historical subjects were his favorites, and copies of his work, such as "Wandering Thoughts," "At the Inn," or "Between Two Fires," hung in homes on both sides of the Atlantic. Despite his American birth, Millet now lived in the Cotswolds, by all accounts a happy man.

There was one other American officer aboard the Boat Train, Col. Archibald Gracie. An amateur military historian of private means, he had just published a book on one of the lesser known campaigns of the Civil War, called *The Truth About Chickamauga*. Although it was the sort of book that only another military historian could love, filled with seemingly endless accounts of troop movements and dispositions, and the comings and goings of countless officers and men, it had entailed a tremendous amount of detective work, and now Colonel Gracie was taking a well-earned rest.

Not all of the famous passengers aboard the Boat Train were Americans. There were several Englishmen of note as well, among them Henry Forbes

Julian, one of the leading metallurgists of the day, who had created new processes for recovering precious metals from ores, and Christopher Head, former mayor of Chelsea and currently a member of Lloyd's of London. But there was one among them who, at the height of his powers, wielded more influence than even J. P. Morgan.

William T. Stead was characterized by Geoffrey Marcus as "half charlatan—half genius." Barbara Tuchman called him "a human torrent of enthusiasm for good causes. His energy was limitless, his optimism unending, his egotism gigantic." In the 1880s Stead had been the editor of the *Pall Mall Gazette*, a Liberal daily, and his crusades had garnered a readership for the *Gazette* so great that at one time it even included the Prince of Wales. The range of his campaigns included railing against life in Siberian labor camps, decrying Bulgarian atrocities in the Balkan wars, and denouncing slavery in the Congo. He espoused with equal passion the causes of baby adoption, housing for the poor, and public libraries. Stead became the center of a national scandal when he published an article entitled "The Maiden Tribute of Modern Babylon," in which he described how for £5 he was able to purchase the services of a thirteen-year-old prostitute. The article resulted in Stead's arrest and conviction on a charge of abduction, for which he was compelled to serve a brief prison term, but the resultant public outcry over his sensational revelation resulted in his quick release and a subsequent act of Parliament that raised the age of consent from thirteen to sixteen.

In 1890 Stead founded his own monthly journal, the *Review of Reviews*, and quickly made it one of the most influential publications of its day. He had interviewed Tsar Alexander III, Cecil Rhodes, Adm. John A. "Jackie" Fisher, and Gen. William Booth of the Salvation Army. He was a friend of men like Cardinal Henry Edward Manning and James Bryce, and even had lunch with the Prince of Wales, the future Edward VII. His mission, as Stead saw it, was to champion all "oppressed races, ill-treated animals, underpaid typists, misunderstood women, persecuted parsons, vilified public men, would-be suicides, hot-gospellers of every sort and childless parents." Short, ruddy-complected, with piercing blue eyes and a reddish beard, habitually dressed in tweeds, Stead presented almost a caricature of the quintessential English eccentric. "He was very nearly a great man," *Truth* would later declare of him, "and certainly a most extraordinary one." To T. P. Connor, he was "a Peter the Hermit preaching the Crusades out of his time." Now he was in his sixty-fourth year, his energy still as boundless as ever, but an increasing fascination with spiritualism was slowly robbing him of his influence and eroding his credibility (he regularly communed with a spirit known only as "Julia.") But even in decline, William Stead was still formidable. Even now he was traveling to New York, at President Taft's personal invitation, to speak at a great international peace conference scheduled to open April 21.[8]

Not all those aboard the Boat Train were wealthy or influential. In one of the Second Class cars, for example, Mrs. Allen Becker was keeping a careful eye on her three children, Ruth, Marion, and Richard. Ruth, a tall, pretty, but serious-looking girl of twelve, was less than thrilled at the prospect of another ocean voyage: she, along with her brother, sister, and mother, had just spent a month making passage from India. Allen and Nellie Becker were missionaries in India, and there all three Becker children had been born. But little Richard, just twenty months old, was a sickly child, and his parents had been told that the only way the boy would survive would be to take him away from the harsh Indian climate. So Mrs. Becker made arrangements for herself, Richard, Marion, who was just four, and Ruth to go home to Benton Harbor, Michigan. For her it would be a homecoming; for the children, America was a foreign land.

Another family traveling Second Class was Thomas William Brown, his wife Elizabeth, and their fifteen-year-old daughter Edith. Mr. Brown had been a real-estate broker and land speculator in South Africa. The Browns had left Capetown because the real-estate market there had gone into a serious decline and now were bound for Seattle, Washington. Traveling Second Class was something of a novelty for the Browns, who were affluent enough to travel First Class anywhere, but in this case there were no more First Class bookings available on the *Titanic*.[9]

The Boat Train rolled out of London and through the slate-roofed, redbrick buildings of Surbiton, Woking, Winchester, Eastleigh, and Southampton; a world that Stead knew intimately, but would have been completely alien to men like Astor, Hays, or Guggenheim. It was the world where the small businessmen, bank clerks, accountants, brokers, bookkeepers, merchants, and shopkeepers who worked in the city lived with their wives and families. They were men and women who guarded their social station with as much determination as the aristocracy did their own, whose class was obsessed with respectability—always watchful never to say or do something that even hinted at a lack of good manners or proper breeding, or would somehow suggest that the individual involved was actually nothing more than a puffed-up member of the working class.

As a result they embraced the values of patriotism, education, hard work, and piety, and were as prim and proper as the upper classes were profligate. But while they might appear to be stolid and unimaginative, they were hardly docile: the Liberal party, which had just forced passage of the Parliament Bill that emasculated the House of Lords, had won its overwhelming majority in the Commons in 1908 because the middle class had wholeheartedly endorsed the Liberals' program of social reforms at home and imperial reforms abroad—reforms that the upper classes had doggedly opposed. They inhabited row upon row of neat, tidy townhouses, each with its own back garden, where in April the narcissus, daffodils, and tulips would be in bloom, the hedgerows in leaf, and the cherry trees in blossom. Spring had come early in 1912, and the whole country seemed to burst with shades of green and bright colors.

Before long, the train rolled into the Surrey countryside; the brick and slate of the suburbs gave way to dressed fieldstone, half-timbering, and thatch. It was the world of the landed gentry; of the manor house, the village church, and the clusters of cottages; of vast fields of grass and heather, broken by stands of spruce and beech, birch and oak. Here men would listen for the call of the blackbird and the cuckoo, and sharpen their long-bladed scythes in anticipation of the thick spring grasses. Here life moved to a rhythm little changed for centuries, in a world of farmers, shepherds, blacksmiths, weavers, and tanners—men who rose with the sun and retired with it. Their work was hard, for mechanization was still a dream for most. They worked the land and tended their animals much as their great-great-grandfathers had. Occasionally a stolen afternoon would be spent fishing for trout in the Itchen, and most evenings would find the men rewarding themselves with a well-earned pint at the local pub, but always there would be an ear cocked to the wind, an eye glancing at the sky, for all it took was one of those terrible North Sea gales to roll in from the east and wash away an entire spring's planting or sweep away a flock of sheep in a sudden flood. It was a world undisturbed by the comings and goings of the rich and powerful, and it had precious few summers left.

There was a third landscape that existed outside the windows of the Boat Train, but it was far removed from the gently rolling countryside of Surrey, both in geography and character. To the north were the industrial cities of the Midlands, where the vistas were of apparently endless corrugated-iron factory roofs, forests of belching smokestacks, and endless warrens of sooty red-brick row houses that gave shelter to the men, women, and children who toiled their lives away in the textile mills or the steel works. This was the economic heart of the British Empire, and like its counterparts in the Ruhr, Le Creusot, or Pittsburgh, it was the home of passions, hopes, and hatreds that would soon reshape Western society.

Many of these row houses had deteriorated to slums, where a family of eight might share two beds and a pair of thin blankets among them, with little or nothing in the way of sanitary facilities, and subsist on an inadequate diet that left the children stunted, pale, and apathetic. Few children completed even the most basic education: by the age of eight they would be working, usually in a textile mill, where their small and nimble fingers were best suited to work amid fast-moving mechanisms. Wages were rarely more than a few shillings a week, and injuries and fatalities involving a child snatched into the maw of a great weaving or spinning machine were commonplace and considered unremarkable by management, since replacements were always readily at hand.

The adults fared little better, often working in mine shafts or before open-hearth steel mills for as little as four pence an hour, in a twelve-hour shift with no lunch break (lunches were eaten at the workplace), seven days a week. Taking a day off without permission in advance could result in a worker being jailed in some industries. Disease was rife among them, chiefly tuberculosis, and limited and meager diets often resulted in stunted bodies and minds. (It is a matter of official record that the minimum height requirement for the British Army was of necessity reduced in 1900 from five feet, three inches to five feet.)

Labor unions had made some inroads in alleviating the worst of the workers' lot, but poverty and its accompanying deprivations were still the rule in the life of most industrial workers' lives. A blacklist even existed in some industries: a worker dismissed for labor agitation could be barred from rehire, sometimes just within the industry, sometimes in the entire city. To souls such as these, hopelessness was a permanent condition, and the idea of paying £1,000 to rent a suite of rooms on a steamship for five days was beyond their comprehension. Somehow, all the great material and technical progress that had been the hallmark of the Victorian Period had done little to ameliorate the lot of the people whose labors had made them possible. It was a social and economic imbalance that would produce pressures on society which, like a head of steam in an overheated boiler, would one day blow that society apart.

There had been warnings, for those observant enough to take note of them, the most recent being the Great Coal Strike, which began in January 1912 in the coalfields of Wales. By March more than a million miners from Glasgow to Newcastle had walked out of the mines. The basic issue was pay, when the average wage for a miner was less than £1 ($4.80) for a sixty-hour week. The labor was backbreaking, with the men working doubled over or lying on their sides, covered with coal dust, in temperatures usually well over 100°F., sometimes working in two or three inches of water, with poor light and little ventilation. Ultimately it was killing work—most miners died from some form of lung disease before the age of fifty if they weren't killed by an explosion or a cave-in first. Believing they could break the back of the Miners' Union, the mine owners refused to bargain, deciding instead to wait the miners out.[10]

It was a disastrous decision for both sides. The whole of the British economy was dependent on coal, from the steel industry to shipping, not to mention the basic requirements for heating and cooking in nearly every home. As the weeks passed, supplies ran short and prices rose astronomically until only the upper-class and the wealthiest middle-class households could afford to buy what little coal remained. Far from generating sympathy among the working class, as the Transportation Strike had done in the fall of 1911, the Coal Strike created bitter resentment toward both sides.

Hardest hit of all was the shipping industry. In 1912 fully half of all the gross registered shipping tonnage in the world was British, some ten million tons in all. As coal became more and more scarce, more and more ships were tied up at dockside, their cargoes rusting or rotting in warehouses on the piers, their crews sent ashore, idle, unemployed. In Southampton alone more than 17,000 stokers, trimmers, firemen, greasers, seamen, and stewards were out of work by mid-March. With the unions' emergency funds rapidly being drained, many families were beginning to wonder how they would be able to put food on their tables. Already some landlords, with an almost Dickensian lack of sympathy, were beginning to serve eviction notices on those families whose rent was in arrears. Though the strike was actually settled on April 3, it would be nearly two weeks before coal reached the cities and seaports and the hardships would begin to ease.

Ironically, the disruption caused by the strike had touched the lives of the upper classes hardly at all, while it had caused innumerable problems for most of the people it had been meant to benefit. Ultimately all the Coal Strike had done was to underscore the near-total lack of understanding the two sides had for each other. In hindsight it was quite clear that the strikers had no real idea how little sympathy the mine owners and their peers had for the laborers. For their part, the Astors, Guggenheims, and Hays of the world—or the Pirries, Morgans, or Ismays, for that matter—would have found it nearly impossible to comprehend the reasons behind the strike in the first place, just as surely as they never would have understood the stolid life of the suburbs or the pastoral life of the country, and would have been utterly incapable of imagining a Birmingham, a Manchester, or a Sheffield.[11]

The Boat Train sped across the great moors of northwest Surrey toward the long ridge of the Hog's Back, reaching the high plateau beyond Basingstoke. Beginning the long downward incline toward Eastleigh and rushing through the chalk cuttings and short tunnels of the Hampshire Downs, the train was now approaching speeds close to seventy miles an hour. It passed by Winchester and at the end of its eighty-mile run from Waterloo station, it coasted into Southampton, through the Terminus Station, and across the Canute Road. A few hundred yards beyond, it came to halt at the platform built on the White Star Line's Ocean Dock. There, just a short distance away, lay the *Titanic*.

For more than a week now the ship had been the center of attention in Southampton Harbor, the scene of almost constant activity. First came the provisions and foodstuffs for the voyage, being delivered daily in almost staggering quantities. For the five-day voyage to New York, the *Titanic* required the following supplies for her galleys:

Fresh meat	75,000 lbs	Potatoes	40 tons
Fresh fish	11,000 lbs	Onions	3,500 lbs
Poultry and game	25,000 lbs	Rice, dried beans	10,000 lbs
Salt and dried fish	4,000 lbs	Lettuce	7,000 heads
Bacon and ham	7,500 lbs	Tomatoes	$2^3/4$ tons
Sausages	2,500 lbs	Fresh green peas	2,250 lbs
Fresh eggs	40,000	Fresh asparagus	800 bundles
Flour	200 barrels	Oranges	180 boxes (36,000)
Sugar	10,000 lbs	Lemons	50 boxes (16,000)

Coffee	2,200 lbs	Grapefruit	50 boxes
Tea	800 lbs	Hot house grapes	1,000 lbs
Cereals	10,000 lbs	Fresh milk	1,500 gal
Fresh cream	1,200 qts	Condensed milk	600 gal
Ice cream	1,750 qts	Fresh butter	6,000 lbs
Sweetbreads	1,000	Jams and marmalade	1,120 lbs

Equally well stocked were the *Titanic*'s cellars, holding some 20,000 bottles of beer, ale, and stout; 1,500 bottles of wine; 15,000 bottles of mineral water; and 850 bottles of spirits.

To serve the splendid meals that would be prepared from this vast array of foodstuffs, an equally impressive volume of glassware, tableware, cutlery, and crystal was taken aboard. Included were such items as 3,000 tea cups; 2,500 breakfast plates; 1,500 souffle dishes; 8,000 dinner forks; 2,500 water bottles; 2,000 wine glasses; 12,000 dinner plates; 300 claret jugs; 2,000 egg spoons; 400 toast racks; 1,000 oyster forks; 8,000 cut tumblers; and 100 grape scissors.[12]

While all these items and more were being brought aboard, the messy business of coaling was taking place. Ordinarily coaling was a routine if tiresome affair, but in April 1912 it was a far from routine procedure. The Great Coal Strike was now in its sixth week, and supplies were growing short. In order to avoid delaying the *Titanic*'s maiden voyage again, the White Star Line decided that she would sail with full bunkers (she burned 650 tons a day), even if it meant taking coal from other White Star ships and leaving them tied up at their piers. That is exactly what happened; the *Oceanic* and *Adriatic* had their crossings canceled and their passengers transferred to the *Titanic*. The coaling was completed at almost the last minute, the last few tons being loaded on the morning of April 10. In all the haste to get the coal aboard, the crew hadn't had time to properly wet the coal down. Dry coal and coal dust were a perpetual fire hazard, and a smoldering fire broke out in the starboard bunker of Boiler Room No. 6. Despite the best efforts of the boiler room crew to put the fire out, the bunker would continue to smoke throughout the voyage.[13]

For most of the passengers transferred from other ships this was a happy exchange, since they were sailing on a brand new vessel, the biggest and most luxurious in the world, but had only paid for passage on the smaller, older vessels. But some of them felt a certain apprehension about the whole affair, resulting in a few last-minute cancellations among those passengers who were to be transferred.

Similarly there were notable absences among those who had made reservations for the *Titanic*'s maiden voyage. The most prominent was J. P. Morgan, who had every intention of making the trip until he had come down with an illness remarkably similar to influenza a few weeks prior. His physician subsequently decided that the old man was too weak to make the crossing.

Also absent on the *Titanic* would be Jack Binns, probably the best-known wireless operator in the world. Back in 1906 when the White Star's

Republic, caught in a heavy fog, had been rammed by the small steamer *Florida*, Binns, the *Republic*'s wireless operator, sent out a distress call within minutes. For the next thirty-six hours Binns stayed at his post, helping to coordinate the efforts of the rescue vessels. Although the *Republic* eventually sank, all of her passengers and crew, except for the four unfortunates who were killed in the collision, were safely transferred to the flotilla of vessels that had rushed to the stricken liner's side in response to the wireless call Binns had sent out. Binns subsequently spent two years on the *Adriatic* under Captain Smith, and had intended to sail on the *Titanic*, but he had a job waiting for him in New York and he didn't want to wait until April 10 to depart, so he sailed on the *Minnesota* on April 6.

Alfred Gwynne Vanderbilt, one of the few men in the world whose net worth rivaled that of John Jacob Astor, had also booked passage on the *Titanic*, but changed his mind at the last minute. It would prove to be a short-lived reprieve, though, for Vanderbilt would go to a watery grave on the deck of the *Lusitania* little more than three years later.[14]

While the coaling was still underway, Capt. Maurice H. Clarke of the Board of Trade began the mandatory surveys of the ship. Distress rockets, flares, and other "fireworks" were examined and approved; lifeboats and floats were tested; charts and instruments were inspected. Second Officer Charles Lightoller recalled ruefully:

> The Board of Trade Surveyor, Captain Clarke, certainly lived up to his reputation of being the best cursed B.O.T. representative in the South of England at that time. Many small details, that another surveyor would have taken in his stride accepting the statement of the officer concerned, was not good enough for Clarke. He must see everything, and himself check every item that concerned the survey. He would not accept anyone's word as sufficient—and got heartily cursed in consequence.

Captain Clarke passed the *Titanic* as being in compliance in all particulars with Board of Trade regulations.[15]

Chief among these were regulations concerning lifeboats, and though the idea that she was unsinkable had become so firmly entrenched in the public's mind that it was believed that lifeboats were no longer necessary, the *Titanic* still had to comply. The Board of Trade had concocted a complicated formula for determining the lifeboat requirements of British registered vessels. Specifically this stated that any ship over 10,000 tons must carry sixteen lifeboats with a capacity of 5,500 cubic feet, that is, space for 550 people, plus enough rafts and floats to equal 75 percent of the capacity of the lifeboats. For the *Titanic* this worked out to a required capacity of 9,625 cubic feet, room for 962 persons. Actually, the *Titanic*'s lifeboat capacity exceeded the Board of Trade requirements, since the White Star Line had added four Englehardt collapsibles, wooden keels with folding canvas sides, to the ship's complement of boats. Together with the required sixteen boats they gave the *Titanic* a capacity of 11,780 cubic feet, room for 1,178 people. Nobody at the time seemed to realize the discrepancy between the number of people the *Titanic* could carry—over 3,000—and the number of people she had lifeboats for. Unfortunately the regulations had been written for ships a quarter of the *Titanic*'s size and had never been revised.[16]

When the ship was being built, Alexander Carlisle, one of the managing directors at Harland and Wolff, had pointed out that the new geared Welin davits the *Titanic* was being fitted with could each handle up to three life-boats, giving the ship the potential to carry up to forty-eight boats. Carlisle himself recommended that the number of boats be doubled, but he didn't press the point, so the suggestion was turned down by the White Star Line as being too expensive. Besides, the *Titanic* not only complied with the Board of Trade regulations, but by being "unsinkable," she had made them obsolete.[17]

Just how firmly this was believed Mrs. Albert Caldwell learned firsthand that morning when she was watching a group of deck hands carrying luggage aboard the *Titanic*. Impulsively, she stopped one of the men and asked him, "Is this ship really nonsinkable?"

"Yes, lady," he replied, "God Himself couldn't sink this ship."[18]

These deckhands were under the supervision of the chief bosun, Alfred "Big Neck" Nichols, who seemed to be everywhere, watching everything. At the same time, the marine superintendent was making his rounds, inspecting hatches, winches, derricks, and fenders. The arrival of the Boat Train meant that sailing time was not far off, and the deck crew did everything they could to shepherd the latest arrivals into the ship.

For First and Second Classes the first stop was the Purser's Office. The duties of a purser on any large passenger vessel were much like those of the manager of a large hotel ashore and required many of the same talents: a good head for business; tact, charm, and diplomacy for dealing with tem-peramental passengers; and the ability to delegate authority without relin-quishing responsibility among subordinates. All these qualities the *Titanic*'s purser had in abundance. Hugh McElroy was a tall, well-built man, who had become so popular among frequent travelers on the North Atlantic—that some passengers made a point of traveling on ships he was assigned to. His table in the First Class Dining Saloon was often as popular as that of the cap-tain, for McElroy was one of those rare individuals who seemed to know everybody and everything, from the latest shipboard gossip to the current stock market tips. The very soul of discretion, he was often the confidant of passenger and crewman alike. As the passengers quickly passed through his office to have their tickets processed, he managed to have a smile or a kind word for each of them.[19]

The procedures for Third Class were somewhat different. At the head of each Third Class gangway was posted a team of surgeons under the direction of the *Titanic*'s Chief Surgeon, Dr. F. W. N. O'Loughlin. Like Purser McElroy,

O'Loughlin was an Irish Catholic, and the two men had served together for many years, beginning on the *Oceanic*, then the *Baltic*, the *Adriatic*, the *Olympic*, and now the *Titanic*. The purpose of the surgeons Dr. O'Loughlin posted at the gangways was to conduct a quick but thorough examination of every steerage passenger attempting to board. Every immigrant was checked for signs of trachoma, a highly infectious and potentially blinding disease of the eye. By folding back the upper eyelid of each Third Class passenger boarding, the doctors could quickly spot the white scar tissue that invariably indicated presence of the disease. Anyone showing such signs was instantly and summarily turned back—American immigration laws forbade admission of anyone with trachoma into the country. (One other requirement of American law was that locked barricades be set up between steerage and the other passengers— originally intended to prevent the spread of disease, like the out-of-date lifeboat regulations this provision had never been modified, and as in every other particular the *Titanic* complied fully.)[20]

Once admitted by the surgeons, the steerage passengers were handled as expeditiously as possible. R. A. Fletcher left a description of the process in his book *Travelling Palaces*:

> Once on board . . . it is astonishing how quickly the stewards direct the passengers to their quarters. No sooner are the passengers past the medical men at the head of the gangway, than they are taken care of. "Single men this way, please," a steward reiterated incessantly. "Ticket number so-and-so, thank you. Straight along the passage. You will find a steward a little further on who will direct you."
>
> That steward is probably standing near the head of a staircase. "Go down the stairs and turn to the left. Here, you sir, you to the right. You all together? All from the same town, eh? Yes, to the right. I'll see you again by and by." And so on, directing them to their quarters where other stewards are in attendance to see that each man is shown to his cabin and berth with as little delay as possible. The tickets are numbered to correspond with the numbers of the berths, and thanks to this arrangement and the careful direction of the stewards, the early arrivals are soon back on deck watching the other passengers arrive.[21]

Noon was rapidly approaching when the Trinity House pilot, George Bowyer, came aboard and had the pilot's flag hoisted at the foremast. Bowyer had been the pilot at Southampton Harbour for nearly forty years, the latest of a long line of Bowyers who had been harbor pilots at Southampton since the time of the Napoleonic Wars. The ship's whistle gave a series of short sharp blasts, a warning for the visitors, friends of passengers, and assorted vendors and reporters to begin making their way ashore. One by one the gangways were pulled away as the harbor tugs began moving into position.

Just as the last gangway was being lowered, a half dozen stokers, who had slipped ashore earlier to pay one last visit to a nearby pub, came rushing up, trying to get back aboard. The *Titanic*'s master-at-arms barred the way, turning them back, and the stokers missed the boat, so to speak.[22]

At noon exactly, one long, deep-throated blast from the *Titanic*'s whistles signaled the nearby tugs to stand by. "Make fast the tugs!" George Bowyer's booming voice rang out across the bridge. There was a jangle of ringing bells as the brass engine room telegraph rang down to signal "Slow Ahead," and the water at the stern of the ship began to churn as the three great screws began to turn.

Pilot Bowyer quickly checked to make sure that all the ship's officers were properly stationed: Chief Officer Wilde in the fo'c's'le (forecastle) head in charge of moorings, with Second Officer Lightoller assisting him as well as seeing to the forward spring lines; First Officer Murdoch aft at the auxiliary bridge on the poop deck, in charge of the moorings there, assisted by Third Officer Pitman; standing beside Murdoch was Fourth Officer Boxhall, who would be passing the telegraph orders down to the engine room, while at the same time recording all movements in the log; Fifth Officer Lowe was on the bridge with Pilot Bowyer, manning the telephones; Sixth Officer Moody was supervising the removal of the last gangway. As soon as that gangway was clear, Bowyer began to call out a rapid series of orders: "Let go the stern ropes! . . . Let go your head rope! . . . Let go your after spring! . . . Tow her off aft! . . . Let go your for'ard spring!" The tugs began to pull the ship away from the side of the dock, and the passengers and crowd watching on the quay let out a cheer as a gap began to open up between the *Titanic* and the side of the quay. Bowyer called for the after tug to let go, and the huge liner slowly moved forward into the River Test.

In the First Class Dining Saloon the ship's orchestra played an air from the musical "The Chocolate Soldier," while Pilot Bowyer gradually worked the ship up to a speed of six knots as she moved down the channel. The immense bulk of the liner displaced an incredible volume of water in the narrow channel, creating a powerful suction in her wake. As she approached the entrance to the channel, the *Titanic* drew abreast of the small American liner *New York*, which was moored side by side to the White Star's *Oceanic*. Both ships had been immobilized by the coal strike, and neither had steam up. As the *Titanic* passed, the suction of her wake drew the two smaller vessels away from the dock where they were tied up. The strain on the six lines mooring the *New York* to the *Oceanic* grew too great, and with a series of loud cracks they parted in rapid succession as the *New York* was pulled helplessly toward the *Titanic*. For a moment a nasty collision seemed inevitable as the stern of the *New York* swung to within three or four feet of the bigger liner's hull.

Quick thinking on the part of Captain Gale of the tug *Vulcan* and prompt action on the *Titanic*'s bridge by Captain Smith averted an accident. The *Vulcan* quickly passed a line to the stern of the *New York*, and, throwing its engines full astern, managed to slow the wayward liner and drag her away from the *Titanic*. At the same time, Captain Smith ordered "Half Astern" on the engines, the sudden wash thrown up along the *Titanic*'s side by the huge propellers providing the extra thrust needed to push the *New York* away. As soon as she was clear Smith brought the *Titanic*'s engines to a halt. The danger wasn't over yet, for the *New York*, still without power, was now drifting down the narrow space between the motionless *Titanic* and the *Oceanic*. Other tugs rushed to aid the struggling *Vulcan*, and in a little less than forty-five minutes the *New York* was being nudged safely back alongside the *Oceanic*. (Later, a barge that had sunk in that same channel was found to have been dragged neary a half mile underwater by the suction of the *Titanic*'s wake.)

None of the three ships was damaged, but during the time it took to get the *New York* securely moored, and before the *Titanic* resumed her passage down the channel, Captain Smith ordered a quick inspection of the ship. Some of the passengers were disturbed by the incident. Renee Harris, wife of the American theatrical producer, suddenly found a stranger standing at her side, asking, "Do you love life?"

"Yes, I love it."

"That was a bad omen. Get off this ship at Cherbourg, if we get that far. That's what I'm going to do."

Mrs. Harris just laughed, believing, like so many others, in the unsinkability of the *Titanic*, but later she would recall that she never saw the man on board again.[23]

Finally the *Titanic* was clear of the docks and steaming down the Southampton Water at half speed. Soon she came up to Calshot Spit, where she slowed to make the difficult turn to starboard into the Thorn Channel. A few minutes later came the sharp right-angled turn to port around the West Bramble buoy, leading into the deep-water channel that flowed past the Cowes Roads, Spithead, and the Nab. As the *Titanic* passed the Royal Yacht Squadron at West Cowes, passengers and crew noticed crowds lining the promenade to catch a glimpse of the beautiful new White Star liner, while sitting out in the Solent roads in a small open boat, a local pharmacist and amateur maritime photographer named Frank Beken waited patiently for the great ship to pass. Camera at the ready, he was to take some of the most memorable photographs of the *Titanic* ever made. Captain Smith recognized the young man from previous encounters in the Solent Roads, and he knew Beken's work, so with a smile gave four blasts on the *Titanic*'s whistle in a salute. It was a moment that Beken would never forget.[24]

Sweeping past Spithead, the *Titanic* dipped her colors to the squadron of destroyers anchored there, then steamed past Ryde, past the Lloyd's lightship, past Selsey Bill, and on to the Nab lightship. At the lightship the *Titanic* stopped to drop Pilot Bowyer, then turned toward the English Channel and the open sea.[25]

CHAPTER 3

Maiden Voyage

*When you shall pass through the waters . . . they shall
not overwhelm you.*

—Isaiah 43:2

THE SHIP'S ORCHESTRA WAS PLAYING IN THE FIRST CLASS DINING SALOON AS
the ship's bugler sounded the call for luncheon. The fresh April winds had
kicked up a mild chop in the Channel, but the *Titanic* never felt it. Already
the passengers were commenting on how smooth the ship's engines were—
scarcely any vibration could be felt, a tribute to the care and attention to
detail the Harland and Wolff engineers had lavished on them. Off to starboard lay the Isle of Wight, its landmarks easily visible in the bright sunshine. In short order Culver Cliff, Sandown Bay, Shanklin Cline, and
eventually St. Catherine's Bay and its high chalk cliffs were left behind as the
Titanic ran down the Channel, making for her first port of call, Cherbourg.

Though he was almost an hour behind schedule as a result of the incident with the *New York*, Captain Smith decided that it might be a good time
to familiarize himself a little better with how the new ship handled. Whether
he had always planned on this, or if it was a response to the near-accident in
Southampton will never be known, but that afternoon Smith had the
Titanic put through several S-turns and other maneuvers to get a feel for her.
After an hour or so of these exercises he ordered the ship back on her course
for Cherbourg, expecting to arrive there in the early evening.[1]

While the passengers were settling in, Thomas Andrews and his assistants were moving about the ship, beginning the slow process of locating the
inevitable problems, faults, and breakdowns that always plague new ships. In
the case of the *Titanic* it appeared that these would be far fewer than usual—
the experience gained with the *Olympic* and incorporated into the *Titanic*
had been invaluable. There were a few niggling details that most men
wouldn't have noticed or bothered with, but Andrews was a perfectionist.
Before long he decided that the color of the pebble dashing on the private
promenade decks was too dark; he thought the coathooks in the staterooms
used too many screws; and he discovered trouble with the hot press in the

First Class galley. Aside from such details, the *Titanic* promised to be, as Bruce Ismay had said about the *Olympic*, "a marvel."[2]

Likewise the crew were going about the business of establishing a shipboard routine. Down on D Deck the masseuse, Maud Slocombe, was busy collecting the odd beer bottle or half-eaten sandwich left behind in the Turkish Bath by the shipyard workers. George Symons, one of the ship's lookouts, approached Second Officer Charles Lightoller, with a more serious concern.

"Yes, Symons, what is it?"

"Sir, we have no lookout glasses in the crow's nest."

"All right, I'll look into it directly." Lightoller quickly made inquiries as to the whereabouts of the missing binoculars, but was unable to bring Symons good news. The glasses could not be found. When Symons told this to his fellow lookouts, there was considerable consternation: the White Star Line hired men specifically for the post of lookout, rather than simply rotating deck hands to lookout positions, and to these men binoculars were necessary for their job. Several of the *Titanic*'s lookouts had sailed on the *Olympic*, where the glasses were stored in a special locker in the crow's nest, and the omission on the new ship didn't sit well with them.

Actually, the binoculars were aboard, but nobody knew it at the time. There had been a last-minute reshuffling of the officers aboard the *Titanic*, and the officer responsible for the glasses was no longer on board. What had happened was this: William M. Murdoch had been assigned as chief officer, but his limited experience with big ships concerned Captain Smith, who asked for Henry Wilde, his chief officer aboard the *Olympic*. Murdoch was bumped down to first officer, which meant that Lightoller, originally the first officer was moved down to second officer. The man Lightoller replaced, David Blair, was left behind in Southampton. For some reason, Blair had ordered the binoculars removed from the crow's nest and shut up in a locker in his cabin. The shuffling about of the senior officers' assignments was done at almost the last minute, Wilde arriving just hours before sailing time, and in the confusion Blair either forgot to tell anyone where the glasses were, or else whoever he told forgot about them. In any case the binoculars were not where they were supposed to be, and nobody had any idea where they were.[3]

The sun sank low on the horizon, bathing the approaching chalk cliffs of the French coast in a reddish glow. Soon a lighthouse perched at the end of a long breakwater appeared, marking the entrance to Cherbourg Roads. Dropping anchor in the Roads, just off the Cap de la Hogue, the *Titanic* was met by the tenders *Nomadic* and *Traffic*. A late-afternoon squall sprang up, kicking up a swell strong enough to cause the two tenders to bounce rather alarmingly up and down as they the drew alongside the *Titanic*, striking the side of the ship occasionally. Edith Russell, who was boarding the ship at Cherbourg, wondered with more than just idle curiosity if the passengers and their luggage would be transferred safely. Nevertheless, the passengers, baggage, and mail were taken aboard without incident, and by 9:00 P.M. the *Titanic* had turned around and left Cherbourg behind, shaping a course for Queenstown.

Edith Russell (her real last name was Rosenbaum, but she had Anglicized it for business reasons) was a fashion correspondent for *Women's Wear*, and already an experienced Atlantic traveler. Originally she had intended to return to the United States on the *George Washington*, which had been scheduled to sail from Cherbourg on April 7, but when she found out that she could book passage on the *Titanic*, which didn't sail until April 10, she was overjoyed. The extra three days would allow her to cover the Easter Races in Paris and still arrive in New York the same day the *George Washington* would have. Alarmed by the squall at Cherbourg, she told Nicholas Martin, the Cherbourg agent for the White Star Line that she'd decided to take another ship, regardless of when it would arrive. Martin told her that it would be possible, but since her luggage was already on board the *Titanic*, she would have to sail without it. Miss Russell took a rather dim view of the prospect since her luggage contained not only her wardrobe but also $3,000 worth of business orders.

Furthermore, her mascot was in her luggage. A few years earlier her mother had given her a little toy pig, made of porcelain covered with white fur. It had a tail that was attached to a music box inside the pig, which, when the tail was turned, played the song "Maxixe." Edith's mother had given it to her after Edith had been in a near-fatal automobile accident, which, along with several other life-threatening incidents, convinced her that Edith was accident prone. "Carry it with you always," her mother had said, since the pig was a symbol of good luck in France, and Edith appeared to need all the luck she could muster. When Nicholas Martin informed her that she would have to leave her luggage aboard the *Titanic*, her first thought was to ask about additional insurance on it. Martin was nearly incredulous. "Ridiculous," he said, "this boat's unsinkable."

Miss Russell laughed and said, "My luggage is worth more to me than I am, so I had better stay with it." With that, she made her way aboard the *Titanic*, feeling somewhat better since she and her mascot wouldn't have to part company.[4]

Also boarding the ship at Cherbourg was one couple who had booked passage under assumed names—with good reason. It would have been inadvisable for "Mr. and Mrs. G. Thorne" to admit that they were not married. They were George Rosenshine and Maybelle Thorne, traveling together in First Class, who were posing as man and wife.

Boarding at the same time were Sir Cosmo and Lady Duff Gordon. Sir Cosmo was a member of a moderately distinguished branch of the Scottish nobility, imbued with a sense of obligation to uphold the rights and privileges of the aristocracy against the repeated and growing infringements of the common masses. Sir Cosmo went through life oblivious to anything going on around him that did not relate to him personally or affect his prerogatives as a British peer. Lady Duff Gordon was known throughout European and American society as Madame Lucile, owner of "Lucile's," one of the most expensive and exclusive women's fashion salons. Her original shop in London now boasted branches in Paris and New York, and Lady Duff Gordon's clientele included some of the best-known names on both sides of the Atlantic, making her one of the most sought-after designers. Her creations were tasteful, elaborate, and prohibitively expensive (one of her designs used thirty yards of silk at the hem), but everybody who was anybody knew who Madame Lucile was and coveted her dresses. Strangely enough, Sir Cosmo and Lady Duff Gordon were trying to travel incognito, registering under the name of "Mr. and Mrs. Morgan"—strange because Lady Duff Gordon was so well known among the passengers they would be joining.[5]

By evening the ship had begun to settle down into a working routine. Watches were set, work crews were detailed, and stewards busied themselves laying out the First Class passengers' clothes for dinner or directing Second and Third Class passengers to appropriate dining rooms. Second Officer Lightoller was just beginning to feel confident, after almost two weeks on board, that he could finally make his way from one point in the ship to another by the most direct route.

Charles Herbert Lightoller was very much the popular image of a steamship officer. Tall, sun-bronzed, handsome, and with a deep, pleasant speaking voice, Lightoller was a good officer and an outstanding seaman. He had gone to sea as a boy on a clipper on the Australian run under the legendary Old Jock Sutherland, one of the most notorious "crackers-on" Liverpool had ever produced. (A "cracker-on" was a hard-driving master who would push his ship through a full gale without ever reducing sail.) Lightoller had experienced fire at sea, been a castaway, stood as second officer on a three-skysail clipper, and passed for a Master's certificate, all by the age of twenty-three, and later had been involved in the Yukon Gold Rush.

After Lightoller joined the White Star Line, an incident in Sydney Harbor during the Boer War in which he had contrived to fire a salute to the colors at Fort Dennison while simultaneously hoisting the Boer flag led to his transfer to the North Atlantic run. He had served under Captain Smith several times before and had been first officer of the *Majestic* and later the *Oceanic* before being assigned to the *Titanic*. Now , he was more than a little miffed at being bumped out of the first officer's slot to allow room for Chief Officer Wilde: in the narrowly confined world of a steamship line, the first officer's position was usually a guarantee of a command in the not-too-distant future, so Lightoller regarded his supersession as a sort of demotion.

Oddly enough, Lightoller had a distinctly uneasy feeling about the *Titanic*; he wasn't sure why, but he felt that she was not destined to be a happy ship. Perhaps he was simply upset about being moved down to second officer, but years later he would recall how sailors develop a "sense" about their ships:

> It is difficult to describe exactly where that unity of feeling lies, between a ship and her crew, but it is there, in every ship that sails on salt water. It is not always a feeling of affection, either. A man can hate a ship worse than a human being, although he sails on her. Likewise a ship can hate her men, and she frequently becomes known as a "killer."[6]

The man who had replaced Lightoller, after being bumped himself from chief officer to first, was William Murdoch. A short, wiry man with a pleasantly plain face and a ready smile that heralded boundless good humor, Murdoch was a Scot from Dalbeattie in Galloway, the son of a seafaring family. Like Lightoller, he had done his apprenticeship in sail, earned all his certificates, then joined the White Star Line, serving first in the Australian trade, then moving to the passenger liners of the North Atlantic. He had served on an impressive succession of distinguished ships, the *Arabic*, the *Adriatic* under Captain Smith, then the *Oceanic*. Most recently he had been Captain Smith's first officer for two months on the *Olympic*, so he felt far more at ease with the *Titanic* than did Lightoller. Like Lightoller, though, he was less than happy about being replaced at the last minute. But Murdoch was a conscientious officer, and as he had amply demonstrated over the years, he was an excellent seaman, with nearly faultless judgement and iron nerves. Captain Smith was certain to be glad Murdoch was on board.[7]

Captain Smith, of course, was Capt. Edward J. Smith. Solidly built, slightly above medium height, he was handsome in a patriarchal sort of way. His neatly trimmed white beard, coupled with his clear eyes, gave him a somewhat stern countenance, an impression immediately dispelled by his gentle speaking voice and urbane manners. Respectfully and affectionately known as "E. J." by passengers and crew alike, he was a natural leader, radiating a reassuring combination of authority, confidence, and good humor.

Captain Smith had, like most of his officers and most skippers on the North Atlantic, gone to sea as an apprentice at the age of twelve, signing on as a cabin boy on a square-rigged ship. After getting his certificates he signed on with the White Star Line at the age of twenty-seven, and his career had been an uninterrupted series of successes ever since. The captain of a passenger vessel on the North Atlantic run was expected to mingle socially with the First Class passengers, and Smith's dignified manner and warm personality made him instantly popular on White Star ships. Some passengers thought so much of him that they booked crossings only on ships he commanded.

White Star rewarded him for generating such a loyal following by giving him command of most of their new ships, so that a maiden voyage with Captain Smith in command became something of a tradition for the line.

He also was much admired among professional circles for his seamanship. "It was an education," Lightoller would later recall, "to see him con his own ship up the intricate channels entering New York at full speed. One particularly bad corner, known as the Southwest Spit, used to make us fairly flush with pride as he swung her round, judging his distances to a nicety; she was heeling over to the helm with only a matter of feet to spare between each end of the ship and the banks." Despite such spectacular ship handling, Smith's career was remarkable for its near-total absence of any accidents or incidents—its contrast to Lightoller's catalogue of experiences, for example, was remarkable. In 1907 after he brought the brand new *Adriatic* to New York on her maiden voyage, he granted a request by New York papers for an interview. When asked about his career at sea, he responded:

> When anyone asks me how I can best describe my experience of nearly forty years at sea, I merely say, uneventful. Of course there have been winter gales, and storms and fog and the like, but in all my experience, I have never been in any accident of any sort worth speaking about . . . I never saw a wreck and never been wrecked, nor have I been in any predicament that threatened to end in disaster of any sort.

Smith was asked about the safety of the ships he commanded. He gave his answer with absolute assurance: "I cannot imagine any condition which would cause a ship to founder. I cannot conceive of any vital disaster happening to this vessel. Modern shipbuilding has gone beyond that."[8]

Only one blemish marked Captain Smith's otherwise spotless record: in February 1912 he had been in command of the *Olympic* when she was involved in a controversial collision with the Royal Navy's cruiser HMS *Hawke*. Although an Admiralty inquiry found that the 46,000-ton *Olympic* had pulled the 7,000-ton *Hawke* into the liner's wake, forcing the cruiser into the liner's stern quarter, the White Star Line rejected the inquiry's finding as self-serving and rewarded Smith with the command of the new *Titanic*. He was now fifty-nine years old, commodore of the White Star Line, and he had decided it was enough. After forty-five years at sea, thirty-two of them with the White Star Line, once he took the *Titanic* to New York and brought her back he would retire. It seemed to be, by anybody's reckoning, a fitting climax to a brilliant career, commanding the largest, safest, most opulent ship afloat.[9]

As the *Titanic* pulled away from Cherbourg, the more experienced passengers soon settled in, while those new to transatlantic travel wandered about the ship, taking in all the marvels of this wonderful new vessel. As the First Class passengers were sipping their after-dinner liqueurs or coffee, the ship's orchestra began playing on A Deck, the first of what was to be a nightly occurrence, the after-dinner concert.

As with everything else aboard the *Titanic*, the White Star Line spared neither effort nor expense to assemble what was regarded as the finest ship's orchestra afloat. This was the day of Fritz Lehar and his great operettas, *The Merry Widow*, *The Count of Luxemburg*, and *Gypsy Love*; when Oscar Strauss continued to write waltzes in the great Viennese tradition; English musicals such as *The Country Girl*, *Our Miss Brooks*, and *Miss Hook of Holland* provided melodies everyone knew; and the new American rage, ragtime, was in constant demand by the huge numbers of Americans crisscrossing the Atlantic. The strains of light melodies accompanying lunch and dinner and providing a backdrop for the day's shipboard activities were always one of the most enduring memories for transatlantic travelers.

Wallace Hartley, the bandmaster, most recently had been bandmaster on the Cunard line's *Mauretania*, but in early 1912 White Star wooed him away to the *Titanic*. Hartley's violin was well known for its rich, warm sound by many First Class travelers. Equally accomplished was his second violinist, Jock Hume, who had been part of the band on the *Olympic*. (Jock's mother had urged him not to go back to sea, but the pay on the new ship was good, especially for a young man who was soon to be wed.)

Pianist Theodore Brailey and cellist Roger Bricoux had come over from the *Carpathia*, another Cunard ship, while the bass-viol player, Fred Clark, had never been to sea before. The ensemble was completed by George Krins, who played the viola, J. W. Woodward, another cellist, and P. C. Taylor, a pianist.

Usually, the band played as two separate ensembles: a quintet under Wallace Hartley's direction that played at teatime, after dinner, and at Sunday services; and a trio, consisting of piano, violin, and cello, that played in the Reception Room outside the Café Parisien and the *à la carte* Restaurant on B Deck.

The band's position was a curious one, for the members were not part of the *Titanic*'s crew. Technically they were employed by the Liverpool firm of C. W. and F. N. Black, who the White Star Line paid for the musicians' services, while the Blacks actually paid their salaries. As a result they were berthed as Second Class passengers and dined in the Second Class dining saloon. They were still required to sign the ship's articles, however, which subjected them to the authority of the ship's officers like any other crew member. (In a similar "neither fish nor fowl" situation were the French and Italian employees of the *à la carte* Restaurant on B Deck. The restaurant was not operated by the White Star Line, but by Monsieur Gatti, who ran it as a concession.)[10]

By 11:00 P.M. the concert had run its course, and the passengers began to drift off, some to retire for the night, others to relax with friends in one of the smoking rooms or lounges, while others set out for further exploration. Even as jaded a palate as William Stead's was impressed. In a letter posted at

Queenstown the next day, he wrote in frank admiration, "This ship is a monstrous floating Babylon."[11]

— ◆◆◆ —

In the late morning of April 11 the *Titanic* steamed within sight of the Irish coast as the grey mountains of Cork slowly rose over the horizon. It was a cold morning, and few passengers were inclined to brave the brisk wind to sun themselves on the open decks, preferring to watch the approaching shore from one of the enclosed promenades or public rooms. The south coast of Ireland is one of the loveliest landfalls in Europe, with its high granite cliffs, often topped by a lonely, ruined castle or signal tower standing like a sentinel over innumerable coves and beaches and the impossibly green fields and pastures stretching out behind them. Soon the Old Head of Kinsale hove into view, a familiar sight to any transatlantic traveler, with its rocky promontory topped by a tall lighthouse, often used by the skippers of passenger liners as a landfall and navigational fix. Just around the headland lay Cork Harbor.

As the *Titanic* approached the Daunt Lightship, a few miles south of Queenstown, she slowed to take on the pilot, then proceeded majestically toward the harbor. The passengers could now see the twin forts guarding the entrance to the harbor, as well as the crowds of people lining the shore who had come out to watch the new ship being guided into Queenstown.

They had started gathering hours before, some coming from as far away as Cork City, by land a twenty-mile trek around Cork Harbor. This was a seafaring crowd, every bit as knowledgeable as the one that had seen the *Titanic* off at Southampton the day before, and it watched with admiration as the new ship glided in past the Heads, slowly rounded Roche Point, and dropped anchor two miles off shore.[12]

The twin tenders *Ireland* and *America* drew alongside the *Titanic* and began transferring passengers and mail. There were about 130 new passengers taken on, young Irish men and women who for the most part had never been farther than one or two days' journey away from their homes, as well as almost 1,400 sacks of mail. The handful of passengers that had only booked passage as far as Queenstown left the ship, including Mrs. Lillie Odell, who had made the short voyage with her two brothers, her sister-in-law Kate, and a nephew, along with an invited guest, Francis M. Browne. Browne, thirty-two years old, a schoolteacher and a candidate for the Jesuit priesthood, was what a later generation would call "a shutterbug." He had brought his camera with him on the trip to Queenstown and had taken a remarkable series of photographs of shipboard life on the *Titanic*, including some amazing pictures of the near-collision with the *New York*.

A small flotilla of bumboats followed in the wakes of the two tenders, filled with vendors of various sorts hawking their wares. Several of the more respectable looking people were allowed on board, and for an hour or so the after Promenade Deck was transformed into an impromptu open-air market for Irish laces, linen, ceramics, and porcelains. John Jacob Astor was so taken by a lace jacket that he paid $800 for it on the spot.[13]

Winnie Troutt (her real name was Edwina, but nobody ever called her that), a schoolteacher from Bath, was far more interested in lunch than in tenders or bumboats. Not that the food, which was uniformly excellent, was the attraction, but she was interested in the company at her table. Assigned to a table seating eight, Miss Troutt had, much to her delight, discovered that her dining companions were friendly, intelligent, and articulate, and so had quickly formed a new circle of friends. She had become particularly fond of Jacob Milling, an industrialist from Copenhagen who manufactured locomotives. He was traveling to America to learn as much as possible about how Americans built locomotives so he could apply their expertise to his enterprise. He confessed to Winnie that although he had only known her for a day, he felt so comfortable in her company that he felt he had known her all of his life. Of course, the forty-eight-year-old businessman's intentions were entirely honorable, for he was careful to point out to Winnie that he had even written to his wife telling her about his new friend. He had just posted the letter on the tender here at Queenstown.[14]

There was one odd incident in Queenstown Harbour. As the two tenders drew alongside, one of the *Titanic*'s firemen climbed up the ladder inside the fourth, aftmost funnel (it was a dummy, used for ventilating the engine room), and suddenly stuck his head up out of the funnel, his soot-covered face grinning wickedly down at the passengers on the deck of the liner and the tenders below. Although intended as a mere practical joke, it was in poor taste, for few people knew that the fourth funnel was nonfunctional, and the sudden appearance of this man in such an unexpected place caused considerable consternation among those who saw him. The culprit was never identified, but the more sensitive people took the apparition as another "bad omen." One young fireman named John Coffey, suddenly seized by a sense of foreboding, took the opportunity to desert and stowed away on one of the tenders just before it withdrew from the *Titanic*'s side.[15]

As soon as the last passenger and sack of mail had been transferred, the *Titanic*'s whistles gave a long blast, a signal for the tenders, bumboats, and any nearby small craft to stand clear. Gangways were dropped, lines cast off, and, with a ringing of telegraph bells, the great ship got under way again. Another stop at the Daunt Lightship to drop off the pilot, and the *Titanic* was clear of the Irish coast, standing out into the Atlantic. Captain Smith continued to shape his course just a few miles off the coastline, to give his passengers the full benefit of the splendid view. In short order the *Titanic* had left the Old Head of Kinsale behind, followed by Courtmacsherry Bay, the Seven Heads, and the well-known massif of Galley Head. By midafternoon she was past the Stags and Kedge Island, and around teatime the Fastnet Light was in sight. For years afterward the tale would be told around many a supper table, beside an evening fire, or at the bar of the local pub about how father, son, daughter, or wife had seen the *Titanic* that day. The image of her grace and beauty would remain indelibly etched in their memories as she raced past, her upperworks gleaming in the bright April sunshine.

By nightfall Ireland had been left behind and many of the Irish immigrants gathered on the stern to catch a last glimpse of their homeland. Whatever fortunes would befall them in America, it was doubtful that many of them would ever have the money or the opportunity to return. Eugene Daly said his farewell on his pipes, playing the haunting "Erin's Lament." Once the Irish coast was left behind, they turned and made their way back to their cabins, filled with a thoroughly Irish determination to make a better life for themselves in America.[16]

They were not the only ones to catch that last glimpse of land with some feeling of regret. Nine-year-old Franky Goldsmith, Jr., sat at the stern with his mother Emily watching Ireland slowly disappear. Franky's father, Franklin, Sr., was a machinist from Kent who was taking his family to Detroit, Michigan, where there was plenty of work at good wages, something he was finding hard to come by in Kent. Franky and his mother watched the British Isles slip below the horizon with mixed emotions: Franky, though as excited as any nine-year-old at the thought of traveling to a foreign country, was saying goodbye to the only home he had ever known; Mrs. Goldsmith's sadness ran deeper, for she was still mourning her youngest child, who had died of diphtheria only a few months before.

Chief Officer Wilde was less than happy as well, but for quite different reasons. He had written to his sister in a letter posted at Queenstown that he was feeling distinctly uneasy about his latest assignment. "I still don't like this ship. . . . I have a queer feeling about it."[17]

Henry Tighe Wilde was not considered a man given to flights of fancy. A tall, powerfully built man, just thirty-eight years old, he too had worked his way up, from a ship's apprentice in the old square-rigged ships, through the ranks until his appointment as chief officer of the *Olympic* in May 1911. The White Star Line's management held him in high regard, and Captain Smith valued his skill and experience enough to ask that he be assigned to the *Titanic* for her maiden voyage, moving Murdoch from chief officer to first. With his usual tact and diplomacy the captain had broken the news to Murdoch, explaining that he didn't doubt Murdoch's ability, but Wilde's nearly year-long experience on the *Olympic* would be especially valuable in shaking down the new *Titanic*.

Wilde, on the other hand, wasn't particularly keen on the idea. He disliked the thought of bumping his friend Murdoch out of his new berth, and like Lightoller, he never felt comfortable with the *Titanic* herself. Eventually his friends and family persuaded him to overcome his reluctance to take the appointment, arguing that with Captain Smith retiring this would put him in line to succeed him as captain of either the *Titanic* or the *Olympic*. After much consideration, he finally agreed to go, but as the letter to his sister showed, he was still apprehensive about the new ship.[18]

Together, Captain Smith, Chief Officer Wilde, First Officer Murdoch, and Second Officer Lightoller were the watch-keeping officers. To assist them were four junior officers: Third Officer Herbert Pitman, Fourth Officer Joseph Boxhall, Fifth Officer Harold Lowe, and Sixth Officer James Moody. Pitman had spent nearly nine years at sea, five of them with the White Star Line. He had a particular talent for administration and a comfortable, friendly manner in dealing with passengers. Boxhall, like Pitman, had been with the Line for five years now. Boxhall came from a seafaring family, and indeed there must have been something nautical in his genes, for he had already acquired a reputation as being an outstanding navigator. Captain Smith had so much confidence in his skill that he assigned Boxhall the responsibility of keeping the ship's charts up-to-date, including any position, weather, or ice reports the *Titanic* might receive.

Harold Lowe was a self-described "hard case" who had gone to sea at the age of fourteen. Actually "gone to sea" wasn't quite correct: he had been apprenticed by his father to a Liverpool businessman, but Lowe announced that he "wouldn't work for anybody for nothing" and promptly ran away to sign on as a cabin boy on a schooner. He soon moved up to square-rigged ships, earned all his certificates while spending five years sailing up and down the West African coast, and finally joined the White Star Line in early 1911.

The most junior of the officers, James Moody, had also spent a fair amount of time in sailing ships before joining the White Star Line. His first ship with the line was the *Oceanic*. The assignment to the *Titanic* seemed like a godsend to him, although he found her size somewhat imposing. While still in Belfast, he had written home, "I have been here a week, chiefly occupied trying to find my way about the big omnibus." Moody was disappointed that the new position didn't offer any increase in pay, but there were compensations: he wrote excitedly to his sister that at last he had a cabin, though small, all to himself. With the weather expected to be clear and calm for the next few days, none of the *Titanic*'s officers anticipated anything more than a routine crossing, with, of course, the usual teething troubles that accompany any new ship. Yet even those seemed more noticeable by their absence. Harland and Wolff had done a splendid job on this new ship, and the *Titanic*'s officers, staff, and crew settled into a routine of daily shipboard duties.[19]

Still, there were a few members of the crew who exercised the age-old sailor's right to find something to grouse about in their ship, no matter if she was brand new. Arthur Paintin, Captain Smith's steward, was typical when he wrote to his parents in a letter posted from Queenstown, "what a fine ship this is, much better than the *Olympic* as far as passengers are concerned, but my little room is nowhere near so nice, no daylight, electric light on all the time, but I suppose it's no use grumbling."[20]

For the next three days the *Titanic* steamed calmly across the Atlantic, fair weather accompanying her the entire way. The passengers had quickly grown accustomed to the new ship, and the experienced travelers had indulged in what had become a ritual on the transatlantic liners: the first night out they consulted the passenger list, looking for familiar names. The list itself had been printed in a neat little booklet for them, the White Star Line being used to their wealthier clients' habits.

Of course the list included all the prominent names, but also included were the thirty-one maids, valets, and personal servants accompanying the various First Class passengers. These servants were indispensable to the upper classes of the day, and often were valued friends and confidants of the men and women they served. The Line also recognized the somewhat nebulous status these men and women held—obviously it wouldn't do to treat them as First Class passengers, which they clearly were not, but they couldn't be treated like any ordinary working class folks either. White Star solved the dilemma by including a separate promenade and dining room reserved exclusively for the maids and menservants of the First Class passengers.[21]

A few people traveling First Class had their names deliberately omitted from the printed list. Missing were the names of George Bradley, C. H. Romaine, and Harry Homer. All three men were sailing on the *Titanic*, but under aliases. They had a very good reason for doing so: all three were notorious cardsharps, hoping to make a maiden voyage killing. A fourth professional gambler, Jay Yates, was also making the crossing, under the name "J. H. Rogers," though neither name was on the passenger list.

Such professional gamblers were and continue to be a fixture on passenger liners. Most were known to the pursers and assistant pursers on the larger liners, but as long as the stakes never went too high or no one appeared to be victimized by his or her losses, the gamblers' activities were largely ignored. The White Star Line did take the precaution of issuing a warning, inserted in the passenger list, that professional gamblers might be aboard and discouraging "Games of Chance, as being likely to afford these individuals special opportunities for taking advantage of others." Admittedly this warning was more for the self-protection of the White Star Line than the welfare of the passengers, to keep the Line from being implicated should anyone lose too heavily.[22]

Another ritual that took place early in the voyage was the custom of gentlemen traveling alone to formally offer their services to "unprotected" ladies, that is women who were single, widowed, or traveling alone. Usually this involved nothing more strenuous than fetching a deck chair or calling for a steward to "bring the lady another hot tea." It also ensured a dinner companion and often some interesting conversation. As a prelude to a shipboard romance, however, the custom was a dismal failure, despite seemingly being tailor-made for such a prospect, since the unwritten, unspoken code of conduct of the day demanded that the gentleman be exactly that, and almost invariably the men complied.

So it was, for example, that Mrs. William Graham and her daughter Margaret, along with Margaret's governess Miss Shutes, were taken under the "protection" of Washington Augustus Roebling, the heir to the New York engineering and steel firm, and Howard Case, the London manager of Vacuum Oil. Colonel Gracie nearly outdid himself, beginning by taking Mrs. E. D. Appleton, Mrs. J. Murray Brown, and Mrs. R. C. Cornell under his wing. Gracie later told how these three women, who were sisters, were returning from England, "where they had laid to rest the remains of a fourth sister, Lady Victoria Drummond." Finally, he would extend his services to young Miss Edith Evans, not to mention the remarkable Mrs. Candee.[23]

Mrs. Helen Churchill Candee was every bit as well protected as Colonel Gracie was overstretched. An attractive widow of considerable charm, Helen Candee was born out of her time. By 1912 she was already a successful author: in 1900 she had published a book based on a thoroughly startling premise, expressed in its title, *How Women May Earn a Living*, followed by a western, *An Oklahoma Romance*, and a cultural guide entitled *Decorative Styles and Periods*; she was due to have a history of tapestry published in the fall. She was independent, intelligent, and strong willed—thoroughly capable of succeeding in a man's world.

It was her habit to spend her mornings reading on the Promenade Deck forward, taking two chairs, "one for myself and the other for callers—or self-protection," as she put it. No less than six different gentlemen came forward at various times the first two days of the voyage to offer their services: Colonel Gracie, of course, the very model of the Edwardian gentleman; an Englishman named Hugh Woolner, the son of a sculptor, who probably appealed to Mrs. Candee's artistic leanings; Edward A. Kent, a Buffalo, New York, architect who had been recommended to her by a mutual friend; Clinch Smith, a Long Island socialite and one of Colonel Gracie's best friends; E. P. Colley, from Ireland; and Bjorn Steffanson, a dashing Reserve lieutenant in the Swedish Army.

Mrs. Candee "felt divinely flattered to be in such company," while the six gentlemen in turn were all fascinated by this attractive, dynamic woman. Furthermore, the reason for her sailing on the *Titanic* added to her mystique: her son had been injured in an airplane accident—an unusual event in 1912—and she was hurrying to meet him. While it seemed that Mrs. Candee had a few more gentleman escorts than she needed, she in no way discouraged the attention. Indeed the entire custom of a gentleman offering his "protection" to an unescorted woman, which would bring howls of protest from various quarters in later, more "enlightened" times, could come in very handy.[24]

Colonel Gracie would later refer to this handful of people as "our coterie" and they all got along famously. The colonel, a kind and well-meaning sort, occasionally could be a bit much: he had even pressed a copy of his book *The Truth About Chickamauga* onto Isador Straus. Mr. Straus, a model of tact, told Gracie he would read it "with intense interest," although what interest he would find in 462 pages of overly detailed military minutiae was questionable. Nonetheless, Gracie was having such a good time that, uncharacteristically for him, he neglected his exercise regimen to spend time with his new friends.[25]

The morning of Sunday, April 14, Gracie decided to do something about his lack of exercise. A prebreakfast game of squash with Fred Wright, the ship's squash pro, was followed by several laps in the swimming bath, then up to the First Class Dining Saloon for a big breakfast. Later that morning he planned to attend the Divine Services, which Captain Smith, as was customary, would be conducting.

Meanwhile Mrs. Candee, in the company of Hugh Woolner, had gone exploring. At one point in their excursion through the ship they found themselves up on the Boat Deck, where they found T. W. McCawley, the gym instructor, inside the gleaming new gymnasium. They spent the better part of an hour riding the mechanical horses and pedaling furiously on the stationary bicycles, which were hooked up to big red and blue pointers on a large dial on the wall, showing how far each rider had pedaled. They even took turns on a mysterious contraption called a mechanical camel. Later they retired to the First Class Lounge, where stewards served hot tea and buttered toast. All in all it was a pleasantly quiet Sunday.[26]

For Dickinson and Helen Bishop, Sunday was one more wonderful memory to add to their recollections. Young newlyweds from tiny Dowagiac, Michigan, they had been taken with the idea of closing their honeymoon with a First Class passage on the maiden voyage of the largest, most luxurious ship in the world. It had been a wonderful choice.[27]

Benjamin and Esther Hart were traveling in Second Class, along with their daughter, seven-year-old Eva. They were bound for the province of Manitoba, Canada, where Mr. Hart was going to start a new business. Father and daughter were almost inseparable, it seemed, and together they had great fun exploring the ship over the past three days. Mrs. Hart couldn't share their enthusiasm: she didn't believe for a minute that the ship was "unsinkable," despite what the press said, and had feelings of foreboding from the moment she set foot aboard the *Titanic*. Mr. Hart humored her, and he must have been a patient man, since Mrs. Hart was convinced that catastrophe would strike at night, so she slept during the day, and spent her nights sitting up reading or knitting.

Little Eva was also busy making new friends, and soon found herself frequently playing with six-year-old Nina Harper, once Mr. Hart settled a squabble between the two girls and solemnly informed Eva to share her precious teddy bear with Nina. Nina was traveling with her father, the Rev. John Harper, a Baptist minister from Scotland who had recently become a widower. Accompanying him and his daughter was his sister-in-law, Miss Jessie Leitch.[28]

Another clergyman traveling in Second Class was the Rev. Earnest Carter, vicar of the tiny parish of St. Jude in East London. He was accompanied by his wife Lilian. He was trying to make the best of the voyage, as he was fighting off a headcold he had picked up before the ship sailed. As luck would have it, the Carters had made the acquaintance of Miss Marion Wright, a young woman bound for America and marriage to an Oregon fruit farmer, who possessed a beautiful soprano singing voice; but of more immediate interest to Reverend Carter, she also had a supply of tablets that helped alleviate his cold. Since Reverend Carter had already been asked to lead the traditional Sunday night hymn singing in the Second Class Dining Saloon, he asked Miss Wright if she would grace the gathering with a solo. Flattered, Miss Wright agreed.[29]

In Third Class, although without such amenities as squash courts, stationary bicycles, or a mechanical camel, the steerage passengers had made themselves very much at home. Suddenly finding themselves with more leisure time on their hands than they had ever had before, the English, Irish, Swedish, Finnish, German, and Italian immigrants slowly began to try to get to know each other, often with generations of suspicion and prejudice, not to mention language barriers, to overcome. It was not an easy process, and for the most part the various nationalities tended to stick together. But there seemed an inordinate number of musicians among the steerage passengers, and almost every night there were dances in the common areas of Third Class. The steerage passengers seemed quite happy with their accommodations and there were remarkably few complaints. There was one odd deficiency though: the ship had only two bathtubs for all of Third Class, in this case over seven hundred people. Worse, both of them were located in the stern, a bit of hard luck for those berthed forward who had to make the long trek aft.

No one could deny that the poop deck, at the stern of the ship, offered some of the most spectacular views of the sea. Because it was an exclusively Third Class area, the steerage passengers would gather there in large numbers during the day. This was where young Kathy Gilnagh was sitting early that Sunday afternoon when she found herself intrigued by Eugene Daly, the young Irish piper, playing the bagpipes on the after well deck, just forward and one deck below her. The keening wail of the pipes recalled for her the Ireland she was leaving behind, filling her with melancholy.[30]

For the crew, after breakfast was over, came a faithfully followed Sunday ritual of a passenger ship at sea: the captain's inspection. It was an impressive sight with Captain Smith leading the way, followed by the department heads—the chief officer, the chief engineer, the chief steward, and the purser, all in their best uniforms. From top deck to bottom, bow to stern, and through all the public rooms, they visited every accessible part of the ship. Normally after the captain's inspection would come boat drill, but to the crew's less than secret relief, this Sunday the boat drill was inexplicably canceled.[31]

In truth, even had the boat drill taken place, it would have done little good. The boat drill as outlined by the Board of Trade only required a ship's officers to supervise a picked crew, mustered beforehand, to uncover a designated lifeboat on each side of the ship, swing it out over the ship's side, and climb aboard. Some officers would require the crewmen to examine the oars, mast, sail, and rigging that were stowed in each boat; others weren't so demanding. Once this was accomplished, the crewmen would climb out of the boat, swing it back inboard, pull the cover back on, and go back to work. On the *Titanic* only the crew had boat stations, and these were merely assignments telling the crewmen which boats they were supposed to assist in loading and lowering. As for the passengers, there were no lifeboat assignments of any kind.

At precisely 11:00 A.M. Captain Smith held Divine Services in the First Class Dining Room. On this occasion Second and Third Class passengers were permitted in the First Class areas. The ship's orchestra provided the music, and instead of the Book of Common Prayer, a special company-issued Book of Prayer was used. Sometimes the captain would turn the service over to one of the clergymen on board, but this time he took the service himself. In his strong, measured voice he led the assembled passengers through the General Confession and the Prayer for Those at Sea, along with other psalms and prayers, concluding with Hymn Number 418, "O God, Our Help in Ages Past."[32]

With the Divine Service over, the captain returned to the bridge, and the stewards rearranged the tables and chairs for the afternoon luncheon. While the galley was busy with preparing the food, Captain Smith was attending to his navigation.

At noon every day, the captain and his officers would gather on the port bridge wing, each with a sextant in hand. They would each take a series of sun sightings to work out the ship's precise position, which would then be recorded in the ship's log, along with the distance covered in the previous twenty-four hours. As with most other liners of the day, the *Titanic* held a sweepstakes for the passengers to wager on the day's run. Once the noon sun-sightings were taken and the distance known, the ship's siren blew and those passengers who had placed bets would gather in the First Class Lounge to await the results. A rumor had sprung up that the ship was going faster than it had yet, and when the day's figure was posted it seemed that it was true, for the ship had covered 546 miles in the past day, a speed of nearly $22^1/_2$ knots—bettering the previous day's run of 519 miles, and making the day before that—a mere 386 miles—seem positively poky by comparison.[33]

Bruce Ismay for one took considerable satisfaction in that figure. Earlier in the voyage he had given Captain Smith a list of the various speeds he wanted the ship worked up to at specific points in the crossing, and the *Titanic*'s performance so far had been as close to flawless as could be hoped for. Early that afternoon, as he and Captain Smith were sitting together in the First Class Lounge, Ismay announced his intentions: "Today we did better than yesterday, and tomorrow we shall do better still. We shall beat the *Olympic*'s time to New York and arrive Tuesday night!" It would be a terrific publicity coup for the White Star Line, with their newest and most luxurious ship arriving ahead of schedule—and doing so in time to make headlines in the Wednesday morning papers.[34]

Ismay saw nothing wrong in his usurping some of the captain's authority, although Captain Smith may have seen it differently. Ismay believed that as the owner's representative he had the right to interfere with the ship's operations and navigation. It was typical of him then, when he sat down to lunch with Captain Smith around 1:30 P.M., to take a message that the captain had shown him, sent by the liner *Baltic*, stick it in his pocket and apparently forget about it. Of course the message hadn't been forgotten: later that afternoon Ismay encountered Mrs. Thayer and Mrs. Ryerson, two of the most socially prominent women on board, and in the course of the conversation, Ismay (who liked to remind people that he was the chairman of the White Star Line) took the message out and read it to them. It said, "Icebergs and large quantity of field ice in 41.51 N 49.9 W." The two ladies were suitably impressed.[35]

For all his arrogance, though, Ismay could also be a compassionate man, as Mrs. Ryerson and her husband were to learn on their way to New York. When Ismay learned that the death of their son in America was the reason for their crossing aboard the *Titanic*, he arranged to have an extra cabin placed at their disposal and a steward permanently assigned to them.

The noon luncheon was quite an affair. The menu set before Ismay would have done any hotel on either side of the Atlantic proud:

R.M.S. *Titanic*

April 14, 1912

LUNCHEON

Consomme Fermier	Cockie Leekie

Fillets of Brill
Egg a l'Argenteuil
Chicken à la Maryland
Corned Beef, Vegetables, Dumplings

FROM THE GRILL

Grilled Mutton Chops
Mashed, Fried & Baked Jacket Potatoes
Custard Pudding

Apple Meringue	Pastry

BUFFET

| Salmon Mayonnaise | Potted Shrimps |
| Norwegian Anchovies | Soused Herrings |

Plain and Smoked Sardines

Roast Beef
Round of Spiced Beef
Veal & Ham Pie
Virginia & Cumberland Ham
Bologna Sauce   Brawn
Galantine of Chicken
Corned Ox Tongue
Lettuce   Beet Root   Tomatoes

CHEESE

Cheshire, Stilton, Gorgonzola, Cheshire
Camambert, Roquefort, St. Ivel,
Cheddar

Iced draught Munich Lager Beer 3d. & 6d. a Tankard[36]

——◆◆◆——

That message about ice that was sitting in Ismay's pocket during lunch was the third one the wireless operators aboard the *Titanic* had received that day. The senior and junior operators who constituted the wireless section of the *Titanic*'s crew were a couple of busy young men. Wireless in 1912, while something less than the "erratic novelty" that it has sometimes been depicted as being, was still new enough that it could be considered in its childhood, if not its infancy. True, ranges were limited, the performance of some sets was marginal, and there was a shortage of skilled operators, but the rapidly growing number of conventions and etiquette were adding a much-needed measure of discipline to wireless communications. What was most noticeably lacking was standardization—there were a half dozen types of equipment; two different Morse codes, American and International; no regulations concerning the hours wireless watch was to be kept; and no definite order in the ships' crew organizations as to where the wireless operator belonged.

This was due in part to the fact that the wireless operators did not actually work for the shipping line that owned their particular vessel. Instead there were four private companies that controlled the wireless industry and hired out the services of their operators to the steamship lines: Compagnie General Telegraphique of France, Telefunken of Germany, and the twin companies of American and British Marconi Marine. Though the two wireless operators aboard the *Titanic* had signed the ship's articles and took orders from the ship's officers, they were actually employees of British Marconi.[37]

The senior operator, John "Jack" Phillips, was a serious young man from the village of Farncombe, near Godalming in Surrey. He had just turned twenty-five on April 11, and had been with British Marconi for six years. Phillips graduated top of his class at the Marconi training school in Liverpool, and subsequently had worked on the *Teutonic, Lusitania, Mauretania, Campania,* and *Oceanic.* In addition, he spent three years at the high-powered transmitting station at Cliffden in Ireland. Like many young men who become involved with emerging technologies, Phillips was enthralled by wireless, quite knowledgeable about the theory behind it, and adept at turning a practical hand to getting the best performance out of his sometimes temperamental equipment.

His assistant, the junior operator, was only twenty-two. Harold Bride hailed from Bromley in Kent, and had only been with Marconi about eighteen months, his first assignment being the *Haverford* in the summer of 1911, followed by short stints on the *Lusitania,* the *Lafranc,* and the *Anselm.*

Both Phillips and Bride had learned a great deal more at the Marconi school in Liverpool (the students there called it the Tin Tabernacle) than simply the dot-dash rudiments of Morse. Courses in electricity, magnetism, radio-wave propagation, troubleshooting of equipment, and the new regulations of the Radiotelegraphy Convention were all included. An enduring complaint about wireless of that era was the deliberate interference often caused by operators of one company with the signals of another. While such incidents did happen, they were the exception rather than the rule, since such interference could work both ways. (The worst offenders were the German Telefunken operators.) The Radiotelegraphy Convention was very clear about how wireless operators were supposed to conduct themselves, and quite explicit about certain types of transmissions. One type of message that was absolutely forbidden to be interfered with was a distress call.

The courses in radio wave propagation explained to the operators the effect of the ionosphere on wireless transmission and why both transmission and reception were clearer and longer ranged at night than during the day. Of course, this benefit in range and clarity meant that the majority of the wireless operator's work was done during hours when most of the rest of a ship's crew would be asleep, though not always. There was no requirement for a twenty-four-hour wireless watch to be maintained by any ships, so the wireless operators usually worked a schedule set for them by the ship's captain. On the *Titanic,* this meant that Phillips and Bride alternated shifts, twelve hours on, twelve off, seven days a week. Smaller vessels with only one operator usually had a fifteen to eighteen hour shift.

The work was not difficult in the conventional sense, but the long hours of enforced immobility and intense concentration as the operator sat at his table, key at hand and headphones on, were exhausting. The pay did little to compensate for this: Phillips, for example, as senior operator, only made £8 a month, Bride only £5. It was the knowledge that they were part of a small, select fraternity, capable of snatching messages seemingly out of the thin air with their ungainly looking apparatus that kept most operators at their stations.[38]

Of course that ability fascinated others as well. Passengers especially took an almost childish delight in sending messages to friends and families from the middle of the Atlantic Ocean. As a result, a good deal of Phillips's and Bride's time was taken up with private messages that had nothing to do with the ship itself, mostly of the "Having a wonderful time, wish you were here" variety. The messages had to be handled, since the passengers were paying for the service, but they tended to cause the work to get piled up and occasionally interfered with traffic important to the safe navigation of the ship. Unfortunately there was no set procedure for handling messages on the *Titanic*—or any other ship, for that matter—unless the message was specifically addressed to the captain. Otherwise, Phillips and Bride took care of any incoming messages as best they could.

April 14 was no exception. The *Titanic*'s wireless was a brand new unit—1.5 kilowatts, powerful for the day and relatively long ranged—but a bit balky, so Phillips had trouble all day getting his messages sent. About 9:00 A.M. he took down a report from the Cunard liner *Caronia* that told of "bergs, growlers, and field ice at 42N, from 49 to 51W." He sent Bride to the bridge with the message, and Fourth Officer Boxhall plotted the position on the chart, as well as posting the message in the wardroom. About twenty minutes before noon the Dutch liner *Noordam* reported ice in much the same area, and at 1:42 P.M. the message from the *Baltic* was received. This one went directly to Captain Smith, who showed it to Ismay, who in turn pocketed it. The *Amerika*, a German ship, sent a warning about ice a few minutes after the *Baltic*, mentioning that she had passed two large bergs at 41.27 N, 50.8 W. The *Amerika*'s message was addressed to the U.S. Hydrographic Office, but her set wasn't very powerful, so she asked the *Titanic* to pass it on, and Phillips did so, keeping a copy for the ship.[39]

If anyone on the bridge had bothered to plot all the positions in these reports, he would have seen an immense belt of ice seventy-eight miles wide stretching across the *Titanic*'s projected course. Instead the messages were scattered across the ship, one already plotted by Fourth Officer Boxhall, another languishing in Ismay's pocket, the rest somewhere in limbo between the wireless office and the bridge.

About midafternoon the *Titanic*'s set went on the blink and Phillips spent the next four hours locating the fault and making repairs. It was frustrating because the traffic kept piling up, and there would be a huge backlog once the set was fixed. Just a little after 7:00 P.M. he got the wireless working again, and he began to attack the stack of messages on his desk. At 7:30 the Leyland liner *Californian* called to warn the *Titanic* about "three large bergs five miles to southward of us" and gave her position as 42.3 N, 49.9 W. That meant the ice was only fifty miles ahead of the *Titanic*.[40]

CHAPTER 4

Ten Seconds

Every matter has its time and way.
                                        —Ecclesiastes 8:6

AT 6:00 P.M. ON SUNDAY, APRIL 14, SECOND OFFICER LIGHTOLLER CAME ON watch, relieving Chief Officer Wilde on the bridge. Wilde commented to Lightoller that it felt rather colder than usual, and indeed it seemed that the temperature had plummeted once the sun had set. Lightoller agreed, and after a while decided to call up Jim Hutchinson, the ship's carpenter. Remarking that the temperature had fallen four degrees in the past hour, Lightoller told Hutchinson to watch out for the ship's fresh water supply—if the temperature continued to fall, there was a chance it could freeze. Hutchinson agreed to keep an eye on it. Catching the attention of Trimmer Samuel Hemming, Lightoller told him to secure the forward fo'c's'le hatch; otherwise the glow of light coming up from below was enough to ruin the night vision of the lookouts in the crow's nest.[1]

Lightoller was sharing the watch with Sixth Officer Moody. Recalling the message he had seen posted in the wardroom, the one from the *Caronia*, Lightoller decided to hold an impromptu test of Moody's navigational skills, and asked the young sixth officer when he thought the *Titanic* would be nearing the ice. After a few seconds' thought, Moody answered sometime around 11:00 P.M. Lightoller was disappointed—he had already worked out the answer as being close to 9:30. Clearly, Moody's navigation wasn't up to snuff.

It didn't occur to Lightoller that Moody may have based his answer on a message the second officer hadn't seen. In addition to the *Caronia*'s warning, there were the warnings sent by the *Noordam* and the *Amerika*, which had been sent to the bridge, although no one later seemed to know exactly what happened to them. There was also the message from the *Baltic* still sitting uselessly in Bruce Ismay's jacket pocket. And, unknown to anyone on the bridge, yet another message had arrived, this one from the Atlantic Transport liner *Mesaba*. She had sent out a detailed warning, reading, "Lat. 42 N to 41.25 N, Longitude 40 W to 50.30 W, saw much heavy pack ice and great number large icebergs, also field ice." The *Titanic* was already inside the rectangle described in the *Mesaba*'s message, and had Captain Smith known this he might have considered changing course or reducing speed. But this last message was still sitting under a paperweight on Phillips's desk, and the other warnings were going unread or unheeded.

Captain Smith was mindful of the danger, however. Already he had laid out a course for the *Titanic* that took her at least ten miles south of the normal shipping lane, a precaution against the ice that had drifted unusually far south this spring. At dinner he tapped Ismay on the shoulder and asked for the *Baltic*'s message back, saying he needed to post it on the bridge, which he then did.[2]

After dinner, George Widener invited Smith to a special reception he was giving to honor the captain's retirement. Smith, who liked Widener and his family, was pleased to attend, and it was with some reluctance that around 9:00 P.M. he excused himself and returned to the bridge, saying that he had to attend to the ship. There he stopped to talk with his second officer as they peered out into the cold April night. It was by all reports an exceptional night—it was extraordinarily clear and calm, conditions that made both Smith and Lightoller less than happy. Smith remarked on the cold.

"Yes, sir," Lightoller replied, "it's very cold. In fact it's only one degree above freezing."

"There is not much wind."

"No, it's a flat calm, as a matter of fact."

"A flat calm. Yes, quite flat."

Lightoller then remarked that it was a pity that the breeze had so completely died, since the chop a breeze usually kicked up would make it easier to spot any ice ahead as it washed up against the base of a berg or growler. Smith was sure that the visibility was good enough that even a "blue" berg, that is, one that had recently overturned, would be spotted before it could present a danger. Just before 9:30, Captain Smith told Lightoller he was going to his cabin. "If it becomes at all doubtful, let me know at once."[3]

The sudden drop in temperature had driven all but the most hardy passengers inside. Since this was the next to the last night out, it was the custom for the First Class passengers to dress in their most resplendent attire for dinner. (The last night out was reserved for packing.) The ladies looked ravishing in their evening gowns; the gentlemen were dashing in their white tie and tails. Even Mrs. Henry Harris put in an appearance, in the best theatrical tradition, though she would have been excused if she hadn't: earlier that day she had tripped and fallen down one of the staircases, breaking a small bone in her arm. Once Assistant Surgeon Simpson had set the arm in plaster, Mrs. Harris gamely insisted on dressing for dinner, earning a compliment from Captain Smith for her pluck.[4]

In Third Class another of the seemingly endless dances was getting under way. In the middle of the merriment, a large rat suddenly appeared out of nowhere, eliciting screams of terror, some real, some feigned, from the young women. A handful of the men dashed after the offending rodent, and the dance was under way again.[5]

After dinner about a hundred Second Class passengers had gathered in their Dining Saloon for the traditional hymn singing, led by the Rev. Earnest Carter, an Anglican priest, while a young Scottish engineer named Douglas Norman played the piano. All of the hymns sung were chosen by request, and Reverend Carter held the little gathering's attention by preceding each selection with a brief bit of information about the hymn's author and some-times a history of how the particular hymn came to be written. When Mar-ion Wright prepared to sing "Lead Kindly Light," he explained that the song had been written in the aftermath of a shipwreck on the North Atlantic.

Kate Buss, who had come to hear her new friend Marion Wright sing, noticed that many of the people gathered in the dining saloon were power-fully moved by Miss Wright's singing, some of the men even having tears in their eyes. At one point, Reverend Carter's wife Lilian was seen covering her face with her hands, lost either in deep prayer or deep emotion. Not surpris-ingly, then, more than a few of the hymns chosen dealt with the dangers of traveling by sea, and Lawrence Beesley, a young school teacher from London who was traveling to see his brother in America, remembered how movingly everyone joined in to sing "Eternal Father, Strong to Save."

> Eternal Father, strong to save,
> Whose arm hath bound the restless wave,
> Who bidd'st the mighty ocean deep
> It's own appointed limits keep.
> O hear us when we cry to Thee
> For those in peril on the sea.[6]

At 10:00 P.M. First Officer Murdoch walked onto the bridge to relieve Lightoller. The first thing he said was, "It's pretty cold."

"Yes it is. It's freezing," was Lightoller's reply. He then went on to tell Murdoch that the ship might be up to the ice any time now, adding that the water temperature was down to thirty-one degrees and still dropping; that the carpenter had been warned not to let the fresh water supply freeze up; that the crow's nest had been specially warned to watch out for ice, specifi-cally small bergs and growlers; and that the captain had left word to be called if "it became at all doubtful." With that, Lightoller, looking forward to a warm bunk, bade Murdoch good night and went off to his cabin. While Murdoch was relieving Lightoller, Quartermaster Hitchens relieved Quarter-master Oliver at the helm. "N 71 W," Oliver murmured, giving Hitchens the *Titanic*'s current course.

"N 71 W," Hitchens repeated, taking the wheel and peering into the softly lit binnacle to make sure the ship was steady on her course. Satisfied that she was, Hitchens gazed out through the wheelhouse windows into the night.[7]

In the crow's nest, Lookouts Jewell and Symons were relieved by Lookouts Fleet and Lee. "Keep a sharp eye out for ice, especially small bergs and growlers!" Symons said, repeating the last orders given to him. Fleet and Lee quickly settled in and began peering intently into the night. Fleet noticed what looked like haze on the horizon, and it seemed that the ship would be in it soon.

"Well, if we can see through that," Fleet remarked, "we'll be lucky."[8]

In the wireless office, just behind the officers' quarters on the boat deck, Phillips finally was making some headway on the backlog of personal messages from the passengers. The day had been so exhausting that Bride had volunteered to relieve Phillips at midnight, a full two hours early. It was typical of Bride, who seemed to possess a bottomless reservoir of good humor and thoughtfulness. Meanwhile Phillips still had more than an hour to go, so he hunched over his key and rapped out his messages to the relay station at Cape Race, Newfoundland.

Suddenly, at 11:00 P.M., the *Californian* burst in, announcing "Say, old man, we are surrounded by ice and stopped." The *Californian*'s operator hadn't bothered to get Phillips's OK to break in on his transmission, and the ship was so close that the message nearly deafened him. Furious, Phillips signaled back, "Shut up! Shut up! I am busy, I am working Cape Race!" The *Californian*'s operator lapsed into hurt silence and Phillips apologized to Cape Race, whose operator, William Gray, was a good friend. The last thing Jack Phillips needed after a day like this was some idiot interrupting his work. Wearily, he resumed sending his messages.[9]

In the crow's nest, Lookouts Fleet and Lee continued to peer determinedly into the night, their concentration total. The mist that Fleet had commented on earlier had disappeared, and now all conversation between the two men ceased as they scanned the waters ahead of the ship. Mindful of Second Officer Lightoller's warning to be alert for ice, neither man wanted the slightest distraction, for though visibility was good, conditions for spotting ice were poor. Despite the crystal clear air, the absence of any moonlight meant that the typically ghost-white icebergs and growlers would be visible only at a much reduced distance, while the calm sea, later described as "as smooth as a piece of polished plate glass," meant that there would be no white wash of water at the base of an iceberg that would ordinarily be kicked up by chop or swell. Fleet in particular sorely missed the binoculars.

It was a little more than twenty minutes before midnight when Fleet thought he saw something straight ahead. The object appeared quite small at first, but grew rapidly in size, and Fleet hesitated for only a few seconds to make sure of the object's identity before reaching up for the pull of the large bronze bell above his head. He gave three sharp tugs, three rings being the signal for "object ahead," then quickly grabbed the telephone in the box on the mast behind him. The bridge answered almost immediately—it was Sixth Officer Moody.

"Iceberg right ahead," Fleet said without preamble.

"Thank you," Moody replied. Turning to First Officer Murdoch, he repeated Fleet's words.[10]

"Hard a-starboard!" Murdoch snapped to quartermaster Hitchens, who stood at the ship's telemotor wheel. Murdoch then stepped over to the bronze engine room telegraph and rang for full speed astern on both engines. Hitchens meanwhile spun the wheel to the right, then all three men waited tensely for the bow to swing clear of the oncoming berg.[11]

Up in the crow's nest it looked as if the ship would never turn in time. Bracing themselves for the shock of a head-on collision, Fleet and Lee breathed a sigh of relief as at the last second the prow swung left, apparently missing the ice. Even so, it looked awfully close, and as the berg brushed past, large chunks of ice thudded onto the foredeck and into the well deck. As the ship glided past, the two men could see why the iceberg had been so hard to spot at first—it was a "blue" berg, recently overturned and still dark with sea water. Over the noise of the falling ice it seemed to the two lookouts that they could hear a faint, metallic ripping sound.

On the bridge Murdoch pulled the switch that closed the watertight doors to the boiler rooms and engine room, then stepped out onto the starboard bridge wing and watched the berg pass by the liner's hull. It was so close he felt he could almost reach out and touch it.[12]

Throughout the *Titanic*, her crew, sensitive as crew members always are to the rhythms and sounds of their vessel, reacted to the collision in a surprising variety of ways and with an equally surprising variety of explanations. Down forward on D Deck, in the crew's quarters, Fireman John Thompson and his mates had woken up only moments before and were preparing to go on watch at midnight. A sudden crash sent those men still in their bunks sprawling onto the deck. Thompson heard a "harsh, grinding sound," then ran out onto the forward well deck, only to find it littered with ice.

Asleep in his bunk in the forward crew's quarters, Seaman Fred Clench was awakened "by the crunching and jarring, as if [the ship] was hitting up against something." Quickly pulling on his trousers and shoes, he too went out onto the forward well deck. As he stood beside the hatch to the No. 1 cargo hold, Clench could hear the sound of inrushing seawater far below.

Four decks below and some ways aft of where First Officer Murdoch was standing, in the First Class Dining Saloon, four off-duty stewards were sitting around one of the tables. The last passengers had long since left and now this small group had the huge dining room all to themselves. A faint but unmistakable shudder that seemed to run the length of the ship interrupted them in the middle of their conversation. That was all, just a shudder, but it was enough to rattle the table settings.

Steward James Johnson thought he recognized it: he had been on the *Olympic* when she had dropped a propeller blade earlier that year, and it felt exactly the same to him. Another steward was apparently of the same mind, and, anticipating a trip back to Harland and Wolff, promptly announced, "Another Belfast trip!"

Just astern of the First Class Dining Saloon was the First Class galley, where Chief Night Baker Walter Belford had just finished baking rolls for the next morning's breakfast. Suddenly for no apparent reason, a pan filled with freshly baked rolls sitting atop an oven tumbled to the deck, startling Belford. Then he too noticed that the ship seemed to shudder, although in his annoyance over the ruined rolls, the thought of another trip to enjoy Belfast hospitality was the last thing on his mind.

One deck lower, on C Deck, four off-duty seamen were relaxing in the forward crews' mess. Seamen Brice, Buley, Osman, and Evans were, as one of them put it, "sitting around smokin' and yarnin'" when they heard three bells ring up in the crow's nest, followed about a half minute later by a slight jar. To Seaman Edward Buley, "it seemed as though something was rubbing alongside her," while Brice thought it felt like "a heavy vibration." Frank Osman went out onto the forward well deck and was confronted by the sight of mounds of ice piled on its starboard side.[13]

Down in the engine room, the only indication Chief Engineer Bell had that anything unusual had happened was the unexpected ringing of the engine telegraph as someone on the bridge suddenly ordered "Full Speed Astern" on both engines. Bell quickly gave the order to stop the center turbine and then threw the reciprocating engines into reverse. A moment later an alarm bell sounded as the watertight doors began to close automatically. For several minutes a bewildered group of engineers, greasers, and artificers looked at each other and wondered just what had happened.

Quartermaster George Rowe had been standing watch on the after, or auxiliary, bridge. This was often a hardship post, for the bridge was really just an open catwalk running across the poop deck at the stern, leaving Rowe completely exposed to the elements. Tonight, though, wasn't all that bad: the absence of any wind kept the cold from becoming unbearable, and Rowe was able to keep reasonably warm by pacing to and fro across the bridge. As he paced he noticed a curious sight—thousands of tiny ice splinters that gave off bright colors as they caught and refracted the glow of the deck lights, a phenomena that sailors call "Whiskers 'round the Light." It stuck in Rowe's mind because it usually occurred only near ice fields.

His reverie was broken suddenly by a slight change in the motion of the ship, as the steady beat of the engines changed. Peering forward he stared at what appeared to be a full-rigged ship, with sails set, passing perilously close by the *Titanic*'s starboard side. After a second or two, Rowe realized that he was actually looking at an iceberg, one that towered over the auxiliary bridge, itself nearly sixty feet above the water. As Rowe watched, the berg passed by swiftly and vanished.[14]

Steward Alfred Crawford was strolling the corridors of B Deck forward when he heard a muffled "crunch" coming from the starboard side of the ship; he ran out to the railing just in time to see "a large black object" passing alongside. Turning to go back inside, he saw Mr. and Mrs. Dickinson Bishop coming out onto the deck. The Bishops had left their cabin, B-47, to see what had happened. Both were shivering furiously in the intense cold, and they walked up and down the deck a couple times before bumping into Steward Crawford. "You go back downstairs," Crawford told them, "there's nothing to be afraid of. We have only struck a little piece of ice and passed it."

The Bishops' experience was typical of most of the passengers': many of them felt *something*, variously described later as a bump, a quiver, or a grinding jar, but few had any idea what it was. Major Peuchen thought a heavy wave had struck the ship. Marguerite Frolicher, a young Swiss girl traveling with her father on one of his business trips, was half asleep and thought of the Zurich ferries' notoriously bumpy landings. Mrs. E. D. Appleton felt little, but heard something disturbing indeed—a ripping sound, as if someone was tearing a long piece of cloth.[15]

In the First Class Smoking Room, located almost at the center of the *Titanic*'s upper deck, the shudder brought all activity to an abrupt halt. A handful of guests from George Widener's party in honor of Captain Smith had left the *à la carte* Restaurant behind and moved into the Smoking Room shortly after the ladies had retired. Now Clarence Moore, Major Butt, George Widener's son Harry, and William Carter were all that were left. In one corner of the room, a handful of young men, Hugh Woolner and Bjorn Steffanson among them, were involved in a rather boisterous game of bridge, while at another table Lucien P. Smith was discovering that his French wasn't up to the complexities of bidding with three Frenchmen.

Suddenly they all felt a shudder, and conversations hung suspended for a moment. Every man was instantly on his feet, hurrying out the aft doors and rushing to the after railing of the Promenade Deck. Hugh Woolner heard someone calling out "We've struck an iceberg—there it is!" Peering intently into the night, Woolner thought he could make out a huge black shape a hundred or so yards astern of the ship, but it was quickly swallowed up by the darkness. The group filed back into the Smoking Room passing comments back and forth about the incident, and just as the last man in was closing the door behind him, someone noticed a new phenomenon—the engines had stopped.[16]

Just a few moments earlier, Mr. and Mrs. Walter Douglas had been strolling past the Grand Staircase. Mr. Douglas had just remarked to his wife that the ship seemed to be going faster than it ever had before, as for once the vibration of the engines was quite noticeable on the staircase. They had arrived at their stateroom, C-68, just as the *Titanic* hit the berg, but to them the shock of the collision didn't seem very great.

Mrs. J. Stuart White didn't think much of it at the time either: the ship quivered as if it "went over a thousand marbles. There was nothing terrifying about it at all." Mr. C. E. Stengel, in C-116, was moaning in his sleep. His wife shook him awake, and just as his head cleared, he heard a "slight clash." Stengel paid it little attention until he noticed a moment later that the engines had stopped. Turning to his wife he said, "There is something serious, there is something wrong. We had better go up on deck."[17]

To Bruce Ismay the shudder meant something serious, though perhaps not dangerous. He had awakened with a start in his deluxe cabin on B Deck, having had enough experience with ships to know that the *Titanic* had hit something. But what?

James McGough, a buyer for Gimbel's from Philadelphia, could have answered Ismay's question. Something of a fresh-air fiend, McGough had left the porthole of his cabin open as he was getting ready for bed. When the iceberg brushed by, several sizable chunks of ice fell into his cabin through the open port.

Of all the passengers' reactions, perhaps that of Mrs. Walter Stephenson was the most ominous. As she lay in her bed, just dozing off, she felt a jolt run through the ship. Instantly it brought to mind the memory of another April, just six years earlier, when she had been lying in bed and felt the same kind of jolt, as the city of San Francisco began falling to pieces around her.[18]

Back up on the bridge, Captain Smith appeared just seconds after the impact. Imperturbable as ever, but with a serious air, he asked, "Mr. Murdoch, what was that?"

"An iceberg, Captain. I ordered hard-a-starboard and rang for full speed astern. I was going to hard-a-port around it, but it was just too close."

"Close the watertight doors."

"Already closed, sir."

"All stop."

"Aye, sir." Murdoch turned to the engine room telegraph and rang down for the engines to stop.

Just then Fourth Officer Boxhall came up to the bridge, and together with Smith and Murdoch, stepped out onto the starboard bridge wing, where for several seconds they peered vainly into the night trying to spot the iceberg. Stepping back inside, Smith sent Boxhall on a quick inspection of the ship. After just a few minutes Boxhall returned, saying he could find no damage below decks. His report didn't satisfy Captain Smith, who told Boxhall, "Go and find the carpenter and get him to sound the ship." As Boxhall ran down the bridge ladder, the carpenter, Jim Hutchinson, pushed past him on his way up to the bridge, blurting out, "She's making water fast!"

Right behind Hutchinson came one of the postal clerks, Iago Smith, calling out, "The mail hold is filling rapidly!"

Boxhall worked his way down to the mail hold and for a minute or two watched the other four mail clerks, standing almost knee deep in water already, snatching letters from sorting racks and stuffing them into bags, while around them floated other bags of mail, already full. Boxhall rushed back to the bridge to report what he had seen. Chief Officer Wilde appeared and asked Captain Smith if it was serious. After hearing Boxhall's report, Smith turned to Wilde and said, "Certainly. It is more than serious." He asked for Thomas Andrews to be brought to the bridge, then turned and checked the commutator, a device showing if a ship is listing to port or starboard, or down by the bow or stern. At that moment the commutator showed the *Titanic* listing five degrees to starboard and two degrees down by the head. Smith stared at it for some seconds, then muttered, "Oh, my God!" so softly that only Boxhall heard him.[19]

Next to appear was Ismay. He had hurriedly thrown a suit on over his pajamas and put on a pair of carpet slippers before setting out for the bridge. Without preamble Smith told Ismay the ship had collided with an iceberg. "Do you think the ship is seriously damaged?" Ismay asked.

"I'm afraid she is."

Smith was waiting anxiously for Thomas Andrews. After dinner Andrews had returned to his cabin, A-36, to go over his notes for the day. When the call came from Captain Smith, Andrews had been poring over blueprints and diagrams of the Promenade Deck—he hadn't even noticed the collision—as he worked out the details of converting the writing room into more staterooms. It was a mildly amusing problem, since, as Walter Lord put it, "The writing room had originally been planned partly as a place where the ladies could retire after dinner. But this was the twentieth century and the ladies just wouldn't retire. Clearly, a smaller room would do."[20]

Moments after Andrews arrived on the bridge, he and Captain Smith were making their own inspection of the damage. Working their way deep into the ship, using mostly accesses and corridors used only by the crew to attract less attention, they found the forward cargo holds flooded, the mailroom awash, and the squash court floor covered with water. As they made their way back to the bridge they passed through the A Deck foyer, their faces set in expressions of inscrutability. Once on the bridge, Andrews reviewed the situation: the forepeak and both forward holds were flooded, the mailroom was awash, Boiler Room No. 6 was flooded to a depth of fourteen feet, and water was entering Boiler Room No. 5. For nearly three hundred feet, as the iceberg bumped and ground along the *Titanic*'s side, seams had been split, plating bent, and rivets popped: the first six of the *Titanic*'s sixteen watertight compartments had been opened to the sea, all in the ten seconds' time it took the berg to brush by.[21]

Down in the bowels of the ship Andrews's diagnosis would have come as no surprise. Fireman George Kemish recalled that the ship was "a good job . . . not what we were accustomed to in old ships, slogging our guts out and nearly roasted by heat." The firemen only had to keep the furnaces full, not bothering with rakes or slicer bars, so the men were taking it easy. Fireman James Barrett was talking to Assistant Second Engineer James Hesketh when they heard a thud, the screech of tearing metal, and the clanging of a warning bell. A red warning light began flashing above the watertight door.

Barrett and Hesketh barely had time to take this all in when with a tremendous bang the whole starboard side of the ship seemed to split open. The sea thundered in, and the two men barely hardly had time to leap through the rapidly closing watertight door into Boiler Room No. 5.

Room No. 5 had its own problems. A gash two feet long extended past the bulkhead dividing No. 5 from No. 6, and water was pouring in. One of the stokers was digging himself out of a bunker the impact had knocked him into, while the rest of the crew in Boiler Room No. 5, along with Barrett and Hesketh, began to rig hoses and start pumps in a valiant effort to keep the water at a manageable level.

Farther astern in the other four boiler rooms and the engine room the rumor quickly started that the *Titanic* had run aground off the banks of Newfoundland. This was quickly quelled when an off-duty trimmer came around, announcing, "Blimey! We've struck an iceberg!"[22]

Far above, in Andrews's cabin, A-36, builder and captain stood over a structural diagram of the ship. Andrews quickly outlined the problem for Captain Smith. All of the ship's six forward watertight compartments were open to the sea. The *Titanic* could float with any two of her sixteen watertight compartments flooded—in an extreme case she could actually float with four of her forward compartments flooded. But at this point a design flaw emerged: the first two watertight bulkheads extended only as high as D Deck, as did the last five, while the middle eight only carried up to E Deck. With the first five—or in this case six—compartments breached, the weight of the incoming water would pull the ship's head down until the water level in the flooded compartments rose above the top of the bulkheads; the water in the fifth compartment would spill over into the sixth, pulling the ship down farther until the water in the sixth compartment spilled over into the seventh, and so on, until the ship inevitably sank.

Smith was stunned. After forty uneventful years at sea the worst nightmare of a captain's career had come for him. How impossibly bitter must have been the memory of six years earlier, when on the bridge of the then-new *Adriatic* he had told reporters "I cannot imagine any accident happening to this vessel. I cannot conceive of any disaster causing this ship to founder. Modern shipbuilding has gone beyond that." Now, he was making his last voyage before retiring, in command of what was supposed to be the largest, safest ship in the world, and the *Titanic's* builder was telling him that she had at the most an hour and a half before she sank.

Even more unbearable must have been the knowledge shared by Smith, Andrews, and a handful of the officers on board: that night the *Titanic* was carrying 2,207 passengers and crew, yet because of the hopelessly outdated Board of Trade regulations there were lifeboats for only 1,178 of them. Andrews's news was not only the ruin of Smith's career, it was a death sentence for half the people on board the ship.[23]

Captain Smith and Thomas Andrews had just become the unwitting victims of the North Atlantic shipping companies' incredible run of good luck. It had been forty years since there had been a passenger ship sunk with a serious loss of life, the last being the *Atlantic*, which struck a submerged rock and sank, with the loss of 491 lives, in 1872. In 1880 the Guion Line's *Arizona* had struck an iceberg head-on in a dense fog, but despite the damage done by the shock of the impact, the *Arizona*'s collision bulkhead had held, and she limped into St. John's, Newfoundland, her crumpled bow apparently mute testimony to the ability of the big ships to stand up to icebergs.

Compounding the folly of that assumption was the sinking of the White Star Line's own *Republic* in 1906, which created in the public's mind a wholly erroneous concept of the role lifeboats were meant to play in an accident at sea. Rammed and mortally damaged by the *Florida*, the *Republic* had remained afloat for nearly thirty-six hours, during which a half dozen other vessels came to her assistance. This provided the ship's crew with more than ample time to load the *Republic*'s passengers into the boats and, working in relays, transfer them safely to the surrounding vessels. When the *Republic* finally sank, the only lives lost had been those unfortunate souls killed in the collision. It had never occurred to anyone at the time that all of the *Republic*'s boats combined could hold only about half of the passengers and crew on board at the time: if the ship had foundered within an hour or two of the collision, the only hope of safety would have been those inadequate lifeboats, and more than five hundred people would have been left on her decks to drown.[24]

With the knowledge that he was facing exactly such a situation, Captain Smith returned to the bridge. At 12:05 A.M. he told Chief Officer Wilde to uncover the lifeboats. Boxhall had already gone to the officers' quarters to rouse Second Officer Lightoller and Third Officer Pitman; Murdoch was organizing the muster of the passengers. Slowly the alarm began to spread through the ship.

CHAPTER 5

A Slow Comprehension

*. . . and a people without understanding shall come to
ruin.*

—Hosea 4:14

SOME PEOPLE DIDN'T NEED TO BE AWAKENED. WHEN FOURTH OFFICER
Boxhall burst into the quarters of Second Officer Lightoller, he found him
lying on his bunk, wide awake. "You know we have struck an iceberg!"
Boxhall exclaimed.

"I know we have struck something," Lightoller replied. At the time of
the collision he was asleep in his bunk, but he woke with a start and ran bare-
foot out onto the Boat Deck to see what had happened. Everything seemed
quiet, although Lightoller noticed Captain Smith and First Officer Murdoch
standing on the starboard bridge wing, staring astern into the darkness.

Lightoller returned to his cabin and lay back down in his bunk, then
noticed that the ship's engines had stopped. Well, he decided, whatever it was
that was wrong, he was off duty, and it wasn't his business to worry about.
(Lightoller was probably still miffed about his supersession as first officer.)
He lay in that pleasant twilight between sleep and wakefulness for nearly a
half hour before he heard a thunderous roar overhead, as the funnels began
venting excess steam, which brought him fully awake. Moments later Fourth
Officer Boxhall came in announcing the collision, adding, "The water is up
to F Deck in the mailroom." Lightoller pulled a sweater and a pair of trousers
over his pajamas while Boxhall went off to rouse Third Officer Pitman.[1]

Pitman, like Lightoller, had been lying in his bunk at the time of the
collision. He had heard a sound like "the chain running over the windlass"
but wasn't much concerned by it. However, he was due to go on watch at
midnight, so he got up, looked out his cabin door, and seeing nothing
unusual, closed the door, lit his pipe, and began getting dressed. He was
nearly finished when Boxhall came in and told him about the iceberg. Drawing on a coat, Pitman followed Boxhall out onto the Boat Deck, where he
ran into Sixth Officer Moody, who told him there was a large amount of ice
in the forward well deck. Pitman made his way forward and stood at the well

deck railing for some minutes, watching some of the Third Class passengers playing in the ice, kicking blocks of it back and forth and starting iceball fights. Pitman then went up to the fo'c's'le, found no sign of damage, and started back across the well deck, heading for the bridge. Halfway there he spotted a group of firemen trooping up from below, their bags slung over their shoulders.

"What is the matter?" Pitman asked.

"Water is coming in our place," one of the firemen answered.

"That is funny," Pitman said, chuckling. Then he looked down the No. 1 hatchway and saw seawater pouring in at the bottom of No. 1 hold; suddenly it wasn't very funny anymore.[2]

Pitman's experience was similar to one Trimmer Samuel Hemming had a few minutes earlier. While lying in his bunk, off duty, he heard an odd hissing sound coming from the forepeak. Getting up, he went forward to investigate the noise, which seemed to be coming from the forepeak chain locker. There he found the chain locker hatch forced upward against its stops, air rushing out from underneath it, forced out by the tremendous pressure of the in-rushing sea below. Just then Chief Officer Wilde put his head around the hawse pipe, and seeing Hemming there called out to him.

"What *is* that, Hemming?"

"The air is escaping from the forepeak tank, sir, but the storeroom is quite dry."[3]

For most of the passengers aboard the *Titanic* it was almost as if nothing had happened. In the First Class Smoking Room, Steward James Witter went off to learn whatever he could about that odd shudder, but his departure was barely noticed by the two tables of bridge players. Lieutenant Steffanson settled a little deeper into his armchair with his hot lemonade, while Spencer Silverthorne remained engrossed in Owen Wister's novel, *The Virginian*.

A few passengers had noticed an odd detail or two. Mr. and Mrs. Henry B. Harris were playing double Canfield in their cabin on C Deck. Mrs. Harris's broken arm had left her in considerable pain and feeling quite fatigued, so her heart wasn't really in the game. As she idly watched her dresses swaying on their hangers in rhythm to the ship's engines, she noticed that they had suddenly stopped moving.

One deck below, in Second Class, Lawrence Beesley lay in his bunk reading. Abruptly the gentle motion of the mattress ceased. On B Deck Jack Thayer had just called good night to his parents and was buttoning up his pajama jacket when he felt the breeze through the half-opened porthole in his cabin drop off, then stop altogether.

More than any shudder or jolt, the stopping of the *Titanic*'s engines attracted the passengers' attention. Bells jangled as passengers rang for their stewards, inquiring as to why the ship had stopped. Mrs. Arthur Ryerson flagged down Steward Bishop in the hallway, who explained, "There's talk of an iceberg, ma'am, and we've stopped so as not to run over it." After hearing this Mrs. Ryerson debated with herself for some minutes as to whether or not she should wake her husband—he was not a good sailor and tonight he was getting his first good sleep since leaving Southampton. Finally she decided that in the absence of any further alarm she wouldn't disturb him.

Lawrence Beesley's steward was deliberately vague, or else simply didn't know what was going on. Beesley asked him, "Why have we stopped?" to which the steward replied, "I don't know, sir, but I don't suppose it's much." Not at all satisfied, Beesley threw on his coat and began to work his way up to the Boat Deck to have a look around.

A similar curiosity infected other passengers. Jack Thayer, having told his parents that he was "going out to see the fun," pulled on an overcoat, still wearing pajamas underneath. Colonel Gracie, more methodical, as befitted a military man, carefully dressed for the cold—including long underwear and woolen stockings—then trotted up to the Boat Deck.[4]

Once on deck all Jack Thayer found was a night that was bitterly cold, stars that were incredibly bright, a sea that was amazingly calm. The *Titanic* lay motionless in the water, brilliantly lit from bow to stern, the three functional funnels blowing off huge clouds of steam with a roar. Other passengers, like Thayer, who had come out to see what had caused the ship to stop, simply milled about, some wandering over to the railings to stare into the empty night. After a while most of them gave in to the cold and sought the warmth of the A Deck Foyer.

There they made quite a contrast to the magnificent surroundings. The elaborate white-enameled wrought iron scrollwork of the skylight, the delicate woodworking of the columns and banisters of the Grand Staircase, the wall clock with its two bronze nymphs representing Honor and Glory crowning Time all presented an odd setting for the knot of passengers variously attired in sweaters, dressing gowns, fur coats, evening clothes, or like Jack Thayer, pajamas and slippers hurriedly covered with overcoats. As they stood exchanging odd snippets of information, Captain Smith and Thomas Andrews passed through, returning from their inspection. Try as the passengers might to read something from the two men's expressions, they learned nothing as Smith and Andrews politely but firmly edged past. Few had any real sense of danger: rather, most were concerned about how long the ship would remain stopped and if it might significantly delay their arrival in New York. When pressed on this point, a steward told George Harder, "Oh, it'll be a few hours then we'll be on our way again."[5]

Some passengers thought they had the answer. Thinking along the same lines as Steward Johnson, Howard Case, London manager of Vacuum Oil, remarked to Fred Seward, "Looks like we've lost a propeller blade, but it'll give us more time for bridge." Harvey Collyer knew exactly what was going on: he explained to his wife Charlotte, "We've struck an iceberg—a big one—but there's no danger. An officer told me so." The Collyer family (they had an eight-year-old daughter, Marjory, who was asleep in the room next door) was making its first trip across the Atlantic—Mr. Collyer had just purchased a fruit farm in Fayette, Idaho—so every experience was exciting for the three of them. Tonight, though, the novelty had worn a little thin for Mrs. Collyer: dinner in the Second Class Dining Room had been too rich for her, and her stomach was still queasy. When her husband reassured her that no one sounded at all frightened, she lay back down on her bunk, trying to quell the upset stomach and get some rest.[6]

"What do they say is the trouble?" asked William Stead. He had been taking a late-night stroll on the portside promenade at the time of the collision, and had gone below to his cabin without realizing anything had happened. Only when the ship stopped and began blowing off steam did Stead reappear on deck.

"Icebergs," was Frank Millet's laconic reply.

"Well, I guess it's nothing serious. I'm going back to my cabin to read."

Father Thomas Byles was standing nearby, breviary in hand, reading his office—it was the one for Low Sunday—and overheard the exchange between Stead and Millet. Like Stead, Father Byles decided the incident was minor and returned to his meditation.[7]

John Jacob Astor had heard about the iceberg and gone up to take a quick look around the Boat Deck. Unimpressed, he returned to his suite, where he explained to his wife, Madeline, that the ship had struck some ice, but it didn't seem serious. Hearing this, Mrs. Astor wasn't alarmed either.[8]

Word of the iceberg spread rapidly, though with little if any sense of alarm. The exchange Peter Daly overheard in the corridor just down from his cabin was typical. One young woman in First Class was excitedly urging another: "Oh, come and let's see the berg—we've never seen one!"

After a short expedition of their own, the Bishops returned to their stateroom. Mrs. Bishop began undressing for bed, while Mr. Bishop started to read, but they were interrupted by a knock at the door. It was Mr. Albert Stewart, part owner of the Barnum and Bailey Circus. He invited Mr. Bishop to "Come out and amuse yourself."

They couldn't see the berg—it had long since drifted off into the darkness—but they could still see plenty of ice: tons of broken, splintered ice had been jarred loose from the berg as it brushed by the ship and fallen into the forward well deck. A surrealistic winter wonderland, the piles of ice soon became a source of amusement for the Third Class passengers who, like their counterparts in First and Second Class, had come on deck to find out what was wrong. Unlike the other classes, the Third Class passengers who were berthed forward hadn't felt a grinding jar or faint shudder. Instead there had been a series of thuds, bangs, and screeches as the berg scraped along the side of the ship. Now up on deck they discovered the ice, and curiosity turned into rambunctiousness as they playfully threw chunks of ice and slush at each other.[9]

Soon the forward railing of A Deck was lined with First Class passengers watching the steerage passengers at play. Major Arthur Peuchen, a wealthy but not socially distinguished chemical manufacturer from Toronto, Ontario, spotted Charles Hays, the president of the Grand Trunk Railway, coming out of his stateroom and called out, "Mr. Hays, have you seen the ice?" Hays replied that he hadn't, so Peuchen replied, "If you care to, I will take you up on deck and show it to you." The major, seizing the opportunity to be seen in such prominent company, decorously escorted Hays forward.[10]

Ice collecting quickly became a widespread if short-lived fad. A steerage passenger presented a bemused Fourth Officer Boxhall with a chunk of ice the size of a small basin. (It's easy to imagine Boxhall wondering "What am I supposed to do with it?") Greaser Walter Hurst lay in his bunk, half awake, when his father-in-law, whom he shared quarters with, mischievously tossed a lump of ice into his lap. In the crew's mess Able Seaman John Poingdestre produced a shard of ice and passed it around, while in the stewards' quarters someone brought in a fist-sized fragment with the comment, "There are tons of it forward!"

Steward F. Dent Ray, unimpressed, rolled over in his bunk, muttering, "Well, that will not hurt anything."

As Colonel Gracie stood in the A Deck Foyer a voice behind him said, "Would you like a souvenir to take back to New York?" Gracie turned and there stood his friend Clinch Smith, holding out his hand. In it lay a small piece of ice, smooth and "flat like my watch," as the Colonel would later remember.

The most bizarre experience, though, belonged to First Class Steward Henry Etches. Making his way forward along an E Deck passageway, he encountered a Third Class passenger headed aft, carrying a block of ice. Before Etches could murmur "Excuse me" as he passed, the passenger threw the ice to the deck, and, as if demanding an answer, shouted "Will you believe it now?"[11]

Whatever it was that Etches was supposed to believe, there were several individuals who already had indisputable proof that something was definitely wrong with the *Titanic*. Antoni Yasbeck and his wife Celiney, married less than two months, were abruptly awakened by a loud crash twenty minutes before midnight. Traveling in Third Class, the Yasbeck's cabin was in the bow, down near the waterline. Frightened by the noise and suspecting trouble with the ship, the Yasbecks decided it would be easier to find out what was wrong by going down below than by making the long climb to the upper decks. Creeping along a corridor until they came to a doorway leading down to the engineering spaces, the newlyweds peered down into Boiler Room No. 6. They decided after one glance that they had seen enough, and hurried back to their cabin to dress. The sight of the boiler-room crew and the engineers struggling against the incoming water convinced the couple that the ship was in danger.

Carl Jonnson, also a Third Class passenger with a berth in the bow, was awakened by the same loud noise that had roused the Yasbecks. Almost as soon as he got out of bed, water began seeping into his cabin from under the door. Jonnson began to dress, and by the time he had finished, the water had risen high enough to cover his shoes. He wasted no more time, but quickly began to make his way topside. Daniel Buckley, a young Irishman who had boarded the *Titanic* at Queenstown, had an even more disturbing experience. He had been awakened, like most of the Third Class passengers berthed in the forward accommodation, by the noise of the collision. Instead of getting up immediately, he lay in his bunk until he heard the murmur of voices in the corridor outside his cabin. When he jumped out of his bunk he landed in water up to his ankles.[12]

Far aft, in one of the Second Class sections near the stern of the ship on F Deck, Mrs. Allen Becker and her three children were awakened by, of all things, dead silence. The engines had stopped, something they hadn't done since the *Titanic* had left Queenstown. Worried, Mrs. Becker inquired of her steward what had happened. "Nothing is the matter," he told her. "We will be on our way in a few minutes." Reassured, Mrs. Becker went back to her bunk and lay down. But sleep eluded her, and the longer she lay there the more concerned she became, since the engines hadn't started up again. Getting up again, she found another steward, who told her "Put your lifebelts on immediately and go up to the Boat Deck."

"Do we have time to dress?"

"No, madam, you have time for nothing."[13]

Like Nellie Becker, Sarah Daniels awoke when the engines stopped. For some reason this disturbed her, and she went to knock at the door of her employer, Hudson Allison. When she voiced her concern to him, Allison, who had been asleep himself, simply told her, "Sarah, you're nervous—go back to bed. This ship is unsinkable." Still worried despite Mr. Allison's assurances, Sarah began dressing as soon as she returned to her cabin.

Mr. and Mrs. Norman Chambers, who had left their First Class cabin on E Deck, now stood at the top of the stairs in an F Deck companionway and watched the five postal clerks struggling to save 200 sacks of mail—some 400,000 letters altogether—from the rising sea water. The *Titanic*'s post office occupied two deck levels: stowage for the mail was on the Orlop Deck and sorting was done just above on G Deck. Within minutes of the impact the postal clerks were working in water up to their knees as they dragged the mail bags up the stairs to G Deck—where less than five minutes later water began lapping over the sill of the companionway, onto the floor of the G Deck mail-room. Temporarily giving up the unequal struggle, the clerks climbed up the stairs to F Deck, and stood by Mr. and Mrs. Chambers, watching the water continue to rise in the mail room. From their vantage point they could also see trunks beginning to float about in the First Class baggage room.

While they watched, Fourth Officer Boxhall came by, peered over their shoulders into the flooding mailroom, then hurried on his way. Boxhall was followed a few minutes later by Assistant Second Steward Wheat, then later on by Captain Smith. Meanwhile the postal clerks climbed down again and went back to trying to save the mail.[14]

Just aft and below where the Chambers and the postal clerks were standing was Boiler Room No. 6. When the alarm had sounded most of the men didn't have time to duck through the rapidly dropping watertight door into Boiler Room No. 5. Instead they had to scramble up the ladders of the escape trunks to the deck above. They were only about halfway there when a voice shouted out, "Shut the dampers! Draw the fires!" and the men returned to their positions. Frantically racing against the rising water, the stokers, trimmers, and firemen worked to shut down the boilers. Thick clouds of steam filled the air, and in just a few minutes the water was waist deep. But the excess steam had been vented and the fires drawn, so when the sea reached the boilers there would be no explosions. Finally the same unseen voice that had called the men back now sang out, "That'll do!" and the men fled Boiler Room No. 6 for the last time.[15]

Boiler Room No. 5 had its own share of problems. Assistant Engineers Hesketh, Harvey, and Wilson were feverishly working to get the pumps going. A fat jet of seawater was shooting from the two-foot gash that extended from the bulkhead along the starboard side. Eventually the three engineers got the pumps working and were able to stay ahead of the incoming water. A few minutes later the lights went out in Boiler Room No. 5, and Engineer Harvey told Fireman Barrett to go aft to No. 4 for emergency lanterns. Since the watertight doors had to remain shut, this meant Barrett had to climb up the escape ladder, cross the deck above, and climb down into Boiler Room No. 4. Once he had the lanterns, Barrett then repeated the performance in reverse, only to find as he climbed back down into No. 5 that the lights had come back on.

Engineer Harvey in the meantime was not taking any chances, and he ordered the boilers in No. 5 shut down. Barrett climbed up the ladder once again, and called down fifteen or twenty of the idle men from No. 6 who were milling around on E Deck to help. Together the crews from Boiler Rooms 5 and 6 began to draw the fires in the five enormous boilers. By midnight, by dint of back-breaking work, they had doused the fires and put on the dampers to keep the steam from rising, while the excess steam was blown off. The lights burned brightly and the pumps thumped away, staying ahead of the incoming water. Certainly there seemed no reason to believe anything was seriously wrong.[16]

Yet the signs were there for those who knew what to look for: the forepeak, the forward cargo holds, and the mailrooms were flooded; water was rapidly rising in the now abandoned Boiler Room 6; and the sea was lapping against the back wall of the squash court on F Deck. Some of the passengers began to get the picture. On D Deck Mrs. Henry Sleeper Harper was trying to get Dr. O'Laughlin to persuade Mr. Harper, who was still ill, to stay in bed. Sadly the old surgeon shook his head, and told her, "They tell me the trunks are floating around in the hold; you may as well go on deck."

One deck above, in cabin C-51, Elizabeth Shutes asked a passing officer if there was any danger. With a reassuring smile he said, "Everything is all right, don't worry. We've only burst two pipes."

"But what makes the ship list so?" she persisted.

"Oh, that's nothing," the man replied and walked away, but before she closed the cabin door, Miss Shutes heard him tell another officer farther down the corridor, "We can keep the water out for a while." Closing the door she turned to see if her nineteen-year-old charge, Margaret Graham, had overheard. She had—Margaret had been nibbling on a chicken sandwich, and now her hand was shaking so badly that, as she later put it, "the bread kept parting company from the chicken."[17]

A few passengers began to slowly comprehend that all was not right with the ship. Up on A Deck, Major Peuchen noticed something peculiar. As he stood with Charles Hays watching the Third Class passengers playing in the ice, he suddenly cried out, "Why, she is listing! She should not do that! The water is perfectly calm and the ship has stopped!"

Hays seemed unperturbed. "Oh, I don't know. You cannot sink this boat." But Major Peuchen was not alone in his observation: not far from where he was standing, Colonel Gracie and Clinch Smith had noticed the same thing, while father aft, in Second Class, Lawrence Beesley noticed he was having trouble putting his feet where he wanted to on the stairs, as if the deck was tilted forward. William Sloper had been walking along the Promenade Deck when he abruptly stopped and remarked to his companion that it seemed as though they were walking downhill.[18]

At 12:05 A.M., after issuing orders to uncover the boats and muster the passengers, Captain Smith left the bridge and walked down the port side of the Boat Deck to the wireless shack. Inside, Phillips and Bride were completely unaware that anything had happened. After such a hectic day, with the transmitter breaking down and creating such a backlog, the exhausted Phillips was still desperately trying to catch up. Even though he wasn't scheduled to come on duty until 2 A.M., Bride had offered to relieve Phillips at midnight to allow the senior operator to get some extra rest. Bride had just finished dressing when Captain Smith walked into the cabin.

"We've struck an iceberg," the captain announced without preamble, "and I'm having an inspection done to see what it has done to us. You'd better get ready to send out a call for assistance, but don't send it until I tell you." By this time Bride had taken Phillips's place at the transmitter, and Phillips was behind the green curtain that separated their bunks from the wireless room itself. After hearing Captain Smith's announcement, Phillips began getting dressed again.

A few moments later Smith returned, this time just sticking his head in the door and saying simply, "Send the call for assistance!" Phillips asked if he should send the regulation call, and Smith said, "Yes, at once!" Then he handed Phillips a slip of paper with the *Titanic*'s position on it, which Fourth Officer Boxhall had worked out moments earlier.

Phillips and Bride switched places again, and Phillips put the headphones over his ears. At 12:15 A.M. he began tapping out the letters "CQD"—the international signal for distress: "CQ—All Stations" "D—

Distress"—followed by "MGY," the *Titanic*'s call letters, and the position "41.46 N, 50.14 W."

"CQD . . . CQD . . . MGY . . . 41.46 N, 50.14 W . . . CQD . . . MGY. . . ."[19]

———

"Get up, lads, we're sinking!" The normally smiling face of Second Steward George Dodd was grave as he stood in the doorway of Assistant Baker Charles Burgess's bunkroom. Further forward Steward William Moss was trying to get the waiters up and moving, but no one was taking him seriously. When Dodd appeared, shouting, "Get every man up! Don't let a man stay here!" the mood of levity vanished and the men scrambled to comply. Just then, as if to reinforce Dodd's warning, Carpenter Hutchinson came up the corridor outside and blurted, "The bloody mail room is full!" In minutes the men were dressed, if somewhat haphazardly. (Baker Walter Belford, for example, who had just come off duty, quickly donned his baker's uniform again—but forgot to put on underwear.) They then rushed out into the companionway toward their work stations.

Trimmer Hemming had returned to his bunk after his trip to the forepeak. Satisfied that despite his odd experience with the chain locker hatch the damage to the ship wasn't serious, he was just drifting off to sleep when the ship's joiner shook him awake, saying, "If I were you I'd turn out. She's making water one-two-three and the racquet court is filling up." A moment later Bosun Nichols came in, calling out, "Turn out, you fellows, you haven't half an hour to live! That's from Mr. Andrews. Keep it to yourselves and let no one know."[20]

The passengers certainly didn't know. Word had spread quickly that Captain Smith had ordered everyone onto the Boat Deck wearing their lifebelts, but nobody really believed it was serious. Lucien Smith had abandoned his bridge game and briefly returned to his cabin to let his wife know that he was, in his words, "going exploring." Reassured by her husband's unworried tone, Mrs. Smith had gone back to sleep after her husband had left.

Suddenly she was aware that the lights in their cabin had come back on and Mr. Smith, smiling, was bending over her. Still without the slightest trace of concern in his voice, he explained to his wife, "We are in the north and have struck an iceberg. It does not amount to anything but will probably delay us a day getting into New York. However, as a matter of form, the Captain has ordered all ladies on deck."

Colonel Astor and his wife were notified by their steward that all women were requested on deck with their lifebelts on, but since her husband had seemed so unconcerned earlier, Mrs. Astor took her time dressing. When she finally emerged on deck she looked as if she were prepared for an afternoon's shopping in London: she wore a black broadtail coat with a sable revers, a diamond necklace, and carried a muff.

Capt. Edward Gifford Crosby, a retired Great Lakes skipper, had first scolded his wife for not responding immediately to the summons to the Boat Deck. Mrs. Crosby was not happy about leaving her warm berth for the frigid exposure of the Boat Deck, and her husband in exasperation cried out, "You'll probably lie there and drown!" A few minutes later he apologized and, noting that nothing seemed seriously wrong, said, "The ship is badly damaged, but I think the watertight compartments will hold her up." But he still insisted that Mrs. Crosby and their daughter Harriet get dressed and go up to the Boat Deck. Resignedly, the two ladies complied.[21]

In the First Class Smoking Room the bridge games had picked up again, despite the departure of Lucien Smith. Lieutenant Steffanson was still buried in his armchair with his hot lemonade, while nearby, Spencer Silverthorne remained engrossed in his novel. One of the *Titanic*'s officers came through, calling out, "Men get on your lifebelts, there's trouble ahead!" Nobody moved; hardly anyone even looked up.[22]

But more passengers were beginning to have presentiments of danger. Dr. Washington Dodge, with only a hunch to go on, quietly awakened his wife and told her: "Ruth, the accident is rather a serious one; you had better come on deck at once."

James Drew was quite firm with his wife when she hesitated momentarily, reminding her that they were responsible for their eight-year-old nephew Marshall. With that Mrs. Drew quickly dressed, then woke up the little boy, announcing that she was taking him up on deck. Despite Marshall's sleepy fussing, Mrs. Drew bundled him up and finally led him to the boats.

Arthur Ryerson wasn't going to get any more sleep, either. Though Mrs. Ryerson was never sure afterward what it was, something convinced her that time was short. So now she was rushing about like a mother hen as she quickly got her husband, her three children, their governess, and the maid, Victorine, up and dressing. But her youngest, Emily, just couldn't seem to get herself dressed. Despairing of the youngster ever being ready, Mrs. Ryerson had Emily throw a blanket over her nightgown; then taking her youngest by the hand, Mrs. Ryerson led her little band up to the Boat Deck.[23]

In some cases the passengers were getting conflicting advice from the crew. The Countess of Rothes and her cousin, Gladys Cherry, were standing in the First Class Entrance Foyer on B Deck when a crewman came up and informed them of the captain's order to go up to A Deck with their lifebelts on. The two women hurried back to their cabin, but on their way encountered their steward. When they asked him where they might find their lifebelts, he informed them that they weren't necessary.[24]

The countess's experience was a bit unusual, though, for most passengers in First and Second Class learned of Captain Smith's orders from their stewards. In those days, on board a crack liner like the *Titanic*, stewards had at most only a half dozen or so cabins in their charge, so that they could devote more time and attention to individual passengers and learn the small details that allowed them to keep passengers happy. As a result, the large number of experienced stewards meant that word spread very quickly through First and Second Class, and their innate tact usually ensured that the passengers were cooperative.

This was why, when William Stead fussed about leaving his cabin, Steward Andrew Cunningham gently but firmly stood his ground with the old curmudgeon, and finally got him into his lifebelt. It was why in B-84, after fitting Benjamin Guggenheim into his lifebelt, Steward Henry Etches insisted, despite the smelting baron's protests, that he put on a heavy sweater before going out on deck—it was much too cold, Etches maintained, for Guggenheim to go without it. And it was why when Alfred Crawford, who had spent thirty-one years on the North Atlantic liners, went in to help Mr. Albert Stewart into his lifebelt, he heard no argument. Once the lifebelt was on, Steward Crawford bent down to tie the elderly gentleman's shoes.[25]

Mrs. Lucien Smith, for one, was in no hurry whatsoever, as she carefully dressed for the cold April night: wool dress, high shoes, two coats, and a knitted hood. The whole time she was dressing, Mr. Smith kept up a steady stream of cheerful small talk, carefully avoiding any mention of the collision (no one really knows just how much he knew for certain at this point). Mrs. Smith announced that she was ready, but just as they were closing the door to their cabin, she realized that she was leaving some of her jewelry behind. This brought her husband up short—this was no time to be concerned with what he termed "trifles"—and Mrs. Smith suddenly realized how serious the situation was. Relenting slightly, Mr. Smith allowed his wife to pick up two favorite rings, then closed the cabin door with a certain finality and hurried his wife to the Boat Deck.[26]

Major Peuchen, like Mrs. Smith, was also slow to realize the danger, although he had noticed that the ship was listing. An accomplished yachtsman (Peuchen was the vice commodore of the Toronto yacht club), he was more sensitive to such things than the average passenger, but after a moment's initial alarm, he decided that he was in no immediate peril, so he began to make his way back to his cabin. As he passed through the A Deck Foyer one of the First Class stewards informed him that the captain had ordered all passengers to the Boat Deck with their lifebelts. Having already experienced the cold, the major decided it would be wise to dress warmly first.

The stewards were doing their best to pass on the captain's instructions, though their civility wasn't always returned. For several minutes Steward Etches had stood at the door of C-78, trying to explain the situation. The door was locked, and when Etches knocked he received no reply. After knocking loudly with both hands, Etches heard a man's voice ask, "What is it?," then a woman call out, "Tell us what the trouble is." Etches repeated Captain Smith's order, then asked them to open the door. The couple inside refused, and after a few minutes Etches gave up and moved down the corridor to another cabin. He never knew who the couple were or if they ever unlocked the door.[27]

Down on E Deck another locked door, new and stiff, had jammed, trapping a man inside the cabin. Several passengers had tried to force the lock without success. In desperation Norris Williams, the tennis pro, broke down the door, freeing the trapped passenger. No sooner had he done so than a steward appeared, who promptly announced that everyone there would be charged with damaging company property as soon as the *Titanic* reached New York.[28]

The steward was quite serious, and at 12:15 A.M. such a threat didn't seem like a laughing matter. Captain Smith's orders still seemed to be hardly more than a precautionary measure, typical of such an experienced old seadog. Fewer than a half dozen people on board knew for certain how badly damaged the *Titanic* was. Her lights were still bright, her cabins were warm, and except to a few shrewd observers like Major Peuchen or William Sloper, her decks still seemed level.

There were some passengers who were taking no chances, at least as far as their valuables were concerned. In the C Deck foyer Purser McElroy was busy removing the contents of the ship's safes, while a clutch of passengers clamored for their jewels, cash, and other valuables. One such young man, Adolf Dyker, handed his wife a small satchel containing 200 Swedish *kroner*, a sapphire necklace, two gold watches, and two diamond rings. He then escorted her to the Boat Deck. All the while McElroy was urging the passengers to hurry and get to the boats. It remains uncertain whether McElroy knew the ship was sinking yet, but given all the years that he and Captain Smith had served together, coupled with the urgency of his warnings, it's quite likely that he did.[29]

In steerage, the Third Class stewards were just as busy spreading the word as their First and Second Class counterparts, but here the form differed somewhat. Usually the door to a cabin would be rather unceremoniously thrown open, the lights flicked on, and with a bellow the steward would announce: "Everybody up! Get your lifebelts on and get everybody on deck!" Most of the steerage passengers who were berthed forward were already up, having been awakened by the crash of the collision. In some places sea water had already started creeping in, as Daniel Buckley, Carl Johnson, and others had discovered; and soon a steady stream of single men and married couples, often with their luggage in hand, headed aft down the long straight corridor that ran nearly the whole length of E Deck, nicknamed "Scotland Road" by the crew, making for the Third Class areas in the stern.

Once there, most of them settled in the Third Class Smoking Room or the General Room, while a few hardy souls ventured out onto the after well deck. Those who had made for the forward well deck, single men for the most part, found the same Arctic seascape that had confronted Seaman

Clench and Fireman Thompson. Literally tons of ice in chunks of all sizes and descriptions were strewn across the deck. It wasn't very long before the Third Class men, especially the Irish, began the impromptu soccer matches that Major Peuchen and Charles Hays found so entertaining.

In the stern, the noise caused by the newcomers from the bow had already awakened many of the women and families quartered there. Soon everyone was roused as the stewards moved from cabin to cabin. The problem now was that the steerage passengers were awake, but what were they to do and where were they to go?

Steward John Hart had been making certain that all the forward Third Class cabins were empty, and now as he was making his way down "Scotland Road" to the stern he noticed that one of the doors on E Deck that led to the Second Class staircase had been left standing open—normally it was closed and locked. What struck Hart as unusual was that every one of the Third Class passengers who had come down that passageway had passed by it without so much as a glance, none of them realizing that the staircase led to the upper decks and eventually to the lifeboats It was clear to Hart that if any of the Third Class passengers were going to reach the Boat Deck, they would have to be guided there. Hart called Interpreter Muller over to him and immediately the two men began to get the steerage passengers organized.[30]

———————

On the Boat Deck sat the sixteen lifeboats, eight to a side, numbered fore to aft, even numbers to port, odd numbers to starboard. Under Boats 1 and 2 sat Collapsibles C and D respectively, while Collapsibles A and B were lashed upside down atop the officers quarters, abreast of the forward funnel. Ordinarily the Boat Deck served as the open air promenade for First and Second Classes, the forward two-thirds of the deck being reserved for First, the rest for Second, so now small groups of First and Second Class passengers began gathering in their respective deck areas. The Third Class passengers were still gathering in the after well decks at the end of the superstructure, waiting for instructions. Small knots of crewmen began to swarm over each boat, removing canvas covers, discarding the masts and spars, clearing the lines, and fitting cranks to the davits. A dozen of the ship's bakers appeared, trailing behind Chief Baker Charles Joughin, each carrying four loaves of bread, which were quickly distributed among the boats. Others checked the kegs of water or tossed in lanterns or tins of biscuit.

The passengers stood quietly by as one by one the boats were swung out and lowered until they were level with the Boat Deck, or in some cases with the Promenade Deck below. First Officer Murdoch and Third Officer Pitman were both pleasantly surprised by how easily the davits worked, with little of the sticking and jamming that characterized older designs. The boats would certainly handle much easier when it became necessary to lower away.[31]

Still, no order had been given to begin putting the passengers into the boats, so the passengers and crew continued to mill about on the upper decks. Few were dressed properly for the night air. Robert Daniel, a Philadelphia banker, wore only woolen pajamas; Mrs. John Hogeboom had a fur coat over her nightgown; Second Officer Lightoller wore a greatcoat and a sweater over his pajamas; Mrs. Turrell Cavendish wore a wrap and her husband's overcoat; Steward Ray had on his shore suit; Bruce Ismay was clad in his dressing gown and slippers; Mrs. Washington Dodge's high-button shoes flopped open with every step she took because she hadn't bothered to take the time to button them.

Jack Thayer looked very stylish in a green tweed suit and vest, but there was more than style to his choice of clothes. Underneath he wore a mohair vest and over it all he had thrown his overcoat—like Major Peuchen, he had already experienced the cold firsthand. The major himself, when he had gone back to his cabin after his encounter with the steward in the A Deck Foyer, carefully donned two sets of long woolen underwear, as well as several layers of warm clothing. As he dressed he occasionally glanced at a tin box sitting on a table beside his bed. In it were $200,000 in bonds and $100,000 in preferred stock. Finished changing, he took a last look around the room, then firmly closed the door behind him. Seconds later he was back. Quickly he picked up three oranges and a good luck pin, then left for good. The tin box was still on the table.[32]

The odd assortment of belongings that people did take with them said much about how serious they believed the situation to be. Mrs. Bishop, apparently convinced that she would be returning left behind $11,000 worth of jewelry in her cabin, but insisted that her husband return for her muff. Harvey Collyer was so certain that he would be back, he left his watch on his pillow; his wife had casually tied her hair back with a ribbon and wrapped a steamer blanket around their daughter Marjory. By contrast, Norman Chambers was anything but optimistic: he put a revolver in one pocket and a compass in the other. Two Second Class passengers brought books: Lawrence Beesley crammed the pockets of his dressing gown, which he was carrying over his shoulder, with the novels he had been reading before the collision; and Stewart Collett, a theology student, took the Bible he had promised his brother he would always carry. Edith Russell, who had been looking out of her cabin porthole at the time of the collision and had watched the iceberg glide by, apparently only feet away, almost forgot her musical pig, the good-luck mascot given to her by her mother, and later had to rush back to her cabin for it at the last minute. The casual air displayed by most of the passengers simply reflected not only their ignorance of the peril the ship was in, but also their unwillingness even to entertain the idea that the *Titanic* could be in danger.

It was an exchange between Marguerite Frolicher and her steward that seemed to epitomize the general attitude of the passengers. Bumping into Miss Frolicher in a corridor on C Deck, the steward recalled her teasing him a few days earlier when he'd put a lifebelt in her cabin. Why bother, she had asked, if the ship was unsinkable? It was purely a formality, had been his reply; she would never need it. Now almost defensively, he smiled and told her, "Don't be scared, it's all right."

"I'm not scared," the nineteen-year-old Swiss girl replied, "I'm just sea-sick."[33]

But the lifebelts were the one constant in this procession, and they didn't escape the perceptive eye of Mrs. Helen Candee: "On every man and every woman's body was tied the sinister emblem of death at sea, and each walked with his life-clutching pack to await the coming horrors. It was a fancy-dress ball in Dante's Hell."[34]

Kate Buss, the young Englishwoman from Sittingbourne who was traveling to America to join her fiance Samuel Willis in San Diego, shared her Second Class cabin on E Deck with two other unmarried young women. She had been sitting up reading a newspaper when the collision occurred, but, like so many others, it was only when the *Titanic's* engines stopped that she noticed anything amiss. Putting on her dressing gown and slippers, she stepped out into the corridor and soon encountered one of her dinner companions, a physician by the name of Ernest Morawick. Dr. Morawick announced that he was off to find out what was happening, so Miss Buss promised to wait for him to return. While she was standing in the hallway a group of musicians hurryied by, clutching their instruments. This unusual sight so roused Kate's curiosity that, forgetting Dr. Morawick, she knocked on the door of Marion Wright's cabin, and the two of them together made their way to the Boat Deck.

Once there, the two young women were joined by Douglas Norman, the soft-spoken young Scot who had accompanied Marion on the piano at the hymn-sing earlier that evening. Norman explained to them that the ship had struck an iceberg, which made sense out of all the activity on the Boat Deck. After standing at the after end of the deck for several minutes, shivering in the bitter cold, Norman suggested that they go below and put on some warmer clothing, an idea Kate and Marion quickly endorsed.[35]

Down in Third Class, Steward John Hart and a dozen crewman had begun to mobilize the steerage passengers. Spreading out as quickly as they could, they told everyone to get their lifebelts on and go up on deck. They helped where they could, adjusting lifebelts, and rousing sleepy children. Shortly they were relieved by several stewardesses, and Hart and his men then set about closing the watertight doors on F Deck, sealing off the forward compartments. (The watertight doors Murdoch had closed automatically from the bridge when the ship struck the iceberg were only the ones on the lower decks—the boiler rooms, engine rooms, and machinery spaces—while the doors on E, F, and G Decks had to be closed manually.)

It was just then that a twenty-six-year-old Norwegian fisherman named Olaus Abelseth, coming from his berth in the bow, reached the Third Class

General Room. Heading for a South Dakota homestead he had never seen, Abelseth had been given charge of the daughter of an old family friend for the duration of the voyage. The girl was barely sixteen, and as the minutes passed Abelseth's concern grew, for the growing crowd made the task of finding her increasingly difficult. At last they spotted each other, and in the company of Abelseth's brother-in-law and cousin, set out for the after well deck.[36]

The tension on the Boat Deck began building slowly as the passengers continued to wait for further instructions. A few tried to make light of the situation: bumping into Fred Wright, the *Titanic*'s squash pro, Colonel Gracie recalled that he had a game scheduled for 7:30 A.M. the next morning and asked, "Hadn't we better cancel that appointment?"

"Yes, we'd better," replied Wright lamely. Of course, he already knew that the squash court was under water by now, and the colonel didn't. Mrs. Vera Dick would always remember the remark a stranger made as he helped her fasten her lifebelt: "Here, try this on—it's the latest thing! Everybody's wearing them." Colonel Gracie's friend Clinch Smith, refusing to stray from character no matter how dire the straits, remarked to a young girl carrying a Pomeranian puppy, "Well, I suppose we ought to put a life preserver on the little doggie, too."[37]

But the quips and jokes only served to underscore the disorganization that was already beginning to make itself felt and would continue to frustrate the efforts of the *Titanic*'s officers and crew throughout the night. For some reason, Captain Smith, usually so decisive and swift to action, was slow to react to what he knew to be an impending disaster—the commands he was giving were sound as far as they went, but often they didn't go far enough. After ordering the passengers on deck and the lifeboats uncovered, he seemed hesitant to give the command necessary to start putting the passengers in the boats. The presence of Chief Officer Wilde did little to help the situation either: he had never served with First Officer Murdoch or Second Officer Lightoller before, and his last-minute addition to the officers' roster disrupted what had been a fairly well-coordinated staff; at the same time, he was demonstrating very little initiative of his own, seemingly content to pass on Captain Smith's instructions, but never expanding on them or clarifying them as he saw fit, and rarely issuing any orders of his own. It wouldn't be long before Lightoller, usually very strict about adhering to the chain of command, would begin ignoring Wilde altogether.[38]

In the meantime, as the crew finished clearing the boats away, the passengers continued to gather on the upper decks. Just off the Boat Deck, in the gymnasium, Colonel and Mrs. Astor sat side by side on the mechanical horses. The colonel had his penknife out, and was slicing open one of the lifebelts to show his wife what was inside.

By 12:20 A.M. Captain Smith, with his inspections complete, the certainty of the ship's fate clear in his mind, and the wireless now sending out calls for assistance, finally decided to put First Officer Murdoch in charge of the starboard boats, Second Officer Lightoller in charge of the port side. Chief Officer Wilde had no specific assignment, apparently being expected to act as a sort of overseer. When Lightoller, though he didn't yet believe the ship was in mortal danger, asked for permission to swing the boats out, Wilde told him to wait. After a few minutes Lightoller went to the bridge and got permission directly from Captain Smith. Then when Lightoller asked Wilde if he could begin loading the boats, Wilde again told him to wait. So Lightoller again went to the bridge. After a moment's silence, Captain Smith gave Lightoller a quick nod: "Yes, put the women and children in and lower away."

Captain Smith also suggested that Lightoller might find it easier to get the women and children in the boat if it were lowered to the level of the Promenade Deck and loaded from there. The Second Officer then went back to Boat 4, and ordered the boat lowered down to A Deck. Too late he remembered what Captain Smith apparently had forgotten: unlike the *Olympic*, the *Titanic* had the forward half of her Promenade Deck enclosed, and the windows were all shut.

Quickly he detailed some of the crew to go down to A Deck and open the windows. In the meantime, Boat 4 would have to wait, so he moved aft to Boat 6, and prepared to load it instead, this time from the Boat Deck. Standing with one foot in the boat and one on the deck, Lightoller called for women and children. The response wasn't even half hearted—it seemed no one was willing to forfeit the warmth and bright lights of the *Titanic* for the chill of an open boat. Why should they? There was no apparent danger, the ship seemed to be perfectly sound, and besides, if the *Titanic* really was unsinkable, there wasn't any need to bother with lifeboats.[39]

Suddenly, as if to heighten the sense of security aboard the ship, there was music playing. Bandmaster Wallace Hartley had assembled the *Titanic*'s orchestra in the First Class Lounge and quickly launched into a set of lively ragtime: "Great Big Beautiful Doll," "Alexander's Ragtime Band," "Can't You Hear me Caroline?" "A Little Love, a Little Kiss," and "Moonlight Bay." The tempo was fast, the tone light and cheerful.[40]

Third Officer Pitman, who was working on the starboard side of the Boat Deck with First Officer Murdoch, was standing by at Boat 5, waiting for further instructions from the bridge, when a middle-aged passenger rushed up to him and shouted, "There is no time to lose!" Pitman ignored him—he had more important things to do than pay attention to busybody passengers in pajamas and slippers. The stranger then urged him to begin loading the boat with women and children. This annoyed Pitman. He turned to face the passenger directly (he had no idea who this stranger was) and calmly announced, "I await the *Captain's* orders," then resumed working on the boat.

Taken aback by such apparent *lese majeste*, Bruce Ismay retreated down to Boat 7. Pitman, who had never met Ismay before, had in the meantime realized just who the meddling stranger might be, and went forward to the bridge to ask Captain Smith if he should do as Ismay had ordered. Smith nodded and said, "Carry on!" Quickly returning to Boat 5, Pitman jumped in and called out, "Come along ladies!"[41]

The first to climb into the boat were Mrs. Crosby and her daughter Harriet. Her husband, Captain Crosby, no longer had any illusions about the *Titanic*'s safety. The Crosby ladies were followed by Mrs. Washington Dodge and her five-year-old son, a stewardess, Mrs. F. M. Warren, then Helen Otsby. Someone in the crowd shouted, "Put the brides and grooms in first!" so a few husbands were allowed to go with their wives, including newlyweds John and Nelle Snyder of Minneapolis, and then a few single men. Like Lightoller on the port side, Pitman was finding it difficult to persuade many passengers to leave the relative warmth and safety of the *Titanic*'s decks.[42]

Right aft of Boat 5, at Boat 7, First Officer Murdoch tried mightily to get as many people into the boat as he could. Ismay came bustling up, shouting, "Gentlemen, please get back!" Dorothy Gibson, a star of serial motion pictures, got in along with her mother. Their bridge companions of the evening, Frederick Seward and William Sloper, were persuaded to join them. When the shout went up at Boat 5, "Put in the brides and grooms first!" Murdoch seemed to think that this was a good idea, so the Bishops and the Greenfields, both newlyweds like the Snyders, stepped into Boat 7. J. R. McGough had just remarked to a companion that "We are certainly safer here than in that little boat!" when he felt a pair of powerful hands grab his shoulders from behind—he never saw the man, though it may have been Murdoch—while a gruff voice said "Here, you're a big fellow; get in that boat." McGough found himself being pushed forward into the boat, and a few other men got in after him.

Seaman Hogg was crawling about the bottom of the boat, trying to replace the drain plug, while Steward Etches was frantically trying to keep the passengers' feet from getting tangled up in the falls. At 12:45 Murdoch felt he could wait no longer and ordered Boat 7 lowered away, the first boat down. With a capacity of sixty-five persons, it held twenty-five occupants.[43]

Assisting Third Officer Pitman now at Boat 5 was Fifth Officer Lowe. Lowe's rather late appearance was due to his propensity for heavy sleeping. He was off duty this Sunday night and taking advantage of it by catching up on some much-needed rest—as he was later to explain, "You must understand that we do not have any too much sleep, and therefore when we sleep we die." Whatever the reason, Lowe slept through the collision, even the venting of the steam. Voices outside his cabin door brought him back to the land of the living: when he looked out the porthole and saw the Boat Deck swarming with passengers and crew, all in lifebelts, he fairly leaped from his bunk, hurried into his clothes, snatched up a revolver (strictly nonregulation), and rushed out on deck. Immediately Pitman put him to work on Boat 5.[44]

First Officer Murdoch told Pitman to take charge of Boat 5, and once the boat had been lowered, to stand by the after gangway to take on more passengers. Evidently Murdoch was concerned that if the boats were fully loaded before they were lowered, the weight of the passengers might cause them to buckle and break in the middle, a concern Lowe shared. (Apparently neither man was aware of the fact that all of the lifeboats had been tested against just such an eventuality before the *Titanic* left Harland and Wolff.) Murdoch shook hands with Pitman, said, "Goodbye, good luck," then turned to Lowe and said, "That is enough before lowering. We can get a lot more in after she's in the water."

About this time Ismay reappeared, and called out, "Are there any more women before this boat goes?"

"I am only a stewardess," came a reply.

"Never mind," Ismay said. "You are a woman—take your place." The stewardess stepped forward and Ismay helped her into the boat. At the same time a heavy-set man, Dr. Henry Frauenthal, leaned over to kiss his wife goodbye, cried out, "I cannot leave you!" and fell into the boat. Furious, Murdoch shouted, "Throw that man out!" but as several crewmen rushed to comply, three more men jumped in, one of them dislocating two ribs of a lady passenger. Murdoch decided to get the boat away before the situation got out of hand. He nodded to Lowe, who began the slow process of lowering the boat.[45]

The paint was still fresh on the pulleys, and the new fall lines were stiff and had a tendency to stick. As a result Boat 5's progress toward the water was anything but smooth. First the bow would drop several feet, then the stern, then the bow again. Anxiously watching from the railing, fearful for his wife and son, Dr. Dodge was "overwhelmed with doubts" that he might be "exposing them to greater danger than if they had remained aboard the ship."[46]

Boat 5's slow progress was a source of anxiety for Bruce Ismay as well. Not satisfied with Lowe's best efforts, Ismay hung onto one of the davits, leaned far out over the water to watch the boat; he then began swinging his arm in huge circles, calling out over and over again, "Lower away! Lower away! Lower away! Lower away!" This was too much for Fifth Officer Lowe, and the fiery Welshman rounded on Ismay.

"If you'll get the hell out of the way, I'll be able to do something!" Lowe shouted in Ismay's face. "You want me to lower away quickly? You'll have me drown the lot of them!" Lowe then turned away in disgust and resumed lowering Boat 5, which shortly reached the water without incident. Stung by Lowe's outburst, Ismay slunk off toward Boat 3.[47]

Obviously Bruce Ismay was having a bad time of it. He was in a particularly unenviable position, being every bit as aware as Captain Smith and Thomas Andrews of the inadequacy of the *Titanic*'s lifeboats, but unlike them, he bore a particular responsibility for the problem. At a conference with senior managers and designers of Harland and Wolff in early 1910, when the details of the design for the *Olympic*, *Titanic*, and *Gigantic* were being finalized, Ismay had been presented with a plan to equip the ships with as many as forty-eight lifeboats, with a total capacity of 2,886 persons. This had been drawn up by Alexander Carlisle, who was then the managing director of the shipyard. Ismay studied the plan for a few minutes, then rejected it on grounds of expense, declaring that the sixteen boats required by the Board of Trade would be sufficient. He then returned to questions about the ship's decor. As Carlisle later put it, "We spent two hours discussing carpet for the First Class cabins and fifteen minutes discussing lifeboats." Now, in the worst way imaginable, Ismay was confronted with the consequences of his offhand treatment of Carlisle's proposal.[48]

Ismay's hysterics were also notable for their uniqueness. Most of the passengers and a good number of the crew still believed that the *Titanic* was safe and that everyone would be rescued in a few hours. Charles Hays, catching sight of his new friend Major Peuchen, who was busy helping clear away Boats 2 and 4, called out, "Peuchen, this ship is good for eight hours yet. I have just been getting this from one of the best old seamen, Mr. Crosby of Milwaukee." Evidently Hays had not seen the haste with which the good captain had put his wife and daughter in Boat 3.

Just as unperturbed as Hays were the four men sitting inside the First Class Smoking Room calmly playing bridge: Frank Millet, Arthur Ryerson, Clarence Moore, and Archie Butt. They seemed determined not to let the noise and confusion of the Boat Deck interfere with their game. At the Smoking Room entrance stood Monsieur Louis Gatti, the *maitre d'* of the *à la carte* restaurant. He was still wearing the white tie and tails he had donned some hours earlier, just before the restaurant opened, and now he was a portrait of Gallic nonchalance, watching the bustle about the Boat Deck.

Farther forward, in the gymnasium, the Astors had abandoned the mechanical horses, but the gym wasn't empty. Two couples, Mr. and Mrs. Smith and Mr. and Mrs. Harper, relaxed on a quartet of deck chairs and chatted amicably.[49]

All this time, back at the stern of the ship, Quartermaster Rowe maintained his chill vigil on the auxiliary bridge. He had noted that shortly after the iceberg had glided by, the ship had stopped and moments later began venting steam. But the activity on the Boat Deck hadn't attracted his attention, and so he was quite startled when about fifteen minutes before 1:00 A.M. he saw a lifeboat only about a third filled, float by on the starboard side.

He telephoned the bridge and asked if they knew there was a lifeboat adrift. The voice at the other end, Fourth Officer Boxhall, with a distinctly disbelieving tone asked who he was. Rowe explained and Boxhall realized that in the excitement Rowe had been forgotten. Boxhall told him to come to the bridge immediately and bring some distress rockets. Rowe pulled a box containing twelve white rockets from a locker on the poop deck, then began making his way forward—quite possibly the last man to learn what was happening.[50]

CHAPTER 6

Partings and Farewells

As you yourself live, I will not leave you.
                                          —II Kings 4:30

DOWN ON F DECK STEWARDESS ANNIE ROBINSON STOOD OUTSIDE THE MAIL room, watching the water rise. Carpenter Hutchinson rushed past her at one point, carrying a lead line. The young stewardess noticed that he looked distracted, almost scared. That was enough for her, and she began making her way to the upper decks. On A Deck she ran into Thomas Andrews, who greeted her with a small scolding.

"I thought I told you to put your lifebelt on," he said.

"Yes, but I thought it rather mean to wear it."

"Never mind that! Put it on—walk about—let the passengers see you."

"It looks rather mean. . . ."

"No, put it on! If you value your life, put it on. Now, I want you to open up all the spare rooms. Take out all the lifebelts and spare blankets and distribute them."

A moment later, Andrews literally bumped into another stewardess, Mary Sloane, whom Andrews was fond of in a brotherly way. Miss Sloane had just been told by Dr. O'Loughlin, "Child, things are very bad," and now she asked Andrews if the ship really was in any danger. Andrews replied, "It is very serious, but keep the bad news quiet for fear of panic." That was his overriding concern now: the last thing the *Titanic* could afford was a panic.

He seemed to be everywhere, still filled with the boundless, driving energy that had characterized the man for so long, trying to imbue everyone with an appropriate sense of urgency. But unlike Ismay's frantic dashing to and fro, he instinctively tailored his counsel to match the nature of the individuals he encountered. That was why he had told Mr. and Mrs. Albert Dick, who had been his dinner companions that evening, "She is torn to bits below, but she will not sink if her after bulkheads hold," even though he knew the ship was doomed. To Mr. and Mrs. John B. Thayer, whom he knew wouldn't panic and could keep a confidence, he was completely candid: in his estimation, he said, he didn't give the ship "much over an hour to live."[1]

Some of those on board had already come to a similar conclusion. It was just after midnight when Daniel Buckley, who had been kicking chunks of ice about the forward well deck, heard one of the stewards repeating the order for all passengers to go to the upper decks with their lifebelts on. Deciding to go back to his cabin on F Deck to retrieve his, he dashed down the staircase that led to E Deck and abruptly stopped when he found the bottom three steps already underwater. Forgetting about his lifebelt, he turned and fled up "Scotland Road" toward the stern. About this same time Steward Ray went down to his quarters on E Deck to fetch a warm overcoat and decided to make his way back up using the forward main staircase. The corridors in the forward part of the ship were now quite empty; the firemen and steerage passengers that had earlier filled them were long since gone farther aft. When Ray reached the foot of the staircase he was disturbed to hear the sound of water sloshing back and forth behind a partition just forward of where he was standing.

Assistant Second Class Steward Joseph Wheat had a more personal encounter with the encroaching sea water. His room on F Deck was just aft of Steward Ray's on the deck above. When Wheat went to fetch his valuables, everything seemed secure and dry. But as he made his way back to the stairs leading topside, he ran across an unnerving sight: water was flowing down the stairs from the deck above, E Deck. It wasn't much, just a trickle about a quarter inch or so deep, but it didn't take Wheat long to figure out what it meant: the compartment forward on F Deck had filled up completely, and just as Andrews had predicted, the water was slopping over the top of the watertight bulkhead on E Deck and had begun filling up the next compartment. For Steward Wheat it was time to go.

A bit later, around 12:30 A.M., Able Seaman John Poingdestre had gone down to the fo'c's'le in E Deck to get his rubber sea boots. He had just pulled them on when the wooden wall between his quarters and some of the Third Class accommodations forward collapsed and the sea rushed in. Frantically Poingdestre fought his way free of the swirling water that rapidly rose to his waist.[2]

Down below, though, there was still a lot of work to be done. In the portside reciprocating engine room, Greaser Thomas Ranger, at the direction of Chief Engineer Bell, began turning off forty-five large fans that were part of the massive refrigeration machinery. Earlier Bell had switched on the emergency dynamos now that Boiler Rooms 5 and 6 were shut down, but he was being careful to conserve every amp of power for the lights and the wireless, and so had told Ranger to shut the refrigeration plant down. While Ranger went about his task, Electrician Alfred White began brewing coffee, and Bell began organizing his men to get as many of the pumps working as possible.

In Boiler Room 5, the situation appeared to be fairly under control. The sea was still pouring in through the two-foot-long gash in the starboard bulkhead, but the boilers had been shut down and the fires drawn, and most of the stokers and firemen had been sent topside. Now Engineers Harvey and Shepherd, with Lead Fireman Barrett and a few others helping them, were working amid the swirling clouds of steam that rose from the dampened fires, trying to get the pumps going. Under Harvey's direction Barrett had just lifted a manhole cover of the starboard floorplates so Harvey could make adjustments to the pump controls.

The steam had reduced visibility to only a few feet, and that was why Shepherd, hurrying over to assist Harvey, never saw the open manhole, fell in, and broke his leg. As gently as possible Harvey, Barrett, and Fireman George Kemish lifted Shepherd from the hole and carried him to the pump room at the forward end of the compartment. After making the injured man as comfortable as they could, they went back to work. Orders had come from the bridge for everyone to report to their boat stations, so Barrett saw the rest of his firemen off, except for Kemish, then went back to work at the valves with Harvey.

After a few more minutes' work the pumps were going strong, the deck of the boiler room was nearly dry, and the steam had nearly dissipated. Without warning the sea suddenly came rushing into Boiler Room 5 as the bulkhead between No. 5 and No. 6 gave way. Harvey shouted for Kemish and Barrett to make for the escape ladders, while he turned and ran forward to try and reach Shepherd. In seconds both Harvey and Shepherd were swept under by a rising flood of water.[3]

Up on the Boat Deck there was still little urgency in loading the boats, most people still believing that the fuss was just precautionary. John Jacob Astor summed it up best when he echoed J. R. McGough, remarking while watching Boat 5 being lowered, "We are safer on board the ship than in that little boat." No one was aware that the bulkhead between Boiler Rooms 5 and 6 had collapsed; very few knew the extent of the damage done by the iceberg; even fewer knew that there were boats for only half as many people as were on board. Only Phillips, Bride, and the *Titanic*'s officers knew that the ship was sending out the international distress call. From bow to stern the *Titanic*, sitting motionless in the water, was ablaze with bright lights, their glow lighting the ocean for hundreds of yards in every direction. Bouncy, up-tempo ragtime floated across her decks, while passengers and crew milled about in a calm, unhurried fashion. The ship was beginning to list noticeably down by the head, but even that didn't seem to cause much concern. Certainly few people aboard considered the situation dangerous.

All that changed in an instant a few minutes before 1:00 A.M., just as Boat 5 was being lowered. Without warning a bright flash and a loud hiss came from the starboard bridge wing, and a few seconds later a shower of brilliant white stars burst high over the *Titanic* with a tremendous bang. (Fifth Officer Lowe was to retain the memory of Bruce Ismay's startled expression—staring high into the air, mouth open in disbelief—for the rest of his life.) White rockets at sea meant only one thing: distress. Now everyone knew that the *Titanic* needed the help of any ship close enough to see her: she was in mortal danger.

At 11:50 P.M. the lookout bell in the crow's nest had rung once, signaling that a ship was spotted nearby off to port. The stars had been so bright, even down close to the horizon, that the lights of this ship hadn't been clearly seen until the *Titanic* had turned around the iceberg and swung her bow around to the north. When Fleet and Lee saw the other ship, they had immediately called the bridge, where Sixth Officer Moody had taken their report. He passed it on to Fourth Officer Boxhall, who ran out onto the port bridge wing and through his high-powered glasses saw a steamship about a third of the *Titanic*'s size a half-point off the port bow. She appeared to be motionless and not more than ten or twelve miles away, her green (starboard) running light showing clearly. Boxhall informed Captain Smith as soon as he had returned to the bridge from his inspection with Thomas Andrews, a few minutes past midnight. Smith acknowledged Boxhall's report, but did nothing until Quartermaster Rowe arrived on the bridge carrying the box of rockets forty-five minutes later. Smith then told Boxhall to try contacting the ship by Morse lamp, and ordered Rowe to begin firing the rockets, letting one go every five minutes or so.[4]

In the Marconi shack Phillips and Bride were unaware that Rowe had started firing the rockets, although if he had known Phillips probably would have felt better. News from other ships had been discouraging. At 12:18 the first ship to respond to the *Titanic*'s CQD was the Norddeutscher Lloyd's *Frankfort*. Her response to Phillips's call was a curt "OK—Stand by." A few moments later, though, the Canadian Pacific's *Mount Temple* responded that she was changing course to meet the *Titanic*, as did the Russian steamer *Birma*, as well as the Allen Line's *Virginian*, but none of them was particularly close.

At 12:25 Phillips got his first piece of good news. The wireless operator of the Cunard liner *Carpathia* had missed the *Titanic*'s first CQD, so when he casually asked Phillips if he knew there was traffic waiting for him at Cape Race, Phillips brushed his query aside, rapidly tapping out, "Come at once. We have struck a berg and require immediate assistance. It's a CQD, old man [CQD OM]. Position 41.46 N, 50.14 W." After a moment's pause the *Carpathia*'s operator asked whether to tell his captain. Phillips replied, "Yes, at once!" A few minutes later, the news came that the *Carpathia* was only fifty-eight miles away and "coming hard."

At 12:34 the *Frankfort* called again, this time with a position—one hundred fifty miles away. Phillips asked, "Are you coming to our assistance?" The German liner asked, "What is the matter with you?" Patiently Phillips tapped back, "Tell your captain to come to our help. We are on the ice."

At this moment the *Olympic* barged in. She was five hundred miles away, but her powerful wireless easily put her in touch with her stricken sister. Phillips asked her to stand by. Captain Smith had just come in the cabin to get a first hand report of the situation. Phillips told him about the *Carpathia*.

"What call are you sending?" Smith asked.

"CQD," Phillips replied.

That jogged Bride's memory. Recently an international convention had introduced a new distress call to supersede the traditional CQD. It had chosen the letters SOS—not because they stood for anything in particular, but because they were simple enough for even amateurs to send and receive. Bride suggested to Phillips, "Send SOS; it's the new call, and besides this may be your last chance to send it!"

Phillips, Smith, and Bride all laughed together, and at 12:45 A.M. April 15, 1912, the *Titanic* sent out the first SOS in history. Phillips would continue to send the new signal, interspersed with the traditional CQD call, as long as the power lasted.[5]

Outside, on the Boat Deck, the mood had shifted dramatically once the rockets started going up. The lights were still bright, the music was still cheerful, but Lightoller and Murdoch found that they no longer had to coax people into the lifeboats. The hardest thing now was looking away while the goodbyes were being said.

"Be brave. No matter what happens, be brave!" were Dr. W. T. Minahan's parting words to his wife as he helped Mrs. Minahan into Boat 4. Adolf Dyker watched his wife climb into one of the boats, handed the little satchel containing their valuables across to her, and simply said, "I'll see you later." He then faded back into the crowd.

"Walter, you must come with me!" cried Mrs. Walter Douglas. Shaking his head, Mr. Douglas replied, "No, I must be a gentleman," and stepped back onto the Boat Deck. "It's all right, little girl," Daniel Marvin told Mary, his bride of three weeks. "You go and I'll stay a while." As the boat was being lowered he blew her a kiss.

Mark Fortune saw his wife and three daughters into a boat, then reassured them that he and his son Charles would be fine. "We're going in the next boat," he explained. One of the girls called back, "Charles, take good care of Father!"

Thomas Brown brought his family out onto the Boat Deck and quickly saw them into Boat 14, then stepped back and calmly lit a cigar. When Mrs. Brown urged him to get into the boat, he shook his head and said, "I'll see you in New York."

Mr. and Mrs. Turrell Cavendish said nothing as Mrs. Cavendish climbed into the waiting boat. Turning to her husband, she kissed him, held him close for a moment, then kissed him again. After a few moments she let him go and he turned away.

Sometimes the husbands had to be firm with their wives. Arthur Ryerson told Mrs. Ryerson in no uncertain terms that "You must obey orders. When they say 'Women and children to the boats' you must go when your turn comes."

Mrs. Lucien Smith didn't want to give in to Mr. Smith, and tried appealing to the captain. As Captain Smith stood out on the bridge wing, Mrs.

Smith ran up to him asked if he would make an exception and let her husband go with her. Not having the heart to refuse her directly, Captain Smith instead raised his megaphone and shouted, "Women and children first!" down the starboard Boat Deck.

Embarrassed, Mr. Smith stepped between them, saying, "Never mind, Captain, I'll see that she gets in a boat." Then taking his wife by the arm, he guided her down the Boat Deck, explaining, "I never expected to ask you to obey, but this is one time I must. It is only a matter of form to have women and children first. The ship is thoroughly equipped and everyone on her will be saved." They stopped by Boat 6 and Mrs. Smith asked him if he was being completely truthful. He said yes, they kissed, then she climbed into the boat.

There were sons who sometimes had to be as firm as husbands. When Alexander Compton heard his mother exclaim that she would sooner stay behind than leave her son, he brought her over to Boat 14 and told her, "Don't be foolish, Mother. You and Sara go in the boat—I'll look out for myself." Mrs. Compton gave in and the two women climbed into the boat.[6]

Some women simply refused to get into the boats without their husbands. Mrs. Hudson Allison clung fiercely to Mr. Allison, and nothing would change her mind. Together they stood on the starboard side of the Boat Deck, their daughter Lorraine sheltered from the cold in her mother's skirts. Further aft, unknown to the Allisons, their nurse, Alice Cleaver, had managed to get into Boat 11 with the Allison's infant son Trevor. Alice had deliberately separated Trevor from his parents in an act of desperation: she was terrified that her past, which she had concealed from the Allisons, would catch up to her, and she would be dismissed and then deported from Canada, where she was hoping to make a new life in the Allisons' service. Three years earlier she had been convicted of murdering her own infant son. After being released on the grounds that it had been an act of desperation after being deserted by her common-law husband, Alice Cleaver had falsely presented herself as a trained nurse to gain her employment with the Allisons. As long as little Trevor remained in her custody, she convinced herself, her situation remained secure, and she would do whatever it took to keep him with her, even if it meant abandoning the rest of the family.[7]

Despite the new sense of urgency, there still hung over the ship an almost haunting air of formality, as if the manners and genteel conduct of polite Edwardian society were expected even in this eventuality. Miss Marie Young, who had once been the music governess to Theodore Roosevelt's children, was escorted to Boat 8 by Major Butt who, she later recalled, "wrapped blankets about me and tucked me in as carefully as if we were going on a motor ride." He then stepped back, and lifting his hat to her, gave her a message for his family. "Goodbye, Miss Young. Good luck to you, and don't forget to remember me to the folks back home." Young Victor de Satode Penasco carefully gave his seventeen-year-old bride into the care of the Countess of Rothes, who saw the girl safely into Boat 8.

"The whole thing was so formal," Mrs. J. J. Brown would later tell the *New York Times*, "that it was difficult for anyone to realize it was a tragedy. Men and women stood in little groups and talked. Some laughed as the first boats went over the side. All the time the band was playing. . . . I can see the men up on deck tucking in the women and smiling. It was a strange night. It all seemed like a play, like a dream that was being executed for entertainment. It did not seem real. Men would say 'After you' as they made some woman comfortable and stepped back."[8]

Sarah Daniels, Mrs. Allison's maid, had no sooner come on deck than a seaman took her arm and pulled her toward Boat 8. She had returned to the Allison's cabin on C Deck to persuade Mr. Allison of the seriousness of the situation, but instead all she received for her efforts was an upbraiding from him for disturbing the family a second time. Now as the sailor was helping her into the boat, she began to protest, saying that she must look after her employer's family. Only when the man assured her he would see to the Allisons' safety did she relent and climb in the boat. Sarah had no idea that the Allisons were just a few yards away on the other side of the Boat Deck, nor that she would never see them again.[9]

Quickly now the boats began to fill with women, wives being escorted by their husbands, single women by gentlemen who had offered their services to "unprotected ladies" at the beginning of the voyage. It was this convention that saw Mrs. William Graham, her daughter Margaret, and Margaret's governess, Elizabeth Shutes, brought up to Boat 8 by Howard Case, the London manager of Vacuum Oil, and Washington Augustus Roebling, the president of the steel-making firm. Likewise, Clinch Smith was careful to see Constance Willard safely into Boat 8, while Martin Gallagher was shepherding Mary Glynn into Boat 13.

Colonel Gracie was a busy man: Mrs. E. D. Appleton, Mrs. R. C. Cornell, Mrs. J. Murray Brown, and Miss Edith Evans were all under his care, and he couldn't find any of them. Perhaps he was too distracted by his search for Mrs. Candee, who he was also unable to find.

When Edward Kent found Mrs. Candee shortly after the collision, she had given him an ivory miniature of her mother for safekeeping and assured him that she was all right. A short time later Hugh Woolner and Bjorn Steffanson, the dashing Swedish army lieutenant, escorted her into Boat 6. As the boat was being lowered Woolner waved goodbye and assured her that he and Lieutenant Steffanson would be waiting to assist her back on board as soon as the *Titanic* "steadied herself." Moments later Colonel Gracie, along with Clinch Smith, rushed up, still looking for Mrs. Candee, and Woolner promptly informed them that the lady had already been seen safely into a boat. Gracie nodded absently, then rushed off to look for the rest of his charges.[10]

The slant of the decks began to grow more ominous as the bow continued to fill. Gus Cohen went forward to fetch his few valuables from his Third Class cabin on D Deck and found his room already under water. The same thing happened to Celiney Yasbeck. Lightoller was using a long, narrow staircase that ran along the funnel trunking from the Boat Deck down to E Deck—it was an emergency escape route for the boiler room crew—to gauge how fast the ship was sinking: the foot of the staircase was completely under water and the sea was rising past D Deck. It made for an eerie sight: the lights, enclosed in protective waterproof housings, still glowed brightly under the rising water. To Lightoller, time was getting short.[11]

Thomas Andrews clearly was of the same mind. Moving from boat to boat, always with a sense of quiet urgency he continued to yell for the women to hurry, repeating to them, "Ladies, you must get in at once! There is not a moment to lose! You cannot pick and choose your boat! Don't hesitate, get in!" His exasperation was understandable. At Boat 9 an elderly lady caused a scene as she was being helped into the boat by pulling away from her assistants and running away from the boat altogether. Steward Witter tried helping a woman into Boat 11, but the woman became hysterical, lost her footing, and knocked Witter into the boat, falling heavily on top of him. While waiting to climb into Boat 8 a young girl suddenly cried out, "I've forgotten Jack's picture! I must go back and get it!" Despite the protests of the those around her she quickly ran below, returning moments later, picture clutched in her hands, to be unceremoniously hustled into the lifeboat.[12]

On the port side, at Boat 6, Major Peuchen had lent a hand clearing away the mast and spars, then stepped back onto the deck. Lightoller quickly put all the women he could into the boat, put quartermaster Hitchens in charge and at 12:55 ordered it lowered. One of the women who hadn't yet made up her mind about getting into a boat was Molly Brown, who was standing to one side watching Boat 6 being put down. Suddenly she felt a pair of strong hands on her shoulders and heard someone she couldn't see saying "You are going, too." Propelled forward, speechless for probably the only time in her life, Mrs. Brown abruptly dropped four feet into the slowly descending lifeboat.

Lightoller turned toward Boat 8, then spun around again as a woman's voice called up from Boat 6, "We've only one seaman in the boat!"

Lightoller was short of seamen, and had none to spare for Boat 6, so he called into the crowd, "Any seamen there?" Major Peuchen, stepped forward.

"I will go, if you like," he said.

"Are you a seaman?"

"I am a yachtsman."

"Well, if you're seaman enough to get out on that fall, you can go." At that, Major Peuchen climbed over the railing, leaned out to catch the forward fall and lowered himself down into Boat 6. Once he had reached the boat, Hitchens told him to find the drain plug and make sure it was tapped firmly in place. While Peuchen was fumbling about in the dark at the bottom of the boat, Hitchens shouted, "Hurry up! This boat is going to founder!" Peuchen thought he meant the lifeboat—Hitchens meant the *Titanic*.[13]

Lightoller's shortage of proper seamen had come about because of a plan to have some of the portside boats stand by the lower gangways after they were lowered, and complete the loading from there: Lightoller, it seems, was as concerned about the lifeboats buckling while being lowered as Murdoch, and just as much in the dark about the Harland and Wolff tests. Ismay could have informed the Second Officer that the boats were tested and sound, as could Andrews, but Ismay was on the other side of the Boat Deck and Andrews was somewhere farther aft, so Lightoller went ahead and sent the boat away only half-filled.

The idea of loading passengers from the gangways never had a chance: the boats that were supposed to stand by instead rowed off into the darkness, and the gangway doors were never opened. When a number of passengers went down to one of the gangways to be used on C Deck, they nearly became trapped there when a crewman who didn't know of the plan locked a companionway door behind them. Fortunately they were released a few moments later, but it had been a terrifying experience.

Something similar must have happened to a group of a half-dozen seamen, led by "Big Neck" Nichols, the bosun. They were sent below by Lightoller to open the gangway doors and were never seen again. This was a grievous loss to Lightoller, who was forced to start rationing his remaining crewmen.

Victorine Chandowson, the Ryersons' maid, was nearly trapped in the same way. Returning to her cabin, she had been hurriedly gathering up her few valuables when she suddenly heard the "click" of a key turning in her cabin door: a steward was locking the doors to prevent looting and didn't know she was inside. Her shriek of terror kept the man from locking her in. Enough was enough, she decided, and empty handed she ran back up to the Boat Deck.[14]

The starboard side of the Boat Deck seemed less frantic. The band had come out on deck, still playing dance tunes. One passenger was overheard remarking that he had been told by an officer that the ship wouldn't sink for at least eight or ten hours, and by then the *Titanic* would be ringed by rescue ships. While Lightoller was strictly enforcing the Captain's "Women and children first" order on the port side, on the starboard side First Officer Murdoch was a little more accommodating: women and children first, then if there were no more ladies, married couples and single men. Mrs. Graham watched as Henry Harper carefully climbed into Boat 3, accompanied by not only his valet and his dragoman, but Harper was also carrying his Pekinese, Sun Yat Sen. At 1:00 A.M. Boat 3 was lowered, with the same jerky motion that Boat 5 had experienced. Like Boat 5, Boat 3 had a capacity of sixty-five persons, but also like Boat 5, she was loaded with less than half that number.[15]

Right aft, down on E Deck, a growing crowd of Third Class passengers gathered at the foot of the main steerage staircase, which led to the after well deck. They had been there ever since their stewards had begun rousing them shortly after midnight. At first the crowd consisted of mainly families and single women but its ranks were soon swelled by growing numbers of single men and married couples fleeing the rapidly flooding Third Class accommodations forward. As the crowd grew so did the noise, and a rising babel of voices speaking a half dozen different languages made it difficult for the stewards to relay instructions. Interpreter Muller was doing his best with the Germans and Scandinavians, but it was slow going.

The rising clamor attracted the attention of Minnie Coutts. A young mother traveling in Third Class with her two small boys, eleven-year-old William and eight-year-old Leslie, to join her husband in New York, she had felt only the slightest tremor when the *Titanic* hit the iceberg and paid little attention to it. It was not until the mass exodus of steerage passengers from up forward began passing her cabin that she took notice and became somewhat alarmed. Careful not to disturb her sons, who were fast asleep, she stepped out into the corridor and stopped a passing steward, inquiring about the cause of the commotion and was told that the ship was in no danger. Nearly an hour would pass before another steward finally came along with the order for everyone to put on their lifebelts.

At this Mrs. Coutts found herself in an awkward strait: there were only two lifebelts in her cabin, and she couldn't find a third, since all of the other Third Class passengers seemed to be looking for lifebelts as well. She began frantically asking every person who passed by if they knew of any extra lifebelts, but no one did. One crewman frankly informed her that there were no extra lifebelts available anywhere. In the hope that something would turn up, she quickly dressed her sons, strapping a lifebelt onto each of them, then stepped back out in the corridor and ran into the same crewman who had just moments before told her there were no more lifebelts. Desperately she explained her predicament and this time the man calmly replied, "Follow me."

He led the three of them forward through a maze of passageways, through First Class and into the crews' quarters. There, he took his own lifebelt, fastened it around her and said quietly, "There, now, if the ship goes down, you'll remember me." Minnie asked if the situation was really that dangerous and the crewman replied that it was. He then gave her directions to the boat deck and left.

Minnie and her boys set out for the upper decks, only to find their way blocked by a locked door. She was just beginning to feel the first tinges of panic when another crewman appeared and quickly led them to the Boat Deck. It wasn't until she and her boys were safely in Boat 9 that Minnie realized that she had never learned the name of the crewman who had given up his lifebelt. She never saw him again.[16]

At half past midnight the word came down to Third Class to send the women and children up to the Boat Deck. Steward Hart, who had realized early on that the Third Class passengers had almost no chance of negotiating the passageways and corridors that were usually inaccessible to steerage if left to themselves, began to organize his charges into little groups. Around 12:50

he set off for the Boat Deck, leading a score of women, some with children in tow. Other stewards continued to organize and reassure the rest of the Third Class passengers. It wasn't an easy trip: the design of the ship, because of those outdated American immigration laws that required Third Class physically separated from the other classes of passengers, allowed no direct route from the Third Class berthing areas to the Boat Deck, and access to what routes there were was very limited. That was why Hart had to lead his group up the stairs to the Third Class Lounge on C Deck, across the after well deck, past the Second Class Library, into First Class, along a stretch of corridor that led past the surgeon's office and the private dining saloon for the First Class' servants, and finally out to the Grand Staircase, which carried them up to the Boat Deck.

Once on deck Hart led his charges to Boat 8, where as quickly as he got them in, several jumped right back out and ran inside where it was warm. Exasperated, Hart gave up after a few minutes and began the long trip back to Third Class.

It was well after 1:00 A.M. when he got back to E Deck and prepared to set out with his second group. This time many of the married women refused to go without their husbands, while several of the men, some rather forcefully, demanded to go along. But Hart had his orders—women and children only—and after firmly reinforcing the order, he set off, reaching the Boat Deck around 1:15. This time he led his group to Boat 15, but was stopped by First Officer Murdoch when he started back down for steerage again. Overriding Hart's protests, Murdoch ordered him to go with Boat 15 when it was ready to be lowered.[17]

Hart's efforts underscored the fact that, despite later accusations to the contrary, there really was no deliberate policy of discrimination against Third Class. What there was, and what may have been all the more insidious by being purely unintentional, was that simply no policy or procedure for looking after the Third Class passengers existed. Instead, they were left to shift for themselves, not because they were being purposely ignored, but rather because they had simply been overlooked.

Future generations would have a hard time understanding how this could be, preferring instead to attribute it to the innate snobbery of the Edwardian society, but the truth was far less malign and much more tragic. Somewhere in the chain of command communications had broken down, and as had happened so many times before on this night, when Captain Smith had given no specific instructions, Chief Officer Wilde seemed incapable of initiating any actions himself. The other officers were already thoroughly occupied and had little time to spare for wondering about what or who the captain and the chief officer may have overlooked. That discrimination was never intended by the White Star Line lay in the fact that none of the women and children from steerage who reached the Boat Deck were prevented from getting into the lifeboats. The problem was that so few made it there.

Nevertheless, a lot of them tried. Singly and in small groups, some steerage passengers began to make their way to the upper deck. A few of the barriers that closed off Third Class from the rest of the ship were down, and some of the steerage passengers began to work their way into the ship, unsure of where they were going, but certain that if they kept climbing, eventually they would reach the Boat Deck.

But most of the barriers were still up, confining Third Class to the forward and after well decks, where there were no boats. At this point, two components of the geography of the ship defeated the efforts of many of the Third Class passengers to reach the Boat Deck. The first was in the design of the *Titanic*: there were only a handful of exits from the Third Class areas that gave access to the upper decks—seven to be exact; all of them, be they doors, gates, or hatchways, by law were required to be kept locked. The second was the interior layout of the ship: the complex route that Steward Hart followed when leading his group of women passengers up to the boats was actually the most direct route to the Boat Deck, but for the Third Class passengers, it was a venture into *terra incognita*, abounding with dead ends and circuitous passages.

A sense of the growing danger they were in communicated itself to some of the steerage passengers and they started finding ways up to the Boat Deck. Soon a thin but steady stream of Third Class passengers could be seen crawling up onto a cargo crane in the after well deck, inching across the boom to a railing on B Deck, then clambering over the railing and on up to the Boat Deck.

Some of them got lost and wandered into the Second Class promenade on B Deck, which turned out to be an apparent dead end. The only way out was an emergency ladder, meant for the crew's use only, that passed very near the First Class *à la carte* restaurant. The restaurant, which was still brightly lit, could be seen through the French doors, with table after table already set with gleaming china, sparkling crystal, and freshly polished silver in preparation for the morning's breakfast. Anna Sjoblom, one of those who got lost, would always remember how the sight had taken her breath away—she had never seen anything like it growing up in Finland.

Two decks below them, another group of young women from steerage found their way barred by a locked gate, this one guarded by a seaman. The three young colleens—Kate Murphy, Kate Mullins, and Kathy Gilnagh—frantically pleaded with the man, who refused to allow them to pass through (regulations were regulations, after all). Suddenly a big, tough-looking Irishman from the girls' home county, Jim Farrell, the piper, came up the corridor. He took one look at the girls, at the gate, and at the seaman, then bellowed "Good God, man! Open the gate and let the girls through!" Thoroughly intimidated, the sailor meekly complied, then ran off.

A larger group was clamoring at another guarded gate barring the way to the upper decks, this one down on E Deck by the Second Class staircase. As Daniel Buckley approached the barrier, the man ahead of him was roughly shoved back by the seaman standing before the gate. Howling in fury the man charged forward again. The seaman promptly ducked through the gate, locked it behind him, and fled. The passenger broke the lock, then took off in pursuit of the offending seaman, shouting that he would chuck the sailor into the sea if he caught him. Buckley and dozens of others rushed through the open gate and hurried up the stairs.

Yet they were only a handful—there were still hundreds of steerage passengers walking about aimlessly in the after well deck or at the foot of the staircase on E Deck. Also left behind on E Deck were most of the Second and Third Class kitchen staff, along with chefs and waiters from the *à la carte* restaurant. The majority of them were French and Italian, and, owing to a longstanding British animosity toward France and Italy, were objects of suspicion in 1912. No one knows who, if anyone, actually gave the order, or why it was given, but about an hour after the collision they were shepherded into their quarters by members of the deck crew, locked in, and promptly forgotten.

Many of those steerage passengers left behind returned to their cabins; others turned to prayer: around 1:30 Gus Cohen passed through the Third Class Dining Saloon and saw a large number of them gathered there, many with rosaries in their hands, "huddled together, weeping, jumping up and down as they cried to their 'Madonna' to save them." August Wennerstrom, also a Third Class passenger, later observed bitterly:

> Hundreds were in a circle with a preacher in the middle, praying, crying, asking God and Mary to help them. They lay there, still crying, till the water was over their heads. They just prayed and yelled, never lifting a hand to help themselves. They had lost their own willpower and expected God to do all their work for them.[18]

Clearly not all of the barriers for Third Class were of the physical kind. It is a difficult concept to grasp from the late–twentieth–century perspective of an egalitarian, socially mobile society, but it was an undeniable reality that in the first decade of this century feudal society was far from dead. The rigid class structure that had shaped, driven, and defined Europe for more than a thousand years still exerted an overwhelming influence on the lives of almost everyone born into it, dictating every aspect of life: an individual's vocabulary, diet, education, clothing, housing, profession, even choice of friends were to greater or lesser degrees prescribed or proscribed by their position in society.

And nowhere was that rigidity more prevalent than in the working class. Sons and daughters followed the life paths of their fathers and mothers, each generation putting its successor on the treadmill. Centuries of being the source of an endless supply of labor led to an ingrained mindset among the majority of working men and women whereby they expected to be told where to go, what to do, and when to do it—initiative was never expected of them. Leaving behind the strictures of their working-class origins was equally unthinkable: though Great Britain's recently formed Labour party had as its proclaimed goal the amelioration of the worst physical conditions of the workingman's lot, it was not yet ready to articulate the idea of creating a society that would overcome all the poor conditions of the workingman's life.

This is not to say that the working class viewed itself as oppressed, ready to spring to the barricades in defiance of the patriciate. The working men and women of the early twentieth century—the steel and textile mill workers, chimney sweeps, tanners, coachmen, dustmen, butlers, and maids—were no more ready to rebel than the serfs from whom they had descended. They were good at what they did and proud of it. A contemporary American, Richard Harding Davis, wrote in *Our English Cousins*:

> In America we hate uniforms because they have been twisted into meaning badges of servitude; our housemaids will not wear caps, nor will our coachmen shave their mustaches. This tends to make every class of citizen more or less alike. But in London you can always tell a 'bus driver from the driver of a four-wheeler, whether he is on his box or not. The Englishman recognizes that if he is in a certain social grade he is likely to remain there, and so, instead of trying to dress like someone else who is in a class to which he will never reach, he "makes up" for the part in life he is meant to play, and the 'bus driver buys a high white hat, and the barmaid is content to wear a turned-down collar and turned-back cuffs, and a private coachman would as soon think of wearing a false nose as wearing a mustache. He accepts his position and is proud of it, and the butcher's boy sits up in his cart just as smartly, and squares his elbows and straightens his legs and balances his whip with just as much pride, as any driver of a mail-cart in the Park.[19]

Third Class then may have been descriptive of these people's level of accommodation on a transatlantic liner, but not of the way they viewed themselves. There was nothing fatalistic or resigned in their willful acceptance of their station and of the consequences of that acceptance: they were behaving according to beliefs and values handed down to them by their parents, their grandparents, and their great-grandparents. And if, as far as August Wennerstrom was concerned, they showed little or no inclination to take matters into their own hands, it was because they believed until it was too late that the people in charge, the officers and crew, knew what they were doing. When that belief finally proved false, there would no time for anything but prayer.

In the engine and boiler rooms everyone was too busy to think of prayer, let alone getting away to the boats—there was too much work to do. Chief

Engineer Bell was determined to keep the power going for as long as possible—the lights would stay lit, the pumps keep going, the wireless would still work. To make things easier for the engineers to move about he had opened the watertight doors aft of Boiler Room 4. When the water reached that far, he reasoned, it would be easy enough to close them again.

Bell must have been proud of his men; they worked so hard: Trimmer Thomas Dillon dragging long sections of pipe forward to Boiler Room 4 to get more suction from the pumps there; Greaser Ranger shutting down forty-five ventilation fans, which required him to scramble among hot, exposed moving machinery; Greaser Fred Scott freeing a trapped shipmate from one of the propeller shaft tunnels, caught there when the watertight doors had closed.

The stokers and trimmers in Boiler Room 4 worked frantically to draw the fires in the five huge double-ended boilers. Back and forth they dragged their rakes and slicer bars as they pulled the burning coals from the fireboxes. Soon the embers were falling, hissing, into ankle deep water as the sea began to seep through the floor plates, but the men toiled on: there would be no explosions when the cold sea water reached the boilers. The rising water was past Trimmer George Cavell's knees when he decided he'd had enough and headed for one of the escape ladders. But halfway up, a nagging feeling that he was leaving everybody else behind caused him to stop and go back down. But by then Chief Engineer Bell was satisfied that the fires were sufficiently drawn, and had ordered Boiler Room 4 evacuated, so when Cavell returned, he found it empty. Satisfied that he hadn't run out on his mates, Cavell headed for the upper decks.[20]

Lightoller loaded Steward Hart's first group into Boat 8 as quickly as he could, then looked around for other women. Mrs. Stuart White noticed Captain Smith ordering a pair of stewards into the boat to act as oarsmen, and Dr. Alice Leader would later recall that they didn't seem to know their places in the boat. Just before Lightoller was to give the order to lower away, Mr. and Mrs. Straus walked by, and Mrs. Straus stopped and began to climb into the boat. At the last second she changed her mind, turning to her husband saying, "We have been living together for many years; where you go, I go." Colonel Gracie and Hugh Woolner overheard her, and tried to get her to change her mind, but she was adamant. Finally Woolner turned to Mr. Straus and said, "I'm sure no one would object to an old gentleman like yourself getting in."

"I will not go before the other men," Straus replied firmly, and for husband and wife the issue was settled. Mrs. Straus turned to her maid and helped the young woman into Boat 8, giving the girl her fur coat, saying, "Here, take this. I won't be needing it." The old couple stepped away from the boat and settled into a pair of nearby deck chairs to await the end together. Feeling vaguely embarrassed at having overheard all this, Lightoller gave the order to lower away at 1:10, then started aft.[21]

Just as Boat 8 had slipped its falls and was pulling away, Chief Officer Wilde tapped Lightoller on the shoulder and asked, "Where are the firearms?" Somewhat taken aback, Lightoller said, "Come with me." Wilde followed as Lightoller led him to the arms locker, where Captain Smith and First Officer Murdoch were already waiting. Opening the locker, Lightoller passed out a half-dozen revolvers and some ammunition to Wilde, who then distributed them to the other officers. Just as Lightoller was about to return to the boats, Wilde shoved one of the revolvers and a half-dozen shells into Lightoller's hands with the remark, "Here, you might need this." The second officer nodded a bemused acknowledgement and hurried back out to the Boat Deck.[22]

Captain Smith returned to the bridge where Fourth Officer Boxhall and Quartermaster Rowe were firing off the rockets. When Captain Smith handed Boxhall a revolver, the young officer looked at his captain in frank disbelief—he still hadn't accepted the fact that the *Titanic* was sinking. "Captain, is it *really* serious?" he asked.

"Mr. Andrews tells me that he gives her an hour to an hour and a half."[23]

Men were still faring far better on the starboard side of the Boat Deck than on the portside, since First Officer Murdoch's enforcement of "women and children first" was far more lax than Lightoller's. Of course this meant that a male passenger's chances of getting off the sinking ship might depend entirely on which side of the Boat Deck he was on. No one objected when two Frenchmen, sculptor Paul Chevré and aviator Pierre Marechal, climbed into Boat 7, or a pair of buyers from Gimbel's found seats in Boat 5. Dr. Washington Dodge had earlier seen his wife and son safely into Boat 5 when he was spotted by Steward Ray, standing near Boat 13. Ray felt responsible for the family since he had urged the Dodges to sail on the *Titanic* in the first place, so now he rather unceremoniously propelled Dr. Dodge forward, bundling him into Boat 13, saying, "You'd better get in here," just before the boat was lowered.

An almost flagrant abuse of Murdoch's less stringent concept of "women and children first" created one of the most sensational incidents of the night. Up at the forward end of the Boat Deck, at Boat 1, Sir Cosmo Duff Gordon was standing by, along with his wife and secretary, almost as if they were waiting to be formally invited to climb into the lifeboat. Finally Sir Cosmo asked Murdoch, who had just ordered Boat 3 put down, if they could get in Boat 1. Murdoch nodded and said curtly, "Yes, jump in!" (Sir Cosmo, ever the stickler for observing the proprieties, especially where the aristocracy was involved, would later recall Murdoch's words as, "Oh, certainly do. I'd be very pleased." Somehow this seems doubtful.)

As the baronet, his wife, and secretary stepped into the boat, two Americans, Abraham Solomon and C. E. Stengel, came rushing up and were told by Murdoch to get in. Solomon managed this nicely, but Stengel, obviously no acrobat, had trouble negotiating the railing. Finally he got over it and simply rolled into the boat. The nimble and surefooted Murdoch laughed hard, exclaiming, "That's the funniest thing I've seen all night!"

Looking about, the first officer saw that with Boats 3, 5, and 7 gone, most of the passengers had moved aft. Quickly he told six stokers standing nearby to get in, then put Lookout George Symons in charge, telling him, "Stand off from the ship's side and return when we call you." What Murdoch had in mind isn't clear; certainly he knew that the passengers wouldn't be returning to the *Titanic*, and the idea of loading the boats from the gangways had come to naught. Whatever his thinking, Murdoch signaled to the men at the davit cranks and Boat 1—capacity forty persons, occupants twelve—began its descent to the sea below.

It was just then that Greaser Walter Hurst, released from duty in the boiler rooms, had come out onto the forward well deck. He watched Boat 1 coming down the *Titanic*'s side, and noticing that it was nearly empty he turned to one of his mates and remarked, "If they are sending the boats away they might as well put some people in them." It was 1:15 A.M.[24]

CHAPTER 7

Desperate Exodus

*. . . but behold, distress and darkness, the gloom of
anguish. . . .*

—Isaiah 8:22

BY 1:15 PHILLIPS WAS BEGINNING TO WORRY. WHERE WAS EVERYBODY? IT
had been nearly an hour since the *Carpathia* informed him that she was
putting about and "coming hard" but that had been the only good news he'd
had so far—and even that had come with a depressing qualification: the
Carpathia was fifty-eight miles away and it would be nearly four hours
before she arrived. Phillips knew that the *Titanic* didn't have four hours left
to live. Anxiously he continued tapping away, hoping that some ship—any
ship—would be closer and finally answer. (It is easy to imagine Phillips wondering where that damned fool was who had nearly blown his ears off just a
couple hours ago.)

Up on the bridge Captain Smith seethed with a frustration similar to
Phillips's as he continued to stare at the light on the horizon, so tantalizingly
close. Smith, Fourth Officer Boxhall, and Quartermaster Rowe all agreed that
it was a ship: while the three men watched as the rockets were being fired, she
had slowly swung around, as if drifting on the current until both her green
(starboard) and red (port) sidelights showed, indicating that she was bow on
to the *Titanic*. For a moment Boxhall thought this meant she was steaming
toward the stricken liner, but it soon became disappointingly clear that this
wasn't the case. Yet even if that ship couldn't hear the tremendous bangs of
the *Titanic's* rockets bursting surely she must be able to see the rockets themselves. Why didn't she respond? Boxhall finally gave up on trying to reach her
by Morse lamp, but Rowe was eager to try so Captain Smith gave him permission. Once he thought he saw a reply, but after studying the stranger
through the captain's glasses he decided it was only her masthead light flick-
ering. Discouraged, Rowe went back to firing off the rest of his rockets.[1]

In the wireless shack the strain was starting to show on Phillips. It didn't
seem possible to the other ships that the "unsinkable" *Titanic* could be in
mortal danger, and in vain Phillips was trying to make them understand.

When at 1:25 the *Olympic* asked, "Are you steering south to meet us?" Phillips tapped back in exasperation, "We are putting the women off in the boats," feeling that should make the situation clear enough to anyone. The *Frankfort* broke in with "Are there any ships around you already?" Then, a few seconds later: "The *Frankfort* wishes to know what is the matter? We are ten hours away."

Phillips jumped up, tearing the head phones from his ears, shouting, "*The damn fool!* He says, 'What's up, old man?'!" Furiously he tapped back, "You are jamming my equipment! Stand by and keep out!"[2]

Every few minutes Captain Smith would drop by to see if Phillips was having any success raising any ship closer than the *Carpathia*—clearly that motionless ship on the horizon was on his mind—and provide Phillips with further information. It was a quarter past one when Smith informed Phillips that the power was beginning to fade, maybe ten minutes later when he told him the water was reaching the engine rooms. At 1:45 A.M. Phillips again called the *Carpathia*, this time telling her, "Come as quickly as possible, old man; engine room filling up to the boilers."[3]

—◆◆◆—

Just a few minutes past midnight on the small Cunard liner *Carpathia*, the wireless operator, Harold Thomas Cottam, had just handed some wireless messages to First Officer Dean on the bridge and was returning to his wireless cabin. Once there he remembered some traffic he'd been listening to earlier that night, including some messages for the new White Star liner *Titanic*. He thought he would remind Phillips, whom he knew professionally, about those waiting messages. It took a few minutes for the set to warm up, then he politely tapped out a call to the *Titanic*, quickly receiving a curt "Go ahead."

"Good morning, old man [GM OM]. Do you know there are messages for you at Cape Race?"

What Cottam heard next made his blood run cold. Instead of the expected jaunty reply came the dreaded "CQD—CQD—SOS—SOS—CQD—MGY. Come at once. We have struck a berg. It's a CQD, old man [CQD OM]. Position 41.46 N, 50.14 W."

Stunned, Cottam did nothing for a moment, then asked Phillips if he should tell his captain. The reply was immediate: "Yes, quick." Cottam raced to the bridge and breathlessly told First Officer Dean. Dean didn't hesitate—he bolted down the ladder, through the chartroom and into the captain's cabin, Cottam hard on his heels.[4]

For Capt. Arthur H. Rostron, such indecorous behavior was a bit much; people were expected to at least knock before barging in on the captain, especially when he was asleep. But the reprimand died on his lips when a clearly anxious Dean told him about the *Titanic*. Rostron swung his legs out of bed and then seemed lost in thought for a few seconds as he digested the news.

"Mr. Dean, turn the ship around—steer northwest, I'll work out the course for you in a minute." As Dean sped back to the bridge, Rostron turned his attention to Cottam. "Are you sure it's the *Titanic* and she requires immediate assistance?" he asked.

"Yes, sir."

"You are absolutely certain?"

"Quite certain, sir."

"All right, tell him we are coming along as fast as we can." Cottam left and Rostron began dressing, his mind racing.

Forty-three years old, Rostron had spent the last thirty of them at sea, the first ten in sail. He had joined Cunard in 1892 and had risen steadily, if unspectacularly, up the company ladder. (Cunard captains are never expected to be spectacular. The conscientiousness and circumspection of Cunard skippers was—and still is—legendary.) He was an experienced mariner, known and respected throughout Cunard as "the Electric Spark" for his decisiveness and boundless, infectious energy. He was also noted for his piety; he neither smoked nor drank, was never heard to use profanity, and in a day and age when recourse to the Almighty was not regarded as quaint or a sign of weakmindedness, was known to turn to prayer for guidance.

In January 1912 he was given command of the *Carpathia*, a 14-knot, 13,564-ton liner that plodded along the Atlantic track between New York and the Mediterranean. This cold April morning she was three days out of New York, carrying approximately 800 passengers in three classes, on what had been up to now an uneventful crossing. In all of Rostron's years at sea, he had never been called upon to carry out a rescue. This was to be his first real test.

As he straightened his tie and set his cap square on his head, Rostron settled the last few details in his mind. Striding out into the chartroom he began working out the details of the *Carpathia*'s new course. After a few minutes he made a quick trip up to the bridge to give the helmsman the new course—North 52 West—then called down to the engine room to order Full Speed Ahead. At the *Carpathia*'s top speed of fourteen knots she would cover the distance between herself and the *Titanic* in four hours, which was not good enough for Rostron. Now he swung into action.

Returning to the chartroom he called for Chief Engineer Johnstone. Speed, he told Johnstone, he wanted more speed than the old *Carpathia* had ever mustered. Call out the off-duty watch to the engine room, get every available stoker roused to feed the furnaces. Cut off the heat and hot water to passenger and crew accommodations, put every ounce of steam the boilers made into the engines.

Next he spoke to First Officer Dean and gave him a list of things to be done: all routine work knocked off; the ship prepared for a rescue operation; swing out the ship's boats; have clusters of electric lights rigged along the ship's sides; all gangway doors to be opened, with block and tackle slung at each gangway; slings ready for hoisting injured aboard and canvas bags for lifting small children; ladders prepared for dropping at each gangway, along with cargo nets; forward derricks to be rigged and topped, with steam in the winches, for bringing luggage and cargo aboard; oil bags readied in the lavatories to pour on rough seas if needed.

Dean set to immediately and Rostron turned to the ship's surgeon, Dr. McGhee: the three surgeons aboard to be assigned to specific stations—McGhee himself in First Class, the Italian doctor in Second, and the Hungarian doctor in Third. All three were to be supplied with stimulants and restoratives and first aid stations to be set up in each dining saloon.

To Purser Brown: see that the chief steward, the assistant purser, and the purser himself each covered a different gangway to receive the *Titanic's* passengers and crew; get their names and classes and see to it that each one went to the correct dining saloon for a medical check.

Chief Steward Henry Hughes received an additional set of instructions: every crewman was to be called out; coffee was to be available for all hands. Also, soup, coffee, tea, brandy, and whiskey should ready for those rescued; the smoking room, lounge, and library were to be converted into dormitories for survivors. All the *Carpathia's* steerage passengers were to be grouped together; the extra space would be given over to the *Titanic's* steerage passengers.

Finally Rostron urged everyone to keep quiet: the last thing they needed was the *Carpathia's* passengers lurking about while there was work to be done. To help keep the passengers where they belonged, stewards were stationed along every corridor to shepherd the curious back into their cabins. An inspector, a master-at-arms, and several stewards were sent down to keep the steerage passengers in order—no one was sure how they would react to being herded about in the wee hours of the morning.[5]

His instructions issued, Rostron quickly reviewed everything he had ordered, trying to think of what he had overlooked. There didn't seem to be anything, so he quickly strode to the bridge and began posting extra lookouts. He was determined that the *Carpathia* was not about to meet the same fate as the ship she was rushing to aid. Rostron had an extra man posted in the crow's nest, two lookouts in the bow, extra hands posted on both bridge wings, and Second Officer James Bisset, who had especially keen eyesight, posted on the starboard bridge wing.

Now having done all he could do, Rostron faced the toughest task—waiting. But there was one last detail Rostron did not overlook. Second Officer Bisset noticed it first; then so did the others on the bridge—the captain standing toward the back of the bridge holding his cap an inch or two off his head, eyes closed, lips moving in silent prayer.[6]

Down in the boiler room the extra hands were put to work shoveling coal into the furnaces of the boilers. First the safety valves were closed off, then the engineers began to systematically shut off steam to the rest of the ship, ducting it instead into the reciprocating engines. Up, down, up, down, up, down, the pistons pounded, as the chief engineer watched the revolutions steadily increasing. Faster and faster the ship drove ahead—14 knots . . . 14 1/2 . . . 15 . . . 16 . . . 16 1/2 . . . 17 knots. The old *Carpathia* had never gone so fast.

The deck crew was soon roused by First Officer Dean and put to work collecting extra blankets, shifting furniture in the dining saloons, and rigging the extra equipment ordered by Captain Rostron. It all seemed utterly bewildering to the crew since no explanation had been given for this flurry of activity, but Dean felt explanations could wait.

Chief Steward Hughes thought his men could do a better job if they had an idea of what was happening, so at 1:15 A.M. he gathered all his stewards in the main dining saloon. Quickly, quietly, he told about the *Titanic*, explained how the rescue was up to the *Carpathia*, then pausing dramatically and eyeing each man directly, solemnly intoned: "Every man to his post and let him do his duty like a true Englishman. If the situation calls for it, let us add another glorious page to British history." The stewards immediately set to work, determined that when they arrived at the *Titanic*'s side, they would be ready for anything.[7]

Phillips was still bent over the wireless key, mechanically tapping out his call and hoping that by some miracle a closer ship would suddenly respond. Even if the *Frankfort*, the *Olympic*, or any of the other ships didn't realize it—though thankfully Cottam on the *Carpathia* seemed to understand how serious the situation was—Phillips knew that the ship was doomed.

The news was spreading. Ships within range of the *Titanic* passed the word on to other ships that weren't, and the station at Cape Race was able to pick up Phillips's signals directly. Soon the operator there relayed the *Titanic*'s messages inland, where they were picked up by the wireless station atop the *New York Times* Building in New York City. In Philadelphia, Wannamaker's department store had recently installed a wireless office, capitalizing on the public's interest in the new technology. The office had actually been set up in one of the store's front windows, and this was where a young wireless operator named David Sarnoff caught the signals from Cape Race. He in turn quickly passed the word on to other stations farther inland; slowly the New World was awakening to the unfolding tragedy in the North Atlantic.[8]

The *Titanic* had slowly begun listing to port, and now there was a yawning gap nearly three feet wide between the deck and the sides of the lifeboats on the port side of the ship. A young French woman tried to jump across into Boat 10 but missed. Desperately she clutched at the gunnels of the lifeboat while her feet caught the railing of the deck below. She was quickly pulled back aboard, and she tried again, this time successfully. Meanwhile children were being rushed into Boat 10, Seaman Evans later recalled that some were just "chucked in," one baby being caught by a woman passenger who snatched at the child's dressing gown. Shortly Boat 10 was ready to be lowered, and as the boat began its descent, a man rushed to the rail. To Fifth Officer Lowe, who tried to stop him, he looked like a "crazed Italian"— although to Lowe, anyone who tried to rush a lifeboat was either a "Dago" or an "Italian." In this case Lowe couldn't stop the man, who jumped into the boat just as it was dropping below the level of the deck.

Lowe crossed to the opposite side of the ship, where a knot of Second and Third Class women passengers were waiting on A Deck to get into Boat 11, and immediately began helping the women get aboard. Edith Russell came rushing up, clutching her toy pig, which she had wrapped in a blanket. A steward took her pig, and thinking it was a baby, tossed it to one of the women in the boat, then helped Edith climb over the rail and into the boat.[9]

Mrs. Allen Becker had just put her two youngest children into the boat when it suddenly began to lurch downward. "Please let me go with my children!" she cried. She was quickly rushed up and into the boat. At the last second she realized that her eldest daughter Ruth was still waiting on the deck. Mrs. Becker called out to the girl, "Get into the next boat!" as Boat 11 descended. As the boat reached the water, someone up on deck called down, "Is there a seaman in the boat?" When there was no reply, Seaman Brice slid down the after fall and cast off from the ship.[10]

Kate Buss couldn't bear to watch as the boats were being lowered: it was such an emotionally wrenching sight to her that she deliberately averted her eyes from the boats. Standing on the starboard side of the Boat Deck, once again joined by Marion Wright and Douglas Norman, Kate pondered her chances of being rescued along with her friends. Shortly the trio was joined by another shipboard acquaintance, Dr. Alfred Pain. When the cry came up from Boat 9 of "Any more ladies there?" the two men hustled Marion and Kate forward to the waiting boat. Miss Wright stepped across and into the boat without a word, and as Miss Buss was climbing aboard, she noticed a number of men already seated in the boat. She beckoned to Norman and Pain to follow, but crewmen barred the two men from joining her, and the boat was quickly lowered.

Aghast, Kate rounded on Seaman Haines, who was in charge of the boat, and demanded to know why her friends had been kept from joining her. Haines replied, "The officer gave the order to lower away, and if I didn't do so he might shoot me, and simply put someone else in charge, and your friends would still not be allowed to come." Horrified at the apparent callousness, Kate was speechless. She never saw Douglas Norman or Dr. Pain again.[11]

Now a rising hysteria began to creep along the Boat Deck as Boat 13 was being loaded. A fat woman shrieked, "Don't put me in that boat! I don't want to go in that boat! I've never been in an open boat in my life!" Steward Ray, who had just bundled Dr. Dodge rather unceremoniously into Boat 13, turned to her and said sharply, "You have got to go and you may as well keep quiet." Someone tossed an infant to Ray, who was standing in the stern of the boat. Turning to the women in Boat 13, he called out, "Who'll take this babby?" A young woman volunteered and the "babby" (it was ten-month-old Alden Caldwell) was passed forward.

Following her mother's instructions, Ruth Becker came up to Boat 13 and asked if she could get in. Fifth Officer Lowe said, "Sure," and helped her over the rail, then turned to the deck and called for any more women. None came forward so Lowe ordered the boat put down. Just as the boat began to drop, some Second Class male passengers, among them Lawrence Beesley, the young schoolteacher, stepped forward and jumped into the boat.

About halfway down the *Titanic's* side someone looked over the side of the boat and saw that the boat was being lowered directly into the condenser exhaust pouring out from the side of the ship. Ordinarily this three-foot-thick jet of water was created by the spent steam being discharged by the center turbine's condenser, but this flow came from the pumps in the boiler rooms, fighting their losing battle to stay ahead of the rising water. It would have swamped Boat 13 in seconds, capsizing the boat and tossing everyone aboard into the sea. Desperately the crewmen and the male passengers grabbed at oars and spars, pushing the boat clear. Seconds later she hit the water, and everyone aboard her breathed a sigh of relief.

Boat 13's troubles weren't over yet, though. The wash from the condenser exhaust pushed the boat aft, and now she found herself underneath Boat 15, which was rapidly descending. Frantically calling up to the deck to stop lowering, the crewmen in Boat 13 rushed to clear the falls. The men on deck heard the cries coming up from below, and halted Boat 15 with only a few feet to spare, while the men in Boat 13 were finally able to get the falls released. Seconds later Boat 13 rowed away into the night as Boat 15 gently splashed into the water.[12]

Another rocket shot up into the sky. Quartermaster Rowe had fired off a half-dozen already, going to the Morse lamp occasionally, still vainly trying to get the attention of that ship on the horizon. Like Rowe, Captain Smith was convinced that she couldn't be more than ten or twelve miles away, and he muttered something to Rowe about wanting a six-inch naval gun to "wake that fellow up." Rowe didn't catch all of the captain's remark, but he silently agreed with the gist of it. Rowe's frustration, like Phillips's, was beginning to build, but like the wireless operator, he kept at his work, hoping for a miracle.[13]

———◈———

About 1:20 in the morning of April 15, 1912, a dozing copy boy was jolted awake when the basket came crashing down the shaft of the dumbwaiter that connected the wireless station on the roof with the editorial offices of the

New York Times. The startled copy boy snatched up the sheet of paper in the basket, read it, then took off for the office of the managing editor, Carr Van Anda. Van Anda read the message, frowned in disbelief, then read it again. From Cape Race in Newfoundland, the bulletin read:

> Sunday night, April 14 (AP). At 10:25 o'clock [New York time]
> tonight the White Star Line steamship "Titanic" called 'CQD' to
> the Marconi station here, and reported having struck an iceberg.
> The steamer said that immediate assistance was required.[14]

Van Anda quickly called the New York office of the White Star Line, then contacted *Times* correspondents in Montreal and Halifax in an effort to learn more. At the moment the facts were sparse: about a half hour before midnight (New York time), the Allen Line had received a transmission from their steamer, the *Virginian*, which had picked up one of the *Titanic*'s early distress calls and had altered course to rush to the stricken liner's aid. The White Star ships *Olympic* and *Baltic* were also putting about, as were the *Birma*, the *Mount Temple*, and the *Carpathia*. Cape Race was monitoring the wireless transmissions between these ships as well as keeping a close watch on the messages coming from the *Titanic*. Cape Race had heard nothing from the sinking liner since 12:27 A.M., when a blurred and abruptly cut off SOS was heard.

Van Anda had a good head for news, and quickly began reshaping the morning mail edition of the *Times*. The political feud between President Taft and Theodore Roosevelt, which had dominated the news for the three past months and had originally been given preeminence on the front page, was instantly relegated to the inside pages, and taking its place would be the accident to the *Titanic*. Van Anda sensed that a tremendous story was breaking and at the same time, a terrible dread was looming in the editor's mind. The *Titanic* hadn't been heard from in nearly an hour—as more reports came in, he learned that the women and children were being put into the lifeboats and that the ship's engine room was flooding. What Van Anda began to suspect was the worst—the "unsinkable ship" had sunk.

There was no confirmation yet, so the story Van Anda prepared for the early edition was cautious. He simply presented the facts as they were known at that early hour, as well as whatever information was available about the ship and her passengers. But the four-line headline itself shouted:

NEW LINER TITANIC HITS AN ICEBERG;

SINKING BY THE BOW AT MIDNIGHT;

WOMEN PUT OFF IN LIFEBOATS;

LAST WIRELESS AT 12:27 A.M. BLURRED

That would do for the morning editions, but now Van Anda decided to play his hunch: when the city edition went to press, it announced that the

Titanic had sunk. It would be several hours before he would know for sure, but if he was right, then the *New York Times* would have "scooped" every other paper in the country—quite an accomplishment for a newspaper that in 1912 was just another New York daily. Although he didn't know it at the time, Van Anda was about to secure claim to a position of preeminence for the *New York Times* among American newspapers that it would never relinquish.[15]

Fifth Officer Lowe would have traded every newspaper in America for a few more lifeboats. After seeing Boat 13 safely into the water at around 1:30, he crossed to the port side of the Boat Deck with Sixth Officer Moody, stopping at Boats 14 and 16. "I've just sent five boats away without a single officer in any of them," he told Moody, "so there had best be an officer in one of these two."

"You go," Moody replied. "I'll find another boat."

By the time Lowe began loading Boat 14, the situation on board the Titanic was clear. Clearly the *Titanic* was doomed, and there was no longer the time to ask or cajole the women into the boats. Two seamen grasped Charlotte Collyer, one by the arm and the other by the waist and pulled her toward Boat 14. As she struggled to get free, her husband Harvey cried out, "Go, Lottie! For God's sake, be brave and go! I'll get a seat in another boat!"

A young man, barely more than a boy, climbed over the rail into Boat 14 and tried to hide beneath the seats among the women already in the boat. Furious, Lowe drew his revolver, dragged the young man out of his hiding place, and ordered him back onto the ship. The boy pleaded with Lowe, saying that he wouldn't take up much room, but Lowe thrust the gun in his face and said, "I'll give you just ten seconds to get back onto that ship before I blow your brains out!" Sobbing, the boy only pleaded harder, and Lowe suddenly changed tactics, saying, "For God's sake, be a man. We've got women and children to save."

By now the women in the boat, already thoroughly frightened, began crying. Eight-year old Marjory Collyer anxiously tugged at Lowe's arm, whimpering, "Oh, Mr. Man, don't shoot, please don't shoot the poor man!" Lowe smiled at her and shook his head. Somehow Lowe's mixture of threat and appeal worked, for now the young man had crawled out of the boat and was lying face down on the deck. (In all the excitement, the fifth officer failed to notice eighteen-year-old Daniel Buckley, who was sitting among the women in Boat 14 with a woman's shawl over his head.)

Just seconds later another male passenger tried to rush aboard Boat 14, but was caught and thrown back by Lowe. It was this malefactor's misfortune to land among several Second Class men, who began to beat him senseless. Another wave of Lowe's "Italians" tried to force their way into the boat. Lowe yelled, "Look out!" to Seaman Scarrott, who drove them back using the tiller bar like a club. Lowe drew his gun again, and shouted, "If anyone else tries that this is what he'll get!" and fired three times along the side of the ship. The crowd fell back, Lowe stepped into the stern of Boat 14, and the boat was quickly lowered.[16]

At Boat 15, Steward Hart had just finished loading the last women from the second group he had brought up from steerage. Although he was prepared to go back again, First Officer Murdoch told him to stay with the boat. It was a wise decision, for just then a half-dozen men rushed the boat. Murdoch and Hart struggled to hold them back, Murdoch shouting at the men, "Get back! Get back! It's women first!" Breathlessly the first officer gave the order to lower away.[17]

August Wennerstrom had escorted two Swedish girls to Boat 15, then crossed over to the port side of the Boat Deck, and stood near the fourth funnel, puffing away on a cigar and watching Boat 16 being loaded. Of all the boats put down, Boat 16 was probably the one loaded and launched with the least amount of fuss. Wennerstrom noticed that almost all the people getting into the boat were Second and Third Class women and children. Once Boat 16 was gone, Wennerstrom began to make his way forward. Up at the forward end of the superstructure there were a few boats left. It was nearly 1:45 A.M.[18]

Through it all, the sounds of ragtime, familiar dance tunes, and popular waltzes continued. Bandmaster Hartley and his musicians, all wearing their lifebelts now, were playing by the forward entrance to the Grand Staircase. They had been playing for close to an hour now, but if Hartley ever had any thought of stopping, he gave no sign of it. This was exactly what Wallace Hartley had always conceived of his duty as orchestra leader to be: years before, when a friend had asked him what he would do if he found himself standing on the deck of a sinking ship, he replied, "I would gather the band together and begin playing." No one is certain, of course, if Hartley or anyone else in the band knew that there were too few boats and their chances of getting away very slim, but not one of them stopped playing.[19]

In spite of the desperation beginning to wash over the Boat Deck, some individuals on board persisted in displaying a remarkable calm. A diehard foursome in the First Class Smoking Room—Major Butt, Arthur Ryerson, Clarence Moore, and Frank Millet—seemed completely imperturbable: despite the alarmingly tilting deck, their bridge game went on uninterrupted. Perhaps it was a defense mechanism, a denial of a reality that they did not want to face. At any rate the bidding, tricks, ruffs, and finesses continued.

Nearby, William Stead sat ensconced in a leather armchair, completely absorbed in his book. The ongoing commotion outside on the Boat Deck disturbed him not one whit; he never made any attempt to put on a lifebelt nor even expressed the slightest curiosity about the state of the ship. Doubtless he recalled that in the course of an after-dinner conversation Friday night he had defied superstition by telling a tale about a cursed Egyptian mummy, deliberately drawing the tale out until he was able to conclude it after midnight, then gleefully drawing his audience's attention that it was now the thirteenth of April when he finished. It was equally probable that he was well aware he would soon be experiencing firsthand the spiritual world in which he so ardently believed.

Charles Hays, standing off to one side on the Boat Deck, was probably recalling an after-dinner conversation he'd had with Colonel Gracie a few hours earlier. Just before Gracie retired for the night, Hays had remarked, "The White Star, Cunard, and the Hamburg-Amerika are now devoting their attention to a struggle for supremacy in obtaining the most luxurious appointments for their ships. But the time will soon come when the greatest and most appalling of all disasters at sea will be the result." Whatever his thoughts, Hays seemed singularly resigned to remaining on board to the end: after seeing his wife into Boat 3, he never went near any of the lifeboats.

Jay Yates, the professional gambler who had been on board hoping to make a maiden-voyage killing, would be remembered by many survivors as working as hard as any man on board to get as many women and children as he could into the lifeboats. Certainly he had no illusions about his fate: quickly tearing a page from his appointment book, he scribbled a hasty note, then thrust it at a woman climbing into one of the boats. Signed with an alias, it read, "If saved, please inform my sister Mrs. F. J. Adams of Findlay, Ohio. Lost. J. H. Rogers." (The note eventually would find its way to Yates's mother, who broke down when she received it. "Thank God I know where he is now," she sobbed. "I had not heard from him in two years. The last news I had from him he was in London.")[20]

Benjamin Guggenheim outdid them all, though. Sometime between 12:30 and 1:00, he disappeared from the Boat Deck, only to reappear about 1:30. He no longer wore the warm sweaters that Steward Etches had insisted on earlier. Missing too was his lifebelt. Instead he and his secretary had donned white tie and tails. And now, standing calm and dignified on the Boat Deck, he gave Steward Johnson a message for his wife:

> I think there is grave doubt that the men will get off. I am willing to remain and play the man's game if there are not enough boats for more than the women and children. I won't die here like a beast. Tell my wife, Johnson, if it should happen that my secretary and I both go down and you are saved, tell her I played the game out straight and to the end. No woman shall be left aboard this ship because Ben Guggenheim was a coward.

When pressed as to why he had laid aside his lifebelt and changed into evening clothes, he said simply, "We've dressed in our best and are prepared to go down like gentlemen."[21]

CHAPTER 8

"She's Gone!"

Flee from the midst of Babylon, let every man save his life!

—Jeremiah 51:6

IT WAS NOW 1:45 A.M. THE *TITANIC* HAD DEVELOPED AN UGLY LIST TO PORT as her bow dipped under and the sea began pouring through the hatch covers and ventilators of the forward well deck. Standing by the bridge Chief Officer Wilde bellowed, "Everyone on the starboard side to straighten her up!" Passengers and crew dutifully trooped across the Boat Deck and the ship swung slowly back.

About this time Phillips turned the key over to Bride, left the wireless office and took a quick walk around the forward half of the Boat Deck. He watched the frantic efforts of the crew as they tried to maintain order in loading the lifeboats. For the first time that night he heard the ragtime and waltzes being played by the band. When he returned to the wireless shack a few minutes later, all he could do was shake his head as he took over from Bride again and mutter, "Things look very queer outside, very queer indeed."[1]

At one point Phillips had watched the sea sweep over the foredeck and begin to flood into the forward well deck, washing past the foot of the foremast and swirling around the winches and cranes. Though he probably couldn't have known it, as he watched the sea begin to pour down the hatch-covers of Number 1 and Number 2 holds, the *Titanic* was sinking faster, as now the water could enter the ship by a way other than the ruptured hull below. More critical, the cargo hatches gave the sea a way into the ship that was above all the watertight bulkheads. The end was not far off now.

There were precious few lifeboats left. Near the bridge a scuffle broke out around Collapsible C, which had been fitted into the davits of Boat 1. A mob of stewards and Third Class passengers rushed the boat, trying to climb aboard. Purser McElroy drew his revolver and fired twice into the air, while First Officer Murdoch tried to hold the crowd back, shouting, "Get out of this! Clear out of this!" Hugh Woolner and Lieutenant Steffanson heard the gunshots and rushed over, just in time to see two stewards slip past McElroy and Murdoch and jump into the boat. Woolner and Steffanson promptly dragged the culprits back out and threw them onto the deck. Under the watchful eyes of the four men—the two officers and two passengers—Collapsible C was quickly but calmly loaded.[2]

A much steadier Bruce Ismay was doing his best to help, having recovered his composure after suffering Fifth Officer Lowe's earlier outburst. He had spent most of his time shepherding as many passengers into the lifeboats as possible. Now he was working with Murdoch and McElroy, trying to get any women or children they could find into Collapsible C.

Finally McElroy was satisfied that the boat was full and called out to lower away. From the starboard bridge wing the chief officer asked who was in command of the boat. Before McElroy could reply, Captain Smith, also standing on the starboard bridge wing, turned to Quartermaster Rowe—still vainly firing his rockets—and told him to take charge. Rowe fired off his eighth and last rocket, then noticed that now he could see only the strange ship's red sidelight. Clearly she wasn't underway, but only drifting with the current. Disgusted, he left the four remaining rockets and jumped in the stern of the collapsible. McElroy nodded to the deck hands at the davits, and they began turning the cranks to lower Collapsible C to the sea. Just as the boat's gunwale reached the level of the deck, Bruce Ismay stepped forward, and without so much as a glance at the other men on the Boat Deck, jumped into an empty spot near the bow.

The lowering continued and as the boat made her way down the ship's side, the *Titanic*'s list returned, causing Collapsible C's wooden keel to catch on the rows of rivet heads protruding from the hull plates. The passengers desperately pushed the boat away from the side of the ship, using oars as fenders, until Collapsible C reached the water. The falls were quickly freed and the boat drifted off into the night.[3]

Ismay's example was ignored by most of the First Class men. A little farther up the Boat Deck, Arthur Ryerson, Major Butt, Clarence Moore, and Walter Douglas, having abandoned their bridge game, stood together talking quietly. Jack Thayer, standing on the starboard side of the Boat Deck with Milton Long, didn't know that his father, John B. Thayer, was only a few yards away on the other side of the Boat Deck, chatting with George Widener. A dozen or more of the First Class men were helping Lightoller and Murdoch load the lifeboats and free Collapsibles A and B, which were still lashed to the roof of the officers' quarters.[4]

On the port side of the Boat Deck, Lightoller was getting Boat 2 ready for loading. After Quartermaster Rowe had finished firing off the rockets, Fourth Officer Boxhall had remained on the bridge waiting for orders. Captain Smith told him to take charge of Boat 2, so Boxhall had crossed to the port side, where Lightoller was getting the boat loaded. Only moments before the second officer had discovered a large group of men—passengers and crewmen—already huddled in Boat 2. Furious, Lightoller drew his revolver and leveled it at them, shouting, "Get out of there, you damned cowards! I'd like to see every one of you overboard!" There was a mad scramble as the men fled the lifeboat: they had no way of knowing that Lightoller's gun wasn't even loaded—and they had all heard shots fired further down the deck just a few minutes before! Lightoller moved back to Boat 4 and Boxhall took charge of Boat 2. In short order twenty-five women, one male passenger from steerage, and Boxhall, along with three crewmen, had climbed into the boat. At one point one of the women pleaded with her husband to come with her, but he gently pushed her away, saying "No, I must be a gentleman." An embarrassed Boxhall witnessed the exchange, then turned and told the men at the davits to lower away. Slowly Boat 2 creaked its way down to the sea.[5]

Boat 4 had been a problem all night, but now Lightoller had no choice—he had to use it. Originally the plan had been to load the boat from the Promenade Deck, but the windows there had proven particularly difficult to open. Then someone noticed that the *Titanic*'s sounding spar projected from the hull immediately below the boat. While Seaman Sam Parks and Storekeeper Jack Foley went below to get an axe to chop away the offending spar, Lightoller had moved on to other boats. Now the spar was gone, the windows were opened, and a stack of deck chairs served as makeshift steps to the window sills. Standing with one foot in Boat 4 and one foot on the sill, Lightoller called for the waiting women and children to climb aboard.

They had certainly waited long enough. Among those in the crowd were the Ryerson family, Mrs. Thayer, Mr. and Mrs. Carter, and of course, Colonel and Mrs. Astor. For more than an hour they had shuttled back and forth between the Boat Deck and the Promenade Deck as various plans for loading the boat were made, altered, then discarded. After being ordered up to the Boat Deck a second time, only to have Second Steward Dodd tell them to go back down to A Deck again, they were understandably frustrated. "Just tell us where to go and we will follow!" exclaimed Mrs. Thayer in exasperation. "You ordered us up here and now you are sending us back!"

The shuttling was over now and Boat 4 was being loaded just as quickly as Lightoller, assisted by Clinch Smith and Colonel Gracie, could pass the women and children through the open windows. John Jacob Astor helped his wife negotiate the deck chairs, saying, "Get into the lifeboat, to please me." He then asked Lightoller if he could join her, explaining that she was "in delicate condition."

"No, sir," Lightoller replied firmly, "no men are allowed in these boats until the women are loaded first."

"Well, what boat is it?"

"Boat 4, sir." At that Astor turned to his wife and said, "The sea is calm. You'll be all right. You're in good hands. I'll meet you in the morning," then stepped away and made his way back up to the Boat Deck.

As Arthur Ryerson was helping his wife and their maid, Victorine, across the deck chairs, he noticed that the girl had no lifebelt on. Quickly stripping his off, he fastened it around the frightened young woman, then saw her into the boat. When Jack Ryerson made to follow her, Lightoller suddenly called out, "That boy can't go!"

Mr. Ryerson bristled. Placing his arm around Jack's shoulders he said, "Of course the boy goes with his mother—he's only thirteen." Jack climbed through the window into the boat, leaving Lightoller muttering, "No more boys." He didn't notice ten-year-old Billy Carter, Jr., wearing a girl's hat, climb past him as Mrs. Carter got in the boat. Ryerson, like Colonel Astor, returned to the Boat Deck.

Just then Colonel Gracie noticed a young woman standing off to one side, holding a baby. Who she was he had no idea, but from the expression on her face, she was clearly frightened of going near the edge of the deck but was equally terrified of being left behind. Gracie assured her that he would hold her child while she climbed into the boat and the woman accepted his help. No sooner had she taken her seat than she cried out, "Where's my baby?"

"Here's your baby, miss," Gracie said gently, and handed the child over. Gracie never forgot his own fear at that moment, worried that the boat might be lowered before he could return the infant, and wondering how he would manage in the water with a child in his arms.[6]

From up on the Boat Deck a voice called down, "How many women are there in the boat?"

Lightoller did a quick count and called back, "Twenty-four."

"That's enough, lower away." At 1:55 Boat 4 dropped to the water—just fifteen feet below.[7]

It was clear now to those in the lifeboats that, no matter what they had believed or hoped before, the *Titanic* was doomed. The ship was visibly moving now, and from somewhere inside her a series of intermittent crashes began, sounding like huge stacks of china being shattered. First Officer Murdoch was finally convinced that it was hopeless. As he watched Collapsible C pull away from the ship, he turned to Steward John Hardy and said quietly, "I believe she's gone, Hardy."[8]

Lightoller had been convinced of it for some time: each glance down that emergency stairway showed the sea rising steadily higher. Now it was up to C Deck. Despite the bitter cold, Lightoller's exertions had worked him into quite a sweat, and great beads of perspiration stood out on his forehead. Gone was his greatcoat—working now in only his pajamas he supervised the crewmen who were slinging Collapsible D in Boat 2's now empty davits. Assistant Surgeon Simpson, seeing that the second officer was wringing wet with sweat, couldn't resist a good-natured, if ill-timed, jibe, calling out, "Hello, Lights, are you warm?" Lightoller ignored him.[9]

It's uncertain whether or not Lightoller had been aware of the discrepancy between the number of people aboard the *Titanic* and the capacity of the lifeboats she carried; or, if he was aware of it, if he had thought of it in anything more than terms of abstract numbers. Whatever the case, the awful truth of that disparity was driven home to him now. Before him, on the *Titanic*'s decks, were more than 1,500 people; behind him was the last lifeboat, with seats for forty-seven. Recalling that when the crowd had rushed Boats 14 and 15 as well as Collapsible C, they had barely been held back, Lightoller took no chances: gathering all the crewmen he could find, plus a few trusted passengers, he had them form a ring around Collapsible D, arms locked together. Only women and children would be allowed through.

Winnie Troutt had been watching the boats being lowered for some time without making the slightest move to get into one herself. She felt she had seen too many husbands and wives forcibly separated so that single women such as herself could be given preference in the boats. At least, she thought, her family would be spared the cost of a funeral for her.

Suddenly a man she had never seen before came up to her and held out a baby to her, saying, "I don't want to be saved, but will you save this baby?" Winnie took the child, then realizing that now she had to find a place in one of the boats, she headed for Collapsible D. The men forming the barricade around the boat let her pass through, but as she did so, a woman Winnie didn't know looked at her and the baby and cried out, "Oh, you['re] so fool[ish]! The ship's about to sink."

"Why, you nasty thing!" Winnie snapped furiously. She turned to a crewman and asked, "What will become of us?"

"Don't worry, madam, the White Star Line will take care of you." Satisfied, Miss Troutt climbed into Collapsible D.

A man who had been calling himself "Mr. Louis Hoffman" during the voyage brought two small boys to the ring and passed them through. His name was actually Michel Navatril, and he had kidnapped the boys—his sons, Edmond, just two, and Michel, not quite four—from his estranged wife, hoping to escape to America where she would never find them. As he let go of Michel's hand, he said, "Tell your mother I love her." Right behind him came Colonel Gracie with Mrs. John Murray Brown on one arm and Miss Edith Evans on the other. Henry B. Harris brought his wife Renee up to the ring, passed her through, and was told he could not follow. "I know," he sighed, "I'll stay."

The Goldsmiths came up to the ring and stopped. Mr. and Mrs. Goldsmith said a quiet goodbye, then Mr. Goldsmith gave nine-year-old Franky an affectionate squeeze on the shoulder, saying, "So long, Franky. I'll see you later." A traveling companion gave Mrs. Goldsmith his wedding band, remarking, "If I don't see you in New York, see that my wife gets this." A steward pulled Mrs. Goldsmith and her son toward the boat, then turned to sixteen-year-old Alfred Rush. "No!" the lad cried, "I'm going to stay with the men!" Just behind Mrs. Goldsmith and Franky a talkative group of Syrian women, many with babies, climbed into the boat.

Lightoller and Hardy were helping the women make the climb over the railing into the boat. The boat was about half full when Chief Officer Wilde strolled over from the starboard bridge wing and called out, "You go with her, Lightoller."

"Not damn likely," the second officer shot back, and continued to help women into the boat. Somehow in the shuffle Mrs. Brown and Miss Evans hadn't yet gotten into the boat. When they finally reached the railing there was only one seat left. Miss Evans turned to Mrs. Brown and said simply, "You go first. You have children waiting for you." Mrs. Brown climbed aboard and Lightoller called out to lower away.

One deck below, at the forward end of the Promenade Deck, Hugh Woolner and Bjorn Steffanson began to realize just how tight their situation was. They had spent the past hour and a half rushing to and fro about the Boat Deck and the Promenade Deck, helping with loading and launching the boats, dealing with those cowards in Collapsible C, making sure the women in their charge were seen safely aboard the lifeboats. Now the rising sea was only a few feet away, and the last lifeboats were leaving. Just as they were resigning themselves to their fate, they saw Collapsible D being lowered right beside them. Steffanson thought there was enough room in the bow and jumped for it, followed seconds later by Woolner, who landed half in, half out of the boat. Steffanson pulled him aboard. An instant later, the boat hit the water. As the falls were freed and the boat began pulling away from the *Titanic*, Seaman William Lucas looked up at Edith Evans and called out, "There is another boat going to be put down for you." It was 2:05 A.M.[11]

With all the boats gone and the ship obviously only moments away from foundering, there was one last, painful duty for Captain Smith to perform. First he walked up the port side of the Boat Deck to the wireless shack, where he found Phillips still hunched over his key, tapping away. Quietly, Smith told Phillips and Bride, "Men, you have done your full duty. You can do no more. Abandon your cabin. Now it's every man for himself." Phillips glanced up at him, then went back to Morsing. The Captain continued: "You look out for yourselves, I release you. That's the way of it at this kind of time." Then he turned and left the wireless shack for the last time. Without a word Phillips continued to tap out his distress call.[12]

Now Captain Smith moved about the Boat Deck, speaking quietly to whatever crew members he found. To the knot of men struggling atop the officers' quarters to release Collapsibles A and B, he called up, "You've done your duty, men. Now it's every man for himself." To a small group of stewards gathered near the First Class entrance he said, "Men, do your best for the women and children, and look out for yourselves." And again, to some of the boiler room crew that made it to the Boat Deck, he said, "Well men, I guess it's every man for himself."[13]

The boiler room crews had been released by Chief Engineer Bell. He had told his engineers that they were released too, but in their determination to keep the lights burning and power supplied to the wireless, none of them left the engine room. By now it was too late, and Bell and his men would remain at their posts until the end.[14]

It would be interesting to know what his second officer thought of the Captain's sentiments. There were two collapsibles, A and B, lashed upside down to the roof of the officers' quarters, and as long as there was a lifeboat to fill, Lightoller wasn't about to give up. Quickly mustering the nearby crewmen and a few willing passengers such as Colonel Gracie, he set some of them to untie the lashings holding the boats in place, while others set up makeshift ramps of oars and planking to slide the boats down from the roof. Among them was Trimmer Hemming, who Lightoller recalled having told to go with Boat 6.

"Why haven't you gone yet, Hemming?"

"Oh, plenty of time yet, sir."

Lightoller's efforts weren't entirely successful. The men were able to get Collapsible A to slide down the improvised ramp, and were hurriedly trying to fit the falls from Boat Number 1's davits to her, but Collapsible B broke through its ramp and landed on the Boat Deck upside down. Each collapsible weighed more than two tons and Lightoller just didn't have the manpower to right it.[15]

In the wireless shack Bride took Captain Smith at his word and had gathered up all the papers and the wireless log. Just after the Captain left, a woman who had fainted was brought into the shack and placed in a chair. A moment or two later she revived and left with her husband. The lights were starting to take on an orange glow as the power began slowly fading. Phillips was tinkering with the set, trying to adjust the spark to make it stronger. At 2:10 he sent out two "V"s, which were picked up faintly by the *Virginian*; they were the last transmission anyone heard from the *Titanic*.

Slipping behind the green curtain to gather up his money and a few personal belongings, Bride stepped back into the wireless room to find a stoker bending over Phillips. Phillips, headphones still on his head, was lost in intense concentration, totally unaware that the stoker was surreptitiously unfastening his lifebelt. With a shout Bride leaped at the stoker.

Phillips, startled, jumped up and the three men grappled. After a brief scuffle, Bride was able to pin the stoker's arms while Phillips beat the man senseless. Dropping the unconscious man to the floor, Bride reached for the logbook, but Phillips shouted, "Let's get out of here!" and dashed out the door, Bride hard on his heels. Phillips ran aft, while Bride turned and made his way forward.[16]

Back at the base of the second funnel, on the roof of the First Class Lounge, Bandmaster Hartley tapped his bow against his violin and the ragtime ceased. A moment later the solemn strains of the hymn "Nearer, My God, to Thee" began drifting across the water. It was with a perhaps unintended irony that Hartley chose a hymn pleading for the mercy of the Almighty, as the ultimate material conceit of the Edwardian Age, the ship that "God Himself couldn't sink," foundered beneath his feet. As the band played, the slant of the deck grew steeper, while from within the hull came a rapidly increasing number of thuds, bangs, and crashes as interior furnishings broke loose and walls and partitions collapsed.[17]

Higher and higher the *Titanic*'s stern rose out of the water, until the great bronze propellers, motionless now, slowly emerged from the sea. As the stern rose, the liner seemed to begin to sluggishly move forward, as with a series of dull booms (mistaken by some passengers for exploding boilers) the watertight bulkheads began to give way under the inexorable pressure of the inrushing sea. Within the ship the emptiness of the public rooms was almost oppressive—it seemed unreal for all the smoking rooms, saloons, and lounges to be deserted.

But they weren't entirely empty. The foursome in the First Class Lounge had returned to their bridge game and were still doggedly playing, seemingly oblivious to the increasingly steep slant of the table top. Around 2:10 Steward John Stewart glanced inside the First Class Smoking Room and was astonished to see Thomas Andrews standing in the center of the room with his arms folded across his chest. At last the tremendous drive and energy were gone, and he stood motionless before the fireplace, his face devoid of expression. Puzzled, Stewart called out, "Aren't you even going to try for it, Mr. Andrews?"

Andrews never replied—he simply continued to gaze at a painting before him, "The Approach to Plymouth Harbour," as if he never heard the question. His lifebelt lay carelessly tossed across a green-topped card table apparently forgotten.[18]

At 2:15 the bridge dipped under, sweeping Captain Smith into the sea. A wave of water rushed back along the Boat Deck as the *Titanic* began to pivot on a point somewhere just aft of amidships. The calm dignity of "Nearer, My God, to Thee" began to be lost in the clamor of a great ship entering her death throes. Just as the sea washed over the bridge, the superstructure gave a sickening lurch, momentarily interrupting the music, when the forward expansion joint collapsed. Running athwart the superstructure even with the positions of Boats 5 and 6, the joint gave way as the ship's center of gravity shifted. The two aftermost stays supporting the forward funnel, anchored aft of the joint, now went slack, and the remaining eight stays were suddenly forced to carry the weight of the huge funnel in an attitude for which they were never designed.[19]

The sounds of the ancient hymn still carried across the water, and those in the lifeboats felt a certain horrible dignity about the moment. Pierre Marechal, sitting in Boat 7, would later relate: "When three-quarters of a mile away we stopped, the spectacle before our eyes was in its own way magnificent. In a calm sea, beneath a sky moonless but sown with millions of stars, the enormous *Titanic* lay on the water, illuminated from the waterline to the Boat Deck. The bow was slowly sinking into the black water."[20]

Aboard the ship though, an almost hysterical air gripped those who remained: that lurch of the superstructure when the expansion joint collapsed acted as a signal for those still on the upper decks to begin a mad rush toward the stern. As the water rolled up the deck, Peter Daly, the Lima representative for Haas & Sons of London, found a woman he didn't know clutching at him, crying, "Oh, save me! Save me!"

"Good lady," he replied, "only God can save you now." But the woman persisted, and Daly consented to make the jump into the freezing water with her. Taking her by the arm he helped her to the Boat Deck railing, just as a big wave came sweeping up the deck, washing him clear and pulling the woman from his grasp. Daly didn't see her among the survivors.

Steward Brown was among those still struggling to launch Collapsible A when the sea surged up around his feet. Realizing that the boat would soon be floating off, he jumped in the stern and cut the lines there, yelling for someone to cut the forward falls as well. Somebody did and at that moment the wave washed Collapsible A from the deck.[21]

Up on the roof of the officer's quarters, Second Officer Lightoller saw First Officer Murdoch one deck below still working desperately to get Collapsible A's falls attached to the davits. He watched as the water rolled up the Boat Deck, engulfing Murdoch, as the bow sank lower and the stern continued to rise. As the water advanced, the crowd retreated before it, struggling "uphill" against the ever-steepening tilt of the deck. As Lightoller looked on in horror, the slow, the aged, or the merely clumsy were one by one overtaken by the rising sea, while others rushed to the stern, gripped by the drive of self preservation, prolonging their lives for a few minutes more. After a moment, Lightoller turned his back on them, and dived into the surging water.

Surfacing, he saw just ahead of him the crow's nest, now level with the water. Some irrational instinct seized him, and for a few seconds he swam toward it, thinking it a place of safety. Quickly snapping out of it, Lightoller turned and began to swim clear of the ship, but she wasn't ready to let him go. Tons of seawater pouring down the ventilator shafts in front of the forward funnel created an irresistible suction, which pulled him back and pinned him against a grating just below the surface of the water. "Now we'll see if Christian Science really works," he thought as he realized that he was trapped and would be taken down with the wreck. Almost idly he wondered how long he would last, or if the grating would break from the pressure before he drowned, dragging him inside the hull of the sinking ship.

He never found out. From somewhere deep within the ship a burst of hot air surged up the ventilator shaft, forcing him to the surface. Sputtering, Lightoller barely had time to take a deep breath before he was sucked under again, held against another grating and spit back up, like some sort of latter day Jonah. Gasping, Lightoller struck out away from the ship toward the overturned Collapsible B.[22]

The unfortunate boat was the object of a good deal of attention from those who had been standing on the forward end of the superstructure. Harold Bride had grabbed an oarlock as the boat was washed off, and suddenly found himself swept underneath it. A dozen other men quickly scrambled atop the overturned keel, unaware of Bride struggling in the air pocket beneath it. The collapsible seemed dubious safety at best as it bobbed close to the sinking liner. In a matter of seconds those huge funnels—large enough for two railway coaches to pass through side by side—would plunge under, swallowing huge gulps of seawater and anything floating in it.

The terror of being sucked down into the ship never materialized for Collapsible B, though. As the tilt grew steeper, the strain became unbearable for the remaining eight stays supporting the forward funnel. With a series of pistol-shot cracks, the stays parted, and accompanied by the groan of twisting steel, the funnel collapsed, falling over the starboard side of the ship amid a shower of sparks. For Lightoller and the men clinging to Collapsible B it was a blessing, for when it hit the water, the falling funnel kicked up a wave that washed them thirty yards clear of the ship. Others were less fortunate, for when it fell the funnel landed on a knot of swimmers struggling in the sea beside the wreck.[23]

Now the sea was sweeping over the forward skylight and around the base of the second funnel. Colonel Gracie, nearing exhaustion, lay at the foot of the second funnel and suddenly found himself caught up in a swirling maelstrom of seawater, which threatened to pull him under like it had done with Lightoller. Terrified of being swallowed by one of the funnels, Gracie gave a mighty kick and broke free of the ship, surfacing some twenty yards from the *Titanic*.[24]

Jack Thayer and Milton Long, a shipboard acquaintance who had spent most of the evening in the company of young Jack, were still standing by the starboard rail just aft of the second funnel. Earlier they had watched the uproar at Collapsible C, and both were convinced that particular boat didn't stand a chance. So they decided to wait a little longer before abandoning the *Titanic*. Now as they stepped out of the way of the frantically retreating crowd, they watched the advancing water close in on them. The time had come, they agreed, to jump. They shook hands, wished each other luck, then straddled the railing together. Long looked at Thayer, who was pulling off his overcoat, and asked, "You are coming, boy?"

"Go ahead, I'll be right with you," Thayer replied. Long slid down the side of the ship, and a few seconds later Thayer stood up on the railing and jumped out as far as he could. When Thayer came to the surface Long was nowhere to be seen. He had been dragged under by the sinking ship.[25]

The slant of the decks had become so steep that people began to lose their footing. Chef John Collins had been trying to help a woman from steerage who had two children with her, rushing from one side of the Boat Deck to the other, trying to find a lifeboat. Collins, carrying one of the children, heard someone call out that their best chance was in the stern. Turning he began to struggle "uphill" along with the woman and the other child, finding it nearly impossible to stand upright. All four of them were caught by the rising water, and the child was swept from Collin's grasp. He never saw mother or children again.[26]

Back by the fourth funnel, Olaus Abelseth braced himself for the on-rushing wave, but it never reached him. Huddled together on the raised roof over the First Class Smoking Room, Abelseth, his cousin, and brother-in-law were all clinging to a rope slung from one of the davits as a lifeline. The *Titanic* continued to pivot just forward of where the three men were standing, and they found themselves watching in dismay as one by one the passengers and crew remaining on the Boat Deck slid down into the water just a few feet below where they were standing. Despite the repeated urgings of his brother-in-law, Abelseth had postponed jumping off the ship until the last possible moment. Now with the sea only feet away, the three men joined hands and jumped in. Abelseth's legs were snarled by a rope, and to free himself he had to let go of the other's hands. They were swept away while Abelseth fought to get loose, all the time thinking "I'm a goner." At last, his lungs near bursting, he kicked free of the last tangle of line and struggled to the surface. The other two men were never found.[27]

The *Titanic's* lights were glowing a dull red now, and it was difficult for those in the lifeboats to see what was happening aboard the ship. There was a growing knot of kneeling supplicants, most of them Third Class, at the very stern, gathered around Father Byles, their voices murmuring in prayer as the good Father, faithful to the last, offered absolution.

"Hail Mary, full of grace—"

The stern rose higher yet, and the mass of humanity still on board, some 1,500 souls, pressed together toward the tip, clinging to deckhouses, ventilators, cargo cranes, hatchcovers.

"The Lord is with thee—"

The ship herself shrieked with agony, her hull subjected to stresses it was never designed to withstand.

"Pray for us sinners—"

Suddenly every distinction between class and country, passenger and crew, vanished in those last terrible moments.

"Now and at the hour of our death. Amen."

———————

No one ever knew how well or how poorly John Jacob Astor met his end. It would be nice perhaps to say that, like the Thane of Cawdor, "nothing in his life so became him as the leaving of it," but little is certain. Legend has it that Astor placed a girl's big hat on the head of ten-year-old William Carter, saying "Now he's a girl, and he can go." Surprisingly enough it may be true: Astor had already watched Lightoller bar another boy from entering Boat 4, and such a gesture would not be out of place for the eccentric but not entirely unlikable millionaire. Dr. Washington Dodge later stated that Astor and Major Butt went down together, saying, "They went down standing on the bridge, side by side. I could not mistake them." Even though Dr. Dodge was in Boat 13, a good half mile away at the time the bridge went under, there is an element of truth in his statement: if Astor was standing on the bridge when it went under that would explain how he came to be in the water on the starboard side of the ship. When his body was later recovered, it was crushed and covered with soot: Astor had been one of those hapless swimmers caught under the forward funnel as it collapsed.[28]

Likewise the fate of Captain Smith remains a mystery. Later rumors would spring up claiming that he shot himself, but never with any proof. At around 2:10 A.M. Steward Brown saw the captain walk onto the bridge, still clutching his megaphone, but just minutes later Trimmer Hemming found the bridge empty. The most likely situation is that Captain Smith was washed overboard when the forward superstructure went under, for Fireman Harry Senior saw him in the water, holding a child in his arms, just moments before the *Titanic* began her final plunge. Still later, a swimmer approached Collapsible B, encouraging the men struggling atop the overturned lifeboat. "Good boys! Good lads!" he called out over and over again, in a voice tinged with authority, never once asking to be taken aboard. Greaser Walter Hurst tried, holding out an oar for the man to grasp onto, but the rapidly rising swell carried the man away before Hurst could reach him. To his dying day Hurst believed the man was Captain Smith.[29]

There is the nagging possibility that Chief Officer Wilde did indeed take his own life. Eugene Daly and George Rheims would later write to their families, each unknown to the other, describing how each man had watched a senior ship's officer (exactly who they did not identify) put a gun to his head and pull the trigger. Wilde was one of the great mysteries of that night: unlike Captain Smith, First Officer Murdoch, or Sixth Officer Moody, all of whom were also lost, Wilde was almost totally missing in survivors' recollections. No one remembered watching Wilde overseeing the loading of any lifeboats, shepherding any passengers to the Boat Deck, or organizing any crew; instead Wilde seems to have remained near the bridge all night, occasionally giving vague or contradictory orders to some of the other officers. Carl Jansen, a survivor from steerage, did recall later how he "glanced toward the bridge and saw the chief officer place a revolver in his mouth and shoot himself. His body toppled overboard." The mystery is a small tragedy within a greater one, for even if he did not commit suicide, Wilde's apparent inactivity seems to indicate that he alone among the *Titanic*'s officers lost his nerve that night.[30]

Though Archie Butt was later said to have met his fate heroically, the last anyone definitely saw of him was shortly before 2:00 A.M., standing quietly to one side on the Boat Deck, having finally abandoned his card game but taking no part in loading or launching the lifeboats. Though perhaps lacking in superficial glamour, there is a certain dignity about a man quietly accepting his fate, without fuss—but then, he was a soldier.[31]

The rush to the stern had become a stampede as the ship rose higher into the sky. The strains of "Nearer, My God, to Thee" abruptly ceased as the deck beneath the musicians' feet slipped away, and that gallant band—already passing into legend—was pitched into the sea. In seconds the noise became an ear-splitting din as bulkheads, frames, and hull plates began to sheer and break under the strain, while everything movable inside the ship broke loose and plunged toward the bow. Walter Lord, in *A Night to Remember*, described it best:

> There has never been a mixture like it—29 boilers . . . the jew-elled copy of the Rubaiyat . . . 800 cases of shelled walnuts . . . 15,000 bottles of ale and stout . . . huge anchor chains (each link weighing 175 pounds) . . . 30 cases of golf clubs and tennis rackets for Spalding . . . Eleanor Widener's trousseau . . . tons of coal . . . Major Peuchen's tin box . . . 30,000 fresh eggs . . . dozens of potted palms . . . 5 grand pianos . . . a little mantle clock in B-38 . . . the massive silver duck press.
>
> And still it grew—tumbling trellises, ivy pots, and wicker chairs in the Cafe Parisien . . . shuffleboard sticks . . . the 50-phone switchboard . . . two reciprocating engines and the revolutionary low-pressure turbine . . . 8 dozen tennis balls for R. F. Downey & Co., a cask of china for Tiffany's, a case of gloves for Marshall Field . . . the remarkable ice-making machine on G Deck . . . Billy Carter's new English automobile . . . the Ryerson's sixteen trunks, beautifully packed by Victorine.[32]

With a long moan of tortured metal, the *Titanic* stopped moving. The lights, which had been glowing a dark red suddenly went out completely, snapped on again with a searing flash, then went out again forever. From the fourth funnel aft, the *Titanic* stood almost perpendicular, a huge black shape silhouetted against the impossibly bright stars, suspended between the sea and the sky.

It was at this moment that the reckoning came—the culmination of all the terrible "ifs": if the *Titanic's* maiden voyage hadn't been postponed by three weeks; if her departure from Southampton hadn't been delayed by an hour—an hour she never made up; if any of the six ice warnings had been heeded—or if Phillips hadn't cut off the *Californian* in the middle of the seventh; if she'd been moving a knot faster or a knot slower; if there had been moonlight or a choppy sea to illuminate the berg; if the iceberg hadn't been "blue"; if Fleet or Lee had seen the ice ten seconds sooner—or ten seconds later; then there would have never been that dreadful "convergence of the twain," as Thomas Hardy called it, of ice and steel.

And yet—

If the *Titanic* had hit the ice any other way; if she'd been built with a double hull as well as a double bottom; if her watertight bulkheads had carried only one deck higher—she would still have been afloat, crippled, but not dying.

If the White Star Line had listened to Alexander Carlisle; if the Board of Trade's regulations hadn't been so hopelessly outdated; if the ship on the horizon had only come—then 1,500 helpless souls wouldn't be only moments away from eternity.

But all such thoughts were pointless now. The noise died away and a pall settled over the scene. The *Titanic* slowly twisted as if, in Jack Thayer's words, "She turned her deck away from us, as if to hide from us the awful spectacle." Then the weight of the water-filled forward half of the ship began to drag the liner down. She seemed to sag for a moment, as the stern settled back some-what toward the sea: the overstrained hull finally gave way and began to break apart, causing some of those watching in the boats to imagine that somehow she would miraculously right herself, leading others to believe that she had broken completely in two. The *Titanic* began to slip under, gathering speed as she went, as if to hurry and bring an end to this final indignity.

In Collapsible C Bruce Ismay turned his back and hunched over his oar—he couldn't bear to watch. In Boat 1, C. E. Stengel cried out, "I cannot look any longer!" In Boat 14 Esther Hart held seven-year-old Eva tightly, burying her daughter's face in her chest, so Eva wouldn't see her father die. In Collapsible D Mrs. Goldsmith did the same to her son Franky. Standing on Collapsible B, less than fifty yards from the *Titanic*, Second Officer Light-oller heard a sound that would haunt him for the rest of his life: as the ship began her final plunge, he could hear people—husbands and wives, brothers and sisters, parents and children—crying out to one another, "I love you."

Little more than twenty seconds after the liner began moving, the waters of the North Atlantic closed over the Blue Ensign at the *Titanic*'s stern. An eerie silence settled over the sea for some seconds, as if everyone, passengers and crew, those in the boats and those in the water, were momentarily unable to accept that the ship had vanished. Finally someone in Boat 13 sighed, "She's gone, that's the last of her." In Boat 4 Ada Clark overheard someone murmur, "It's gone." In Number 5, Third Officer Pitman glanced at his watch and quietly announced, "It is 2:20 A.M."[33]

CHAPTER 9

The Lonely Sea

There is sorrow on the sea: it cannot be quiet.
—Jeremiah 49:23

THE STARS SHONE DOWN ON A SCENE OF ALMOST UNBELIEVABLE HORROR. The sea around the spot where the *Titanic* had disappeared was covered with a mass of tangled wreckage, and struggling in the midst of it were hundreds of helpless passengers and crew, swept off the ship as she took her final plunge. Over everything a gray mist hung just a few feet above the water. To Colonel Gracie it recalled the waters of Lithe in the *Aeneid*.

The water where the ship had gone under was still troubled, as every few seconds a bubble of air released from the wreck welled up from below, or more wreckage and debris popped to the surface. Some of these pieces may well have been lethal—among the handful of swimmers that reached the lifeboats, a number had been injured by wreckage coming up from below, which included balks of timber, solid wood doors, sections of paneling and furniture, heavy deck chairs, and large chunks of cork.

This upwelling continued for some minutes as the field of wreckage began to spread out across the surface of the sea. For many thrashing swimmers, the debris proved a godsend as they desperately clutched at casks, gratings, deck chairs, writing desks, doors, or planking, frequently fighting one another for possession of some scrap of buoyant material in the slim hope of keeping their heads above water long enough for a lifeboat to come and pluck them out of the water.[1]

Far below the swimmers, everything on the *Titanic* was disintegrating rapidly. Those who had huddled at her stern in the last minutes of her life were quickly swept away once the liner plunged below the surface. With the possible exception of some passengers and crew—the French and Italian restaurant staff still locked in their cabins on E Deck, or the gallant engineers—trapped below decks, the ship was deserted. Powerful forces now took hold of the wreck as it began its long descent to the bottom of the North Atlantic.

The flow of water around the hull began to force the bow onto a more or less even keel. The pressure bent the hollow foremast back across the bridge, while the second funnel was torn from its mountings. All the while the huge pocket of air trapped in the stern kept trying to lift the hull back into a vertical position. A fierce elemental battle raged between air and water for some seconds until the hull of the *Titanic*, which had been distorted and partially broken in two during her incredible headstand just before she went under, gave way. Between the third and fourth funnels, at the after bulkhead of Boiler Room 1, just forward of where the engines were mounted, the keel buckled and the ship jackknifed, the stern bending up at nearly 90 degrees to the rest of the ship. The decks of the forward section at the break collapsed on one another like a bellows, the keel sheared away, and the bow and stern separated.

As they parted huge pieces of machinery spilled out of the break. The forward cylinders of the reciprocating engines broke off their casings and plummeted to the bottom, along with the five single-ended boilers from Boiler Room No. 1, followed by a shower of coal from the ruptured bunkers.

The water-filled bow section drifted off serenely into the depths, gliding down on a more or less even keel. Seven and a half minutes after the *Titanic* had vanished below the surface of the North Atlantic, the great bow plowed into the silt of the ocean floor. A huge mound, some fifty feet high, of rocks, mud, and boulders was pushed up by the prow, and the wreck's momentum caused the hull to buckle just forward of the bridge as it settled.

The stern fared far worse. Unlike the bow, the after section was subjected to an instantaneous inrush of seawater. The trapped air pocket was forced out of the hull with almost explosive violence, splitting sections of plating and ripping decking away from the poop. Cargo cranes, deck fixtures, large sections of hull plating, even the entire fourth funnel, were all flung away from the shattered stern. Slowly spinning like a falling leaf, the stern section drifted to the bottom, impacting there some minutes later with enough force to bury the three screws, causing the broken structure of the stern to collapse even further on itself.

For the next few hours, debris from the wreck continued to settle around and between the two halves of the wreck. The *Titanic* would remain unseen and undisturbed for the next seventy-three years.[2]

—◆—

On the surface, the saddest act of the entire tragedy was being played out. The temperature of the water was only 28 degrees, cold enough to sap the life out of a human being in less than twenty minutes. Second Officer Lightoller likened the sensation of being suddenly plunged into the water to that of "a thousand knives" being driven into his body. Years later Baker Walter Belford would "still shudder and suck in his breath" when he described what he called the "stabbing cold" to Walter Lord. Hundreds of swimmers struggled in the water, clutching at the wreckage—and sometimes each other—desperately trying to stay afloat and fight off the insidious cold. Olaus Abelseth was pulled under by a man who refused to let go until Abelseth was forced to kick him off. Steward Edward Brown was almost dragged down by someone clinging to his clothes. What happened to him, Brown never knew—not a strong swimmer, it was all he could do to keep his head above water.[3]

For the handful who could make it, only Collapsibles A and B were close enough to offer a chance of rescue. Of the two, Collapsible A seemed a better choice. After floating off the Boat Deck nearly swamped, Collapsible A had been washed clear of the wreck by the falling funnel, and now a trickle of half-frozen, exhausted swimmers began to strike out for it. Hauling themselves over the low canvas sides, one by one they sprawled in the bottom of the boat. Eventually some two dozen swimmers made it to Collapsible A, but not all of them had the strength to pull themselves aboard. Among the ones who actually made it were Fireman John Thompson, who had badly burned his hands earlier that night; Mrs. Rosa Abbott, a Third Class passenger who had actually gone down with the ship but had been washed off the stern and up to the surface; Norris Williams, who weirdly enough had swum away from the ship wearing his fur coat—it was lying beside him on a thwart; Peter Daly, who had been washed off the *Titanic*'s deck; a pair of Swedish passengers, also from Third Class; and First Class passenger Thomson Beattie, who for some reason was wearing only his underwear. Two crewmen who had reached the boat would die during the night before anyone could learn their names.

As Collapsible A drifted off into the night, farther and farther from where the *Titanic* had gone down, the swimmers became fewer and fewer until they ceased altogether. The handful of survivors, standing in almost knee-deep water, tried to raise the canvas sides, but found it impossible as some of the iron stays for holding the sides in place were broken and in some places the canvas had been torn, the result of being lowered down the makeshift ramp from atop the officers' quarters. Collapsible A bobbed gently in the rising swell, seemingly alone.

Olaus Abelseth was one of those lucky enough to make it. When he drew up alongside the collapsible, he found nearly a dozen others already in the boat. No one gave him a hand climbing aboard, but no one stopped him either. Later he recalled someone muttering, "Don't capsize the boat." One of the last swimmers to reach Collapsible A was August Wennerstrom. He and his friend Edvard Lindell reached the boat almost together, but Wennerstrom noticed Lindell's wife was missing. Looking back, he saw the woman behind him; he climbed aboard the boat and held his hand out to her, only to find that he didn't have the strength to haul her aboard. Desperately he hung on, hoping someone would help him, but finally his strength gave out, and Mrs.

Lindell slipped into the water. Heartsick, Wennerstrom turned to Mr. Lindell, afraid to tell him what had happened. It wasn't necessary: by this time, Mr. Lindell had frozen to death.[4]

Collapsible B was still floating upside down just a few yards from where the wreck had gone under, with Harold Bride trapped underneath it. The boat had been pushed thirty yards clear of the *Titanic* when the forward funnel collapsed. Quickly the strongest swimmers began converging on the overturned collapsible. Among the first to arrive and climb onto the keel of the boat were young Jack Thayer, Greaser Walter Hurst, Second Officer Lightoller, and three or four others. They had a grandstand view of the *Titanic* as she took her final plunge. Within moments swimmers from every direction were trying to climb onto the boat. (One of them, Algernon Barkworth, a justice of the peace from Yorkshire, showed up wearing a fur coat, looking like some waterlogged sheepdog standing on Collapsible B's keel.) Colonel Gracie hauled himself aboard, having first tried clinging to a section of planking, then an overturned crate, before striking out for the overturned boat. Soon more than thirty men huddled on the keel of Collapsible B.

Some of the men had grabbed oars from the water, but they weren't using them to propel the boat anywhere. Instead they were swatting at anyone else who was trying to climb aboard. Steward Thomas Whiteley had to duck a couple of times before he was able to scramble up onto the stern, while Fireman Harry Senior, one of the last to arrive, was smacked on the head and had to duck under the boat to the other side and climb up from there.

Bride, still trapped underneath the boat, was in an extremely tight spot. As each newcomer struggled up onto the keel of the boat, it sank a little lower in the water, and the air pocket underneath it got a little smaller. Finally deciding it was now or never, Bride took a deep breath, dove down, and kicked his way out from under the boat. Gasping for air, he finally managed to climb aboard near the stern.

Gradually, Lightoller began to assert his authority and bring order to the boat. One of the men lying across the keel suggested, "Don't the rest of you think we ought to pray?" and Lightoller agreed it might be a good idea. A quick poll showed there were Presbyterians, Methodists, Episcopalians, and Catholics aboard—and of course Lightoller himself was a Christian Scientist. The Lord's Prayer seemed like a good compromise, and they all began reciting it in chorus.[5]

As the words floated out over the water, they became mingled with the cries of those still struggling amid the wreckage. Over and over again the cry "Save one life! Save one life!" was heard, rising above the nearly continuous pleadings of people in distress. To Jack Thayer it sounded "like locusts on a midsummer night." To Mrs. Candee in Boat 8, it was "a heavy moan as of one being from whom final agony forces a single sound." When Third Officer Pitman tried to describe the sound to the U.S. Senate Inquiry, his eyes filled with tears as he recalled "a continual moan" that lasted "for about an hour." Nine-year-old Franky Goldsmith would carry the memory of the sound with him the rest of his life: living in Detroit near Tiger Stadium, the roar of the crowd every time a home run was hit would take him back to the North Atlantic and the cold morning of April 15, 1912. Even Lightoller was affected. Years later he admitted that he had never allowed his thoughts to dwell on those agonized pleas for help, and he honestly believed that some survivors died premature deaths because they were never able to erase from their minds the memory of those cries.[6]

In Boat 5, Third Officer Pitman finally decided he could not ignore the sound of so many pleading for help. Standing in the stern of the boat, he called out, "Now men, we will pull toward the wreck!" Immediately the women in the boat began protesting, fearing that it would be swamped by swimmers trying to climb aboard.

"Appeal to the officer not to go back!" one woman begged Steward Etches. "Why should we lose all our lives in a useless attempt to save others from the ship?" Pitman finally gave in and told the men to lay by their oars, but he would feel guilty for the rest of his life about not going back.

In Boat 2 the same thing happened when Fourth Officer Boxhall suggested that the boat should go look for survivors. To Boxhall it seemed inexplicable: only a short while before these women had been in anguish over being compelled to leave their husbands behind, pleading with Captain Smith to let the men into the boats so they could row; now many of these same women were raising a cry of protest at the idea of going back to help those people struggling in the water.

In Boat 8, when Seaman Thomas Jones, who was in charge of the boat, also suggested going back, only the Countess of Rothes, Miss Gladys Cherry, and one other woman favored the idea; everyone else in the boat, including the three men at the oars, demurred. Seaman Jones, unlike Pitman, wasn't about to have those lives on his conscience, and scolded those in the boat: "Ladies, if any of us are saved, remember *I* wanted to go back. I would rather drown with them than leave them."[7]

Probably the most inexplicable inactivity of all was that of Boat 1. Fireman Charles Hendrickson announced, "It's up to us to go back and pick up anyone in the water," but no one agreed with him. With Sir Cosmo and Lady Duff Gordon, her secretary Miss Francatelli, and nine other men aboard, the boat easily had room for another thirty people. But Lady Duff Gordon was violently seasick—she lay at the bottom of the boat, vomiting all night—and Sir Cosmo seemed singularly incapable of exercising any leadership. Lookout Symons, who was nominally in charge of the boat, wasn't any better, for despite his later description of his station, repeatedly describing himself at both the American and British inquiries as "being the master of the situation," he had no more inclination to take any action than Sir Cosmo.

Actually, it's easy to believe that if Sir Cosmo had tried going back, he would have botched the job, for everything he did that night, no matter how well-intentioned, seemed to go wrong. First, he found himself in a boat that could hold forty people but had only seven crewmen and five passengers in it—and all First Class passengers at that. Then, no one in Boat 1 seemed to favor going back to pick up any survivors, or even attempting to do so. Finally, he was drawn into a ridiculous conversation with Fireman Pusey that would nearly ruin Sir Cosmo's reputation. The conversation began between Pusey and Lady Duff Gordon. As she watched the *Titanic* go under, Lady Duff Gordon remarked to Miss Francatelli, "There is your beautiful night-dress gone." Pusey overheard the remark and told her, "Never mind that, you have saved your lives; but we have lost our kit."

A little later, Pusey turned to Sir Cosmo and said, "I suppose you have lost everything?"

"Of course."

"But you can get more?"

"Yes."

"Well, we have lost our kit, and the company won't give us any more. And what's more, our pay stops from tonight!"

Sir Cosmo, more than a little peeved, decided to end the conversation as charitably as he could, and snapped, "Very well, I will give you a fiver each to start a new kit!" He was as good as his word, but when the story got out about how Boat 1 failed to pick up swimmers, the promise suddenly appeared to be some sort of payoff, and Sir Cosmo would eventually have to resort to legal action to clear his name.[8]

One man did go back, and not surprisingly he was Fifth Officer Lowe. The self-described "hard case" was also a man of considerable resource and determination. Once Boat 14 had pulled away from the *Titanic*, he began rounding up as many of the other boats as he could find. Soon Boats 10 and 12 and Collapsible D were gathered around Lowe's boat. Standing in the stern of Boat 14, he quickly ordered the boats tied up together, bow to stern, then began transferring his passengers to the other boats and getting some strong backs in Boat 14 to row. When Boat 4 drifted by, Lowe added it to his little flotilla.

Hopping from boat to boat in the darkness wasn't an easy thing to do, and when an elderly woman with a shawl over her head in Boat 14 seemed a bit too spry, Lowe reached out and yanked the shawl away. A frightened young immigrant (Lowe thought he was another "Italian"; others said he was Irish) stared up at the fifth officer, who said nothing but shoved the man into the bottom of Boat 10 as hard as he could. This incident was also notable for its relative lack of verbal fireworks: Lowe wasn't a patient man and possessed the full range of a sailor's vocabulary. It wasn't surprising that when young Daisy Minahan hesitated in stepping across the gap between two of the boats Lowe suddenly shouted, "Jump, damn you, jump!" Later, some of the women in the lifeboats, shocked at the language Lowe used when he was getting the boats organized, started a rumor that he was drunk. Lowe, a lifelong teetotaler, later found the canard highly amusing.

It took three quarters of an hour before the shuffling of passengers was complete and Boat 14 was finally able to row back to the wreckage. Lowe had originally intended to let the crowd "thin out," though he never explained exactly what he meant by that, but he had badly overestimated how long people could survive in the frigid water, and by now the cries for help were few and faint. The first person they found was a First Class passenger, W. H. Hoyt. A big man, it took the combined efforts of everyone in the boat to bring him aboard. Hoyt was unconscious and bleeding from the nose and mouth—he had been taken down with the wreck, only to be released when the ship began breaking up. But the depth that he had been dragged to had been too great, and Hoyt died within an hour from internal injuries caused by decompression. Other voices called in the darkness, but it was like chasing a will-o-the-wisp, and Boat 14 never seemed to reach those calling for help in time.

Eventually they found Steward John Stewart, who gradually revived after they were able to rub him down and massage his limbs. An Asian man who had lashed himself to a door came floating by, but since he was lying face down with the swell washing over him periodically, Lowe was inclined to pass him by, with the characteristic remark, "What's the use? He's dead, likely, and if he isn't there's others better worth saving than a Jap!" But then Lowe had second thoughts, and ordered the man brought aboard.

Fifth Officer Lowe was about to be taught a lesson about his prejudices. A few moments after being pulled from the water, the man came to, chattered away in his native tongue at the other men in the boat (though nobody could understand a word he said, not even his name), then stood up, stretched, and began stamping his feet to get his circulation going. Minutes later he had his hands on an oar, pulling hard. "By Jove, I'm ashamed of what I said about the little blighter!" exclaimed a startled Lowe. "I'd save the likes of him six times over if I had the chance!"

But Lowe would not have the chance. He continued looking for another hour but didn't find anyone else alive. Finally he told his men to lay by their oars, and Boat 14, along with the other boats, drifted in the darkness, riding up and down on the rising swell, twenty boats in the middle of a lonely sea.[9]

For those left behind in the water, death came quickly. The cold swiftly numbed their hands, their feet, their heads, and they soon lost consciousness. The icy sea sapped the warmth from their bodies until their hearts could take no more and, giving up the unequal struggle, finally stopped. Bodies floated motionless and silent, slowly being swept off by the current, away from the great ice floe and into the open waters of the North Atlantic.

According to the ship's clock on the *Carpathia's* bridge, it was almost 3:30 A.M. and she was drawing close to the *Titanic's* position. Captain Rostron's heart was sinking: try as he might to keep his hopes up, he knew he was too late.

For a while it hadn't seemed so. Around 2:40, while talking to Dr. McGhee, Rostron had caught a glimpse of green light—clearly a flare of some sort—on the horizon just off the port bow. "There's his light!" Rostron exclaimed. "He must still be afloat!" Minutes later, Second Officer Bisset spotted the first iceberg, dimly lit by the reflected light of a star, then a second one, then a third. Carefully timing his helm orders, Rostron began working the *Carpathia* through the fringes of the ice field—but he never slowed down. Occasionally another flare would be seen, but no sign of the *Titanic* herself. Hoping to give some hope to those aboard the sinking ship, Rostron began firing colored rockets, interspersed with Cunard Roman candles, every fifteen minutes. Down below the stokers and firemen shoveled coal like they never had before and every plate and rivet in the ship shook with the exertion as the *Carpathia* thundered on. As one crewman later quipped, "The old boat was as excited as any of us."

Rostron, though, was nearly certain that the *Titanic* was gone. It had been nearly two hours since Cottam had last heard from her. The last message he received had been at 1:50 and had pleaded, "Come as quickly as possible, old man; the engine room is filling up to the boilers." Cottam had told Rostron that the *Titanic*'s signals had been getting weaker; with that last message and the ominous silence afterwards, Rostron feared the worst. Those flares, he decided, couldn't have come from the *Titanic* herself after all. At 3:50 he rang down to the engine room to "Stand By"; at 4:00 he rang for "All Stop." The *Carpathia* was at 41.46 N, 50.14 W. There was nothing to be seen but darkness: the *Titanic* was gone.[10]

As the cries from those left behind in the water slowly faded away and the twenty lifeboats drifted in the rising swell, an odd quiet settled over the survivors. In Boat 2, Fourth Officer Boxhall began firing off green flares. The flares confused people in many of the boats: some thought they came from an approaching steamer, and others used them as beacons to row toward. Soon Boats 5 and 7 came across each other and tied up together; Boats 6 and 16 did the same. Fifth Officer Lowe finally gave up looking for any more survivors, and now Boat 14 rejoined the others. All they could do now was wait for dawn and the rescue ships everyone prayed would arrive.

The survivors did what they could to occupy themselves. It would only be a matter of time, but the magnitude of what they had just seen happen hadn't yet sunk in. So there was something almost idyllic about Edith Russell entertaining a little child in Boat 11 with her toy pig, the one that played the "Maxixe" when its tail was twisted; or Hugh Woolner in Collapsible C feeding cookies to four-year-old Michel Navatril; or Lawrence Beesley tucking the end of a blanket around the toes of ten-month-old Alden Caldwell, only to discover the woman holding the child, Miss Hilda Slayter, and he had mutual friends in Clonmel, Ireland. In Boat 4, Jean Gertrude Hippach idly watched the night sky; she had never known the stars to shine so bright or had seen so many shooting stars. Unbidden, came the memory of a legend she had once heard: that whenever there was a shooting star, someone dies.

There were some people who, though not necessarily mean-spirited, couldn't help but bicker. Mrs. J. Stuart White was particularly offended that the stewards in her boat should be smoking cigarettes—she was so put out that she would formally complain to the American inquiry about the stewards smoking, as she put it, "on an occasion like that!" In Boat 3, the women sniped at each other over petty annoyances—nobody ever remembered exactly what. For some strange reason a woman in Boat 11 kept setting off an alarm clock until Maud Slocombe, the *Titanic's* masseuse, angrily rounded on her and told her to stop.[11]

In Boat 6, Quartermaster Robert Hitchens, who was nominally in charge, indulged in a singular display of childishness. The boat's problems began when Major Peuchen slid down the fall from the *Titanic's* deck to round out the boat's crew. Hitchens, who apparently resented Peuchen's presence and thought that the major would try to take charge of the boat, decided to let everyone know who was in command, and he immediately began ordering Peuchen about. Peuchen, who was used to giving orders, not taking them, demanded that Hitchens turn the tiller over to one of the women and help with rowing the boat. Hitchens would have none of it, telling Peuchen that he was in charge and that Peuchen was to pull at his oar and keep quiet.

With just Lookout Fleet and Peuchen rowing (the only other man in the boat, a Third Class stowaway, had an injured arm), the boat made painfully slow progress away from the *Titanic*, with Hitchens all the while criticizing them for not pulling harder and claiming the boat would be sucked under when the ship went down. At one point he shouted at Fleet, "Here, you fellow on the starboard side, you're not putting you oar in the water at the right angle!" Like many a petty tyrant, Hitchens' newfound authority went to his head, causing him at one point to disobey a direct order from Captain Smith. Just after Boat 6 reached the water, Smith, standing on the port bridge wing, shouted down through his megaphone, "Come alongside the gangway!" Hitchens stared up at the bridge for several minutes, then put the tiller over and said, "No, we are not going back to the boat. It's our lives now, not theirs."

After the ship went down, several of the women in the boat, with, predictably, Molly Brown as their leader, began demanding that Hitchens turn the boat around so that they could go back and pick up at least some of those hapless souls struggling in the water. Hitchens refused, giving a lurid description of masses of frenzied swimmers clutching at the sides of the boat, overloading and eventually overturning it. Peuchen added his voice to the protests, but Hitchens shouted him down, saying, "There's no use going back, 'cause there's only a lot of stiffs there." Peuchen lapsed into a hurt silence, and Hitchens told the men to stop rowing and let the boat drift.

This was too much for Molly Brown. Hitchens had settled himself in the stern, pulling the sail around him for warmth, and Mrs. Brown got up, pushed her way passed him, and grabbed the tiller bar. The women, whose husbands and fathers were the "stiffs" Hitchens wanted to leave behind, demanded that Hitchens let them row so they could keep warm. He only wanted to let the boat drift. Mrs. Brown told the women to start rowing, and when Hitchens made a move toward her, she told him if he took one more step she'd throw him overboard. Even Hitchens knew not to call Molly's bluff, so he sank back under the sail, announcing that all was lost: they had no food, no water, no compass, and no charts. Mrs. Candee pointed out the North Star to him, Mrs. Edgar Meyer called him a coward, and Molly told him to shut up. Hitchens swore at her, and a stoker who had transferred from Boat 16 suddenly spoke up, saying, "I say, don't you know you're talking to a lady?"

"I know who I'm speaking to," Hitchens yelled back, "and I'm in command of this boat." But apparently Hitchens had enough—or else he realized it was a losing battle and he lapsed into a sulking silence. While all of this quarreling had been going on, the cries for help had gradually diminished and faded into silence. There was no point in going back now, so Boat 6 rowed on into the night, with "the unsinkable Molly Brown," as the American press would soon christen her, standing like an Amazon at the tiller.[12]

Collapsible B had its share of squabbles, too, but for the most part the thirty-odd men were more concerned with the common problem of survival. As the swell began to rise, the overturned keel began to pitch, and with each roll a little more of the air trapped underneath escaped, lowering the boat still further into the water. If they were going to make it, they needed leadership. They got it.

It took some time for Second Officer Lightoller to collect his wits—the cold of the sea had truly been numbing—but before long the old habits of command reasserted themselves and Lightoller began to get the men organized. Careful not to disturb the equilibrium of the boat, he had all the men stand up and form two parallel rows, one on each side of the centerline, facing the bow. As the swell rolled the boat from side to side, Lightoller would call out to the men "Lean to the left" . . . "Stand upright" . . . "Lean to the right"—whatever was required to counteract the motion of the boat. From time to time the men called out "Boat ahoy! Boat ahoy!" in unison but received no replies, and after a while Lightoller told them to stop and save their strength.

Even more than the handful of survivors in Collapsible A, the men atop Collapsible B suffered severely from the cold. Standing in water that at first only washed across the boat, then rose gradually to their ankles and then to their knees as the air pocket under the boat slowly leaked away, the men had

The *Titanic* on the ways at Harland & Wolff. The figure leaning on the railing gives a good indication of how big the ship was. Careful examination of the photograph has shown that the name was added after the picture was taken. *Mariners' Museum, Newport News, Virginia.*

The *Titanic* leaving Southampton, April 10, 1912. *Mariners' Museum, Newport News, Virginia.*

Bruce Ismay, chairman of the White Star Line, in a 1911 portrait. *Amereon House, Mattituck, New York.*

Thomas Andrews, managing director of Harland & Wolff. Responsible for supervising the construction of both the *Olympic* and the *Titanic*, he regarded the *Titanic* as his finest work. *Ulster Folk and Transport Museum, Belfast.*

Captain Edward J. Smith, in the summer of 1911, standing on the *Olympic's* Boat Deck, just aft of the bridge. *Southampton City Heritage Services, Southampton City Museum.*

Second Officer Charles Herbert Lightoller. *Southampton City Heritage Services, Southampton City Museums.*

John "Jack" Phillips, senior wireless operator aboard the *Titanic. GEC Marconi, Ltd.*

Harold Bride, junior wireless operator. *GEC Marconi, Ltd.*

The Grand Staircase on A Deck. The bas-relief at the head of the stairs is actually a clock; the two figures represent Honor and Glory crowning Time. *Mariners' Museum, Newport News, Virginia.*

No photograph of the *Titanic*'s boiler rooms is known to exist. This photograph of the boiler room of the Union Line's *Moor*, though she was much smaller than the *Titanic*, gives an excellent idea of the working conditions of a coal-fired ship. *Southampton City Heritage Services, Southampton City Museums.*

The *Titanic*'s orchestra. Concertmaster and first violinist Wallace Hartley is at the center. Other members are, clockwise from upper left: Fred Clarke, bass-viol; Percy C. Taylor, piano; Theodore Brailey, piano; J. W. Woodward, cello; John Law "Jock" Hume, second violin; George Krins, viola. Not shown is another cellist, Roger Bricoux. *Southampton City Heritage Services, Southampton City Museums.*

"Women and Children First," a lithograph produced in 1912. Though somewhat romanticized, it nevertheless conveys a sense of the powerful emotions present on the Boat Deck of the *Titanic* as the lifeboats were being filled and lowered. *Mariners' Museum, Newport News, Virginia.*

Captain Arthur H. Rostron on board the *Carpathia*, wearing the medal for heroism given to him by the U.S. Congress. *Mariners' Museum, Newport News, Virginia.*

The *Carpathia*. She was fifty-eight miles away when she received the *Titanic*'s distress signal. Her top speed was officially only 14 knots, but Captain Rostron pushed her to 17 knots as she dashed to the aid of the sinking *Titanic*. *Mariners' Museum, Newport News, Virginia.*

Survivors in a dangerously overloaded Boat 12, the last lifeboat to be picked up by the *Carpathia*, are assisted aboard. Boat 12 had picked up the thirty men who had spent the night standing atop the overturned Collapsible B. *Southampton City Heritage Services, Southampton City Museums.*

Lord Mersey (right), the wreck commissioner, and Captain Bigham, the secretary of the Wreck Commission, on their way to a session of the British Inquiry. *Southampton City Heritage Services, Southampton City Museums.*

Fairview Cemetery in Halifax, Nova Scotia. Of the victims recovered, 129 of them are buried here. A special trust fund, set up by the White Star Line and still active, provides for the maintenance of the graves. *Author's collection.*

This is almost certainly the iceberg struck by the *Titanic*. It was photographed by the chief steward of the liner *Prinze Adelbert* on the morning of April 15, 1912, just a few miles south of where the *Titanic* went down. The steward hadn't yet heard about the *Titanic*: what caught his attention was the smear of red paint along the base of the berg, indicating that it had collided with a ship sometime in the previous twelve hours. *The Walter Lord Collection.*

no protection from the freshening wind, and their constant movement back and forth to keep the boat steady was using up what reserves of strength they had. Soon some of the men could no longer fight off the cold, and one by one they would sink to their knees, then slowly roll over on their sides, to finally slide off the overturned boat and into the sea, where the swell would carry them away.

Colonel Gracie was particularly suffering, for the effects of prolonged immersion in ice-cold water were hard on a young man, let alone one of fifty-four, no matter how fit. Even his hair was matted down and frozen to his scalp. When the colonel noticed a man wearing a wool cap standing next to him, he asked if he might borrow it for a few minutes to warm his head. "And what would I do then?" was the man's incredulous reply. (The immersion in the ice-cold water would eventually lead to complications for the colonel, whose health would never recover from the ordeal, and he would be dead before the year was out.) A sailor offered Gracie a pull from his flask, which he politely refused, suggesting that Greaser Hurst, shivering violently a few feet away, might benefit from it. Hurst accepted the flask gratefully and took a long pull—and nearly choked: he thought it was whiskey, it was essence of peppermint.

Lightoller discovered that Jack Phillips had somehow made it to Collapsible B, and was standing toward the stern, near Harold Bride. When Lightoller asked what ships were coming, Phillips told him the *Carpathia*, the *Mount Temple*, the *Olympic*, and the *Baltic*—and that the *Carpathia* would probably arrive around daybreak. This was particularly good news to Lightoller, who realized that even his best coordinated efforts couldn't keep Collapsible B afloat indefinitely. Even now the boat had sunk so low in the water that the larger swells were washing across it. Ominous gurgling sounds were heard from under the boat, and it was only a matter of time before it sank.

Lightoller didn't know it, but Phillips had performed his last service for the passengers and crew of the *Titanic*. The long twelve-hour work shift on Sunday, the nerve-wracking two hours bent over the wireless key, trying to summon any ship to the stricken liner's side, and the immersion in the frigid water before reaching Collapsible B had completely sapped the young man's energy. Sometime around 4:00 he silently collapsed and died, his body sliding off into the sea.[13]

The cold was vicious to everyone. In Boat 6, Mrs. Brown wrapped her sable stole around the legs of a stoker who sat shivering uncontrollably as he pulled at his oar. In Boat 4 Mrs. Astor lent her shawl to a steerage woman whose little girl was softly crying from the cold; Third Officer Pitman had to wrap the sail about Mrs. Crosby in Boat 5. Charlotte Collyer passed out, numb from the cold, in the bottom of Boat 14; as she fell, her scalp caught in an oarlock and a big piece of her hair was yanked out, but she didn't feel a thing. In Boat 12, Lillian Bentham noticed that a stoker who was clad only in his uniform jumper was sitting with his feet in a pool of freezing water that had collected at the bottom of the boat. The keel beneath her seat was dry, so with a forcefulness that belied her nineteen years, she insisted that the man trade places with her.[14]

The crew did what they could for the passengers. Steward Ray had snatched up a half-dozen handkerchiefs before leaving his cabin, and now as he sat in Boat 13 he showed how to tie a knot in each corner and turn the handkerchiefs into six caps. Just behind him Fireman Beauchamp, clad only in his work jumper, turned down the offer of an extra coat an elderly woman had brought along, saying that it should go to a young steerage girl farther back in the boat who had been whimpering from the cold. In Boat 5, Mrs. Dodge was shivering violently and her feet were almost numb: she hadn't bothered to button her shoes before she left her cabin on the *Titanic*, and now, with the nearest buttonhook two miles below on the floor of the Atlantic, there was no way they could be fastened. Seaman Olliver, seeing this, took off his stockings and handed them to Mrs. Dodge, with the comment, "I assure you, ma'am, they are perfectly clean. I just put them on this morning."

In Boat 4, Trimmer Thomas Dillon, who had clearly had too much to drink, suddenly produced another bottle of brandy and offered it to those around him, but Quartermaster Walter Perkis promptly seized it and threw it overboard. Dillon was tossed, but not very roughly, to the bottom of the boat. Seaman Diamond, who was in charge of Boat 15, stood at the tiller, an exposed position, shivering violently and muttering curses about the cold that those in the boat couldn't help but overhear.[15]

Soon the initial shock of what the survivors had witnessed a few hours before began to wear off, the awful reality set in, and with it for a few came hysteria. In Boat 8, seventeen-year-old Signora de Satode Penasco began screaming for her husband of three weeks, Victor. The young man, like so many of his elders, had stayed behind after seeing his wife safely into a boat. The strangest reaction though, was from Madame de Villiers: she kept crying out for her son, whom she thought was lost, but who hadn't even been on the *Titanic*.[16]

Some of the women were more subdued in their grief. In Boat 9, Kate Buss and Marion Wright sat together and mourned for Douglas Norman and Dr. Pain, and hoped that Reverend and Mrs. Carter had been saved. In Boat 6, some of the women who had left husbands or fathers behind embraced each other and quietly wept. Sitting in the bow of Boat 3, Mrs. Hays kept calling out to every passing boat, "Charles Hays, are you there?" hoping for a reply. It never came. Aft of where Mrs. Hays was maintaining her vigil a woman from steerage kept saying over and over again to Mrs. Vera Dick, "Oh my poor father! He put me on this boat, and wouldn't save himself! Why didn't I die? Why can't I die now?"[17]

But most of the women sat mute, their grief so intense that it couldn't be vocalized—women like Mrs. Ryerson or Mrs. Thayer, or Daniel Marvin's young bride Mary, wed, like the Signora Penasco, only a few weeks ago, or Celiney Yasbeck who left behind a husband she had married just fifty days before. Those who could did their best to cheer up the ones who were grieving the hardest. In Boat 8, the Countess of Rothes, a dark, pretty, delicate-looking woman, had been handling the tiller, but she turned it over to her cousin, Gladys Cherry, and sat down beside the Penasco girl, calming her and spending the rest of the night trying to comfort her.

The Countess had been given the position at the tiller, normally reserved for the person in charge, by Seaman Jones, who had been given command of the boat. Her courage and determination made quite an impression on Jones, and when he decided to leave the tiller and take a turn at one of the oars, he quickly decided that the Countess should be his replacement. He later explained his reasoning to *The Sphere*, saying, "When I saw the way she was carrying herself and heard the quiet, determined way she spoke to the others, I knew she was more of a man than any we had on board." (When they arrived in New York, Jones had the numeral 8 removed from the gunwale of the boat, framed, and presented to her as a keepsake. The countess, in turn, would remember Jones at every Christmas after that.)[18]

On Collapsible B, Lightoller's attention was focused to the southeast, where sometime around 3:30 he had seen a flash of light, followed some seconds later by a faint "boom." He knew from what Phillips had told him that the *Carpathia* was steaming hard from the south, and Lightoller was hoping it was a signal from the oncoming liner. People in the other boats had seen it too. In Boat 13, Fred Barrett, who was nearly unconscious from the cold, suddenly sat bolt upright and shouted, "That was a cannon!" In Boat 6, Margaret Martin saw a brief glimmer of light on the horizon and cried out, "There's a flash of lightning!" while Hitchens muttered, "It's a falling star."

But a few minutes later another flash was seen, and shortly after that, the masthead light of an oncoming steamer. Soon the ship's green sidelight could be seen as the vessel loomed over the horizon, still firing rockets, still coming hard. In Boat 9, Paddy McGough, a big, strapping deck hand, called out, "Let us all pray to God, for there is a ship on the horizon and it's making for us!" and nobody dared disagree with the suggestion. In Boat 3, someone lit a rolled up newspaper and waved it wildly as a signal, followed a few minutes later by Mrs. Davidson's straw hat. In Boat 8, Mrs. White, who now had something to distract her from those stewards and their cigarettes, swung her cane, which had a battery powered light in it, over her head for all she was worth. In Boat 2, Fourth Officer Boxhall lit the last of his green flares.[19]

———◆◆◆———

Captain Rostron's heart leaped when he saw a green flare light up directly ahead of the *Carpathia*. In the pale wash of light he could make out a lifeboat less than a quarter mile away. Quickly he ordered "Slow Ahead" on his

engines and began to swing the ship to starboard, so he could pick up the
boat in the shelter of his portside, which was to leeward. No sooner had the
Carpathia's bow begun to swing to the right then Bisset spotted a huge dark
iceberg to starboard, and Rostron had to put his helm over to avoid it. The
boat was now on his windward side, and as the morning breeze picked up,
the swell had become choppy, causing the boat to bob up and down like a
cork. A voice called up to the *Carpathia*, "We have only one seaman in the
boat, and can't work it very well!"

"All right!" Rostron shouted back, and began edging the liner closer to
the boat. Turning to Bisset, he told him to go down to the starboard gangway
with two quartermasters and guide the lifeboat as it came alongside. "Fend
her off so that she doesn't bump, and be careful that she doesn't capsize."

"Stop your engines!" The voice was Boxhall's, and Boat 2 was now drifting toward the *Carpathia*'s starboard gangway. Suddenly another voice, a
woman's, cried out, "The *Titanic* has gone down with everyone on board!"
Boxhall turned to the woman, Mrs. Walter Douglas, and told her to shut
up. She lapsed into silence, but apparently no one aboard the *Carpathia* heard
her anyhow. (Boxhall later apologized: Mrs. Douglas understood and refused
to take offense.) Lines were dropped and the boat was made fast. A rope ladder was let down from the gangway, along with a lifeline that Boxhall would
secure under the arms of each passenger before they began climbing up.

The first was Miss Elizabeth Allen who, as she neared the gangway, was
lifted onto the *Carpathia* by Purser Brown. She stepped aboard at 4:10 A.M.
Brown asked her what had happened to the *Titanic*, and she told him it had
sunk. More survivors followed her up the ladder, the last being Boxhall. Rostron sent word that he needed to see Boxhall on the bridge immediately.

When the Fourth Officer appeared, Rostron, hoping to get this painful
duty over with as quickly as possible, asked him directly, "The *Titanic* has
gone down?"

"Yes"—Boxhall's voice broke—"she went down about 2:30."

"Were many people left on board when she sank?"

"Hundreds and hundreds! Perhaps a thousand! Perhaps more!" Boxhall
went on as grief began to get the better of him. "My God, sir, they've gone
down with her. They couldn't live in this cold water. We had room for a
dozen more people in my boat, but it was dark after the ship took the
plunge. We didn't pick up any swimmers. I fired flares. . . . I think that the
people were drawn down deep by the suction. The other boats are somewhere near."[20]

Rostron nodded, the formalities taken care of, and sent Boxhall down to
the First Class Dining Saloon. Dawn was breaking and now the *Carpathia*'s
captain could begin to see the rest of the *Titanic*'s boats, spread out across
four or five miles. The *Carpathia*'s passengers were beginning to stir now, and
those who were already up were lining the rails, looking down at the pitiful
handful of survivors in Boat 2 or gazing out across the water at the other

boats. Mrs. Louis Ogden, a First Class passenger on board the *Carpathia*, would later recall that the lifebelts most of the survivors wore made everyone look as if they were dressed in white. She remembered what her husband had told her about the *Titanic*—he had heard the news from a quartermaster in the early hours of the morning, but both he and his wife were skeptical. Seeing the White Star emblem on the side of Boat 2 now made the truth clear. She felt heartsick.[21]

In the growing light, maybe five miles off, stretching from the northern horizon to the western, was a vast, unbroken sheet of ice, studded here and there with towering bergs, some as much as 200 feet high. Smaller bergs and growlers dotted the open water between the ice floe and the ship, presenting the passengers of the *Carpathia* with a spectacle they would never forget. The sun edged over the eastern horizon, its morning rays playing across the ice, turning it shades of pink, blue, gray-green, and lavender, lending a peculiar beauty to its menace.

One of the male passengers, Charles Hurd, apparently a heavy sleeper who hadn't been aroused by the *Carpathia*'s thundering dash north, awoke to find the ship stopped in the middle of the ocean. He hunted up his stewardess to demand an explanation. The woman was weeping, and before the man could say a word, she pointed to a cluster of haphazardly dressed women making their way into the Dining Saloon, and through her tears said, "They are from the *Titanic*. She's at the bottom of the ocean."[22]

The sky was brilliantly clear, with the sun's golden rays fanning out across the blue. A pale sliver of light appeared, causing Firemen Fred Barrett to cry out in sheer joy at being rescued, "A new moon, boys! Turn your money over, that is, if you have any!" (Barrett had a point: the crew's pay stopped the moment the *Titanic* went under.) As the growing dawn made it clear that the *Carpathia* had indeed stopped to rescue the *Titanic*'s survivors, shouts of relief rose up from some of the boats. Others gave organized cheers as they began pulling for the liner. In Boat 13 they sang "Pull for the Shore, Sailor" as they rowed toward the *Carpathia*.

But some boats were very, very quiet. In Boat 7, Lookout Hogg told his charges, "It's all right, ladies, do not grieve. We are picked up." The women, though, just sat there, speechless with the grief of the silently relieved.[23]

There were no cheers from the freezing men on Collapsible B either— it took too much effort just to stay afloat. As dawn broke, Lightoller spotted Boats 4, 10, and 12, along with Collapsible D, tied together just as Fourth Officer Lowe had left them, about a third of a mile away. Concerted shouts of "Ship ahoy!" produced no results, but when Lightoller found an officer's whistle in his pocket and gave it three sharp blasts, that got the attention of everyone.

Seaman Clinch in Boat 12 and Quartermaster Perkis in Boat 4 quickly cast off from the other two boats and brought their boats alongside Collapsible B. The overturned boat was wallowing badly now, the men almost knee deep in water, and when Boat 4 came alongside, it nearly washed everyone off. Lightoller, taking no chances, especially now that rescue was so close at hand, warned the men not to jump all at once. One by one, they scrambled into two waiting lifeboats, Colonel Gracie crawling aboard Boat 12. He was afraid of losing his footing and being pitched into the water again. Jack Thayer was so cold that as he sat shivering in Boat 12 he didn't notice his mother, equally cold and miserable, huddled in Boat 4 only a few feet away.[24]

Lightoller was the last man off Collapsible B, carefully climbing into Boat 12 , taking charge of the now dangerously overloaded boat, and guiding her toward the *Carpathia*. Fifth Officer Lowe was equally as busy. He had hoisted the sail aboard Boat 14 as soon as the *Carpathia* hove into view, taking advantage of the early morning breeze. Not every sailor could do that, for as he later explained at the Senate Inquiry, "Not all sailors are boatmen, and not all boatmen are sailors." Lowe was both, and taking advantage of the skills he had learned sailing up and down the Gold Coast, he soon had Boat 14 cutting along at close to four knots. He noticed that Collapsible D was particularly low in the water, and swung his boat over toward her.

"We have about all we want!" Hugh Woolner called out to Lowe. He thought the Fifth Officer was going to transfer more passengers to the already wallowing collapsible, but Lowe quickly told him to tie Boat 14's painter to Collapsible D's bow, and he would tow her to the *Carpathia*. Woolner gratefully complied.

Lowe then spotted Collapsible A, almost a mile and a half off, looking like it could sink any minute. More than half the thirty people who had taken refuge in Collapsible A during the night had frozen to death and fallen overboard. Now only a dozen men and Mrs. Abbott were left. Lowe wasted no time and got them aboard Boat 14 as quickly as possible, then put about for the *Carpathia*.[25]

The whole straggling fleet of boats was now converging on the *Carpathia*. It was 4:45 when Boat 13 tied up at the portside gangway, a half hour after that when Boat 7 pulled alongside. There was a tearfully happy reunion when Dr. Washington Dodge, who had been in Boat 13, was brought together with his wife and five-year-old-son by Steward Ray. (Actually, Washington, Jr., in a fit of five-year-old mischievousness, had been trying to keep his mother and father from finding each other. He thought Steward Ray was a spoilsport.)[26]

At 6:00 survivors from Boat 3 began to climb aboard the *Carpathia*. Some used the rope ladders, children were hoisted up in mail sacks, and some of the women, not strong enough to negotiate the rope ladders, were lifted aboard in slings. As Elizabeth Shutes found herself swung up into the air, she heard a voice from somewhere on deck call out, "Careful fellows, she's a lightweight!" When Henry Sleeper Harper stepped into the gangway, accompanied by his wife, his dragoman Hassan Hassah, and his prize Pekinese, one of the first people he saw was an old acquaintance, Louis Ogden. As if it were the most natural thing in the world to meet under such circumstances, Harper walked over to the astonished Ogden and said, "Louis, how do you keep yourself looking so young?" There is no record of Mr. Ogden's reply.[27]

When Collapsible C tied up at 6:30, one of the first people to climb aboard the *Carpathia* was Bruce Ismay, characteristically announcing, "I'm Ismay . . . I'm Ismay." Dr. McGhee approached him with the suggestion that he go down to the Dining Saloon for some hot soup or something to drink.

"No, I don't want anything at all."

"Do go and get something," the doctor urged gently.

"If you will leave me alone, I'll be much happier here. . . . No, wait, if you can get me in some room where I can be quiet, I wish you would."

"Please, go to the saloon and get something hot," McGhee persisted.

"I would rather not."

Giving in, the doctor led Ismay to his own cabin, where Ismay would sequester himself until the *Carpathia* reached New York. Though it was later rumored that he was kept sedated the whole time, there's little evidence to support it. But this self-imposed isolation would indirectly fuel later rumors about Ismay's conduct before and after the disaster until public opinion would so thoroughly pillory him that he ultimately sought refuge in anonymity. Perhaps he didn't know it yet, but Bruce Ismay was a ruined man.[28]

Fifth Officer Lowe conned Boat 14 alongside the *Carpathia* just before 7:00, with Collapsible D still in tow. While the passengers and crewmen made their way aboard the ship, Lowe stayed behind to stow the sail and ship the mast. The boat was still company property and he was still a company officer, after all.[29]

There was a lot of frantic activity on deck (although the *Carpathia*'s passengers and crew were later to remark how quiet the *Titanic*'s survivors seemed) as family members sought one another out, or peered anxiously over the railing as each boat came alongside, looking for familiar faces. Usually the outcome was predictable: the sought-after loved one wouldn't be in any of the boats and the agonizing reality would set in. But sometimes, as in the case of the Dodges, there would be a happy reunion (young Master Dodge notwithstanding). Billy Carter, who had been in Collapsible C, stood staring down at Boat 4 as it came alongside, spotting his wife and daughter, but searching frantically for his son. Finally he called out, "Where's my boy?"

Recognizing his father's voice, ten-year-old William, Jr., lifted the brim of a girl's hat and looked up, saying, "Here I am, Father."

Not all the reunions were as happy. When Mrs. Thayer and her son, Jack, saw one another, they rushed into each other's arms. After a minute though, Mrs. Thayer asked Jack, "Where's Daddy?" All the young Thayer could say was, "I don't know."

Sadder still was the plight of an Italian woman, a steerage passenger, who broke down completely in the Third Class Dining Room, weeping hysterically, and shouting out, "*Bambino!*" over and over again. Soon her baby was found and brought to her, but the crying continued as she held up two fingers to show that a second child was missing. This one was found, too—in the pantry, on the hot press. Someone had put it there so the body would thaw out.[30]

By 8:15 all the boats were alongside, except for Boat 12, which was still a quarter mile away, and moving slowly. The breeze was freshening, and with the boat as overloaded as it was—seventy-four people in a boat designed to hold sixty-five—Lightoller wasn't about to take any chances. Rostron nudged his engines to life and brought the *Carpathia* forward slowly, swinging his bow to starboard a bit to bring the boat into the ship's lee. As he turned, the wind kicked up a squall and a couple of waves crashed over the boat, covering everyone with spray. Gingerly Lightoller put his tiller over, and Boat 12 slipped into the sheltered waters by the *Carpathia*'s side. At 8:30 she made fast to the ship and Lightoller began unloading his passengers. By 9:00 they were all on board.[31]

Now that Captain Rostron had all the *Titanic*'s survivors aboard, he had to figure out what to do with them. A quick inventory of the *Carpathia*'s supplies told him that the only alternative was to turn around and go back to New York. The purser's lists showed that 705 survivors were brought aboard—meaning that 1,502 people had died with the *Titanic*. Heartsick, the deeply religious Rostron decided that though nothing could be done for those lost, a brief service—a combined memorial and thanksgiving—might go a long way toward helping the survivors sort out their grief. Approaching the Reverend Father Roger Anderson, an Episcopalian minister who was one of the *Carpathia*'s passengers, Rostron broached the subject. Reverend Anderson thought it an excellent idea and agreed to preside. The service would be held that afternoon in the main lounge.[32]

The *Carpathia*'s passengers did all they could, too, helping the crew wherever they could, finding extra clothes for the survivors, making room in their cabins for some, giving up their spare toiletries and toothbrushes for many. But there were some burdens they could never ease, never share. As Mrs. Ogden was taking a tray of coffee cups over to two women sitting by themselves in a corner of the *Carpathia*'s upper deck, they waved her off, never taking their eyes from the ice-littered sea. "Go away" they said. "We've just seen our husbands drown."[33]

Meanwhile Rostron returned to the bridge, and ordered as many of the *Titanic*'s boats brought aboard as possible. Six were slung in the *Carpathia*'s davits, seven more were stowed on the foredeck. That was all the *Carpathia* had room for—they would be returned to the White Star Line when the ship reached New York. The other seven boats, including all the collapsibles, were set adrift. While the boats were being hoisted aboard, the *Mount Temple*, another vessel that had come rushing to the *Titanic's* assistance, hove to about six miles away. Rostron quickly appraised the *Mount Temple* of the situation, and asked her to continue the search for survivors. Then he returned to the chartroom to work out a course for New York.

It was about 9:15, as he was laying out his new course, that Rostron was called back to the bridge. A second ship had appeared, steaming up from the southwest. Rostron wondered where she had come from, since Cottam had assured him that, apart from the *Mount Temple*, there wouldn't be any other ships arriving for some time. A brief exchange of flag signals followed, Rostron informing the newcomer that the *Carpathia* had picked up all the survivors and was headed for New York. With that, the little Cunard liner put about and slowly steamed away. The other ship stayed behind for a while, on the off chance that the *Carpathia* had missed anyone, but soon she too was steaming westward. After all, she was already behind schedule—her captain had a reputation for reliability and he didn't want to be too late: the *Californian* was due in Boston in three days.[34]

CHAPTER 10

Watching Eight White Rockets

Watchman, what of the night?

—Isaiah 21:11

ON THE NIGHT OF APRIL 14, 1912, ON THE FRINGES OF AN IMMENSE ICE field in the western North Atlantic, the Leyland Line steamship *Californian* lay dead in the water. Bound for Boston from London, the ship had stopped around 10:30 P.M. Small (6,000 tons), slow (14 knots), and decidedly unglamorous, she was under the command of Capt. Stanley Lord, a fourteen-year veteran of the Leyland Line. He had been the captain of the *Californian* for less than a year and this was his very first encounter with North Atlantic ice.[1]

The *Californian* had been steaming at 11 knots on a course of S. 89 W. true when a few minutes after 10:00 P.M. her third officer, Charles Victor Groves, spotted several white patches in the water dead ahead of the ship; when he mentioned them to Captain Lord, he commented that they were probably porpoises.

Captain Lord knew better: one look was all he needed before he strode to the bridge telegraph and rang for the engines put FULL SPEED ASTERN. The white patches were ice—growlers and small bergs that were the fringe of a huge field of ice ahead. Before long the ship was surrounded by chunks of floating ice. Prudence was Lord's watchword, and as the *Californian* came to a stop, he decided that he would rather deal with the problem of negotiating a passage through the ice in daylight. After all, his ship was a far cry from the crack Atlantic liners like the *Lusitania*, the *Mauretania*, the big German speedsters, or the White Star's new sisters, the *Olympic* and the *Titanic*. They all had precise schedules to maintain: nobody would take much notice if the *Californian* were half a day late. She would stay put for the night.

At 11:00 P.M. Captain Lord went below to the chartroom, intending to pass the night stretched out on the settee there. He left specific instructions with Groves to be called if anything was sighted, although any disturbance seemed unlikely. "Absolute peace and quietness prevailed," Groves later

159

recalled, "save for brief snatches of 'Annie Laurie' from an Irish voice which floated up from a stokehold ventilator." The ship drifted quietly on the current, her bows slowly swinging round until she was pointed almost due east. The sea was amazingly calm and the visibility was exceptional, with the stars standing out in the night sky with diamond-like intensity.

About a quarter past eleven Groves noticed the glare of a ship steaming up over the horizon from the east. Ablaze with lights from bow to stern, the newcomer rapidly came abeam of the motionless *Californian*, passing along her starboard side some ten to twelve miles away. Groves could soon see that she was a large passenger liner, with brightly lit decks piled one on top the other. Around 11:30 he went down to the chartroom, knocked on the door, and told Captain Lord about the newcomer. Lord suggested that Groves try to contact her by Morse lamp, which he did, but gave up after a few moments when he received no reply.

About 11:40 Groves saw the big liner suddenly seem to stop and put out most of her lights. This didn't seem unusual to Groves, who was an old hand of the Far East trade: it was a custom for ships on the Pacific runs to dim their lights around midnight to encourage the passengers to get to bed. He had no way of knowing at that moment that the stranger's lights had gone out because she had made a sudden, sharp turn to port.

Captain Lord too had been watching the new arrival from the port in the chartroom, but unlike Groves, who standing one deck higher and had a much clearer view of the other vessel, Lord didn't believe the ship was much larger than his own *Californian*. He had stepped over to the wireless office at 11:15 and asked his wireless operator, Cyril Evans, if he knew of any other ships nearby. When Evans replied, "Only the *Titanic*," Lord told him to warn her that the *Californian* had stopped and was surrounded by ice. Now, just a few minutes after the stranger had made that sharp turn, he was back on the bridge, peering intently at the distant ship through his glasses. He remarked to Groves, "That doesn't look like a passenger steamer."

"It is, sir," Groves replied. "When she stopped she put most of her lights out—I suppose they have been put out for the night." Carefully Groves ventured his opinion that he thought her to be not more than ten miles off. Lord gave a noncommittal grunt, then announced he was returning to the chartroom, where he was to be informed if any other ships were spotted, the other ship changed bearing, or anything else unusual occurred.[2]

Meanwhile, as soon as the captain had left, Evans slipped on his headphones, adjusted his set, and began tapping out to Jack Phillips on the *Titanic*, "Say old man, we are surrounded by ice and stopped." Evans hadn't bothered to ask Phillips for permission to break into the *Titanic*'s traffic or even properly identify himself, but just barged right in, so it was little wonder that Phillips tapped back furiously, "Shut up! Shut up! You are jamming me! I am working Cape Race!"

Peeved at Phillips's brush off—and perhaps realizing his own mistake—Evans pulled the headphones off and shut down his set. Captain Lord, strangely enough, hadn't asked for an acknowledgment from the *Titanic*, and Evans wasn't about to face Phillips's ire a second time by asking for one, or, an even more frightening prospect, risk his captain's wrath by reporting the consequences of his mistake. Besides, the *Titanic*, wherever she was, was so close that her powerful transmitter nearly blew his ears off when Phillips had responded. So just a few minutes before 11:30, Evans pulled on his pajamas and settled into his bunk with a book.

Just before midnight, the *Californian*'s second officer, Herbert Stone, was making his way to the bridge for the midnight-to-four watch. Stopping by the chartroom, he spoke briefly with Captain Lord, who informed Stone that the ship was surrounded by ice and stopped for the night. He also mentioned the steamer off to the southeast that had come up less than an hour before, and was now showing one masthead light and one red light. Just before Stone climbed up the bridge, Lord gave him one last instruction: to let him know if the other ship's bearing altered in any way, or if the ship moved closer to the *Californian*.

Stone duly relieved Groves at midnight and was soon joined by an apprentice officer, a young man by the name of James Gibson. Gibson trained his glasses on the stranger and could clearly make out her masthead light, her red sidelight, and the glare of white lights on her after decks. He tried to raise the ship by Morse lamp but was no more successful than Groves had been, and after a while he left to attend to the patent log.

Meanwhile Groves, after being relieved by Stone, hadn't gone straight to his cabin, but instead made a short detour and stopped by the wireless office. Evans lay back in his bunk, now glancing idly through a magazine, when Groves came in. Usually Evans welcomed visits from the third officer: young, keen Groves often stopped by to chat with Evans, picking up the latest news of the world or learning something more about wireless.

This night, though, Evans's usual friendly demeanor was somewhat in abeyance. He had a long, hard day—it began around 7:00 A.M. every day, and Evans was the only wireless operator the *Californian* had—and the brush off from Phillips on the *Titanic* had been the last straw. When 11:30 came, his usual shut-down time, Evans had wasted no time in getting off the air. Now he was ready to turn in and didn't feel like being sociable. Groves tried anyhow: "What ships have you got, Sparks?"

"Only the *Titanic*," Evans replied, and Groves nodded, remembering the big passenger liner he had seen overtaking the *Californian* half an hour before. He picked up the headphones and put them on, hoping to catch some traffic. Groves's Morse was getting quite good—Evans was teaching him, and Groves joked that he could now catch one letter in three, though he was actually better than that—but he didn't know enough about the equipment to realize that the *Californian*'s wireless set was equipped with a magnetic detector driven by clockwork, so when he failed to wind it up, he heard nothing. Disappointed, he put the headphones down on the desk and said good night to Evans, turning out the cabin light as he left. It was just after 12:15 A.M. and Jack Phillips had just sent out his first distress call.[3]

While Gibson worked on the log, Stone paced back and forth across the bridge. At 12:40 Captain Lord called up the voice tube from the chartroom, asking if the stranger had come any closer. Stone replied no, everything was the same as before. Lord informed him that he was going to lie down a bit on the chartroom settee. Stone resumed his pacing.

Less than ten minutes later he was startled by a flash of white light bursting above the other ship. Unsure of what he had seen, he watched the stranger closely, and after a few minutes, was rewarded with another white flash—a white rocket bursting high above the unknown vessel, sending out a shower of white stars. Several minutes later he saw another—then later still another—and still another. Five white rockets. . . .

Stone called down the voice tube to Captain Lord and told him about the five rockets. "Are they company signals?" Lord asked.

"I don't know, sir, but they appear to me to be all white."

"Well, go on Morsing."

"Yes, sir."

"And when you get an answer, let me know by Gibson."

"Yes, sir."

Lord returned to his nap on the settee and Stone returned to studying the distant ship. The *Californian* continued to drift, slowly turning to starboard, her bow gradually coming around until it was bearing directly on the other ship. About this time Gibson returned to the bridge, and Stone told him about the strange ship firing rockets. Gibson raised his glasses to his eyes and as he focused on the unknown vessel he was rewarded with the sight of another rocket being fired off. Gibson's glasses, which were more powerful than Stone's, allowed him to see detail Stone couldn't pick up with the naked eye: the white detonating flash, the rocket streaking up into the sky, the near-blinding white flash as the rocket burst, and the spray of slowly falling white stars.[4]

It seemed strange, Stone thought, that a ship would fire rockets at night. As the two officers watched, a seventh rocket climbed into the sky and burst above the stranger. Stone borrowed Gibson's glasses and studied her for some minutes, then handed them back to the apprentice officer, remarking, "Have a look at her now. She looks very queer out of the water—her lights look queer."

Gibson peered at the stranger carefully. She seemed to be listing, and had, as he later described it "a big side out of the water." Stone noticed her red sidelight had disappeared.

The *Californian* continued her slow, drifting turn to starboard until the stranger was now off the port bow. About 1:40 A.M. they saw an eighth rocket burst over the ship. "A ship is not going to fire rockets at sea for nothing," Stone remarked and Gibson agreed. "There must be something wrong with her." Gibson said he thought she might be in some sort of distress.[5]

As the men continued to watch, the stranger slowly began to disappear. To Stone she had seemed to be steaming away from the time she began firing the rockets, and now she seemed to be changing her bearing—Gibson hadn't noticed any bearing change, though he too decided that she was gradually disappearing, but he remarked how she had showed her red sidelight but never her green, as would have been the case with a ship steaming away to the southwest.

At 2:00 A.M. Stone sent Gibson down to wake up Captain Lord. "Tell him that the ship is disappearing in the southwest and that she had fired altogether eight rockets." Gibson knocked on the chartroom door, opened it, and relayed Stone's message. Sleepily, Lord asked, "Were they all white rockets?"

"Yes, sir."

"What time is it?"

"Two oh five by the wheelhouse clock, sir."

Lord nodded, turned out the light, and went back to sleep, and Gibson went back to the bridge. At 2:20 Stone thought he could still faintly make out the strange ship, then her lights seemed to fade away completely. By 2:40 he was certain that the stranger was gone, and whistled down the speaking tube to the chartroom. When Lord answered, Stone told him that the other ship had disappeared to the southwest and was completely out of sight. One last time Lord asked about the rockets, and Stone assured him that there were no colors, "just white rockets." Lord told Stone to record it in the log, then went back to sleep.[6]

Stone and Gibson resumed their watch. For the next hour nothing happened. Then at 3:30 A.M. Gibson suddenly saw another rocket, this one off to the south and farther away than the other rockets had been. Drawing Stone's attention to it, Gibson watched as a second, then a third rocket was launched. The ship firing these rockets was below the horizon, so the two officers never actually saw her, but both men noted that these rockets were company signals, not the white rockets the other ship had fired earlier. Oddly, Stone did not report these new rockets to the captain.[7]

At 4:00 A.M. Chief Officer George F. Stewart appeared on the bridge, relieving Stone. Stone described the night's events—the strange ship to the southwest, the eight white rockets she fired, the ship slowly disappearing, and his informing Captain Lord of these events three different times.

As Stone was talking, Stewart raised his glasses and peering southward spotted a four-masted steamer with one funnel and "a lot of light amidships." He asked Stone if this was the ship that had fired the rockets, and

Stone replied that he had not seen this ship before, and that he was sure that it was not the same one that had fired the first eight rockets. With that, Stone went below, leaving a somewhat bemused Chief Officer Stewart alone on the bridge.

Stewart had an uneasy feeling, a vague sense that "something had happened." Rockets at sea normally meant distress, and Stewart couldn't help but think that may have been the case here. Even so it wasn't until 4:30 that he did anything, and that was to awaken Captain Lord at his accustomed hour. Knocking politely on the chartroom door, Stewart began recounting the night's events as told to him by Stone. About halfway through this recitation Lord stopped him, saying, "Yes, I know. Stone's been telling me."

Once he was dressed Captain Lord went up to the bridge and began to describe to Stewart how he intended to work his way out of the ice field. Stewart asked him if he was going to first try to learn something about the ship that had been firing rockets off to the southwest. Lord raised his glasses and studied the four-masted steamer off to the south and said, "No, she looks all right, She's not making any signals now." For some reason Stewart did not explain to his captain that the ship he was looking at was not the one Stewart was referring to and was not at all the ship that had fired the eight white rockets.[8]

Over the course of the next hour, conversation on the bridge was desultory as the two men waited for the dawn. Finally the feeling that had been nagging at Stewart caused him to run down to the *Californian's* wireless room and wake up Cyril Evans with the words "Sparks, there's a ship been firing rockets in the night. Will you see if you can find out what is wrong—what is the matter?"

Evans fumbled about a bit, then wound up the magnetic detector, slipped on the headphones, and began listening. Within minutes Stewart was racing up the stairs to the bridge, shouting to Captain Lord that a ship had been sunk. A quick dash back down to the wireless office, then back up to bridge with the devastating news: "The *Titanic* has hit a berg and sunk!"[9]

Lord immediately started his engines and began steaming toward the *Titanic's* last reported position. It was slow going for the first four or five miles as Lord picked his way through the heavy field ice that had drifted in during the night and which was frequently studded with bergs. He moved at what he deemed a maximum safe speed—four knots. By 7:00 A.M. the *Californian* was in clear water and carefully worked her way up to her top speed of fourteen knots.

Around half past seven Captain Lord calculated that he had arrived at the *Titanic's* position, but the ship was nowhere to be seen. Only the *Mount Temple*, another ship that had answered the *Titanic's* distress call, was nearby. Some six miles to the east of these two ships sat the Cunard liner *Carpathia*. Evans sent a message to the bridge saying that he had learned that the *Carpathia* was conducting the rescue of the *Titanic's* survivors. Lord decided to make for the rescue ship to see if he could be of any assistance. The ice made a direct course impossible, so the *Californian* had to take a roundabout route, coming up on the *Carpathia* from the southwest. As his ship approached the *Carpathia*, Captain Lord noted that the Cunard vessel had four masts and a single funnel.

The whole crew of the *Californian* was roused by now. Extra lookouts were posted and lifeboats were swung out. Third Officer Groves, awakened by Chief Officer Stewart, stopped by Second Officer Stone's cabin to ask if it was true about the *Titanic*. "Yes, old chap," Stone assured him, "I saw rockets on my watch."

Just on 8:30 the *Californian* hove to alongside the *Carpathia*, and in an exchange of flag signals it was decided that the *Carpathia* would head for New York, while the *Californian* continued to search for survivors.

There was little enough to see—large pieces of reddish cork from the ruptured bulkheads, steamer chairs, cushions, lifebelts, rugs, the abandoned lifeboats, the *Titanic*'s red and white striped barber pole. Captain Lord would later claim that he didn't find any bodies at all, but it is doubtful that he looked very hard. Third Officer Groves later maintained that the search was broken off by 10:30 A.M., though Captain Lord was to say that it was continued until 11:40. Lord's version was the one that went down in the *Californian*'s log, of course, but then Captain Lord's version of many things would find their way into the *Californian*'s log.[10]

Nowhere did the ship's log mention anything about her officers sighting white rockets in the early hours of the morning of April 15, 1912.[11]

CHAPTER 11

Homecoming

But let him remember that the days of darkness will be
many. . . .

—Ecclesiastes 11:8

THE *CARPATHIA*'S RETURN PASSAGE TO NEW YORK WAS MARKED BY BRIGHT,
sunny, and bitterly cold weather and calm seas. The little Cunard liner's passengers were wonderful, digging into their luggage for extra clothing and toi-
let articles for the *Titanic*'s survivors, helping the stewards distribute blankets
and hot drinks, sewing smocks and shifts for children and women out of
steamer blankets, offering spare berths to relieve some of the crowding in the
makeshift dormitories. They did their best to be cheerful and make the
crowded little ship a little less tense. But an almost tangible pall hung over
the ship that no amount of hard work, however cheerfully done, could dispel.

Most of the survivors held themselves somewhat aloof from the passengers aboard the *Carpathia,* not from any sense of snobbery, but rather
because most of them were in varying degrees of shock. The enormity of
what they had experienced was such that no one aboard the Cunard ship, no
matter how sympathetic, could ever understand. And so the *Titanic*'s survivors were polite and accepted the *Carpathia*'s passengers' assistance with
genuine gratitude, but the gulf remained throughout the trip.[1]

Somehow Sir Cosmo Duff Gordon managed to commit yet another
blunder. This one would have been almost comical had it not been so taste-
less. Apparently Lady Duff Gordon had what to her seemed a smashing idea:
why not have a group picture taken of herself, her husband, Miss Francatelli,
the other two passengers, and the seven crewmen who had manned Boat 1
for them? So, the day after they were rescued, all twelve gathered on the
Carpathia's foredeck, the crewmen conspicuous in their lifebelts. Other survivors stared in disbelief as Dr. McGhee, the *Carpathia*'s surgeon, prepared
to take the picture with the words, "Now, smile everyone!"[2]

In the wireless shack Cottam began the laborious task of transmitting the
names of the survivors, along with some brief personal messages from them,
to the White Star Line's New York office. Once Harold Bride had gotten

medical attention for his badly frostbitten feet and a few hours' rest, he began to periodically relieve Cottam at the key, but it was a long process.

One of the first messages Cottam sent was to Philip A. S. Franklin, vice president of the White Star Line in New York:

> Most desirable *Titanic* crew should be returned home earliest moment possible. Suggest you hold *Cedric*, sailing her daylight Friday. . . . Propose returning in her myself. YAMSI.

"YAMSI" was of course a transposition of Ismay, though why the chairman of the line chose to employ such a transparent subterfuge is anyone's guess: he always signed his cables that way. What Ismay didn't know was that the contrived signature coupled with the contents of the message would cause an influential member of the U.S. Senate to suspect Ismay of duplicity, setting into motion a series of events that would ruin Bruce Ismay.

Philip A. S. Franklin had his hands full without worrying about the travel arrangements of the Line's chairman. When Ismay's message arrived, Franklin had an office full of reporters clamoring for news of the *Titanic*. A series of garbled wireless transmissions from ships in the vicinity of the *Titanic* had left the newspapers thoroughly confused. With the *Carpathia* refusing to answer any queries, there were few facts to go on, and the headlines the morning of April 15 were filled with speculation.

The *New York Herald* was typical:

THE NEW TITANIC STRIKES ICEBERG AND CALLS FOR AID
VESSELS RUSH TO HER SIDE

The *New York Times* was prepared to announce in the last edition that the ship had sunk, based on the prolonged silence of her wireless, but no other editor was willing to follow Carr Van Anda's lead. Consequently Franklin was besieged by reporters when he arrived at work in the morning.

At first, Franklin was confident, telling his questioners, "We place absolute confidence in the *Titanic*. We believe that the boat is unsinkable." At the same time though, he was having messages sent addressed to Captain Smith, asking for information about the ship and its passengers.

By midmorning the story of the ship's collision with the iceberg had broken, and now frantic friends and family members of passengers began to gather at the White Star offices: J. P. Morgan, Jr.; W. H. Force, father of Mrs. Astor; Ben Guggenheim's wife; hundreds of others with unknown faces and names. They received the same reassurances that Franklin had given the press earlier in the morning: all was well; everyone would be safe; there was no need for alarm.

It all sounded so convincing. The myth of the *Titanic*'s unsinkability had been repeated so many times by so many different sources that it was inconceivable that any serious accident had happened to her. When the *Evening Sun* ran a banner-sized headline that declared "ALL SAVED FROM

TITANIC AFTER COLLISION," the paper was merely giving voice to what the public—and White Star officials—believed to be true. The latest story had it that the *Titanic*'s passengers were being transferred to the *Parisian* and the *Carpathia*, while the *Virginian* took the wounded liner in tow, bound for Halifax, Nova Scotia.

The White Star Line's positive posture was maintained all day. True, Franklin admitted to reporters, there were rumors that the *Titanic* had been sunk and the loss of life was heavy, but these were rumors, not reliable news. Wireless operators—in some cases amateurs—were catching snippets of transmissions and relaying them on. The news they were hearing wasn't good. But the ships involved, the *Carpathia*, the *Virginian*, the *Parisian*, and others, weren't within wireless range yet, so for news as important as this, Franklin wasn't willing to settle for second- or thirdhand information.

When the official word came at 6:15 P.M. that evening, it was like a body blow to Franklin: the *Olympic*, her transmission delayed for some hours, reported that the *Titanic* had sunk at 2:20 A.M. with more than 1,500 passengers still aboard; the survivors had been rescued by the *Carpathia* and were being brought to New York. Franklin waited three quarters of an hour before he was able to face the reporters. Visibly exerting every bit of self control he could muster, he told them, "Gentlemen, I regret to say that the *Titanic* sank at 2:20 this morning."

That was all he would—or could—say at the moment. It is remarkable that he was able to hold onto his composure for so long, but gradually he admitted that the report "neglected to say that all the crew had been saved," then later that "probably a number of lives had been lost," which eventually became "we very much fear there has been a great loss of life." At 9:00 P.M. Franklin broke down completely—sobbing, he told the stunned reporters that there had been a "horrible loss of life"—it would be possible, he said, to replace the ship, but "never the human lives."[3]

Within hours every major American newspaper carried the story, and the country reeled from the shock. For the next three days, as the papers engaged in endless speculation about what had actually happened, the *Titanic* seemed to be the sole topic of conversation. Invariably the discussion would end with the question "How?" How could a ship declared by expert marine engineers to be unsinkable go to the bottom of the Atlantic two hours after striking an iceberg? How could an iceberg sink a ship? How could a ship not avoid something that big and obvious? And most disturbing of all, how could 1,500 people die when the ship complied with or exceeded every safety regulation on the books? A few minds began thinking very seriously about these questions, and there was going to be hell to pay when they found out the answers.

But those answers would not be forthcoming until the *Carpathia* arrived in New York, and Cottam and Bride were concentrating exclusively on sending the names of the survivors and their personal messages to New York via

Cape Race, refusing to answer any requests for information. This even included those of the cruiser USS *Chester*, dispatched by a worried President Taft. Distraught over the uncertainty of the fate of his friend and aide Archie Butt, Taft had sent out the *Chester* expressly to contact the *Carpathia*, whose wireless didn't have the range to reach New York directly. But despite her repeated attempts, all in the name of the President, the *Chester*'s queries went unanswered, as did those of the various newspapers and wire services hungrily waiting for news.

Predictably, the New York press reacted with calculated petulance. The *World*, for example, proclaimed with an almost audible sniff, "CARPATHIA LETS NO SECRETS OF THE TITANIC'S LOSS ESCAPE BY WIRELESS." The *Evening Mail*'s frustration was even more obvious: "WATCHERS ANGERED BY CARPATHIA'S SILENCE." The *Herald* was miffed, while the *Evening Sun* pouted.

In reality, both Cottam and Bride had been advised by the Marconi office in New York that Guglielmo Marconi himself had concluded a deal with the *New York Times* on behalf of the two young operators that would reward them handsomely for providing an exclusive for the *Times*. For a couple of young men earning the equivalent of $20 a month, the promise of several thousand dollars in exchange for a few hours spent talking to a reporter was irresistible, so sending only survivors' names and messages provided a convenient excuse for turning aside any other inquiries. Neither Bride nor Cottam, or Marconi himself for that matter, were aware that Marconi's apparently benevolent action could appear to be a deliberate attempt to withhold information from an anxious public solely for the *Times*' benefit. In any case, it soon became quite clear that nothing more would be learned from the little Cunarder until her arrival in New York, which was scheduled for Thursday night, April 18.[4]

That Thursday night was cold and rain-filled in New York, the whole of New York Harbor shrouded in a thunderstorm. People began gathering on the Cunard pier around 6:00 P.M.—not many at first, only a few hundred, but slowly the crowd began to grow until by 9:00, more than 30,000 were standing in the cold April rain, another 10,000 lining the battery. Peering through the gloom and mist, a few minutes past 9:00 they spotted a ship in the Ambrose Channel. It was the *Carpathia*. She was greeted by a fleet of steam launches, tugboats, ferry boats, and yachts, led by a large tug containing an official party of the mayor and several city commissioners. As the *Carpathia* hove into sight, the mayor's tug let loose a shrill blast from its steam whistle. Every other boat in the harbor followed by sounding their bells, whistles, and sirens. Captain Rostron stood on the bridge, staring out at the flotilla of boats surrounding his ship and dimly making out the throng gathered at the Cunard pier awaiting the *Carpathia*. Until this moment he had no idea, as he put it later, of "the suspense and excitement in the world."

As we were going up Ambrose Channel, the weather changed completely, and a more dramatic ending to tragic occurrence it would be hard to conceive. It began to blow hard, rain came down in torrents, and, to complete the finale, we had continuous vivid lightning and heavy rolling thunder. . . . What with the wind and rain, a pitch-dark night, lightning and thunder, and the photographers taking flashlight pictures of the ship, and the explosion of the lights, it was a scene never to be effaced from one's memory.[5]

At pierside, people began weeping quietly, but there was no hysteria. The most frenzied behavior was exhibited by the huge numbers of reporters who had gathered along with the crowd on the pier, or had gotten aboard one of the boats that had sailed into the channel to meet the *Carpathia*. When the liner stopped to pick up the pilot, five reporters clambered from their boat over the railing onto the pilot boat, then attempted to force their way past the pilot, up the boarding ladder, and onto the *Carpathia*.

Captain Rostron, once he saw the reception awaiting his ship, anticipated such an eventuality, and had stationed Third Officer Rees at the foot of the boarding ladder. Rees watched in bemused fascination as the small craft gathered around the pilot boat, the reporters shouting questions up to the decks of the *Carpathia* through megaphones, the photographers setting off their magnesium flashes as they took picture after picture. But when one of the newsmen tried to shove the pilot aside and rush up the boarding ladder himself, Rees sprang into action. Grabbing the pilot by the arm, Rees hauled him onto the boarding ladder, then turned and punched the reporter in the mouth, sending him sprawling.

"Pilot only!" he said, in case the other newsmen hadn't got the message. Apparently one missed it, for he immediately started raving about his sister, crying about how he had to see her; when Rees didn't believe his story, he tried to bribe the third officer, offering him $200 to be allowed on board. Rees refused, the pilot was taken up to the bridge, and the journey up the channel resumed.

Somehow one reporter did slip aboard, but he was quickly cornered and brought to the bridge. Rostron, who had no time for such nonsense, informed the man that under no circumstances could he speak with any survivors before the *Carpathia* docked. The man was left on the bridge, after giving his word he would abide by the captain's instructions. "I must say," Rostron later admitted, somewhat astonished, "he was a gentleman."

The crowd gasped with surprise when the *Carpathia* steamed past the Cunard pier toward the White Star dock and stopped. In the nearly continuous lightning and photographers' flashes, the crew of the *Carpathia* could be seen manning several lifeboats and putting them into the water. After a moment the apprehensive crowd realized what was happening: they were the

Titanic's lifeboats, being duly returned to their rightful owners. It was a heartbreaking sight.

After a painfully slow turn, the *Carpathia* made her way back to the Cunard pier, and was carefully warped alongside and made fast. The canopied gangways were hauled into place, and a procession of passengers began to make their way down from the ship to the dock. After a few seconds, the stunned crowd realized that these neatly dressed people weren't from the *Titanic*: Captain Rostron had decided that it would be unfair to his passengers to make them wait and wade through the tumult that would inevitably greet the survivors, so the *Carpathia*'s passengers disembarked first.

Then there appeared a young woman, hatless, eyes wide as she stared at the waiting crowd, the first of the *Titanic*'s survivors. At the foot of the gangway stood a solid phalanx of reporters, each one hungry for a story. Standing unrecognized among them was one man who was after the biggest story of them all: a diminutive figure flanked by two U.S. Marshals, he was Senator William Alden Smith.[6]

—◆◆◆—

Senator Smith would have his moment soon enough, and when he did it would be an unforgettable experience, but there was another homecoming besides the arrival of the *Carpathia* in New York, which would take place over and over again in the days to come, a homecoming of a kind that Senator Smith could know nothing of—and would have been helpless to affect even if he had. Even while the ship was docking at Pier 54, Cottam and Bride were still busy sending personal messages from survivors, and transmitting a list of passengers and crew who were lost in the disaster. One of the great tragedies of the *Titanic*'s sinking that often gets lost is the heavy price paid by the crew—and ultimately by their families. So many statistics and so many numbers would be introduced and paraded before the world in the two great pending investigations that one more recitation of who was lost on the *Titanic* would begin to lose meaning. But within the lists of those missing were the names of the crewmen who lost their lives on board the White Star liner. This was the saddest homecoming of all: the certain news that husbands, fathers, sons, brothers, would not be coming home at all.

Out of 892 crewmen, only 214 survived. Three-quarters of the crew had gone down with the ship, in proportion a far heavier toll than any of the three passenger classes. But what those numbers didn't tell—couldn't tell—was the overwhelming burden of grief that they brought to a single city in England.

Southampton was a city devastated by the *Titanic* disaster. Four of every five crewmen aboard her had come from this proud old seafaring town, whose ties to ships and the sea dated back to Roman times. Entire streets were hung with black crepe, whole rows of houses bereaved. The crowd anxiously awaiting the news was comprised almost entirely of women: young women with bright-eyed babies in their arms; middle-aged women with hands red and worn from work; old women, wrinkled and gray. They gathered outside the White Star Line's Southampton office on April 17. Names were posted as quickly as they came in, but all too often when one of the women would leave to go home, she would be sobbing, sometimes leaning on the arm of a friend, a daughter, or mother-in-law. Sometimes, saddest of all, she left alone. In the April 23 issue of the *London Daily Mail* an unsigned article described how the day closed:

> Later in the afternoon hope died out. The waiting crowds thin-
> ned, and silent men and women sought their homes. In the hum-
> bler homes of Southampton there is scarcely a family who has not
> lost a relative or friend. Children returning from school appreci-
> ated something of tragedy, and woeful little faces were turned to
> the darkened, fatherless homes.[7]

The story went on to tell of the working-class streets in Southampton and the loss they had suffered. It told of Mrs. Allen, whose husband George was a trimmer on the *Titanic*; of a woman on Union Street with three small children; of Mrs. Barnes who lost a brother; of Mr. Saunders, whose two boys were firemen; of an old man on Cable Street who had four sons aboard the *Titanic*; of a young girl, nearly mad with grief, whose husband had been a steward—they had been married only a month; of Mrs. Gosling, who lost her son; and of Mrs. Preston, a widow, who lost her son as well. But the most heartbreaking may have been Mrs. May, whose husband Arthur and eldest son, Arthur, Jr., had both gone down with the ship. There were ten more children left behind, as well as Arthur Jr.'s young wife and six-week-old baby. The father had signed on board the *Titanic* because a leg injury had kept him from sailing on his usual ship, the Cunard Line's *Britannia*. Arthur Jr. had only signed on because the coal strike had put him out of work and he had a family to support. Now Mrs. May had ten children to care for: the oldest was nineteen and brought home a few shillings a week— her youngest was six months old.

The coal strike had wreaked havoc on the shipping industry and put so many men out of work that when the opportunity had come to get a job— any job—on the *Titanic*, there were more men clamoring for them than there were berths, and those who got them counted themselves lucky. Often families were forced to pawn their furniture or what pitiful few valuables they possessed just to be able to buy food, and some landlords were already serv-ing notices to quit to tenants who were in arrears on their rent. Now, for hundreds of families, what had seemed like a godsend when the man of the house had secured a position on the *Titanic* had suddenly become catastro-phe. The *Daily Mail*'s unknown reporter, with a lack of hyperbole remark-able for the day, personalized the tragedy:

Many women who wait for hour after hour outside the White Star offices pathetically cling to the hope that their men, being in the four-to-eight watch have escaped in one of the boats. The twelve-to-four watch was the death watch. One drooping woman was leaning on a bassinet containing two chubby babies, while a tiny mite held her hand. "What are we waiting for, Mummy? Why are we waiting such a long time?" asked the tired child. "We are waiting for news of your father, dear," came the choked answer, as the mother turned away her head to hide her tears.[8]

The grief would take a long time to fade, but fortunately it would only be a few weeks before a number of relief funds were organized to assist the families of the crewmen who perished on the *Titanic*. The assistance said much about the character of the British people as a whole, as well as how deeply the disaster touched the entire nation: contributions to the relief funds came from every part of the country and from every strata of society. The charities ultimately collected nearly £450,000 ($2,160,000) and one of the funds was still functioning, under special circumstances, as late as the 1960s.[9]

But over the years, the enormous number of crewmen lost has somehow been ignored or glossed over, while the plight of the Third Class passengers and the disproportionate loss of life among them when compared to First or Second Class has been heavily emphasized. It is almost as if by some unspoken consent the crew has come to be regarded as expendable, while the steerage passengers are presented as a rare and valuable commodity that was squandered for the benefit of First and Second Class. Yet there was a dynamic that shaped the destinies of those crewmen that was as powerful as any that shaped the fate of the Third Class passengers, and it was every bit as telling about the values of late-Victorian and Edwardian society.

There were a handful of virtues nearly all the Victorians and Edwardians believed in passionately, regardless of class, and whether they were mythical or not they were compelling: respect, almost reverence, for the Crown; the rigidity of the social order; honor; piety; valor; and most of all, duty. Eighty-five years later these values may seem laughable among certain post-modern intellectuals, but at the turn of the century they defined, as absolutely as class determined a man's or woman's station in society, how those men and women would conduct themselves. Indeed the Edwardians' devotion to duty was so deeply ingrained, and so complete, that only after the better part of an entire generation had been slaughtered on the Western Front during World War I would that devotion's validity be challenged. In point of fact, it is only possible to understand how the Tommies were so willing to go over the top and march into the teeth of chattering Spandaus in 1916 by understanding why so many of the crew remained aboard the *Titanic* in 1912.

Yet it is also important to remember that three-fourths of the crew didn't have to die. Though the officers and crew of the *Titanic* were legally obliged to do their best to see the passengers to safety, in practice the officers had little except the force of moral authority to prevent the crew from simply shouldering the passengers aside. The growing power of the Seamen's Union was making it more and more difficult to dismiss crewmen for breaches of discipline. In the years before and after the *Titanic* disaster there have been plenty of examples of crewmen commandeering a sinking ship's lifeboats and leaving the passengers to their fate, a situation still with us as recently as 1965, when the cruise ship *Yarmouth Castle* was engulfed in flames thirty-five miles west of the Bahamas, and the first lifeboat away contained her captain, her bosun, and assorted crew members, but not one passenger.[10]

Yet, on the *Titanic*, aside from a handful of stewards, there isn't a single recorded incident of any crewmen trying to force their way into any of the lifeboats. On the contrary, in two separate instances (Boats 2 and 6) crewmen who had gotten into the boats and were ordered out by an officer complied without protest. Having been raised from birth with the idea that duty came above any other consideration and that obedience and duty were synonymous, it would prove to be too powerful a habit to be broken in a few hours' time.

It was devotion to duty that caused Fireman Cavell to go back to Boiler Room 4 when he thought he might have left too early and was letting his mates down; it kept Quartermaster Rowe on the bridge wing, firing off his rockets and working the Morse lamp, no matter how futile it seemed; it kept Trimmer Hemming on board working at loading and lowering the boats long after his assigned lifeboat had gone; it kept Phillips and Bride at the wireless even after Captain Smith released them; it kept Chief Engineer Bell and the rest of the engineering staff in the engine room even when they knew that it was far too late to reach the upper decks and get away; and it kept Wallace Hartley and the band playing until they were pitched into the sea.

It can't just be ascribed to something as simple as courage; after all, someone once made the observation that, "A hero is simply a coward who got cornered." Instead the inescapable conclusion is that it was a sense of responsibility, of obligation to other people. It was the knowledge that people were depending on them that caused so many of the crew to remain at their posts, even at the cost of their lives. "No greater love . . ." is the most eloquent way it's been put, and it might be too simplistic to ascribe the crewmen's action to love for their fellow men and women, but it's in there somewhere.

Eighty-five years after the disaster, in a different country, within a society that ethnically, morally, and politically is wholly removed from the one that produced the crew of the *Titanic*, it is difficult to believe—let alone understand how—they could knowingly, willingly sacrifice themselves. Yet the evidence is undisputable: aside from the stewardesses, whom nobody ever suggested should stay behind (only three were lost), and a score or so of opportunists who managed to sneak into a boat when one of the officers wasn't looking, the only crewmen who left the *Titanic* in the lifeboats were the men ordered into them by the officers. Compulsion or fear of punishment cannot explain this—the British Merchant Marine was not the Royal Navy, with its ironbound traditions, strict regulations, and rigidly enforced discipline, always backed up by the threat of a defaulter's board or a court-martial.

Instead, it was a matter of individual choice, of a man's sense of responsibility to his shipmates and to the people entrusted to his care; it was the idea that the young, the weak, the infirm, and the unable needed protection from circumstances that they could not ward off for themselves; it was a belief that death itself was preferable to the disgrace of being perceived a coward. These may seem like archaic notions today, but the result was that every crewman who stayed behind made room for one more passenger, one more woman or child, in the lifeboats. That many of those boats left the ship only half full was not their fault.

Nor can it be suggested that the crew members were mindless, unimaginative drudges who went to their deaths because they couldn't think of anything better to do. While centuries of class structure had certainly created in the working class an inherent belief that they were meant to toil at the direction of their "betters" (as the language of the day expressed it), they had never been taught, nor did the upper class ever think, that they were merely expendable. The crew was certainly not under any societal imperative, self-imposed or otherwise, to sacrifice themselves simply for the passengers' sake.

What the crew had was leadership and an example to action. There's no reason to believe that Captain Smith's last words to his crew were, as has sometimes been reported, "Be British, men, be British!"—as if being Anglo-Saxons had given them a particular penchant for dying well—but there can be no argument that the officers, the senior engineers, the pursers, and Thomas Andrews all provided examples for the crew to follow. And follow it they did. And perhaps this was meant to be their lasting homecoming, as real as it was intangible: the example they gave by following. Not every man or woman is meant to be a leader, but it is followers who define the difference between a leader and a lonely fanatic. If there was a lasting legacy from the crew of the *Titanic*, something of genuine meaning that would transcend cliché and platitude that they could leave for their children and grandchildren, it was their willingness to follow men who were doing what was right and noble and good, and in so doing become right and noble and good themselves.

———◆———

Southampton would raise two memorials to those of the crew of the *Titanic* who wouldn't be coming home. One was a classically inspired fountain dedicated to the stewards and other crew members, unveiled in 1915; in 1972 it was moved to the ruins of Holy Rood Church, where it remains in good company. The church, bombed-out by the Nazis in World War II, serves as Great Britain's memorial to her merchant seamen who were lost in both world wars. The other, dedicated in April 1914, was a handsome monument of granite, with panels of bronze bas-relief depicting the engineers, which still stands in Southampton's East Park.

Other cities would put up monuments as well—Liverpool, like Southampton, would honor the engineers, building a column near the city's waterfront. During its construction the design was slightly modified to include a memorial to all the British merchant marine engineers killed during World War I. In New York, the *Titanic* Memorial Lighthouse, sited atop the Seamen's Church Institute, was dedicated on the first anniversary of the sinking. In 1920, Belfast would unveil a graceful statue that depicts two mermaids holding up a victim before a standing figure representing the sea. It would be the summer of 1931 before the Women's *Titanic* Memorial was dedicated in Washington, D.C. A simple, moving sculpture of a man standing with arms outstretched, it can still be found in the city's waterfront park.

Individuals would be commemorated as well. Captain Smith's memory would be honored by a life-sized statue of him, erected near his home in Lichfield, England. A stone tablet commemorating the heroism of Jack Phillips was placed in the memorial cloister in Godalming, Surrey, England. In Comber, County Down, Northern Ireland, Thomas Andrews would be remembered through the efforts of his friends, who oversaw the construction of Thomas Andrews Memorial Hall; today the building is a primary school. In a park in Colne, Lancashire, a bronze bust of Wallace Hartley sits atop a marble pillar, the monument paid for by donations that came from all over England. In New York City, in the quiet shadows of Grace Church, a panel remembers Edith Evans, who gave up her place in Collapsible D so Mrs. John Murray Brown could return to her children; across town, at Broadway and West 106th Street, is a monument to Isador and Ida Straus that was funded by grieving Macy's employees. A marble fountain was erected in Washington, D.C., dedicated to Colonel Archibald Butt. It was paid for from the private funds of President William Howard Taft, who dedicated it to the memory of his lost friend.

But for all the outpouring of love and grief and loss that caused these memorials to be raised, such monuments were beyond the means of most of the friends and families of those who died on the *Titanic*. For them, and for those who had gone down with the ship, all they would ever have would be a rusting hulk lying at the bottom of the North Atlantic, which would serve as memorial, gravestone, and tomb.

CHAPTER 12

Inquests and Judgments

*And I will let loose my anger upon you, and will judge
you according to your ways.*

—Ezekiel 7:3

AS THE PUBLIC'S INITIAL SHOCK OVER THE MAGNITUDE OF THE *TITANIC* DISASter began to fade, indignation took its place. It was almost impossible to grasp the concept, let alone the reality, that more than 1,500 lives had been lost in less than three hours. It was as if a battle had been fought and lost, or a small town had been wiped off the face of the earth. Newspaper editors, using charts, photographs, and any other visual aids they could find, tried to give some meaning to the number and to make the enormity of the casualty list comprehensible to the average person. But it was no easy task, for there had never been a maritime disaster anything like the loss of the *Titanic*. Compounding this sense of incredulity was the fact that ocean travel had seemed to be so safe: in forty years only four passengers had lost their lives on the North Atlantic. Within days of the news breaking about the sinking, government officials, newspaper editors, and the public were all demanding explanations.

Now the moment had arrived for one of the most unusual and unlikely figures to become part of the story of the *Titanic* to take center stage: the junior senator from the State of Michigan, William Alden Smith, a classic Horatio Alger "rags to riches" success story. Born in 1859 in tiny Dowagiac, a logging town in the southwest corner of Michigan's lower peninsula, at the age of twelve Smith had moved with his parents to Grand Rapids, Michigan. It was with that city that he would ever after be associated. His early dream of becoming a newsboy-attaché on a railroad (which developed what would be a lifelong fascination with trains and railroading), had been thwarted by his family's poverty. But like one of Alger's "Luck and Pluck" series heroes, he turned adversity into a challenge, and within a year he had started his own business in Grand Rapids—selling popcorn of all things—and was soon his family's sole means of support, making more than $75 a month, nearly double what the average American family of the day made.

For a while he moonlighted as a correspondent for the *Chicago Times* while serving as a page in the Michigan legislature and discovering the strange but indestructible links between the press and politics. At twenty-one, William Alden, as he was invariably known, returned to Grand Rapids to study law in the offices of Birch and Montgomery, and was admitted to the Kent County bar three years later.

Setting up practice with the offices of Smiley, Smith and Stevens, William Alden quickly became a recognized expert in railroad law. His firm was remarkably successful, and soon Smith was able to buy a small railroad of his own, then a second shortly after, selling them both eventually at handsome profits. At the same time he was laying the foundations of a political career, and 1886 saw him sitting on the Michigan State Central Committee of the Republican party. In 1892 he ran for the Congressional seat from Michigan's fifth district, defeating a popular—and some said unbeatable—incumbent by 10,000 votes. He would represent the state of Michigan in either the House or the Senate for the next thirty-five years.

William Alden Smith was short, about five-feet-six, and had a curiously expressive face, capable of changing from fierce rage to warm affection in seconds. He possessed a great deal of personal charm, a remarkable memory from which he could pluck information almost effortlessly, and an oratorical style that was half persuasive, half coercive. Though he was nominally a Republican, within a short time everyone in Congress knew that William Alden was his own man, bound by no party dogma. He was the quintessential political maverick, and Smith gloried in the role.

He was an American Midwesterner writ large, with all the altruism, naiveté, dreams, hopes, fears, and prejudices of the American heartland. He was not a dupe, for before he became a politician he had been a successful lawyer and businessman; nor was he a rube, for though largely self-educated, he was a more-learned man than many of his colleagues. In no way was he merely an opportunist, for many times before and after his investigation into the loss of the *Titanic*, he was to fight lonely battles for causes many considered lost or hopeless. The *Titanic* inquiry would be Smith's one moment to stand on the world's stage, and he would make the most of it, not for his sake, but for the ideals and people he represented.[1]

When the news of the *Titanic* disaster reached Washington, Smith, like everyone else, was aghast at the enormity of the tragedy. Unlike most people, however, Smith's analytical mind would not rest until he knew how 1,500 people could be left on the decks of the sinking liner. A quick review of the existing legislation regulating the passenger steamship lines on the North Atlantic showed that there were no formal regulations, and the shipping lines were run as *laissez-faire* operations. This situation appalled Smith, who had compiled a considerable record as the sponsor and moving force behind a great deal of the safety and operating regulations of the American railroads passed by Congress in the previous two decades. When he discovered the relationship between J. P. Morgan's railroad interests and Morgan's holdings in International Mercantile Marine, he launched an inquiry. He wasn't sure if there was any evidence of negligence in the navigation, construction, or equipment of the *Titanic*, but if there was, he would find it. Quickly he pushed a resolution through the Senate that authorized the formation of a subcommittee from the Committee on Commerce, of which Smith was a member, naming him chairman. Smith carefully composed the subcommittee with members chosen to make it a politically balanced body, and he was careful to ensure that it possessed the power to issue subpoenas, including those for foreign nationals.[2]

At 3:30 P.M., April 18, Smith, the other six members of the subcommittee, and two U.S. Marshals boarded the *Congressional Limited* at Union Station in Washington, D.C., and arrived in New York just in time to be rushed across the city to Cunard's Pier 54 and meet the *Carpathia* as she tied up. While the *Titanic*'s survivors were making their way down the gangway, Smith, followed by the rest of the committee, rushed up it, and immediately asked the whereabouts of Bruce Ismay. Escorted to Dr. McGhee's cabin, Smith brushed aside Philip Franklin's protests that Ismay was "too ill" to see anyone and informed the chairman of the White Star Line that he would be expected to testify before the subcommittee at the soonest opportunity.

Ismay calmly assured Smith that he would cooperate fully with the investigation, and would appear promptly at 10:00 the next morning, when the subcommittee would begin hearings in the Waldorf-Astoria's East Room. Ismay was as good as his word, for when Senator Smith entered the East Room next morning, Ismay was already seated and waiting for him, apparently recovered from his ordeal.[3]

At 10:30 A.M. Smith opened the proceedings and began by inviting Ismay to tell the committee what had happened, "as succinctly as possible." Ismay responded by giving the figures for each day's run on the crossing, then gave his version of the events of Sunday night: "I was in bed myself, asleep, when the accident happened. The ship sank, I am told, at two-twenty. That, sir, is all I think I can tell you."

Smith didn't believe that was all Ismay could tell him, so he began a lengthy and grueling cross-examination that eventually totaled some fifty-eight pages of testimony. Ismay found himself in the unenviable position of being both a hostile witness and a scapegoat. The faint smile that he wore during the entirety of his testimony seemed to many observers a bit condescending, although Ismay believed, and indeed declared in his opening statement, that he would cooperate fully with the committee. Senator Smith harbored some deep suspicions about Ismay, and the wireless message that Ismay had sent to New York holding up the *Cedric* so that he and the surviving *Titanic* crewmen could immediately sail back to England seemed to Smith a deliberate attempt to evade American jurisdiction. Ismay attempted to explain that he really had the surviving crewmen's best interests at heart when he tried to get them aboard the *Cedric* to return to England. Many of these men had families, and since their pay stopped as soon as the *Titanic* sank, the only way they could support their families was to find a berth on another ship.

Ismay, though, did little to help his case. In addition to the smug air he held about himself while testifying, after being excused by Senator Smith, Ismay complained loudly to several reporters that he questioned the legality of the hearings, whether the American government had jurisdiction over the White Star Line, and the right of the U.S. Senate to subpoena foreign nationals. That the *Titanic* was owned and operated by an American shipping conglomerate, Ismay well knew, since he had sold the White Star Line to Morgan's IMM himself, so there never should have been any doubt in Ismay's mind about jurisdiction, nor should he have questioned the right of the committee to issue subpoenas to British subjects. Smith had made sure he was on solid legal ground before he left New York, receiving assurances from the attorney general that the committee had just such subpoena powers.

The result, in the United States at least, was that Ismay began to look a bit petulant. However much he thought his complaints were justified, he was only hurting himself: the public image of Bruce Ismay was undergoing an ugly transformation, and soon some very pointed questions were being asked in the press about how Ismay, of all people, managed to find a place in a lifeboat. Brooke Adams, a Boston historian of considerable repute, summed up the rapidly growing groundswell of feeling about Ismay when he wrote to Senator Francis Newlands, who sat on the committee:

> Ismay is responsible for the lack of lifeboats, he is responsible for
> the captain who was so reckless, for the lack of discipline of the
> crew, and for the sailing directions given to the captain which
> probably caused his recklessness. In the face of all this he saves
> himself, leaving fifteen hundred men and women to perish. I
> know of nothing at once so cowardly and so brutal in recent his-
> tory. The one thing he could have done was to prove his honesty
> and his sincerity by giving his life.[4]

It was at this time that a particularly devastating cartoon appeared in the *New York American* showing Ismay cowering in a lifeboat, while a liner could be seen sinking in the background. The caption read "Laurels for J. Brute Ismay." During his testimony before the committee, Ismay had taken great pains to place the full responsibility for the running of the ship, and hence the collision, on Captain Smith, maintaining that he had been nothing more than an ordinary passenger. But the *Titanic*'s surviving officers and passengers such as Mrs. Ryerson were to testify that Ismay had played a far different role throughout the voyage, and no matter how hard he tried to shift the blame onto Captain Smith, a cloud of nagging questions of responsibility and cowardice hung over Ismay.[5]

Senator Smith's inquiry lasted nearly six weeks, during which time eighty-two witnesses were called, including all of the *Titanic's* surviving officers, as well Captain Rostron, the officers of the *Californian*, and the wireless operators of both the *Titanic* and the *Carpathia*. When Harold Bride sat before the committee, he created a sensation, not only with his testimony, but also by his appearance: brought into the hearing room in a wheelchair, his frostbitten feet still swathed in bandages, Bride's complexion was pale, his voice weak. There seemed to have been a certain measure of stage managing to this, for Guglielmo Marconi was to appear before the committee when Bride finished his testimony, and Marconi wanted to generate as much sympathy for himself and his company as he could.

The rumor that Cottam and Bride had deliberately withheld details of the *Titanic's* sinking from the press at large in order to sell their story to the *New York Times* as an exclusive rankled Senator Smith. He probed deeply into the ties that existed between Marconi and the *Times*, and questioned if not the legality then at least the propriety of Cottam's and Bride's actions, as well as Marconi's personal part in setting up the deal. This was dangerous ground for Smith to tread on, and he knew it, for there had been a worldwide outpouring of gratitude to Marconi for the lifesaving capability that his invention of wireless now offered. But William Alden Smith was quite firm in his belief that Marconi's popularity should not render him immune from scrutiny. In the end, Smith concluded that there had been nothing illegal in the deal that Marconi had made on behalf of the two young wireless operators, but it was ethically questionable and sorely abused the public's trust. Marconi took the implied warning seriously and amended company policies accordingly.[6]

The *Titanic's* officers collectively and individually created their own sensations. Lightoller, as senior surviving officer, was the first to sit before the committee, and he did what by all accounts was an admirable job in mitigating the White Star Line's responsibility for the accident. Carefully emphasizing the unusual conditions that existed that night, he described how the *Titanic* went down, recounting in thrilling detail how he had made his escape, then successfully conned Collapsible B through the night until the *Carpathia* arrived. Lightoller was able to deflect the Senator's questioning away from the navigational procedures on the bridge, where he might have had a difficult time explaining how six separate warnings of approaching ice could have been so thoroughly ignored; similarly, he was never called upon to explain how or why the lookouts in the crow's nest were never issued binoculars. The tall, sun-bronzed seaman with the deep, manly voice saved White Star from considerable embarrassment.[7]

Significantly, of the eighty-two witnesses called, twenty-one of them were passengers, although, reflecting in part the social prejudices of the day, only three were from Third Class, giving an unbalanced picture of the plight of the steerage passengers as the ship was sinking. But Smith was determined from the start to find out what really happened on the night of April 14–15, and he knew that the passengers, who owed no loyalty to the White Star Line and so would have no reason to hide, alter, or shade facts, would go far in helping his committee form a complete and balanced picture of the sinking of the *Titanic*. Moreover, and in this he was probably acting on the advice of Senator Burton, who had considerable experience with maritime matters, Smith was determined that the investigation would not degenerate into an endless round of technical discussions, which would only leave matters more confused, and by introducing the passengers' testimony he was able to avoid that pitfall.

There were admittedly times when Senator Smith's ignorance of nautical matters seemed to lead him to ask some remarkably odd questions, since the answers seemed perfectly obvious. At one point in the course of Lightoller's testimony, when the second officer was describing how the *Titanic*'s forward funnel had collapsed, falling on a knot of swimmers, Smith asked "Did it kill anyone?" Later, when he was pursuing the subject of watertight compartments, he asked Lightoller if he were able to say "whether any of the crew or passengers took to these upper watertight compartments as a final, last resort?" Lightoller, not believing that Smith had actually asked such a question, replied that he wasn't sure. Still later, he asked one witness if the ship sank by the bow or by the head, and when the feisty Fifth Officer Lowe was testifying, Smith asked him if he knew what an iceberg was made of. "Ice," was Lowe's reply.[8]

It was apparent gaffes like these that were making Smith a laughingstock in Great Britain. At first furious over the sheer effrontery that the committee should think that it possessed the authority to subpoena and detain British subjects, the British press soon began mocking Smith, lampooning him mercilessly, calling him "a born fool." His naiveté, his earnest manner, his persistence, and most of all, the questions he asked, all provided a near-endless source of material for the British satirical press and music-hall comedians. The Hippodrome publicly offered him $50,000 to appear there and give a one hour lecture on any subject he liked, while the music hall stages began to refer to him as Senator "Watertight" Smith.

More dignified but no less upset was the legitimate British press. That the *Titanic* had been the property of an American shipping combine was ignored by a majority of the editors of Britain's dailies. Soon their editorial columns were running over with repetitious protests about Americans overstepping their authority, the general or specific ignorance of things nautical of Senator Smith, the affront to Britain's honor by the serving of subpoenas to the surviving crewmen, and so on. The magazine *Syren and Shipping* questioned the Senator's sanity, while the *Morning Post* declared that "A schoolboy would blush at Mr. Smith's ignorance." It was the position of the *Daily Mirror* that "Senator Smith has . . . made himself ridiculous in the eyes of British seamen. British seamen know something about ships. Senator Smith does not." The *Daily Telegraph* summed up the British attitude best when it declared:

The inquiry which has been in progress in America has effectively illustrated the inability of the lay mind to grasp the problem of marine navigation. It is a matter of congratulation that British custom provides a more satisfactory method of investigating the circumstances attending a wreck.[9]

In other words, this inquiry was something best left to the British Board of Trade, and the Americans had no business conducting such an investigation. The senator was accused of sullying the good name and reputation of the United States Senate, of political opportunism, and of hindering the process of discovering the truth about what happened to the *Titanic*. The outpouring of indignation was so righteous, so consistent, so loud, and so prolonged that the British press was beginning to give the impression that it feared what Smith's investigation might reveal about the British merchant marine.[10]

But not all of the British press joined in the chorus of jeers and condemnation of Smith, while extolling the virtues of a British investigation. G. K. Chesterton, writing in the *Illustrated London News*, was blunt in pointing out the differences:

It is perfectly true, as the English papers are saying, that the American papers are both what we would call vulgar and vindictive; they set the pack in full cry upon a particular man [Ismay]; that they are impatient of delay and eager for savage decisions; that the flags under which they march are often the rags of a reckless and unscrupulous journalism. All this is true. But if these be the American faults, it is all the more necessary to emphasize the opposite English faults. Our national evil is exactly the other way: it is to hush everything up; it is to damp everything down; it is to leave the great affair unfinished, to leave every enormous question unanswered.[11]

The editor of *John Bull* agreed:

We need scarcely point out that the scope of such an inquiry [by the Board of Trade] is strictly limited by statute, and that its sole effect will be to shelve the scandal until public feeling has subsided. *What* a game it is![12]

The *Review of Reviews*, which had lost its founder, William Stead, on the *Titanic*, issued the most stinging rebuke to the rest of the British papers: "We prefer the ignorance of Senator Smith to the knowledge of Mr. Ismay. Experts have told us the *Titanic* was unsinkable—we prefer ignorance to such knowledge!"[13]

In truth, Senator Smith was far from being the bumbling incompetent or the complete rube the British depicted him to be. When he asked, "Did the ship go down by the bow or the head?" he was effectively depriving the

Titanic's officers and owners of one of their more useful defensive ploys, that of falling back on technical jargon and nautical terminology in their answers and hoping to confuse the hapless landlubber. When the Senator asked Fifth Officer Lowe what an iceberg was made of, it was to seek an explanation for those who wondered how an object that was merely frozen water could inflict a mortal wound on a ship with steel sides nearly an inch thick. Fourth Officer Boxhall, when asked the same question, saw what Smith was getting at and replied that he believed that some icebergs did contain rock and such debris, but nothing large enough to matter. Similarly, when asking Lightoller if any of the passengers and crew might have sought refuge in one of the ship's watertight compartments, Smith was not asking for his own enlightenment. In 1911, he had been given a tour of the *Olympic*, conducted by Captain Smith himself, and the Senator had seen firsthand what watertight compartments were on a ship. But there were many thousands of Americans who had never seen an ocean liner and had no idea what a watertight compartment was, who had horrible visions of some huddled knot of survivors trapped at the bottom of the ocean, slowly suffocating in the darkness. Smith had asked a question that he knew to be slightly ridiculous simply to allay those fears.

Nor was Smith above taking steps to educate himself on subjects about which he knew little or was unfamiliar. On May 25 the senator, along with Rear Admiral Richard Watt, chief constructor of the U.S. Navy, and a navy stenographer boarded the *Olympic* in New York harbor. Instructed by P. A. S. Franklin to extend the senator's party every courtesy, the *Olympic*'s skipper, Capt. H. J. Haddock had a crew standing by to demonstrate, at the Senator's request, the method for loading and lowering one of the lifeboats. Smith and his party then made a trek down to Boiler Room 6, where they met Fireman Fred Barrett, who was a survivor from the *Titanic*. In the course of giving his deposition, Barrett showed the senator how the watertight doors worked, and gave a vivid description of what the collision was like in the boiler room that cold April night.[14]

Admittedly, Smith's inquiry was not perfect. Its most obvious flaw was Smith's difficulty in delegating authority to his fellow members, preferring to do most of the cross-examination himself. This territoriality made him enemies both on and off the committee, since it looked like a deliberate attempt on his part to seize and retain control of the limelight. But Smith had approached the investigation with a missionary's zeal, and he wasn't about to let crucial information slip past another member. But his control also created problems, especially as the investigation continued; some members of the committee began attending the hearings only infrequently, and Smith himself, feeling the strain, began to ask some witnesses the same questions more than once.

Nevertheless, Smith discovered some startling information. During the course of his questioning Fourth Officer Boxhall, he learned that there had been another ship nearby, which had not responded to the *Titanic*'s wireless or rockets. Other witnesses confirmed the testimony and Smith became determined to find that ship and find out why. In that he was lucky, for he found her entirely by accident.[15]

The *Californian* had docked in Boston harbor on April 19, the same day that the hearings began in New York. Rumors began flying almost immediately that she had been near enough to the *Titanic* on the night of April 14–15 to watch the ship go down. The newspapers jumped on this immediately, but Captain Lord assured them that his ship had been nearly twenty miles distant from the *Titanic*'s position, well beyond visual range, and had neither seen nor heard anything unusual until the wireless operator came on duty that morning, when the *Californian* then heard of the disaster. When asked about the rumors that some of the crew had seen the *Titanic*'s rockets, Lord smiled and shook his head, saying, "Sailors will tell anything when they're ashore." The reporters took Lord at his word, and the story was buried on the inside pages of the handful of papers that carried it.[16]

One man in Lord's crew was not so easily dispatched. After reading his captain's remarks in the Boston papers, Ernest Gill, one of the *Californian*'s assistant engineers, took a reporter and four fellow engineers to a notary public and swore out a lengthy affidavit, in which he maintained that he personally had seen a ship firing rockets just after midnight on April 15. Moreover, he claimed that the ship firing the rockets was no more than ten miles away, and that he had heard the *Californian*'s second officer saying that he too had seen the rockets, and that the ship's captain had been told about them.

The affidavit was printed in its entirety on the morning of April 23 by the *Boston American*, which also wired a complete copy to Senator Smith in New York. Smith immediately sent his marshals to Boston, to serve Gill, Lord, and the *Californian*'s officers with subpoenas to appear on Friday, April 25, in Washington, where the hearings were being moved. The press picked up the scent of a good story in the making, and Friday morning the hearing room was packed.

Smith had a brief private interview with Gill before the engineer appeared before the committee. At one point the Senator asked Gill outright how much he had been paid for the story. Gill replied $500, but then explained that he would most likely lose his job after his testimony was made public (he did), and he had to do something to secure an income as he had a family to support. But when pressed by Smith about the veracity of his affidavit, Gill budged not an inch—it was all true, he said, and he just wanted to set the record straight about what went on aboard the *Californian* that night. Grateful for the man's candor, Smith had Gill testify to the whole committee. He was taken step by step through his entire affidavit, clarifying some points and expanding on others, with an emphasis placed on the ship firing the rockets. "I am of the general opinion that the crew is," Gill concluded in his testimony, "that she was the *Titanic*."[17]

Captain Lord was the next to testify. Before leaving Boston he had told the *Boston Journal*, "If I go to Washington, it will not be because of this story in the paper, but to tell the Committee why my ship was drifting without power, while the *Titanic* was rushing under full speed. It will take about ten minutes to do so." It took a good deal longer than ten minutes. Lord maintained that he never saw the other ship and that the ship his officers saw, which didn't appear to be in any danger, was too small to have been the *Titanic*. Instead, that unknown ship stopped some ten to twelve miles from the *Californian* about twenty minutes before midnight, then had steamed off around half past two. That was the ship the *Titanic* saw, and not the *Californian*, which was too far away to be seen. Lord also told the Senator that his officers had reported to him only once that the other ship was firing rockets. Why that ship should be sending up rockets Lord had no idea, but he was quite convinced that they weren't distress signals, and that the vessel was in no danger. After letting Lord explain the events of April 14–15 in his own words, Smith began a careful cross-examination that tore Captain Lord's defense to shreds.[18]

Smith drew attention to the fact that any reference at all to the *Californian*'s officers seeing any rockets had been omitted from the ship's log, and that the pages for the early morning of April 15 were missing from the scrap log (an informal log in which entries are kept before their formal entry into the ship's official log), while the rest of the scrap log was intact. He examined Lord on the nature of rockets used as distress signals, causing Lord to describe distress rockets in terms very much like those spotted by his officers that night—that is, white rockets without any colored stars. He then confirmed that Lord had actually seen the other ship as it steamed up over the horizon around 11:00 P.M., had been told three times that a ship nearby was firing white rockets, and that Lord hadn't even bothered to wake up the wireless operator. Smith had even gone so far as to request that the U.S. Navy's Hydrographer's Office supply the committee with all the information it had about ships in the vicinity of the *Titanic*'s final position, and the Navy Hydrographer had found nothing to indicate that there might have been a ship between the *Californian* and the *Titanic*, despite what Lord maintained. All of this could have been overlooked or regarded as simply the accepted practice, given the extremely lax state of regulations for passenger liners and the absence of any requirement for a round-the-clock wireless watch. But while Captain Lord and his officers were testifying, Senator Smith found himself wondering what Arthur H. Rostron would have done in similar circumstances.[19]

Rostron had gone before the committee immediately after Bruce Ismay, and had instantly impressed everyone with his courage, his clear-headedness, his thoroughness, and his compassion. Rostron's dignified and disciplined bearing affected everyone on the committee, and when he described the memorial service held aboard the *Carpathia*, as well as the funeral for four survivors who died shortly after they were rescued, there were tears in his eyes. At the obvious sorrow of this sunburnt seaman, many in the hearing room openly wept.

One point that Senator Smith had wanted Rostron to clarify immediately was whether or not Ismay's position as chairman of the White Star Line would have allowed him to override Captain Smith's authority in matters concerning the handling and navigation of the ship, as rumors suggested. Rostron assured the senator that no one possessed the authority to overrule a captain on board his ship, under any circumstances. This testimony was a singular victory for Ismay, who had maintained that he had taken no part in how Captain Smith ran his ship. Later, Captain Inman Sealby, retired from the White Star Line, would confirm Rostron's assertion of a captain's autonomy. The only other person who could have irrefutably contradicted Captains Rostron and Sealby, and told the committee that Ismay had, in fact, been giving Captain Smith orders was, of course, Captain Smith. Ismay had gotten away with that one.

Senator Smith then asked Rostron to recount the events of the night of April 14–15, and how the *Carpathia* responded to the *Titanic*'s distress call. During the course of describing the *Carpathia*'s frantic dash north to the aid of the *Titanic*, Rostron was asked what preparation he had made to handle the survivors. Almost as if he had anticipated the question, Rostron drew a typewritten list from his coat pocket, on which he had written down all the orders he had given to ready the *Carpathia* for a rescue operation. The alacrity with which Rostron had responded to the *Titanic*, the comprehensive preparation he made, and the courage he had shown by steaming full speed into the ice field to pick up the survivors left an indelible impression on Smith and the other committee members, making Rostron the yardstick by which other ship's captains would be measured. By such a standard, Captain Lord of the *Californian* was found to be woefully inadequate.[20]

In truth, even Captain Smith was found wanting. The senator had discovered that there had been no clear-cut procedure for handling wireless messages on the bridge, so that most of the warnings the *Titanic* had received on April 14 had gone unnoticed. He found that although Captain Smith was aware of some danger of ice ahead of his ship, he had no idea of the magnitude of the ice field stretching across the *Titanic*'s course, and so took no precautions to avoid it. The general attitude of "get on or get out" that prevailed in the North Atlantic steamship lines created an atmosphere that caused ships' captains to maintain high speeds in order to hold to their schedules in even the most dangerous conditions. That no serious accident or incident had yet happened caused a certain air of complacency to surround the navigational practices of the passenger liners. What Senator Smith discovered was that although Captain Smith had handled the *Titanic* no differently than he had every other ship under his command and had followed the accepted practices on the North Atlantic, "standard operating procedure" had been a disaster waiting to happen.

Similarly, the outdated Board of Trade regulations with its absurd formula for computing lifeboat requirements was hopelessly out of touch with the realities of shipping on the North Atlantic. The solution was painfully obvious, though no one had seen the necessity until now: there would be lifeboats for everybody.

Likewise, wireless couldn't be treated as just another business anymore, for there were now too many lives at stake. The instantaneous communications capability that wireless bestowed on ships at sea now meant that it could no longer be treated as a mere toy for the amusement of a handful of passengers or ignored by officers who didn't understand it. The need for a round-the-clock wireless watch was driven home as no argument could have done by the public image of Cyril Evans sleeping peacefully in his bunk while the *Titanic* sank just a few miles away, because his captain never thought—or refused—to wake him up.

With the last witness heard on May 9, Senator Smith began sifting through the testimony and trying to arrive at some conclusion about who was responsible for the *Titanic* disaster. To his utter astonishment, he found that despite the lax and almost reckless way most of the transatlantic liners were run, under the existing laws no one—not IMM, not the White Star Line, not the *Titanic*'s officers and crew—could be found negligent (in the legal sense), so the whole tragedy fell into the category of an "Act of God." To William Alden Smith, it was unthinkable that 1,500 men, women, and children should lose their lives because of carelessness and bureaucratic inertia and no one could be called to account for it. Very well, then—it wouldn't happen again.

When Senator Smith presented his report to the full Senate on May 18, 1912, the gallery was packed and every senator was present to hear Smith's summation. Smith gave one of the best speeches of his career, reasoned yet filled with emotion. He outlined the events leading up to the collision, retold the tale of the sinking liner, and described how the *Carpathia* had rushed at her own peril to come to the survivors' rescue. Then he presented his conclusions.

As much as he admired Captain Smith, William Alden could not hold him blameless. The years of safe navigation had caused the captain to become complacent, he said, just when he needed to be his most cautious. The *Titanic* had been going too fast, with inadequate precautions taken, when she entered the area where the ice was known to be waiting. While Senator Smith would not go very far in criticizing the man who had paid for his mistakes with his life, he hoped that the lesson was clear—accepted practice on the North Atlantic shipping lanes was no longer acceptable. Ships should be required to reduce speed and post extra lookouts when conditions became hazardous, and strict procedures for bringing wireless messages to the bridge and posting them properly once there would need to be implemented.

Lifeboats were dealt with summarily: there would be no more formulas or computations. Ships would carry enough lifeboats to hold every passenger and crewman aboard. Similarly there would be a requirement for twenty-four hour wireless watches to be maintained on all ships equipped with a wireless set.

For all his supposed ineptitude and incompetence, Senator Smith had correctly divined the causes of the disaster and suggested intelligent measures to prevent a similar tragedy in the future. His recommendations, along with his suggestion to create an international patrol of the North Atlantic areas commonly threatened by ice hazards, were seen on both sides of the Atlantic as clearheaded and reasonable. Even the British press was generally approving in tone, although a few papers, refusing to moderate their hostility, suggested that the recommendations had actually come from other members of the committee, implying that the investigation had been productive in spite of Senator Smith.

On the subject of Bruce Ismay, Smith was remarkably restrained. That Smith had little respect for Ismay was evident throughout the hearings, but without solid evidence that Ismay had usurped Captain Smith's authority—and Captains Rostron and Sealby had made it quite clear that legally no one had that prerogative on any ship in the North Atlantic—Smith was not about to make such an accusation. He didn't let Ismay off the hook entirely, though, stating, "I think the presence of Mr. Ismay and Mr. Andrews stimulated the ship to a greater speed than it would have made under ordinary conditions, although I cannot fairly ascribe to either of them any instruction to this effect. The very presence of the owner and builder unconsciously stimulates endeavor. . . ."

There was little hesitation when Smith addressed the subject of Captain Lord and the *Californian*. After extensively reviewing all the testimony of Lord and his officers, of Assistant Engineer Gill, of the *Titanic*'s officers concerning the unknown ship they saw, and the expert findings of the U.S. Navy's Hydrographers' Office, Smith came to a devastating conclusion:

> I am well aware from the testimony of the captain of the *Californian* that he deluded himself with the idea that there was a ship between the *Titanic* and the *Californian*, but there was no ship seen there at daybreak and no intervening rockets were seen by anyone on the *Titanic*—although they were looking longingly for such a sign—and saw only the white light of the *Californian*, which was flashed the moment the ship struck and taken down when the vessel sank. A ship . . . could not have gone west without passing the *Californian* on the north or the *Titanic* on the south. That ice floe held but two ships—the *Titanic* and the *Californian*.[21]

Smith soundly condemned Captain Lord for failing to come to the *Titanic's* assistance "in accordance with the dictates of humanity, international usage, and the requirements of law," and he called upon Great Britain to take action against the owners and master of the *Californian*; then by way of emphasizing his point, he loudly praised Captain Rostron of the *Carpathia* for his heroism, eventually introducing a resolution to award Rostron a Medal of Honor, which Congress passed by acclamation.

His investigation complete, the committee's findings duly entered into the *Congressional Record,* and his recommendations codified in Senate Bill 6976 (which would quickly pass both houses of Congress), Senator William Alden Smith now faded from the scene. His investigation had run for four weeks, called eight-two witnesses, including fifty-nine British subjects, and collected testimony, affidavits, and exhibits totalling 1,198 pages.[22]

What the world was now anticipating was the inquiry by the British Board of Trade, which, as so many British papers had repeatedly pointed out during the Senate investigation, was to be a "more satisfactory method" of arriving at the truth of what had caused the *Titanic* to sink. The inquiry would be conducted in a far more formal manner than the Senate investigation, and be constituted as a court of law under British jurisprudence.

The process began on April 29, when returning *Titanic* crewmen came down the gangway from the liner *Lapland,* which had brought them from New York to Plymouth, only to be put in a quarantine which was just short of imprisonment. They were not released until they were met by Board of Trade representatives waiting to take sworn statements from each of them. The Board of Trade then reviewed their statements, decided as to which crewmen would be called on to testify, and issued formal subpoenas to the ones chosen. The process took several days, during which the crewmen were allowed only limited contact with their families. Despite the bitterness this arrangement caused, not to mention its questionable legality, there were no confrontations between crew members and Board of Trade representatives.[23]

The Board of Trade Court of Inquiry, as constituted by its Royal Warrant, was scheduled to begin sitting in session on May 3, in the London Scottish Drill Hall, near Buckingham Gate, and would consist of a president and five assessors. The assessors were all chosen for their distinguished credentials: Captain A. W. Clarke, an elder brother of Trinity House; Rear Admiral the Honorable Sommerset Gough-Calthorpe, RN (Ret.); Commander Fitzhugh Lyon, RNR; J. H. Biles, professor of Naval Architecture, University of Glasgow; and Mr. Edward Chaston, RNR, senior engineer assessor to the Admiralty. Presiding overall, indeed dominating the court as thoroughly as William Alden Smith had dominated the Senate investigation, would be the fearsome Lord Mersey, Commissioner of Wrecks and formerly president of the Probate, Divorce and Admiralty Division of the High Court. Though Mersey would have the "assistance" of the five assessors, his authority over the Court would be absolute: the areas of investigation, the witnesses called, the admissibility of evidence, and the final findings of the court would all be determined by him.

Lord Mersey—John Charles Bigham, Baron Mersey of Toxteth (Lancastershire)—had first come to prominence as a public figure in Great Britain in 1896 when he headed an inquiry into the notorious Jameson Raid. From the first he exhibited those characteristics which would come to be an inescapable part of any inquest Mersey conducted: he was autocratic, impatient, and not a little testy. Above all, he did not suffer fools gladly, and he was famous for the barbed rebukes he issued from the bench to witnesses or council that he considered were wasting the court's time. (The transcript of the inquiry records show how at one point Alexander Carlisle related that he and Harold Sanderson of the White Star Line often merely rubber-stamped decisions made at a meeting by Lord Pirrie and Bruce Ismay with the words, "Mr. Sanderson and I were more or less dummies." Mersey replied dryly, "That has a certain verisimilitude.") Off the bench, Mersey was a soft-spoken, mild-mannered man of good taste; he was well educated and thoroughly urbane. Politically he was a Liberal, and his company and conversation were much sought after in London social circles. It was to his lasting credit that he did not allow his political views to influence his role as wreck commissioner.[24]

That this was not expected to be the case was a view widely held among professional seamen in Great Britain. The inquiry was being carried out by the Board of Trade, but the board was held by many to be in part responsible, if not for the accident itself, then certainly for the lack of sufficient lifeboats. The idea of the Board of Trade conducting an investigation of itself caused a number of people to suspect that a whitewash brush would be liberally wielded, the "more satisfactory manner" of a British investigation notwithstanding. Second Officer Lightoller homed in on the inconsistency with unerring accuracy: "The B.O.T. had passed that ship [the *Titanic*] as in all respects fit for sea, in every sense of the word, with sufficient margin of safety for everyone on board. Now the B.O.T. was holding an inquiry into the loss of that ship—hence the whitewash brush. . . ." What was to surprise many observers, but not those who knew Lord Mersey well, was the surprising objectivity that the court was to display during the next five weeks. Despite the anticipation of many that the findings would be a whitewashing, when the investigation was over, the Board of Trade would not escape Mersey's keen eye or sharp tongue.

Some people have suggested that the findings of the Senate investigation had some bearing on how Lord Mersey decided to conduct the Court of Inquiry, but that doesn't seem likely. The court began hearing testimony two weeks before Senator Smith released his committee's findings; furthermore, the emphasis of the two investigations were quite different, though complementary. The Senate subcommittee had emphasized asking how the disaster happened; the Mersey Commission asked why. Some twenty-one passengers were called to testify before the Senate investigation; Lord Mersey would call only three. The majority of witnesses appearing before the court would be officers and crewmen from the *Titanic*, *Carpathia*, and *Californian*; various experts in the field of ship construction; and representatives of Harland and Wolff and the White Star Line. In fact, of the three passengers who would testify, none of them would be as material witnesses.[25]

The court sat for a total of thirty-six days over the next eight weeks, called ninety-six witnesses, and asked more than 25,600 questions, the longest and most detailed Court of Inquiry ever held in Great Britain. The transcript was more than a thousand pages, supplemented by exhibits and depositions, and the Report of the Commissioner added another forty-five pages. The entire cost of the inquiry came to nearly £20,000.[26]

Undoubtedly one of the highlights of the inquiry was the intense interrogation on May 14 of Captain Lord and the officers of the *Californian*. The story that had broken in the American papers and been so doggedly pursued by Senator Smith had created an equally huge sensation in Great Britain. The attorney general, Sir Rufus Isaacs, was relentless in his questioning of Lord, pressing over and over again on points in his testimony that Isaacs found unsatisfactory. Lord tried to explain that he had only been told of a single rocket being fired, that he had not seen any of the rockets himself, that he was never informed by his officers that they thought the rocket—or rockets—might be a signal of a ship in distress, and that he had only the vaguest recollection of the night of April 14–15 as he had been asleep in the chartroom at the time. This satisfied neither Sir Rufus nor Lord Mersey, especially when Lord's officers later contradicted him on nearly every important point in their testimony, most significantly about the number of times Lord had been told about the rockets and how many there were. Mersey drew attention to the same discrepancies in Captain Lord's defense that Senator Smith had, notably the suspicious lack of any entries about rockets in the *Californian*'s log and the disappearance of the relevant pages of the scrap log.[27]

An additional factor in the drama came out not in the courtroom but outside it, when the *Californian*'s officers, reproached by the wife of one of the *Titanic*'s officers, openly admitted that they had seen distress signals that night, but had not been able to rouse Captain Lord to take any action. More importantly, it became readily apparent that they tried none too hard, for fear of their captain's temper. The truth finally came out: Captain Lord was a virtual tyrant, sharp-tongued and quick with disparaging remarks, and his officers were utterly cowed by him, to the point that they were bereft of any initiative, leaving all decisions to the captain. The image created in the mind of the public ever since has been of the *Californian*'s officers standing idly on the bridge, so thoroughly intimidated by their captain that they would rather watch another ship sink than run the risk of facing his wrath.[28]

Another of the highlights of the inquiry, for the British public at least, came on May 20, when Sir Cosmo and Lady Duff Gordon were called to testify. Vicious rumors had started after the survivors had been rescued by the

Carpathia that the £5 Sir Cosmo had promised the crewmen in Boat 1 to start a new kit for each of them had in fact been a bribe to keep them from rowing back to the wreck to pick up survivors. The situation was not helped by the ill-conceived idea to have the men from Boat 1 pose for a group picture, complete with lifebelts, for the Duff Gordons on the Boat Deck of the *Carpathia*. Lady Duff Gordon had only wanted the photograph as a memento, but to many of the survivors, still stunned and reeling from the disaster, it appeared as if the Duff Gordons were treating those crewmen like their personal rowing team.

In hopes of quashing the rumors, Sir Cosmo and his wife petitioned Lord Mersey to be allowed to give evidence before the court. Lord Mersey agreed, and everyone who had been in Boat 1 appeared at the Inquiry, where Lord Mersey, Sir Rufus Isaacs, and Henry Duke, K.C., M.P., the Duff Gordons' defense counsel, and other attorneys present subjected them to an intense cross-examination. When Lady Duff Gordon and Sir Cosmo were questioned first by Thomas Scanlan, who represented the National Sailors' and Firemens' Union, then by W. D. Harbinson, who was representing the Third Class passengers, an overt sense of class antagonism crept into their questions. At one point Harbinson's manner grew so antagonistic toward Sir Cosmo that Lord Mersey interrupted the questioning to remind him, "Your duty is to assist me to arrive at the truth, not to try and make out a case for this class against that class."

Harbinson relented, but the feeling was still there, and a short while later he asked Sir Cosmo, "Would I accurately state your position if I summed it up in this way, that you considered that when you were safe yourselves that all the others might perish?" It was an outrageous question under any circumstances, even actionable if it had been asked outside of a courtroom, and Mersey brought Harbinson up short again, asking "Do you think a question of that kind is fair to this witness? I do not! The witness' position is bad enough!" Harbinson, cowed by Mersey's outburst and sensing he was doing his clients no good by antagonizing the wreck commissioner, sat down, and Sir Cosmo was dismissed.[29]

The findings of the wreck commission were delivered by Lord Mersey on June 30. He concluded that the loss of the *Titanic* was due solely to the damage caused by the collision with the iceberg and not to any inherent design flaw in the ship, and that collision was the direct result of the ship steaming into an area known to be hazardous with ice at an excessively high speed. There was an insufficient lookout kept, given the danger of the sea conditions, and that an overall sense of complacency among the ship's officers had contributed to this oversight.

The *Titanic*'s lifeboats, though fulfilling the Board of Trade requirements, were insufficient in number, and a change in the regulations was necessary. The boats themselves had been properly lowered but not properly filled, and had been insufficiently manned with trained seamen. As for the

Duff Gordons, they were exonerated of any wrongdoing, although Lord Mersey made it clear that he believed that they could have acted more responsibly, or at least conducted themselves a little less tactlessly.

On the subject of Captain Lord and the *Californian*, Lord Mersey was merciless. The evidence, he said, made it abundantly clear to him that the ship the *Californian*'s officers saw from their bridge, and watched as she fired rocket after rocket, was the *Titanic*. Captain Lord's excuse that he was sound asleep in the chartroom and couldn't recall having been told about the rockets didn't wash with Lord Mersey, and he believed that Captain Lord had acted most improperly in failing to ascertain what was the matter with that ship and go to the stricken liner's aid. The language of his conclusion was unequivocable:

> There are inconsistencies and contradictions in the story as told by different witnesses but the truth of the matter is plain. . . . When she first saw the rockets, the *Californian* could have pushed through the ice to the open water without any serious risk and so have come to the assistance of the *Titanic*. Had she done so she might have saved many if not all of the lives that were lost.[30]

Mersey was not alone in his judgement of Captain Lord's culpability: even among professional seamen there were serious questions raised about the master of the *Californian*. At one point, after the proceedings were closed but before Lord Mersey drew up his report, Capt. A. H. F. Young, the professional member of the marine department for the Board of Trade, went so far as to press Lord Mersey for a formal inquiry into Lord's "competency to continue as Master of a British ship." Apparently Mersey considered the request, but a legal technicality barred him from taking any action.[31]

Finally, the Board of Trade received a fair amount criticism, despite earlier misgivings in some quarters. In addition to condemning the outdated lifeboat regulations, the court found the board's required "boat drill" procedures laughable: usually one or two boats filled with picked crewmen who would go through the motions of rigging and lowering a lifeboat while the ship was in port. Despite his reputation as the "best cursed B.O.T. representative in Southern England," Captain Clarke received some sharp words for permitting such a lax drill to suffice. Nothing had been done to acquaint the passengers with their boat assignments or any of the lifesaving equipment on board. That too would have to change.[32]

There would be, over the years, observers and writers, mostly Americans, unfamiliar with the usage of British officialdom in the days before World War I, who would conclude that, because Lord Mersey did not explicitly condemn Captain Lord, the White Star Line, or the Board of Trade as resoundingly as Senator Smith did, the whitewash brush had been applied. To do so is to completely misunderstand the quiet, understated language with which Great Britain's senior civil servants expressed themselves. Mersey's report was every bit as damning as Senator Smith's—it was simply less overt.

When it was released, Lord Mersey's report was considered to be far more erudite, comprehensive, and knowledgeable than that of Senator Smith's inquiry. But with the passage of time, Senator Smith's effort has fared far better in the hands of scholars and legal experts. Despite all the pomp and procedural trappings of the Mersey Inquiry, it was not as comprehensive as the American investigation, although in fairness, it has to be said that its warrant didn't permit the scope of inquiry that Smith's committee possessed. Ultimately, the American investigation, for all its seeming informality, or perhaps because of it, learned far more about what happened in those desperate hours than did the British inquiry. The Board of Trade's inquest still has its notable defenders, such as Walter Lord, and on technical matters it far surpassed anything Senator Smith and his colleagues learned, but it was Senator Smith's persistent and perceptive questioning that has left the world with the most vivid account of what really happened to the men and women aboard the *Titanic*.

With Lord Mersey's summation of the Court of Inquiry's findings, the inquests were closed and the investigations completed. Civil suits against the White Star Line by survivors and victims' families would drag on for years, but between the Senate investigation and the British Court of Inquiry, everything constructive that could be done had been done. Lessons were learned and conclusions drawn, and no amount of damages could bring back the dead. It could only be hoped that after the best efforts of legislators, regulating bodies, and the officers and crewmen of the North Atlantic liners were put forward, there would never be a repetition of that awful April night.

CHAPTER 13

Requiem

The land shall mourn, each family by itself. . . .
—Zachariah 12:12

ON GENTLY ROLLING HILLSIDES ON THE OUTSKIRTS OF HALIFAX, NOVA SCO-
tia, far enough from the center of the city that an entirely appropriate atmosphere of tranquility covers everything, sit row upon row of grey granite
stones, all similarly carved and shaped. Some are more weatherworn than
others, some bear names, others are nameless, but all have cut into their
sloping upper faces a date: April 15, 1912. Below the date there is a number.
The number is that given to the body that rests beneath the headstone,
when it was plucked from the North Atlantic eighty-five years ago. They are
all from the *Titanic*.[1]

Late in the evening of April 15, 1912, the Halifax agents of the White Star
Line, A.G. Jones and Company, chartered the Commercial Cable Company's
cable ship *Mackay-Bennett* to recover as many of the victims of the *Titanic* as
possible. Hurriedly placed orders for tones of ice, coffins—more than a hundred of them—as well as embalmers' supplies were quickly filled, and by
morning of April 17, Capt. F. H. Lardner had assembled an all-volunteer crew,
while some forty members of the Funeral Directors Association of the Maritime Provinces had come aboard, and the *Mackay-Bennett* was ready to sail at
noon. (In the days and months to come the White Star Line would be frequently, and sometimes justly, accused of callousness. In contrast, the voyage
of the *Mackay-Bennett* was a genuinely compassionate act: the company was
under no contract to recover any of the victims, especially at its own expense.[2]

Already passenger ships were giving the area where the *Titanic* sank a
wide berth. True, the shipping lane had been shifted some sixty miles farther
south the day after the disaster, but even more compelling was the primal
urge to shun the dead, and what captain would wish to present his passengers with the spectacle of a sea strewn with wreckage and floating bodies?

One skipper, Captain Nelson of the *Volturno*—herself to be immolated in a horrendous fire with terrible loss of life only eighteen months later—withheld news of the sinking ship from his officers, crew, and passengers until the ship made port in New York.

Nevertheless, some ships did pass near the spot where the *Titanic* went down, and the wireless messages guided the *Mackay-Bennett* to the spot. One ship, the *Bremen*, reported nearly a hundred bodies at 42.00'N, 49.20'W. When the *Bremen* docked at New York, several of her passengers were buttonholed by reporters, and among the most memorable of their accounts was that of Mrs. Johanna Stunke, who painted a heartbreaking vignette of unwitnessed tragedy:

> We saw the body of one woman dressed only in her night dress, clasping a baby to her breast. Close by was the body of another woman with her arms clasped tightly round a shaggy dog. . . . We saw the bodies of three men in a group, all clinging to a chair. Floating by just beyond them were the bodies of a dozen men, all wearing lifebelts and clinging desperately together as though in their last struggle for life.[3]

The *Mackay-Bennett* arrived on the scene the evening of April 20, but night fell before the crew could begin work, so the next morning the laborious, back-breaking task of recovering the dead began. The seas were heavy and the wind bitingly chill as the boats were rowed back and forth and each body dragged aboard. All day long they worked, until by dusk the men of the Mackay-Bennett had recovered fifty-one bodies.

As each body was brought aboard the *Mackay-Bennett*, a numbered square of canvas was attached to it. Any valuables or personal effects found were placed in a correspondingly numbered canvas bag. Since few of the dead carried any identification, a complete description of each victim was made—height, weight, age (estimated if not known), hair and eye color, any birthmarks, scars, or tattoos. All this information was meticulously recorded in the hope that it might provide the means to identify the dead. (When Edward A. Kent's body was brought on board, he was still carrying the miniature of her mother that Mrs. Candee had given him for safekeeping. The miniature, which was eventually returned to Mrs. Candee, was one of the items used to confirm Kent's identity.)

The sea had not been kind to the bodies: exposure to the wind and water had seemingly aged many of them—Second Class passenger Reginald Butler, for example, was only twenty-five when he died, but the Halifax coroner would estimate his age at forty-two. Several of the bodies were so badly disfigured after a week's immersion in the sea that the embalmer considered it pointless to carry them all the way back to Halifax. At 8:15 that evening, a burial service was held on the forecastle deck. Afterward, the *Mackay-Bennett*'s engineer Frederick Hamilton, described it in his diary that night:

The tolling of the bell summoned all hands to the forecastle where thirty bodies are to be committed to the deep, each carefully sewed up in canvas. It is a weird scene, this gathering. The crescent moon is shedding a faint light on us, as the ship lays wallowing in the giant rollers. The funeral service is conducted by the Reverend Canon Hind; for nearly an hour the words "For as much as it hath pleased . . . we commit this body to the deep" are repeated and at each interval there comes, splash! as the weighted body plunges into the sea, there to sink to a depth of about two miles. Splash, splash, splash.[4]

Working from sunrise to sunset, by twilight on April 22, the crew of the *Mackay-Bennett* had recovered 187 of the *Titanic*'s dead. Captain Lardner informed White Star's New York office that he would need help, but the Halifax agents had anticipated such an eventuality and had already chartered the Anglo-American Telegraph Company's cable ship *Minia* on April 21. She sailed the next day and by April 26, the two ships were searching together. By noon that day 14 more bodies had been pulled from the sea, and the *Mackay-Bennett* had exhausted her stores. She put about for Halifax with 190 victims aboard, while the *Minia* would continue the search for more corpses until May 3. Between them the two ships recovered 323 bodies (5 more were later picked up by two other ships) and 119 of them were buried at sea.

The *Mackay-Bennett*, her colors at half-mast, arrived at Halifax on April 30 and immediately slipped into Coaling Wharf Number 4 in His Majesty's Naval Dockyard. There, shielded from morbid photographers by high concrete walls and protected by a joint police and naval guard, the bodies were unloaded. Even in death, the careful distinctions of class were observed: first came the crewmen, packed in ice but not embalmed nor sewn in canvas; followed by the bodies of the Second and Third Class passengers, which were sewn up in canvas; last off were the First Class passengers, all embalmed, all in coffins.

The authorities in Halifax had thoroughly prepared for the *Mackay-Bennett*'s return. The Mayflower Curling Rink on Agricola Street, just a few blocks from the dockyard, was turned into a temporary morgue, where sixty-seven canvas-enclosed cubicles had been set up, each holding three bodies. Only people who could produce proof of identity or authorization from next of kin were allowed inside the morgue. The second floor of the rink was converted to a suite of offices for the coroner and his staff, who worked hard at producing the documentation necessary for issuing death certificates. In each case the cause of death was listed as "accidental drowning, S.S. *Titanic*, at sea."

The first body to be claimed and released was Number 124, John Jacob Astor. Despite the condition of the body—crushed and covered with soot (Astor had been caught beneath the forward funnel when it fell into the sea)—identification had been a fairly simple procedure. The records show that he wore a blue serge suit, a blue handkerchief (with, curiously, the initials "A.V." on it), a gold-buckled belt, brown boots with red rubber soles, and a brown flannel shirt with "J. J. A." on the collar. It was this shirt that provided the positive identification of Astor's body, not as commonly believed, the amount of cash he carried. (This included £225 in notes, $2,440 in American currency, £5 in gold, 7s in silver, and 50 francs. Other personal items included a gold watch, gold cuff links, and a diamond ring with three stones.) The body was claimed by his son Vincent, who, along with the family's lawyer, Nicholas Biddle, and the skipper of Astor's private yacht, Captain Roberts, had taken a special train to Halifax.

The purser's list prepared aboard the *Mackay-Bennett*, which the coroner was now using to assist in identifying the bodies, makes for melancholy reading. Some entries are remarkably detailed, which often meant that identification was relatively easy: many others were heartbreakingly stark, making identification nearly impossible. For example: "Number 33; Male, estimated age: 30; blue suit; no marks; brown hair and moustache; no effects." Or: "Number 23, Female, about 25, fair hair. Sum of 150 Finnish marks sewn into clothing." Or: "Number 63; Female, estimated age 22, dark black hair. Clothing—blue dress and blouse, black shoes. Effects—purse with miniature photo; key; few coins; photo locket. No marks on body or clothing. Probably Third Class." Or: "Number 88; Male, estimated age 50, dark hair, moustache light. Clothing—dungaree trousers, flannel shirt. No marks on body or clothing, no effects. Fireman." One particularly sad entry is Number 328—"four feet, six inches, about 14 years old, golden brown hair, very dark skin, refined features. Lace trimmed red-and-black overdress, black underdress, green striped undershirt, black woolen shawl and felt slippers. Probably third class."[5]

In what was probably the strangest twist in the process of identification, the body of Michel Navatril was originally identified as "Mr. Hoffmann," the alias under which he was traveling. It was money that enabled authorities to identify "Mr. Hoffmann" as Michel Navatril: he was being sought by a number of French creditors for outstanding debts. The creditors had issued, on both sides of the Atlantic, a detailed description of Navatril, and this description came to the attention of the Nova Scotian authorities. It matched the body of "Mr. Hoffmann" so closely that the creditors' representatives were called in, and in short order they were able to confirm that the body was indeed that of Michel Navatril. When his body was recovered, the equivalent of several hundred dollars in French francs were found in the various pockets of his clothing. The representatives promptly placed liens on the cash he had been carrying.[6]

Three days after the *Mackay-Bennett* returned, the burials began. Based on instructions from relatives—or in the case of the unidentified or unclaimed bodies, educated guesswork about the victim's religion—those still at the curling rink were designated to be buried in one of three Halifax cemeteries: Fairview, which was a nonsectarian plot; Baron de Hirsch cemetery, right next to Fairview, for those who were Jewish; or Mount Olivet, about a half-mile to the south, for Roman Catholics. All the bodies were properly embalmed, placed in simple yellow-pine coffins, and on Friday, May 3, 1912, the first of a series of funeral services were held.

At 9:30 A.M., a Mass was celebrated at St. Mary's Cathedral, with the Archbishop of Nova Scotia presiding. The cathedral was filled with mourners, which included representatives from the White Star Line, while the coffins of four victims, all young women, rested on a catafalque. At the conclusion of the service, they were taken to Mount Olivet, where they were buried at 4:00 P.M.

At 11:00 A.M. a service began in the Brunswick Street Methodist Church for fifty victims who were to be buried at Fairview. As the service was intended to be nonsectarian, it was conducted by the Halifax Evangelical Alliance. The chancel was covered with floral arrangements, the sanctuary draped in black, and in the congregation sat the lieutenant governor of Nova Scotia, along with officers from HMCS *Niobe* (her crew had provided an honor guard at the curling rink) and from the garrison of the Citadel in Halifax. The scripture read by the Very Reverend Dean Crawford was from Psalm 90 ("Thou dost sweep men away; they are like a dream, like grass which is renewed in the morning . . . in the evening it fades and withers.") The sermon was given by the Rev. Dr. McKinnon of Pine Hill Presbyterian College. At the close of the service, the band of the Royal Canadian Regiment played "Nearer, My God, to Thee" as a recessional while the coffins were carried to waiting hearses.

At this point, in an especially tactless episode involving the *Titanic's* dead, Rabbi Jacob Walter, a leader in Halifax's small Jewish community, took it upon himself to decide that, in addition to those victims already designated for burial in the Jewish cemetery, ten of the bodies intended to be laid to rest in Fairview should go to Baron de Hirsch instead. While the memorial services were being conducted in the city, Walter pried open a number of coffins not yet scheduled for burial and decided that ten of the bodies he inspected were Jewish (how he determined this was never explained). Walter then persuaded workers to move the ten coffins he had arbitrarily selected from Fairview to Baron de Hirsch. Provincial authorities happened upon these transfers as they were taking place and immediately put a stop to them. White Star records later showed that four of the ten bodies Rabbi Walter had picked out were actually Roman Catholic, though they were not intended for interment in Mount Olivet, and the families of the other six had left specific instructions for their burial. What motivated Rabbi Walter to commit such a bizarre act, or what he hoped to gain from it will never be known. To its credit, Halifax's Jewish community repudiated the rabbi for his behavior.

Ironically, one victim who was buried in Baron de Hirsch by mistake was "Mr. Hoffman"—Michel Navatril. Because he had first been identified as Hoffmann, it was believed that he was Jewish, and the error was not discovered until after the burial. Navatril was actually a Roman Catholic, but in a deeply touching act of kindness, the Jews of Halifax chose to allow Navatril to remain among their kin in Baron de Hirsch, and had his correct name cut into his headstone.[7]

Halifax is a seafaring town, and like any seafaring town, beneath its sometimes rough and seemingly uncaring exterior lies a heart as big as the sea itself. That this was so was shown on May 4, 1912, a day any Haligonian can regard with quiet pride. Only one burial took place that day, but it brought out all the concern and sympathy that Halifax could show.

The body of a blonde-haired boy, about two years old, had been picked up by the *Mackay-Bennett* on April 20. The purser's entry was pathetically brief: "No identification; no effects." The sight of the little fellow was enough to move even the tough seamen of the cable ship's crew to tears, and once the word of his plight reached Halifax—no one knew who he was and no one came forward to claim him—the city's heart went out to him. Provincial authorities and White Star officials were inundated with offers to sponsor the boy's funeral. Finally, Captain Lardner and the crew of the *Mackay-Bennett*, who had first requested to take responsibility for the child, were granted permission to sponsor the service.

St. George's Anglican Church was filled that Saturday morning with mourners, and a huge crowd waited quietly outside. The chancel overflowed with wreaths and flowers. After a simple but moving service, six crewmen from the *Mackay-Bennett* shouldered the small white coffin and carried it to the waiting hearse, which then drove to Fairview Cemetery. There on the hillside overlooking Fairview Cove the boy was laid to rest among the others from the *Titanic*. A few years later a granite marker would be placed over the little fellow's grave, with the inscription: "Erected to the Memory of an Unknown Child Whose Remains Were Recovered after the Disaster to the *Titanic*, April 15, 1912." The marker was paid for by Captain Lardner and his crew.

Eventually the boy would be tentatively identified as Gosta Leonard Paulson. He had sailed from Southampton with his mother, two sisters, and a brother. By coincidence, his mother is buried only a few feet from him. His sisters and brother were never found.[8]

Ultimately, six weeks' searching by four ships resulted in the recovery of 328 of the *Titanic*'s dead. Of them, 119 were buried at sea; of the 209 brought back to Halifax, 59 were claimed and taken away for burial elsewhere. The rest remained in Halifax, and the city has been kind to them.

All cemeteries have a certain tranquility about them, but there seems to be a special quietness that surrounds the four rows of marker stones showing where the *Titanic*'s dead lie at Fairview, a quietness that is equally shared by the plots in Mount Olivet and Baron de Hirsch. All three graveyards are well tended—the marker stones are not allowed to fall in disrepair, though the harsh Halifax winters have taken their toll on some. A corner of Thomas Baxter's headstone is deeply fractured and in danger of breaking off, the foundation of the marker over the grave of the little boy has become badly eroded, while fissures have appeared in the bases of other stones.

Every grave is marked with a space on the stone for a name and the words "Died April 15, 1912." Whenever known the name has been inscribed: one in Fairview reads "Jock Law Hume"—he was the second violinist in the orchestra, the young man whose mother didn't want him to sail on the *Titanic*, but who needed the extra money he would earn because he would be getting married in a few weeks. A fellow musician, the bass-violist Fred Clarke, is buried in Mount Olivet. Save for Wallace Hartley, whose remains were sent home to Lancastershire, none of the other musicians from the *Titanic*'s band were ever found—nor were any of the ship's officers or engineers, though more than one of the bodies never positively identified were described in the coroner's report as "probably" or "possibly" an engineer.[9]

In Mount Olivet and Baron de Hirsch cemeteries, all of the stones are identical (there are nineteen victims buried in Mount Olivet, ten in Baron de Hirsch), each stone standing some eighteen inches high, fourteen wide, and seven deep. In Fairview Cemetery, most of the marker stones are of the same design, but a few stones are larger than the others and bear long, elaborate inscriptions.

One is dedicated "In Memoriam—Ernest Edward Samuel Freeman, last surviving son of Capt. S.W. Kearney Freeman, R.N., Husband of Laura Mary Jane Freeman, Lost in the 'Titanic' disaster April 15, 1912. He remained at his post of duty, seeking to save others, regardless of his own life and went down with the ship. Erected by Mr. J. Bruce Ismay to commemorate a long and faithful service." It would be interesting to know if Ismay ever contemplated the irony of that inscription—though in fairness to Ismay it should also be remembered that he set up a lifetime pension for young Freeman's parents.

The inscription on another stone reads:

> In Memory of Our Dear Son, Harold Reynolds, who lost his life in the "Titanic" disaster, April 15, 1912.

> Out of that bitter waste
> Alone with Thee
> Thou didst each hero saint
> From sorrow free
> No human help around I see
> Nearer to Thee
> See angel faces beckon me

Nearer to Thee
In the midst of life we are in death

Even eight-five years later it isn't difficult to imagine the grief of the parents who raised the stone to "George H. Dean, Lost on S.S. 'Titanic' April
15, 1912, aged 19 years. Very deeply mourned by his sorrowing parents Fred
and Mary Dean." A similar heartache comes through the words carved into
the marker for a steward, Herbert Cave:

> In Loving Memory of Herbert Cave, dearly beloved husband of
> Gertrude Agnes Cave, lost in the "Titanic" April 15, 1912, aged
> 39 years.

There let my way appear
Steps unto heaven
All that Thou send'st to me
In mercy given
Angels shall beckon me
Nearer my God to Thee
Nearer to Thee

A stone dedicated to a trimmer reads:

> Sacred to the memory of Everett Edward Elliott of the heroic
> crew S. S. "Titanic" died on duty April 15, 1912. Aged 24 years.

Each man stood at his post
While all the weaker ones
Went by, and showed once
More to all the world
How Englishmen should die.

A trust fund was set up by the White Star Line for the perpetual care of
the graves in Fairview and Mount Olivet—those in Baron de Hirsch are provided for by the Beth Israel Congregation of Halifax. These days the fund is
administered by Cunard, which assumed that responsibility when it took
over White Star in the 1930s. Visitors come quite regularly to Fairview
Cemetery, less frequently to Mount Olivet and Baron de Hirsch. Some leave
flowers, other wreaths, many just stand quietly, trying to imagine what it was
like that cold April night so many years ago. It is a lasting image, the site of
so many graves, holding the remains of people who would have ordinarily
died in obscurity, but now are mourned by total strangers.

CHAPTER 14

Resurrection

Will you draw out Leviathan with a fishhook?
—Job 41:1

THE MIDNIGHT WATCH IN THE CONTROL ROOM OF THE RESEARCH VESSEL *Knorr* was promising to be monotonously routine during the first hour or so of September 1, 1985. "Routine" consisted of one man, in this case Bob Lange, sitting before a television monitor, joystick in hand, while two others, Jean-Louis Michel, the team leader, and Stu Harris, kept close watch on banks of instruments that included monitors for side-scanning sonar, bottom-scanning sonar, and a magnetometer, as well as several additional television monitors.

Back and forth the *Knorr* passed across a rigidly defined sector of the ocean, allowing *Argo*, an ungainly looking underwater survey device, to conduct a thorough search of the bottom. This admittedly dull routine, which required tremendous concentration on the part of the men guiding *Argo*, had been going on for more than three weeks, twenty-four hours a day, with no results to show for it—just endless, unchanging views of the seabed. There was no reason to believe that this watch would be any different. In fact, a certain amount of pessimism was beginning to creep into the attitudes of the men who were controlling *Argo*: the *Knorr* was fast approaching the end of the search area; the calm, clear weather that permitted such a laborious effort, only a few weeks each year in this part of the Atlantic, was about to run out; and they seemed to be no closer to finding their elusive quarry than they had been when they began searching on August 9, three weeks before.

All that changed just twelve minutes before 1:00 A.M. Stu Harris suddenly noticed that there was something on one of his monitors that looked like a big circle. "That looks like a part of it," he said. Lange swung the *Argo* toward the object and the picture grew clearer while the object grew larger.

"That's *big*!"

"Look at it, will you?"

The *Argo* moved closer, and now a clearly discernible pattern of rivets appeared on the object. The watchers could see it was cylindrical, probably

close to thirty feet in diameter, and then they saw it had doors, three of
them, furnace doors at that. Suddenly everybody started talking at once.

"It's a boiler!"

"A boiler?"

"LOOKS LIKE A BOILER!"

"YES! YES! FANTASTIC! IT'S A BOILER!"

"Somebody better go get Bob!"

"Bob" is Robert Ballard, Ph.D., one of the last major players to take
the stage in the drama of the *Titanic*. The boiler seen on the television
monitor was one of the twenty-nine boilers installed in the *Titanic* seventy-
three years before—a single-ended boiler from Boiler Room 1. When the
Argo found it lying on the ocean floor, it marked the culmination of an
ambition that had been driving Ballard for more than ten years: he had
found the *Titanic*.[1]

—◆◆◆—

Almost from the moment she disappeared into the depths of the North
Atlantic, the *Titanic* was the object of wildly imaginative plans and schemes
to raise the wreck. Before too long, though, it became apparent to everyone
that the technology of 1912 wasn't up to the task of even finding the ship, let
alone bringing her back up. All that would be left of her were the few objects
plucked by passing ships from the rapidly dispersing field of wreckage in the
middle of the ocean, the photographs taken of her during her brief life, and
the memories of the survivors.

For a brief time, the *Olympic* enjoyed a rather morbid popularity as passengers would cross the Atlantic on her and vicariously relive the disaster,
pointing out to one another places on board where various incidents had
taken place on the *Olympic*'s sister. Among the great favorites were the spot
near the First Class Entrance on the Boat Deck, where the band stood as they
played their last pieces of music; Lifeboat 8, which Mrs. Straus refused to
enter without her husband; and Boat 2, the position from which Collapsible
D had been lowered, after Edith Evans gave up her seat to Mrs. John Brown.
World War I soon ended this rather bizarre pastime, and when the war was
over and the great liners returned to service, the transatlantic passenger trade
had changed beyond recognition. Gone were the days of the grand floating
palaces: a more casual, egalitarian environment, less concerned with ostentation and more with convenience, replaced the rigid class structures and formal manners of the prewar voyages. By the standards of the 1920s, the
ornate elegance of the *Titanic* seemed pretentious and quaint. The ship and
the disaster faded into a distant recess of the public's memory, intermittently
being revived by the editor of some local newspaper on the occasion of the
death of a survivor who had lived in his hometown; commemorated sometimes by the unveiling of a new monument or memorial, with ever-dwin-
dling crowds in attendance; remembered only by an annual ceremony

conducted by the U.S. Coast Guard, which every April 15 dropped a wreath at 41.46 N., 50.15 W.—a tradition that continues to the present day.

The *Titanic* sometimes made an appearance in literature and more often in film during the years between the two world wars. The most bizarre of these was in Nazi Germany, where a lavish production entitled "*Titanic*" was released in 1938. Like most German films of that time, it was laden with heavy-handed National Socialist propaganda: the hero of the film is one of the ship's officers (German, of course, and entirely fictitious) who pleads vainly with the arrogant and overbearing (British) captain to slow the ship down. After the *Titanic* strikes the iceberg, the German officer takes charge and ruthlessly decides who will and will not be allowed into the lifeboats. Obviously, Mr. and Mrs. Straus never appear in the film.

Far less deluded and far more entertaining was a 1930 movie titled "Atlantic," a screen adaptation of a stage play loosely based on the disaster. Then came the 1932 release of "Calvacade," Noel Coward's paean to the British Empire, which provided one of cinema's great moments, when the newlywed couple walks offscreen to reveal a lifering hanging on the railing behind them, bearing the legend "RMS *Titanic*." The scene became a cliché, of course, but by virtue of the fact that Coward had done his home-work: Richard and Emily were never patterned after any specific couple, but they could easily have been any one of a dozen sets of newlyweds aboard the *Titanic*.

The summer of 1952 saw the release of an American production called "*Titanic*," which starred Clifton Webb and Barbara Stanwyck, with Richard Basehart and Robert Wagner in supporting roles. Although the movie was more fiction than fact (including a scene where the iceberg rips open the *port* side of the ship), there are moments of drama in it every bit as powerful and moving as the actual disaster. At one point, as Miss Stanwyck—in charac-ter—was climbing into a lifeboat after saying goodbye to her once-estranged husband, the actress was overcome by the realization that she was recreating an event that forty years earlier had been all too real. She began weeping uncontrollably. It is also interesting to note that the dilemma of the Third Class passengers who didn't know how to reach the lifeboats is depicted with remarkable accuracy in this film, years before the plight of Third Class became a *cause célèbre* among revisionist historians.

But the real revival in the public's interest in the *Titanic* began in 1955. A young lawyer-turned-author named Walter Lord produced a book about the *Titanic* disaster called *A Night To Remember*. He based much of the nar-rative on interviews with approximately sixty survivors, and the result was a work with such immediacy and realism that the public couldn't get enough of it: to date *A Night To Remember* has never been out of print, having gone through thirty-three editions in hardcover and paperback, and has been translated into over a dozen languages. (In 1986, Lord wrote a sequel, *The Night Lives On*; although it was of immense interest to *Titanic* buffs the world over, it lacked the spark of the original.)

Two years after Walter Lord's book appeared, a film adaption bearing the same title played to packed theaters on both sides of the Atlantic. Starring Kenneth More as Lightoller and David McCallum as Harold Bride, the movie was notable for not only its dramatic impact, which was considerable, but its historical faithfulness as well. Fourth Officer Boxhall, who along with Third Officer Pitman were the last surviving officers from the *Titanic*, was one of the film's technical advisors.

A "fan club" of sorts was formed in 1962 with the rather ill-chosen name "*Titanic* Enthusiasts of America," which was later changed to the "*Titanic* Historical Society," which not only sounded better but was more descriptive of the organization's function. Based in Indian Orchard, Massachusetts, the society is the repository for a great amount of information about the *Titanic* and her sisters, as well as all of the great Atlantic liners. The THS would eventually boast a nationwide membership of over five thousand, and similar organizations would soon appear in Great Britain, Ireland, and Canada.

Suddenly the *Titanic* was a frequent fixture in popular culture: the debut of the American television science-fiction series "Time Tunnel" was set aboard the doomed liner; similarly she was featured in episodes of "The Twilight Zone" and "Night Gallery." The *Titanic* even put in an appearance in "Upstairs, Downstairs," the long-running PBS series about the Edwardian period, centered around the Bellamy household, although no one expected that Lady Marjory Bellamy would be among the great liner's victims.

While the disaster held the attention of screenwriters, a number of authors were exploring the idea of bring the ship up from the bottom of the sea. Arthur C. Clarke devoted an entire chapter of his science-fiction novel *Imperial Earth* to a guided tour of the recovered liner, and books as different as Donald A. Stanwood's murder mystery, *The Memory of Eva Ryker*, and Clive Cussler's thriller, *Raise the Titanic!* were centered around expeditions to salvage or recover the ship. Cussler's book was made into a movie that was released in the summer of 1980. Starring Jason Robards and Richard Jordan, "Raise the *Titanic*!" was, at $45 million, the most expensive movie made up to that time. It was memorable for its spectacular special effects but little else, and the movie vanished almost as quickly as the liner did in 1912. Remarking on how little money the film made when compared to its cost, one observer quipped, "It would have been cheaper to lower the ocean!"[2]

The common thread running through all these works was the firm conviction that the *Titanic* had gone to the bottom in one piece, and that the combination of extreme cold, extreme pressure, low salinity, and very little free oxygen had kept the ship in a sort of deep-sea freeze. Everyone, including oceanographers and marine salvage experts, expected that if the ship were ever found, she would be in a state akin to suspended animation, little changed from the moment she reached the bottom of the ocean on April 15, 1912. What Robert Ballard was about to discover would not only command unprecedented attention, but it would also stun the world.

———◆◆◆———

The son of a NASA engineer, Bob Ballard had to overcome a fear of the water at an early age, and by his teens he was an excellent swimmer. He also discovered that the ocean was the love of his life. An undergraduate degree in physical sciences from the University of Santa Barbara, and graduate school at the University of Hawaii studying geophysics provided him with his academic credentials.

In 1967 Bob Ballard, a fresh young "nugget" (ensign) in the U.S. Navy, specializing in oceanography, joined the Woods Hole Oceanographic Institute (WHOI) in Woods Hole, Massachusetts, one of the leading oceanographic research centers in the country, founded in 1930. Working at WHOI was a dream come true for Ballard, who had always taken a hands-on approach to his discipline. By 1973, Ballard, now a civilian, had earned his Ph.D. in marine geology and geophysics, and was assigned to Project FAMOUS, a joint French–American project set up to map the mid-Atlantic Ridge. It was during this two-year-long project that the idea of finding the *Titanic* first occurred to him.

The idea gave impetus to the development of a concept that Ballard, a leader in the electronics revolution of the early 1970s, had been toying with for some time. He believed that the restrictions on "bottom time"—the time actually spent exploring by deep sea submersible—imposed by limited air supplies, battery power, and crew endurance could be eliminated by taking advantage of the new electronic systems available to the oceanographic sciences. The rapidly expanding capabilities of the various electronic systems should be able to eliminate the necessity for having human beings aboard deep-sea research vessels. Ballard wanted to control the sonars, still cameras, television cameras, and all the manned submersibles that carried and actually did most of their work from a command center aboard a ship on the surface.

After one abortive start with a very primitive form of the device he envisioned (a 1978 expedition sponsored by Alcoa Aluminum that ended in disaster when $600,000 of search equipment was accidentally lost on the ocean floor), Ballard finally received funding from the U.S. Navy, which saw that the system he proposed had real promise for applications in submarine warfare. The exploration equipment he subsequently built went by the name of *ANGUS*, the *A*coustically *N*avigated *G*eological *U*nderwater *S*urvey. Essentially a heavy framework supporting equipment for several sonar units arranged along the three major axes, it also contained high-resolution still cameras that use extremely sensitive film (ASA 200,000). The biggest advantage that *ANGUS* offered was the ability to remain on the bottom indefinitely, being controlled remotely from a mother ship, with guidance signals passed through a cable. To Ballard, this was definitely a more efficient—not to mention more comfortable—method of exploring the ocean floor.

The capability to search the bottom of the ocean for extended periods of time gave Ballard the means to pursue his dream: using *ANGUS*, along with a remote-control, real-time television sled called *Argo*, which complemented the capabilities of *ANGUS*, he could conduct a search for the *Titanic*. Not only would the undertaking provide an extensive field test of *ANGUS* and *Argo*, as well as the feasibility of Ballard's remote-control exploration ideas, a concept he calls "telepresence," but the potential publicity would go a long way toward increasing public awareness of the science of oceanography. The U.S. Navy agreed to sponsor a two-part expedition to test Ballard's equipment in the summer of 1985.

The first part was a highly classified operation off the Azores, an attempt to find the remains of the USS *Scorpion*, an attack submarine lost in 1969, as well as the wreck of the Soviet sub that allegedly rammed and sank her. The second part was a French–American expedition to locate the wreck of the *Titanic*. IFREMER, the French Oceanographic Institute, would provide one of the survey ships, *Le Suroit*, in addition to a number of technicians and scientists.

Le Suroit began the search while the *Knorr* was still off the Azores, but by the end of the first week of August, with her supplies running low, she hadn't found anything, and the *Knorr* took over. Three weeks of patient sailing back and forth across the search area towing the *Argo* behind her, a process the crew christened "mowing the lawn," brought the *Knorr* and her crew to the spot where, a little after 1:00 A.M. on September 1, one of the *Argo*'s controllers looked up and said, "Somebody better go get Bob."

Dr. Ballard dashed to the control room, where Jean-Louis Michel played the videotape of the discovery of the boiler for him. On the live-action monitors, a litter-strewn field of wreckage was passing by. There was no doubt about it—that boiler was from the *Titanic*: only the boilers installed in that great trio of White Star ships had that peculiar pattern of rivets on the faces and that particular arrangement of firedoors. Ballard stood transfixed as the seemingly endless field of debris—it was later determined to be more than 600 yards long—passed under the *Argo*'s cameras: lumps of coal; a silver platter; bottles of champagne; rusty bedsprings; chamber pots; leaded glass panels from the First Class Smoking Room; copper pans from one of the galleys; the corroded remains of a workman's tool kit. Ballard looked at the clock, and unconsciously echoing Captain Smith's words from seventy-three years before, muttered, "Oh, my God."

That got everyone's attention, and Ballard quickly explained, "It's nearly two o'clock, close to the time when the *Titanic* went down. I don't know about anybody else, but at twenty past two, I'll be on the fantail." He then turned and left the control room.

By 2:20, almost everyone had joined Ballard on the fantail, an open area at the very stern of the ship. Atypically, for Ballard is not a modest man, he didn't make a big production out of what he had to say. Instead he spoke quietly for a few minutes, saying that each person could be alone with their thoughts, but that it would be fitting to remember the more than 1,500

people who had died that cold April night. After a short silence, Ballard
urged everyone to get back to work; there was still a lot to do.

The *Argo* had been brought up, since "flying" it just forty feet off the sea
floor ran too great a risk of having it run smack into the wreck itself. It was
time for *ANGUS*, and before the weather forced the team to suspend operations, the camera sled was able to shoot a remarkable amount of footage,
including a complete photo-montage of the wreck.

The rest of Bob Ballard's work on the *Titanic* is easily summed up. In
July 1986, a second expedition was launched, again under the sponsorship of
the U.S. Navy, using the research ship *Atlantis II*. This time a manned submersible, the *Alvin*, went along and made a series of eleven dives on the
wreck, taking hundreds of spectacular—and sometimes heart-breaking—pictures. On three of the dives, Ballard was able to test another of his remote-
control devices, a small self-propelled camera pod called *Jason, Jr.*, or *JJ*. It
was only partially successful, but it did enable Ballard to go inside the wreck
at some points and bring back truly memorable photos and video footage.
On the last dive, the *Alvin* placed a bronze plaque on the stern of the wreck,
a memorial to those who went down with the *Titanic*.

Just as had happened in 1985 when Ballard announced the discovery of
the wreck of the *Titanic*, the 1986 expedition was front-page news all over the
world. The still pictures and video footage taken by *Alvin* and *JJ* were repro-
duced thousands of times in newspapers and magazines and endlessly replayed
on national and local news broadcasts, in almost every language. The public's
endless fascination with what Ballard called the "greatest shipwreck of all time"
was further fueled by new discoveries. For more than two weeks, the *Titanic*,
just as in 1912, dominated the news. Daily newspapers, weekly magazines (the
Titanic even made the cover of *Time* for September 10, 1986), supermarket
tabloids, local and national television news broadcasts, all vied with one
another to provide the latest information about Robert Ballard's discoveries.

What Ballard found left everyone gasping in surprise. The most startling
discovery of all was finding the wreck in two pieces: even though several survivors had stated that the ship had broken in two before she sank, their testimony was inconsistent and sometimes contradictory, and expert opinion had
it that she went under in one piece. Ballard came to the conclusion that the
Titanic did break in two just before she took her final plunge, at a point
somewhere in the Engine Room, where, he theorized, the large openings in
the decks that accommodated the engines had created a weak spot in the
hull. (A later study of the contents of the debris field and the wildly differing
conditions of the two halves of the wreck—the bow almost intact, the stern
badly smashed—would make it clear that though the ship's structure began
to fail during her amazing headstand just before she sank, the actual breakup
took place partway to the bottom.)

For years, it had been an article of faith among those who studied the
disaster that the iceberg had ripped a continuous, 300-foot-long gash in the

Titanic's side. But when Ballard took the *Alvin* down to the bow, he couldn't find any sign of such a grievous wound. Admittedly, most of the bow is buried in a massive pile-up of mud, but what Ballard could make out was a series of split seams, popped rivets, and sprung plates—the result of the iceberg bumping and scraping along the side of hull. When Ballard went back to the records of the British inquiry, he found that the rate of flooding indicated an area open to the sea that totalled little more than twelve square feet. Translated into a continuous gash 300 feet in length meant that the cut could have been only about three-quarters of an inch wide—possible with an acetylene torch, but not an iceberg. Nevertheless, bent plates and open seams in the first five compartments caused by the iceberg grinding its way along the *Titanic's* hull would have had the same effect as a long continuous gash: uncontrollable flooding.

The overall condition of the wreck was also startling. For decades oceanographers and marine archaeologists had believed that the ship was sitting in a veritable deep freeze, with the cold water (only a degree or two above freezing) and the tremendous pressure (six tons per square foot) keeping the free oxygen to very low levels and reducing the salinity of the water, retarding corrosion and rust. It was also thought that there would be a near-total absence of marine life, sparing the wood and fabric furnishings of the ship from consumption. Instead, the expedition discovered that the *Titanic* rests in an area where the oxygen and salinity are higher than normal for such a depth, and that wood-boring worms no one suspected lived at those depths had eaten away almost all of the wood. Instead of a near pristine ship, they found a dilapidated wreck, covered with iron stalactites running down her sides. She was slowly but inexorably decaying. As Ballard put it, "The *Titanic* was unlucky to the last. If she'd fallen almost anywhere else, she'd probably be in perfect condition right now. She couldn't even sink in the right place."

Melancholy settled over Ballard as he and his crew continued to explore the *Titanic*, a deep sadness brought on by the constant awareness that they were, in a sense, exploring a tomb. Ballard gave voice to the feeling at a press conference in Washington, D.C., a few days after his return. As he made his closing statement to the press in an emotional yet subdued way that most press conference statements never are, his voice quavered, then broke with barely restrained emotion.

> The *Titanic* itself lies in 13,000 feet of water, on a gently sloping, alpine-like countryside overlooking a small canyon below. Its bow faces north and the ship sits upright on the bottom. . . . There is no light at this depth. . . . It is quiet and peaceful and a fitting place for the remains of this greatest of sea tragedies to rest. May it forever remain that way and may God bless these found souls.[3]

No one could have foreseen the emotional impact the *Titanic* would have, not just on Ballard, but on the rest of the crew of the *Knorr*, and in

1986, the *Atlantis II*. A pall hung over them, almost as if there had been a death in the family. In 1986, when the *Alvin* finished its last dive, the crew knew instinctively that, for them, no one would ever go back to the wreck.

———◆◆◆———

Others would visit the *Titanic* in the years to come. Ballard had gone on record as being opposed to any kind of salvage or recovery of anything associated with the wreck, but IFREMER already possessed the correct coordinates (which Ballard had refused to release, claiming he was trying to protect the wreck). The French were the first to return to the wreck, with expeditions in 1987 and 1993 that retrieved more than 1,800 artifacts, which included one of Purser Hugh McElroy's safes (it was rusted out and empty), an assortment of tableware and utensils, one of the three sets of steam whistles that were once mounted on the funnels, a small leather satchel that contained a few odd bits of jewelry, a pocket watch, a small bag of coins, and a bracelet with the name Amy spelled out in diamonds.

The artifacts were taken through a careful and exacting process of preservation before being put on display in various museums around the world, where tens of thousands of people flocked to view collections of what would normally be the most ordinary objects—a crewman's straight razor, one of Major Peuchen's calling cards, a pair of eyeglasses, a half-dozen dollar bills, a silver coffee service. The greatest of these exhibitions would open on October 4, 1994, at the National Maritime Museum in Greenwich, England—a display that would eventually be viewed by nearly three-quarters of a million people in its one-year exhibit.[4]

A Canadian–Russian–American group in 1990 filmed the ship and the debris field extensively for the IMAX movie *Titanica*. Financed in part by CBS Television (which was producing a special of its own), by the National Geographic Society, and a number of Canadian business firms, the finished production, shot on 70-mm film and shown in special theaters with seven-story-tall screens, played across the United States for six months to sold-out houses. Including narrative and reminiscences by Eva Hart, whose quiet demeanor belied how deeply the disaster still affected her, *Titanica* presented the reality of the ship, her passengers, and her crew to the audience in a way that left no one who saw it unmoved.[5]

The filmmakers had deliberately refrained from bringing back any artifacts from the wreck, but the recovery of wreckage and debris from the *Titanic* continued to be the subject of heated debate, and none of the salvors was more controversial than a company called RMS *Titanic*, Inc. The successor to *Titanic* Ventures, it is a New York-based salvage firm owned by George Tulloch and Arnie Geller, which commissioned IFREMER to excavate part of the wreck site in 1987, when some 800 artifacts were brought up. In 1992, a drawn-out legal battle left *Titanic* Ventures, now reorganized as RMS

Titanic, Inc., as sole owner of all salvage rights to the *Titanic*. In the summers of 1993 and 1994, an intense schedule of dives resulted in nearly 4,000 items being retrieved from the debris field surrounding the ship.

Among the bits and pieces brought up were a section of one of the *Titanic*'s reciprocating engines, a lifeboat davit, three engine-room telegraphs, kitchen utensils, a megaphone that may have been Captain Smith's, and hundreds of pieces of coal from Boiler Room No. 1. Everything that was recovered was said to have come from the debris field, as Tulloch publicly declared that his firm would never touch the wreck itself, although he had a hard time explaining the film showing his submersible, the *Nautile*, forcibly pulling the warning bell from the foremast. (The crow's nest collapsed while the bell above it was being pulled free.) Tulloch would also go on record to say that none of the recovered artifacts would ever be made available for sale to private collectors, but would remain together as a collection available for exhibition.

It was a pledge that did not long endure, as in mid-1995, Tulloch announced that he (Geller was no longer involved) had begun the preparations for what would be touted as the greatest feat of underwater salvage in history: bringing up a section of the *Titanic* herself. In order to raise the money necessary for such an ambitious project (rumored to be in the neighborhood of $17,000,000, a figure never officially confirmed), RMS *Titanic*, Inc., would begin selling the coal that had been recovered to collectors around the world.

It stirred up a hornet's nest of protest. Two distinct camps formed concerning the treatment of the wreck almost as soon as it was discovered in 1985: the "protectionists," the most vocal of whom was Ballard, who wanted the wreck and the debris field left intact and undisturbed; and the "conservationists" who wanted to recover and preserve artifacts from the around the wreck, though they generally believed that the wreck itself should be left untouched. Tulloch, Geller, and their associates came under fire from both sides, since almost everyone agreed that this latest effort by RMS *Titanic*, Inc., was going too far.[6]

Survivors, survivors' families, and the families of the victims of the *Titanic* were especially outspoken, calling Tulloch and his associates graverobbers and ghouls. They emphatically declared that bringing up anything from the wreck itself, let alone actually raising a part of the *Titanic*, amounted to little more than desecrating a grave. Emotions ran high on both sides of the Atlantic as RMS *Titanic*, Inc., proceeded with its plans to retrieve a section of the starboard hull, some twenty-five feet high and twenty feet long and weighing nearly thirteen tons, that had fallen away from the ship as the *Titanic* broke up.[7]

For some months, however, in an effort to deflect the criticism, Tulloch presented the project as a serious scientific endeavor, where all the proper protocols and formats of marine archeology would be followed and a significant amount of oceanographic research would be carried out at the same time the hull section was to be raised. Before long, though, a carnival atmosphere permeated the entire undertaking and the emphasis shifted toward making the recovery a media spectacular.

First, plans were made for one cruise ship, the SS *Royal Majesty*, then later a second, the MV *Island Breeze* to accompany the salvage vessels to the site of the wreck. Both were packed to the gunwales with reporters, sensation seekers, and *Titanic* buffs. The cruise ships would offer luxury accommodations, at $5,000 per person, including Las Vegas-style shows and casino gambling, along with closed-circuit television in each cabin that would allow the passengers to monitor the progress of the recovery in comfort. Then a group introduced a plan to utilize special underwater lights, originally designed for the production of the Hollywood film *The Abyss*, the idea being to illuminate the forward half of the wreck in its entirety, for the benefit of those on board the cruise ships watching their television monitors, and to allow the wreck to be filmed using purpose-built underwater cameras and super-sensitive film.[8]

Special "showings" of the recovered hull section and artifacts retrieved along with it were scheduled for New York and Boston, accompanied by a number of "Grand Receptions" for VIPs and the media. Finally, several celebrities, some of whom had only marginal associations with the *Titanic*, would be enlisted to add a measure of glamour to the event; among them were actor Burt Reynolds, actress Debbie Reynolds ("The Unsinkable Molly Brown"), and astronaut Buzz Aldrin. (The marketing company selling bookings on the cruise ships went so far as to announce that a world-famous author of two books about the *Titanic* would be part of the expedition, though when queried the gentleman in question stated that he had never been asked to participate, let alone agreed to do so.) Serious marine salvors, marine archaeologists, scientists, and historians quickly raised questions as to whether this expedition was a legitimate scientific undertaking, as Tulloch maintained, or simply a money-making stunt.[9]

Regardless, the salvage vessel *Nadir*, carrying the submersible *Nautile*, left New York harbor on August 26, 1996, along with the two cruise ships, and on August 28 reached the spot where the *Titanic* went down. The salvage efforts got underway almost immediately, despite marginal sea conditions (Hurricane Eduardo was moving up the United States' eastern seaboard and disturbing weather patterns all across the western half of the North Atlantic). The *Nautile* attached a sling of cables to the section of hull chosen for recovery, along with four flotation bladders filled with lighter-than-water diesel fuel. The whole array was carefully brought up from the bottom over a period of several hours to a depth of approximately 200 feet below the surface. RMS *Titanic*, Inc., had planned to have the *Nadir* tow the hull section at that depth until the ship reached the continental shelf, where the piece would be lowered to the bottom (only 250–300 feet down) until the weather cleared. Then the *Nadir* would gradually bring it closer and closer to the surface as the ship approached the coastline until, in a blaze of media-generated glory, the recovered section of the *Titanic*'s hull would emerge from the water in New York harbor.

Nature would have the last word, however, as the seas grew progressively rougher and the vertical movement of the *Nautile* began to place unantici- pated stresses on the floatation bags and the cable sling. At 3:00 A.M. on August 30, at a point about 300 miles south of Nova Scotia, the strain became too much for the chains holding two of the floatation bags to the hull, and they tore free. The loss of buoyancy was too great for the remaining two bags and the supporting cables to bear, and their attachments suddenly parted, sending the section of the *Titanic* plunging to the bottom of the sea again. For those people and organizations who wished to see the wreck remain undisturbed, the news was received as almost a divine endorsement of their views. For those who had supported the effort to recover part of the wreck, it was the ultimate disappointment. What had been one of the most controversial acts of marine salvage in history had ended in dismal failure.

Publicly, Tulloch remained optimistic, pledging to return to the wreck in the summer of 1997 or 1998 to continue the recovery of artifacts and to complete the job by bringing a section of the *Titanic*'s hull to the surface, where it would be preserved and put on public display. Privately, though, experts expressed serious doubts about RMS *Titanic*, Inc., ever raising the money it would need to return to the *Titanic*.[10]

It is unfair, though, to leave the impression that all of George Tulloch's endeavors were motivated by profit or publicity. In the summer of 1991, in a simple, dignified ceremony accompanied by very little media fanfare, Edith Brown Haisman, a quiet, frail woman in her hundredth year, was presented with a polished oak display case about the size of a hardback book. In it was a battered, corroded pocketwatch, its hands forever frozen at 11:04, that RMS *Titanic*, Inc., had recently recovered from the bottom of the North Atlantic. Moved almost beyond tears, Edith acknowledged that, though she knew it well, she had never expected to see that watch again. The watch had once belonged to Edith's father, Thomas William Brown, and he had been wearing it the last time Edith ever saw him. That was very early in the morning of April 15, 1912, and Thomas Brown was waving goodbye to his wife and daughter, who sat in Boat 14 as it pulled away from the side of the *Titanic*.[11]

━━◆◆◆━━

Whether any other salvage experts or entrepreneurs will try to "raise the *Titanic*" in the future, or if the salvage community will content itself with just retrieving artifacts, remains to be seen. Certainly the public's intense interest in both Europe and North America about those bits and pieces that have already been recovered will ensure that recovery efforts of some sort will continue. That the wreck is inexorably decaying and will one day collapse into a pile of rusting scrap is undeniable, though it seems to be a much slower process than some experts have maintained, removing some of the urgency from the claims of the more mercenary salvors. It appears, though, that because of the mountain of technical, logistical, and financial obstacles that have to be overcome by each successive expedition, the number of trips to the wreck will decline in the years to come, leaving the wreck relatively undisturbed in its closing years of decay. Fittingly, then, the final fate of the *Titanic* will be determined not by man, but by the sea.

CHAPTER 15

Revelation

. . .certain persons have made shipwreck of their faith. . . .
—I Timothy 1:19

HISTORY IS NOT COMPOSED OF A SERIES OF DISCRETE EVENTS, INCIDENTS that, like a collection of motion pictures, have clearly defined beginnings and ends. The story of the *Titanic* began long before her sailing day, her launching, her building, even before that summer evening when Lord Pirrie and Bruce Ismay doodled over Havana cigars and Napoleon brandy. She was, during her brief life, the culmination of technological, social, and economic trends that had begun more than a half century before her creation— trends that would continue long after her loss, producing ships with names like *Aquitania, Majestic, Normandie,* and the two *Queens, Mary* and *Elizabeth.* If the world would never again see her equal, that did not mean that it would never again see her kind.

And yet the sinking of the *Titanic,* those hours between 11:40 P.M. on April 14 and 8:30 A.M. on April 15, 1912, was one of those rare finite events that history on occasion does afford humanity. It illuminated with stark, sometimes harsh, clarity the strengths and weaknesses, virtues and flaws of the society that gave impetus to her existence. In those nine hours, the men and women aboard the *Titanic* demonstrated almost every derogatory characteristic of Edwardian society: arrogance, pride, snobbery, prejudice, racism, chauvinism, and maudlin sentimentality. They also showed in equal measure the Edwardians' capacity for self-confidence, self-reliance, self-sacrifice, gallantry, *noblesse oblige,* and devotion to duty. In many ways, what makes the *Titanic* disaster so compelling is that it catches that society at its pinnacle— before the decade was out it would have vanished forever.

For the sinking of the *Titanic* was the first scene in the last act of a drama that had slowly unfolded for centuries. The same energies that powered the Edwardian Age would, like a flywheel spinning too fast, soon tear it apart. When the waters of the North Atlantic closed over the *Titanic*'s stern that cold April night, something changed in the Western world, though no one knew it at the moment. Attitudes, beliefs, and values that had endured for hundreds of years were shaken, overnight as it were, and would remain unsettled more than eighty years later.

Most profoundly disturbed would be mankind's belief in technology. It is almost impossible for people living in this century's last decade to understand the almost mystical reverence people in its first felt for technological progress. The inhabitants of these modern days have had to come to grips with the realization that technology—though it robbed pestilence of much of its potency, greatly increased lifespans, and raised standards of living for many in the world—has been at best a mixed blessing. Hand-in-hand with the advances have come the ravaging of the global ecology, the still-rising threat of nuclear weaponry, and the nightmarish potentials of genetic engineering, which are only beginning to be explored and feared. By contrast, the engineers and scientists of the early 1900s were viewed as benefactors, their products as benevolent gifts that could only improve humanity's lot. The construction of the *Olympic* and *Titanic*, so widely believed to be unsinkable, represented the first sure steps in mankind's eventual, inevitable, triumph over the elements.

After the loss of the *Titanic*, engineers would no longer be hailed as modern-day saviors, their works greeted as panaceas for the assorted ills of mankind, or their efforts the repository of humanity's confidence. Confidence was probably the single outstanding characteristic of the Edwardians, confidence—faith—in the future and in the belief that, no matter how profound the problems, there were answers to all of society's ills, and that they would be found. And nowhere had that faith been given greater expression than in the advances made by science and technology. It was a memorable editorial in the *Wall Street Journal* on April 16, 1912, written while still blissfully unaware of the truth, that gave voice to this faith:

> The gravity of the damage done to the *Titanic* is apparent, but the important point is that she did not sink. . . . Mankind is at once the weakest and most formidable creature on earth. His brain has in it the spirit of the Divine, and he overcomes natural obstacles by thought, which is incomparably the greatest force in the Universe.[1]

But now faith would no longer repose in a ship that steamed blindly into an ice field with no more assurance of its safety than the wise pronouncements of a handful of engineers declaring her to be "practically unsinkable." Science had in the previous century steadily eroded the faith in God that had sustained men for two thousand years, until it seemed that the millennium would be ushered in not by theology but by technology. Yet suddenly what had appeared to be the ultimate accomplishment of science and progress was shown to be helplessly flawed and deadly fragile.

Pulpits on both sides of the Atlantic would ring with the strident rhetoric of an angry clergy denouncing misplaced faith in material objects and human accomplishments. The *Titanic*, it was said, was a heaven-sent warning against the complacency and smug self-satisfaction of the day. "When has such a lesson against our confidence and trust in power, machinery and money been shot through the nation?" asked the Bishop of Winchester. "The *Titanic*, name and thing, will stand for a monument and warning to human presumption." While perhaps not always spurring the masses to flock to churches on Sundays, the sermons drove home a point: humanity had severed its ties with spiritual absolutes, and now its newfound faith in material certainty had been tested beyond the breaking point.[2]

Similarly, privilege would never be the same. As never before, death was perceived as the great leveler it had always been. Forty-two hundred dollars might buy passage in the most opulent suite on board the *Titanic*, but it could no more purchase a seat in a lifeboat than could the thirty-six dollars paid by the lowliest steerage passenger. When John Jacob Astor's crushed and soot-covered body was pulled from the sea, the lesson to the millions who had been adding a touch of vicarious glamour to their lives by faithfully following the actions and antics of the upper classes on both sides of the Atlantic was of the utter senselessness of it all. If almost limitless millions of dollars or pounds sterling could not assure preferential treatment on the decks of a sinking liner, why should it gain the monied and titled classes absolute deference ashore? It would take the cataclysm of World War I before the barricades of class and privilege would begin to crumble, but their foundations were irreparably weakened that April night.

It would be going too far to say that the sinking of the *Titanic* marked the end of an era: the Edwardian Age and the Victorian Era could not be disposed of so easily—but in a way it sounded their death-knell. For centuries the huddled masses had been told that the rich and titled were different, and for a few hours that cold April night, many of them *were* different. There were boors, like Sir Cosmo, but there are always boors. There were cowards, like Dr. Frauenthal, but there are always cowards. There were those whose nerves failed them, like Ismay, but his lack of courage was a deep-rooted character flaw—Bruce Ismay didn't have it in him to be a hero, and it was his lasting misfortune to find himself in a position where he was asked to be one. But they are the exceptions. Instead, the picture is presented over and over again of men in First Class behaving the way the ideal of an upper-class gentleman should, but not always did.

There was Daniel Marvin, reassuring his eighteen-year-old bride of two weeks, "It's all right, little girl," as he helped her into the lifeboat; or Colonel Gracie, working as hard as any crewman to help launch Collapsibles A and B. There were Lieutenant Steffanson and Hugh Woolner helping Purser McElroy, stop a rush on Collapsible C. There was John Jacob Astor, meekly turning away when Lightoller refused to make an exception to "Women and children only" for him; or Isidor Straus refusing to get into a boat before any other man; or Benjamin Guggenheim, dressed in evening clothes, determined to be a gentleman to the end. The coterie that formed the heart of the First Class passenger list took a beating: the last anyone saw of John B. Thayer, Arthur Ryerson, Clarence Moore, George Widener, or Walter Douglas was of them standing in a small group near the portside railing on the forward Boat Deck, none of them going anywhere near a lifeboat.

It was almost as if they had some collective feeling that part of the price for living well was an obligation to die well. It was with a barbed pen that Elbert Hubbard wrote a eulogy for John Jacob Astor, but the barb was meant for those who had been the first to cast stones:

> Words unkind, ill-considered, were sometimes flung at you, Colonel Astor. We admit your handicap of wealth—pity you for the accident of your birth—but we congratulate you that as your mouth was stopped with the brine of the sea, so you stopped the mouths of carpers and critics with the dust of the tomb. If any think unkindly of you, be he priest or plebeian, let it be with finger to his lips, and a look of shame into his own calloused heart.[3]

Critics would be quick to point out that almost as many First Class men were saved as Third Class women, but statements like that can be misleading and manipulative: what they do not say is that more than two-thirds of the First Class men were lost, and that most of them stayed behind voluntarily. Nearly all of the First Class men who got away left the ship in the first four or five boats, when there was little sense of urgency or danger and only a handful of officers knew that there weren't enough lifeboats for everyone on board. Though it is true that none of the First Class men who made it into a lifeboat would later relinquish his place to another passenger, it is significant, perhaps, that not one of the First Class men would demand that someone else give up a seat in deference to him.

It would take too much effort, though, to sustain the image, and by the end of the Great War, the monied and titled upper classes, shocked at having the myth of their own infallibility exposed to the world—and to themselves—had dropped the mantle of leadership. It was a process that didn't begin with the *Titanic*—if there was a moment when the mantle can be said to have begun to irrevocably slip from the shoulders of the upper class, it was the Parliament Bill of 1911. The night the *Titanic* went down was, in effect, their last stand. That some of them botched the job was inevitable, but it shouldn't detract from those who met their obligation in the style their position demanded of them.

Yet more than simple class discrimination was responsible for the deaths of so many Third Class passengers: in the words of Wynn Craig Wade, a clinical psychologist from Michigan State University, "Undoubtedly, the worst barriers were the ones within the steerage passengers themselves. Years of conditioning as third-class citizens led a great many of them to give up hope as soon as the crisis became evident." It was this apparent helplessness that August Wennerstrom, a Third Class passenger himself, had observed and later bitterly commented on, when so many of his fellow passengers in steerage seemed to make no effort at all to save themselves—generations of being at the bottom of the social strata, being told where to go, what to do, and when to do it, had produced a mentality of stoic passivity among many of the peoples who were in Third Class.[4]

This doesn't mean that the steerage passengers simply stood by and let themselves be drowned because they couldn't think of anything better to do: Third Class never got the chance to show their own peculiar brand of courage and self-sacrifice. Unlike the crew, they lacked leadership and an example to action, because no one inside or outside Third Class provided it for them. A handful of men and women in Third Class did succeed in reaching the Boat Deck on their own, but they were lucky—when they left steerage they had no clear idea where they were going or how they would get there. No one will ever know how many others who tried to do the same got lost inside the ship or were trapped in dead ends and taken down with the *Titanic* when she sank. As for the rest, they fell back on old habits, and simply waited in vain for someone "in charge" to come along and lead them to safety.

Their sacrifice, then, would be measured in different terms from those of the officers and crew or the men in First Class who stayed behind—terms far less glamorous, far more harsh. There would be no monuments built or memorials raised to the men and women who faced a cruel fate dictated by the standards of a long-established order. They had put their trust, however misplaced, in the belief that their "betters"—the people in charge, whoever they might be—knew what they were doing. It had always been thus, and they had been raised to believe it would always be so. The steerage passengers didn't know, couldn't know until it was too late, that the circumstances had overwhelmed the very people they were relying on to protect them.

This too was an attitude that would begin a slow but accelerating process of change, as the working classes on both sides of the Atlantic began to exercise more direct control over their lives. In part this would come about because the upper classes would begin their abdication of responsibility for giving direction to the masses, but more so because the working classes would discover for themselves, for the first time in a millennium, and especially during World War I, that the capacity for leadership was not exclusive to the aristocratic and monied men of the world. The age of egalitarianism had begun.

And it would be terribly wrong to imply that the capacity for dying well was the sole preserve of the upper class. The devotion of the five postal clerks, two American and three British, in their vain effort to save the mail from the encroaching sea has been almost forgotten, but the last anyone ever saw of them they were still struggling to bring the sacks of registered mail to the upper decks when they were overwhelmed by the rising water somewhere forward on D Deck.

Likewise the thirty-four engineers and assistant engineers who were released from duty by Chief Engineer Bell sometime before 2:00 A.M., while there was still time to reach the upper decks. None of them left the engine room. The *Titanic* had power and lights until the very end because of the choice made by those electricians, plumbers, artificers, and engineers. Even the Crown was moved by their sacrifice: His Majesty King George V would issue a decree allowing British marine engineers to wear their rank insignia on a background of royal purple, as a tribute to the gallant men on the *Titanic*.

Just as Chief Engineer Bell had done with his engineers, Bandmaster Hartley told the men of the orchestra that they were released, but none of them laid down their instruments. The orchestra continued to play until the *Titanic*'s deck dipped into the water beneath their feet. Like the engineers, none of the band members survived, but they gave birth to a legend of devotion that made them immortal.

Add to that list the firemen, trimmers, stokers, stewards, and assistant stewards, bellboys, deckhands, galley hands, and quartermasters. The death toll among the crew was so high that it could scarcely be believed—678 out of 892. Yet because there are so few references to crewmen involved in the handful of attempts to rush one of the lifeboats—unless it was to help drive the offenders away—the only explanation can be that they deliberately stayed away from the boats.

And perhaps it might have been better for many of those First Class men who survived to have gone down with the ship. Though none of them would suffer the public humiliation of Ismay, few would escape with their good name and reputation intact. Several would be accused of putting on women's clothing in order to get into a lifeboat; one of them, William Sloper, actually contemplated legal action against the *New York Journal* when it identified him as "the man who got off in woman's clothing." He was completely innocent of the slur—all of them were, for there wasn't a single confirmed case of a man in any class getting into a lifeboat dressed like a woman. (At some point young Daniel Buckley acquired a woman's shawl and used it to disguise himself as he sat in Boat 14, but he wasn't wearing a woman's clothes.) For still other First Class men, divorce court awaited. In the proceedings against both William Carter and Dickenson Bishop their wives would cite their conduct the night the *Titanic* went down as part of the supporting evidence for their petitions. In the case of Carter, the rumor began that his wife left him simply because he happened to survive.

At the same time, the sterling performance of women like the Countess of Rothes, Gladys Cherry, and Molly Brown helped gain a good deal of credibility for those who were beginning to explore the idea, novel at the time, that in many roles a woman could be just as effective as a man. Nowhere was this idea being more loudly espoused than within the ranks of the women's suffrage movement. Nevertheless, the loss of the *Titanic* was a grievous blow to the movement and the related cause of women's rights (a concept that, unlike suffrage, existed only in the most nebulous sense, and would not be articulated for another half century). The cry of "Votes for Women!" lost much of its potency when set against that of "Women and children first!" and what could not be denied was that the effort had been made, however ineffectually or haphazardly, and that most of the women aboard had not challenged those words.

The romanticized though not altogether incorrect picture of the male passengers on the *Titanic* standing quietly aside, giving place to the women and children, was so indelibly etched in the public's collective mind—an inevitable and inescapable picture of self-sacrifice—that the protests of the suffragettes went unheeded at best, or met with outright hostility at worst. A huge protest march scheduled to take place in New York City on May 4, 1912, was roundly condemned by some of the suffragettes and their most ardent supporters. Annie Nathan Meyer, who founded Barnard College, summed it up best when she warned the march's organizers, "After the superb unselfishness and heroism of the men on the *Titanic*, your march is untimely and pathetically unwise." Theodore Roosevelt, as always extraordinarily sensitive to which way the political winds were blowing, politely sent his regrets to the march's organizers and withdrew his promised participation.[5]

In England, Mrs. Cecil Chapman might claim that it was the duty of every woman on the *Titanic* to refuse to enter the lifeboats without the men as well, but the sad truth for the women's suffrage movement was that, as Mrs. John Martin of the League for the Civic Education of Women put it, "We are willing to let men die for us, but we aren't willing to let them vote for us." She was merely underscoring the basic hypocrisy of the suffrage movement of the early twentieth century, a hypocrisy that the *Titanic* exposed and that the suffragettes had not considered: equality of rights also entailed equality of risk. The suffragettes lost much of their credibility as a result, as too many of their number, unlike the women of sixty years later, were eager to secure rights without accepting responsibility.[6]

By the end of the first decade of the twentieth century the limits of Western Europe's feudal society could no longer confine the energies that the Industrial Revolution had generated, and the institutions that such a society had evolved over the past five centuries could no longer cope with the demands being placed on them. The Victorian Age and the Edwardian Era had transformed both the aristocracy and the masses in ways that neither readily perceived, and only an event that so starkly highlighted the strengths and weaknesses of both would demonstrate how great those changes were. For the generations to follow, the years of 1914 to 1918 would seem to stretch across the landscape of the past like a curtain, closing them off from the years before, but for those who lived through those days, the turning point would always be the *Titanic*. Many years later, Jack Thayer would remember it this way:

> There was peace, and the world had an even tenor to its way. . . .
> It seems to me that the disaster about to occur was the event that
> not only made the world rub its eyes and awake, but woke it with
> a start. To my mind, the world of today awoke April 15, 1912.[7]

But what really struck home for most people was not that the disaster had occurred, or even the magnitude of it, but the sheer inevitability of the thing. Suddenly everyone knew that there could be no such thing as the "unsinkable ship," and a few hours' observation at any major seaport, combined with some simple arithmetic, would show anyone so inclined to spend the time that there were no ships on the North Atlantic that carried enough lifeboats for everyone on board. But it took the *Titanic* to make them realize that.

Pressing on with all possible speed regardless of weather or sea conditions may have been the standard operating procedure for crack liners on the North Atlantic run, but that didn't reduce the hazards of such practice. Yet because for forty years before April 15, 1912, there had never been a serious loss of life on the North Atlantic caused by such perilous habits, no one realized the danger that such a practice presented. Admittedly, the ramming and sinking of the *Republic* in 1906 should have served as a warning, but the drama of the thirty-six-hour struggle to save the stricken liner overshadowed everything else at the time. It took the tragedy of the *Titanic* to alert people to the danger.

The lack of any clear-cut procedure for getting warnings of ice or other obstacles properly posted on the *Titanic*'s bridge so that all the officers knew of them wasn't peculiar to just the *Titanic*—it was the order of the day on the North Atlantic. William Alden Smith may have looked like a bumptious fool when he decided that the transatlantic passenger trade needed a healthy dose of the same type of regulation that he had brought to America's railroads, but he was merely the point man for an entire populace that realized that a disaster like the *Titanic* would have happened sooner or later.

Though Senator Smith may have made himself the object of ridicule in Britain and come under harsh criticism from certain special interests in the United States, his inquiry had the lasting beneficial effect of no longer permitting shipowners to conduct "business as usual" on the North Atlantic. All the old regulations and Board of Trade formulas would be thrown out, and the question of sacrificing deck space to make room for enough lifeboats to hold everybody on board become moot.

It was true that, as Second Officer Lightoller maintained, the exact circumstances that brought the ship and the iceberg together might never be duplicated in a hundred years, but the popular sense was that the time would have come when the *Titanic* would strike that iceberg, or be rammed, or hit an uncharted rock like the *Great Eastern* did. Or if not the *Titanic*, then the *Gigantic* would, or one of the German leviathans being built even when the *Titanic* sailed, or one of the *Titanic*'s British successors. To most people, sober reflection led to the conclusion that such a disaster was indeed inevitable. In the case of the *Titanic*, it was the glamour of her passenger list, the thrill of her maiden voyage, the sheer breathtaking beauty of the ship itself, and the appalling death toll that combined to heighten the sense of tragedy and loss. All of it underscored the deadly triumvirate of arrogance, vanity, and "o'erweening pride" that led to her destruction. If only the ancient Greeks had known of her, they would have understood the *Titanic* perfectly, for if ever there was a physical expression of *hubris*, it was she.

It took the genius of Thomas Hardy to put such thoughts in terms that many felt but could not express. Hardy had lost a good friend, William T. Stead, on the *Titanic*, and though Hardy didn't share Stead's fascination with spiritualism, he did sense some moving force beneath the surface of the whole affair. With his fine sense of divine inscrutability, he produced the one piece of poetry that among all the reams of literature produced by the loss of the *Titanic* most directly drives to the heart of the tragedy:

The Convergence of the Twain

In a solitude of the sea
Deep from human vanity,
And the Pride of Life that planned her, stilly couches she.

Steel chambers, late the pyres
Of her salamandrine fires,
Cold currents third, and turn to rhythmic tidal lyres.

Over the mirrors meant
To glass the opulent
The seaworm crawls—grotesque, slimed, dumb, indifferent.

Jewels in joy designed
To ravish the sensuous mind
Lie lightless, all their sparkles bleared and black and blind.

Dim moon-eyed fishes near
Gaze at the gilded gear
And query: "What does this vaingloriousness down here?". . .

Well: while was fashioning
This creature of cleaving wing,
That Immanent Will that stirs and urges everything

Prepared a sinister mate
For her—so gaily great—
A Shape of Ice, for the time far and dissociate.

And as the smart ship grew,
In stature, grace, and hue,
In shadowy silent distance grew the Iceberg too.

Alien they seemed to be:
No mortal eye could see
The intimate welding of their later history.

Or sign that they were bent
On paths coincident
Of being anon twin halves of one august event.

Till the Spinner of the Years
Said "Now!" And each one hears,
And consummation comes, and jars two hemispheres.[8]

NEARLY ALL THE PLAYERS HAVE LEFT THE STAGE NOW. ONE BY ONE, THE PAS-sengers and crew have gone, until only a handful are left, and with their passing, along with their contemporaries, go the last living memories of an age when the future still beckoned hopefully, and the skies, while never cloudless, at least were bright.

——◆◆◆——

Lawrence Beesley would publish a book in 1913 about the *Titanic*. It was to be an obsession of his until his death in 1967 at the age of eighty-nine.

The Bishops divorced less than a year after the disaster, in part due to a vicious rumor claiming that Mr. Bishop escaped dressed in women's cloth-ing. After the divorce the former Mrs. Bishop vanished, while Mr. Bishop died in relative obscurity in 1961.

Jack Thayer would go on to graduate from the University of Pennsylva-nia and make a career in banking. Eventually he would return to the univer-sity and serve as treasurer and later as a vice president. But the events of April 14–15, 1912, left a mark on his spirit, until in 1945, still haunted by the *Titanic*, and deeply depressed by the death of his son in World War II, he took his own life. He was 50 years old.

Kate Buss did finally reach San Diego, where she and Samuel Willis were married on May 11, 1912. Their daughter would be named for Lilian Carter. Kate, who was widowed in 1953, would never be able to talk about the *Titanic* without breaking into tears. She died in 1972, at the age of ninety-six.

Billy Carter, like Dickinson Bishop, was divorced by his wife after a sim-ilar rumor started that he too had boarded the lifeboat in a woman's clothes. The quintessential "polo player and clubman" died in Palm Beach in 1940.

Sir Cosmo Duff Gordon, though exonerated by Lord Mersey of any impropriety, spent the rest of his days in the shadow of the *Titanic* and Boat 1. Proud and aloof as ever, he refused to respond to the continuing criticism of his actions on April 14–15, 1912, right up to his death in 1931. However unlikable he may have been, at worst Sir Cosmo was guilty of a monumental lapse into bad taste.

His wife, Lady Duff Gordon, prospered for a while longer in her dress-making business, but World War I spelled the end of the style of fashion "Lucile's" was founded on, and the business folded. Lady Duff Gordon remained spirited right to the very end, continuing to defend her husband, who she finally followed to the grave in 1935.

Rene Harris, the widow of Henry B. Harris, would know incredible prosperity after taking over her late husband's theatrical enterprises, only to lose everything in the Crash of 1929. But her "sunny disposition" never failed her, as Walter Lord put it, and "poor as a churchmouse but radiantly blissful, she died quietly in September, 1969, at the age of 93."[1]

Nellie Becker and her three children, Marion, Richard, and Ruth, found a home in Benton Harbor, Michigan, where they were joined the next year by Mr. Becker. The disaster wrought an emotional trauma on Mrs. Becker, who became nervous and withdrawn, and would never be able to even mention the *Titanic* without bursting into tears. She died in 1961.

Marion contracted tuberculosis and died of complications, just thirty-six years old, in 1944.

Richard went on to live a colorful life, first as a popular singer then as a social worker. He would be twice widowed before his own death in 1975 at the age of sixty-five.

Ruth eventually became a schoolteacher, married and divorced, and never talked about the *Titanic* until her children were almost grown. In March of 1990, at the age of ninety, she again went to sea, taking a cruise to Mexico, the first time she had set foot on board a ship since 1912. She died later that same year.

Helen Churchill Candee would go from strength to strength, becoming a noted author, world traveler, and lecturer—active and feisty until just months before her passing at the age of ninety at her home in York Harbor, Maine.

Mrs. Goldsmith and her son Franky finally reached Detroit, where Mrs. Goldsmith would eventually remarry, finally passing on in 1955.

Marion Wright's marriage to Arthur Woolcott took place as planned on April 20, 1912. They lived in Cottage Grove, Oregon, where they would raise three sons. Marion would only talk about the *Titanic* with her family or close friends, and only on the anniversary of the disaster. She died in 1965.

Colonel Gracie never fully recovered from his ordeal that April night. He wrote *The Truth About the Titanic* in late 1912 and, his health broken, died a few months later, just as the book was going to press.

Mrs. J. J. Brown became known as the "Unsinkable Molly Brown," her sometimes uncouth behavior suddenly becoming charming individualism. She would die in 1942, having become more and more eccentric with each passing year, still not giving a damn if she didn't want to, as colorful and genuine an American article as ever there was.

Eva Hart, deported from the United States because she was indigent—she and her mother had lost everything they owned in the wreck—returned to Great Britain. Eva's mother Esther never remarried and died of cancer in 1928. Eva grew up to become a British magistrate and was honored by Her Majesty Queen Elizabeth for her charitable work. She never forgot her father, and for a long time kept the recollections of that April night locked away in her memory, rarely to be discussed. In her later years, recalling the *Titanic* became easier for her, though she was bitterly outspoken in her opposition to salvaging artifacts from the wreck, calling the expeditions that did so little more than common grave robbers. She died at the age of ninety-one in a hospice in England in February 1996.

During World War I Edith Russell became one of the first female war correspondents, and over her long life, survived automobile accidents, another shipwreck, fire, floods, tornados, and war. Rather than tempt fate any further she refused to ever set foot in an airplane, and maintained to her dying day, in April 1975, that she had survived everything except a plane crash, a husband, and bubonic plague.

Winnie Troutt eventually settled in Southern California, first in Beverly Hills, where she married a baker, then in the town of Hermosa Beach, where she would ultimately outlive three husbands. Like many survivors, it was only with the passage of time that she was able to speak of her memories of the sinking. Proud that she was celebrated in Hermosa Beach more for civic activities than for being a *Titanic* survivor, she passed away in 1984, five months after she turned one hundred.

Bruce Ismay would never be able to live down the whispered accusations of cowardice that followed him almost from the moment the *Carpathia* docked in New York. His accusers had a case: the tradition of a captain being the last to leave a sinking ship had its roots in maritime salvage law, for as long as an owner's representative remained on board, a ship was not considered derelict, the captain usually being the senior representative. While there was no legal imperative for Ismay to stay behind, there was a moral one— one Captain Smith apparently felt compelled to follow. Public sentiment on both sides of the Atlantic felt that Ismay should have as well. Ismay got what many felt were his just deserts, for less than a year after the disaster, he was forced not only to resign as chairman of the White Star Line, which he had planned on doing anyway, but also to step down from the board of IMM, his fellow directors considering him a liability. He became a virtual recluse, rarely leaving the estate he bought in western Ireland, and died there of complications caused by diabetes in 1937. Mrs. Ismay was often heard to remark, "The *Titanic* ruined our lives. . . ."

———

Second Officer Lightoller never did receive a command of his own—nor did any of the surviving officers of the *Titanic*. He retired from the sea in the early 1920s, but never lost his lust for adventure. In 1940 he took his sixty-foot yacht, the *Sundowner*, to Dunkirk, and despite being bombed and machine gunned by the *Luftwaffe*, managed to bring back 131 British soldiers. He died peacefully in 1952.

Third Officer Pitman soon decided that his eyesight had deteriorated badly enough that he could no longer be watch qualified, so he joined the Pursers' Department, still with the White Star Line, at one point serving aboard the *Olympic*. He would spend another thirty-five years at sea before finally retiring to Pitcombe, England, where he died in December, 1961.

Fourth Officer Boxhall, like all the other surviving officers of the *Titanic*, never attained command rank. Over the years the accuracy of the final position he had worked out for the *Titanic* would be questioned by critics, but he defended his position of 41.40 N 50.14 W until the end of his days. His last posting was as First Officer of Cunard's *Aquitania* in the 1930s. After his death in 1963, in compliance with his last wishes, his ashes were scattered over the North Atlantic, at the spot that marks the *Titanic*'s grave.

Fifth Officer Lowe served in the Royal Navy in World War I, then never went to sea again. He retired to his native Wales and died quietly in 1944.

Harold Bride never could cope with the notoriety of being the *Titanic*'s surviving wireless operator. In 1913 he left the Marconi Company and vanished, his whereabouts becoming a mystery for the next three quarters of a century. In 1987 an enterprising private investigator from Michigan named David Norris, who was also an amateur radio enthusiast, traced this lost "silent key." Harold Bride had died in a Glasgow, Scotland, hospital in 1956. He had become a traveling salesman after leaving Marconi, and so successfully concealed his past that even his family did not know who he really was until after his death. No one will ever know what drove Bride to such a self-imposed silence.[2]

Captain Stanley Lord would spend the rest of his life trying to clear his name. Condemned by both the Senate and the Board of Trade Inquiries for failing to come to the *Titanic*'s aid, within months after the disaster he had become enough of an embarrassment to the Leyland Line that he was asked to resign. Though he would find subsequent employment as a master in years to come, his career had effectively ended, as his commands became progressively smaller and slower. Repeated requests by him and on his behalf to the Board of Trade for an inquiry in order to exonerate him were refused. Over the years his case attracted quite a few defenders, some of them very competent and quite clever. But no manipulation of facts, figures, relative positions, curvature of the earth, mystery ships and the like, all of which Captain Lord's supporters have utilized to attempt to exonerate him, can get past the simple fact that there was a ship firing distress rockets near the *Californian* in the early hours of April 15, 1912. Regardless of whether it was the *Titanic* or not, somebody needed help, and Captain Lord refused to go to their aid. He died in 1962, his family to this day still carrying on the fight to have his character rehabilitated.

Arthur Rostron's career was made by his impeccable seamanship in the morning hours of April 15, 1912. In 1915 he was given the *Mauretania*, at the time the most prestigious command on the North Atlantic run, a position he held until 1926. In 1928 he was made Commodore of the Cunard Line, and retired with full honors in 1931. He died in 1940.

———◆◆◆———

The *Californian* continued on for the Leyland Line until she took two torpedoes from a German U-boat in the fall of 1917.

The *Carpathia* would meet a similar fate on July 17, 1918.

The *Gigantic* never left the ways. After the disaster the White Star Line abandoned such pretentious names, so it was as the subdued but dignified *Britannic* that the third sister was launched in April 1914. Extensive modifications were made to her, including a double hull, bulkheads raised to forty feet above the waterline, and cantilever davits that held lifeboats stacked like the cars on a ferris wheel. World War I broke out before she was completed and she was requisitioned by the Royal Navy as a hospital ship. In September 1916, while steaming off the coast of Greece in the Aegean Sea, she struck a mine that ripped open her first six watertight compartments—a coal dust explosion almost blew her bow off—and she sank in an hour and a half. Only plenty of lifeboats and a warm sea kept the death toll down to thirty-five. The *Britannic* was gone before the world ever knew she existed.

Only the *Olympic* was left to carry on for the White Star Line. Her career in World War I was distinguished, to the point of ramming and sinking the *U-103* in May 1918. She returned to passenger service in 1919, becoming one of the best-loved ships on the North Atlantic. But in 1934 she rammed and sank the Nantucket lightship, killing all seven crewmen aboard that hapless vessel. Taken out of service, she was broken up in 1935, many of her interior fixtures and decorations finding their way into houses and pubs in Liverpool, Southampton, and London.

The *Titanic* herself will continue her slow decay at the bottom of the North Atlantic. Despite fanciful talk and wild speculation by salvage firms about raising the wreck, it is most likely that corrosion has so weakened the already over-stressed hull that it would never stand the strain of being raised. Ultimately, her deterioration will cause her great bulkheads to collapse and her decks to fall in, reducing the once proud hull to a mass of twisted steel. Within a century all that will remain of the "unsinkable ship" will be a pile of unrecognizable rust. The porcelain, glass, and ceramic pieces strewn about the debris field, along with the ship's brass fittings, will remain unchanged, alternately covered and revealed by the slowly eddying currents.

But farther to the north, in the Labrador Sea, the icebergs still break off from the Greenland glacier and drift down into the North Atlantic, a force of nature, waiting. . . .

THE *TITANIC*: FACTS AND FIGURES

Dimensions

Length:	882 ft 6 in
Beam:	92 ft 6 in
Moulded Depth:	59 ft 6 in
Height (from keel to top of funnels):	175 ft
Tonnage (Designed):	45,000
Tonnage (Actual):	46,329

Powerplant

Boilers (Double-ended):	25
Boilers (Single-ended):	4
Furnaces (three to each boiler end):	162

Engines:

Two four-cylinder, triple-expansion, direct-acting, inverted-type engines, balanced by the Yarrow, Schlick and Tweedy system, each producing approximately 15,000 shaft horsepower (s.h.p.), driving the wing screws.

One low-pressure turbine, driven by the exhaust steam from the reciprocating engines, producing approximately 16,000 s.h.p., driving the center screw. This turbine could not be reversed.

Performance

Designed Speed:	23–24 kts.
Highest Attained Speed (on April 14, 1912):	22 1/2 kts.
Coal Consumption:	650 tons daily

Crew

Engineer Department

Boiler and Engine Rooms (inc. Firemen, Trimmers, Stokers, and Greasers)	289

Electrical and Refrigeration Engineers	8
Engineers (inc. Engineer Officers)	28

Deck Department

Master and qualified Watch Officers	7
Pursers and Clerks (inc. 1 Purser, 2 Ass't. Pursers)	7
Carpenters	7
Surgeons	2
Bosun, Bosun's Mates, and Quartermasters	8
Able-Bodied Seamen	39
Masters-at-Arms	2
Window Cleaners	2
Messroom Stewards	2

Steward Department

Stewards and Service Staff (inc. Galley Staff)	471
Stewardesses	20
Matron (Nurse)	1
Telegraphists (Wireless Operators)	2
Total Crew	892

(When she sailed, the *Titanic* left behind five stokers who had gone ashore to visit a nearby pub and failed to return to the ship on time. After the disaster, some reports of the total number of lives lost erroneously included these five men. Additionally, the seven engineers from Harland and Wolff who accompanied Thomas Andrews were actually registered as Second Class passengers. Some sources have included them among the crew when recording the number of lives lost, not realizing they were carried on the passenger lists, in effect accounting for them twice.)

Accommodations

	Designed	Carried on Maiden Voyage
First Class	735	337
Second Class	674	271
Third Class	1,026	712
Total Accommodated	2,435	Carried 1,320

Passengers and Crew Lost

	Men	Women	Children
First Class	118	4	1
Second Class	154	15	0
Third Class	381	89	53
Crew	674	3	–
Totals	1,327	111	54

Total Passengers and Crew Lost   1,502

Passengers and Crew Saved

	Men	Women	Children
First Class	57	139	5
Second Class	14	79	23
Third Class	75	76	26
Crew	189	18	–
Totals	335	314	54

Total Passengers and Crew Saved   705

(Some sources quote different figures for the number of passengers aboard the *Titanic* the night she sank, along with correspondingly different numbers of persons lost: these are based on the Board of Trade Report, which still seems to be the most accurate accounting. The number of people saved—705—has never been seriously disputed. Over the years several errors have crept into the figures, the simplest explanation being that the erroneous numbers were based on the published passenger list, which contained the names of several people who cancelled their passage but were never deleted from the list. In addition, there were a number of passengers who were traveling under assumed names for various reasons, who later were added to the passenger lists by their correct names while at the same time their aliases were never removed. Also, as noted above, the seven engineers from Harland and Wolff who accompanied Thomas Andrews were listed as Second Class passengers, but on some lists their names are duplicated in the crew roster, erroneously adding to the total.)

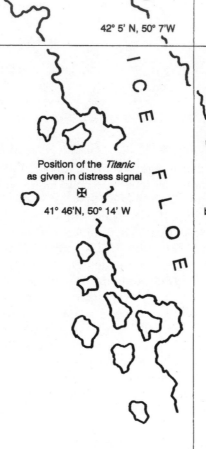

50 ° W

Position of the
Californian
as recorded in her log

⊞

42° 5' N, 50° 7'W

42° N

Actual position of the
Californian
as determined by the
Ministry of Trade in 1987

⊞

41° 53' N, 49° 54' W

Position of the *Titanic*
as given in distress signal

⊞
41° 46'N, 50° 14' W

Actual postition of the *Titanic*
based on the position of the wreck

⊞

41° 43'N, 49° 56' W

I C E   F L O E

The Titanic, the Californian, and the Culpability of Captain Lord

Though all of the principals involved in the controversy over the apparent willful inactivity of the *Californian* and her captain the night the *Titanic* sank are long dead, the debate continues with an intensity that shows little sign of subsiding with the passing years. In the United Kingdom, where the issue is most hotly contested still, the entire incident has become a political football, with all of the attendant distortions, half-truths, and outright deceptions that characterize any dispute where lawyers and politicians displace the original aggrieved parties. Powerful trade unions, which have defended Captain Lord for over three quarters of a century and so stand to lose a great deal of face should Lord be unambiguously found negligent, have intervened and interfered in an official government inquiry and caused the investigators' final report to be materially altered before being released to the public; writers partial to Lord's protests of innocence have been retained to produce books and articles that attempt to "prove" that it was patently impossible for the officers on board the *Californian* the night of April 14–15, 1912, to have seen the *Titanic*'s distress rockets or watch the sinking liner disappear, let alone come to her aid; and other writers who believe the opposite to be true have been warned of potential professional ruin if they press their views too vigorously.

Both sides trot out impressive arrays of experts, armed with reams of various forms, charts, tables, and other paraphernalia. Each camp, those who believe in Captain Lord's innocence and those who maintain his guilt, present their arguments with remarkable lucidity and convincing earnestness. Ultimately, however, the debate over whether Captain Lord failed to come to the aid of the sinking *Titanic* or simply and rightfully ignored a small tramp steamer or fishing vessel nearby comes down to two points: the rockets that were seen from the *Californian*, and the positions of the two vessels.

The issue of the rockets is a major stumbling block for the defense of Captain Lord. The number of rockets fired by the *Titanic* and the number seen by the officers on the *Californian* were identical (eight); the rockets fired by the doomed liner were all white, and the rockets described to Captain Lord three separate times were all white; the times during which

Quartermaster Rowe was firing his eight rockets from the *Titanic*'s bridge and Officers Stone, Groves, and Gibson stood on the *Californian*'s bridge and watched eight rockets burst high over the unknown ship to the south were approximately the same. (The word "approximately" is used because there was a twelve-minute difference between the bridge clocks of the two ships, and the times when certain events took place on board the *Titanic* that night are understandably uncertain. Quartermaster Rowe believed he fired his first rocket at about 12:45 A.M. and his last at about 1:30 A.M., but an error of five to ten minutes either way in his estimate of those times would be quite possible and quite forgivable.) Since no one on board the *Titanic* saw any other ship in the vicinity firing rockets or flares of any kind, although they were desperately looking for some indication from any ships that might be nearby, Captain Lord's oft-repeated defense that there was an unknown vessel (or vessels) between the *Californian* and the *Titanic* firing flares of some sort lacks credibility.

Despite the phenomenal exertions of Captain Lord's supporters over the years, no vessel has ever been found that can reasonably be placed anywhere near both the *Titanic* and the *Californian* in a position where she could be seen from both ships at the same time. The most energetically endorsed candidate for this mystery ship is the little Icelandic fishing smack *Samson*, which had been illegally taking seals in the Grand Banks early in April 1912. A typewritten manuscript, which first appeared in the 1930s and was allegedly based on a handwritten journal kept by one of her crew, asserts that the *Samson* was indeed the vessel seen by both the *Titanic* and the *Californian*, and that the "rockets" observed by the *Californian*'s officers were in fact "signal flares" used to communicate with other fishing vessels in the area. No explanation is offered as to why these "flares" were never observed from the *Titanic*, though. In the end, the case the document puts forward for the *Samson* being the mystery ship collapses completely, as dates, times, speeds, and locations fail to correlate properly or are contradicted by official records. The greatest damage done to the case for the *Samson* is in the log of the customs collector of the port of Reykjavik, Iceland: harbor fees paid by the *Samson* on April 12 and 20 make it devastatingly clear that the little six-knot fishing boat would never have been able to leave Iceland to reach a point anywhere near the *Titanic* and return again in that span of time.

This "second ship" hypothesis of Lord's and his supporters' rests heavily on the second point in the debate over the *Titanic* and the *Californian*, namely the positions of the two ships. Captain Lord's defense has been built over the years around the idea that the *Californian* was too far to the north of the *Titanic*'s position to allow her officers to be able to actually see the stricken liner. Lord maintained that his ship was between nineteen and twenty-one miles away, which would have put the *Titanic* well over the horizon and even made sighting her distress rockets difficult. It was this intervening distance that allowed the "mystery ship" to steam between the *Titanic* and the *Californian*, stop at the same time the *Titanic* struck the iceberg, remain stationary for more than two and a half hours, fire eight white rockets for some obscure purpose, then steam away at the same time the *Titanic* sank. All that was necessary to establish the distance was to compare the *Californian's* position as recorded in her log with the position the *Titanic* gave when sending her distress signals by wireless.

Even allowing for the remarkable number of coincidences such a chain of events would require, and any good historian will vouchsafe to being no stranger to coincidence in history, there are serious flaws in this argument. It was firmly established in 1981 by a research team sponsored by Jack Grimm, a Texas oilman who had hoped, vainly, to be the man who would find the wreck of the *Titanic*, that the bridge clock which Fourth Officer Boxhall was using in calculating the *Titanic's* position had not been reset at the beginning of the last watch, and so was running twenty minutes fast. Using this incorrect time, he estimated that the *Titanic* had traveled fourteen miles farther west than she actually had. This meant that instead of her position being 41°46' N., 50°14' W., she was actually at 41° 43' N., 49° 56' W.; that is, somewhat to the south and east of where Boxhall's figures had placed her.

In the *Californian's* log, her stated position when she stopped for the night at 10:20 P.M., April 14, 1912, was 42°5' N, 50°7' W. This would have put her nineteen miles to the northeast of the position Boxhall had worked out for the *Titanic*, conveniently distant enough to support Lord's contention that the *Titanic* was not visible from his ship. Even when the *Titanic's* correct position is taken into consideration, the *Californian* would still have been nearly twenty miles away. But the *Californian's* logged position was calculated by dead reckoning based on a sun-sighting taken some four hours earlier. What it does not take into account is the 1 1/2 knot current from the north-northwest that caused the ship to drift to the south-southeast as she was steaming, a drift that continued after she stopped at the edge of the icefield, pushing her nearly nine miles away from her estimated position. Factoring that drift into the *Californian's* position leaves her less than eleven miles from the *Titanic*, a position where the sinking White Star liner would have been clearly visible.

There is also a nagging doubt—and a very strong one—about the truth of the entries in the *Californian's* log. A ship's master is ultimately responsible for the contents of his vessel's log, and nothing is entered in it without his approval and permission. For this reason and to avoid errors in log entries, ships keep what is called a "scrap log." This is a record kept during a watch of everything that occurs on board relating to the handling of the ship, including helm and engine orders, signal and navigational information, and status of the crew and stores. It also includes any sightings of other vessels. It is a captain's responsibility to review the contents of the scrap log daily and approve, amend, or correct the entries, after which they are entered into the ship's formal log. The scrap log is kept as a back-up, though, and rarely disposed of. It was noted at the time of both the U.S. Senate inquiry and the Board of Trade investigation that the *Californian's* scrap log for the night of April 14–15, 1912, had vanished, and that the formal log contained no references whatsoever to the ship seen by three of Lord's officers, the rockets that ship fired, or Lord's order to attempt to contact the ship by Morse lamp. The missing sections of the scrap log and the absence of any entries for the night in question were never adequately explained by Captain Lord at either inquest.

It was at these inquests as well that serious discrepancies between the testimony of Captain Lord and his officers appeared, differences so great that at times it gave the impression that these men weren't even on the same ship at the same time. When the true picture finally emerged, it became clear that Lord was a latter-day Captain Bligh, an inflexible tyrant with a powerful temper, given to sarcasm and derisive comments that embarrassed and humiliated his officers, who in turn would go to any length to avoid coming into conflict with their captain. It takes little imagination to envision Captain Lord dictating the exact contents of the log entries for the night of April 14–15, so that they would say precisely what he wished them to say and nothing else.

Nor is it difficult to conceive of Captain Lord falsifying his ship's position in order to more easily exonerate himself. There is some circumstantial evidence that he did so, beyond that of the missing scrap log and the sterile entries in the formal log, evidence that has never been refuted. When Cyril Evans relayed an ice warning to the *Titanic* at 7:30 P.M., he gave her position as 42°3' N., 49°9' W. At this time the *Californian* was on a west-southwest course (S 89° W true), yet when the *Californian* stopped three hours later, the position recorded in the log put her well to the north of where that course would have taken her had she maintained it, and there is no indication that Captain Lord ever ordered a course change: even had he done so, it would have been to the south—changing course to the north would only have carried the *Californian* into even heavier ice than she had been compelled to stop by.

Admittedly, these items are certainly not damning evidence, but they are sufficient to raise enduring questions about Captain Lord and his veracity. What is evident is that Captain Lord was determined not be publicly blamed and stigmatized for failing to come to the aid of the *Titanic*. This is understandable, even forgivable. What is unforgivable is that, even if it was not the *Titanic* seen from the *Californian's* bridge that night, someone was in trouble, and Stanley Lord was clearly unwilling to go to anyone's aid. He would go to extraordinary lengths to ensure that he would not be held responsible for his inaction and that there would be insufficient evidence to suggest that he was.

Try as his family might to rehabilitate his character, and strive as the various special interests may that have made Captain Stanley Lord's case their own, the verdicts of the two inquiries, which echoed each other with devastating precision, have withstood all the legal maneuvering, political posturing, and forensic legerdemain that have attempted to refute them, and so

Lord continues to stand condemned. It may be true, as has often been maintained, that Stanley Lord in person was charming, warm, kindhearted, and a devoted family man, but his demeanor as the master of a merchant ship was forbidding and autocratic to such a degree that his officers and crew were terrified lest they might displease him. Sadder still is the thought that he was a man who refused to undertake the slightest risk to go to the aid of those in peril. Few pronouncements have ever been more damning than the conclusion concerning Captain Lord reached by Sir Rufus Isaacs, the attorney general at the Board of Trade inquiry, when he spoke of Captain Lord:

> I am unable to find any possible explanation of what happened,
> except it may be the Captain of the vessel was in ice for the first
> time and would not take the risk of going to the rescue of another
> vessel which might have got into trouble, as he thought, from
> proceeding through the ice when he himself had stopped.[1]

It was that refusal that would consign Stanley Lord in the world's memory to always being the captain who did nothing, and the *Californian* as being, in historian Leslie Reade's words, "the ship that stood still."

The Conundrum of Captain Smith

The actions of two of the captains whose names have become inseparably linked to the sinking of the *Titanic* have presented history with what is probably a unique set of contrasts. On one hand is the captain who did everything—or nearly everything—right, Arthur Rostron of the *Carpathia*; and on the other is the skipper who did everything—or nearly everything—wrong, Stanley Lord of the *Californian*. Lately, though, the name of a third captain has begun to crop up in discussions about who did what the night the *Titanic* went down and whether his actions were right or wrong—Edward J. Smith.

At the time, the overwhelming majority of the British press, along with quite a few American newspapers, portrayed Captain Smith's conduct as utterly heroic and ultimately self-sacrificing, especially when contrasted with the actions of Bruce Ismay. Smith's reputation, aided by popular books and movies, endured for three quarters of a century. Yet in the past few years questions have begun to be raised, not about Captain Smith's courage, but rather about his judgement and abilities, and how errors he may have made led to the disaster. One noted author specifically suggested that the *Titanic* (along with her sister *Olympic*) were simply too big for Captain Smith to competently handle; other writers have suggested that Smith had become increasingly complacent, even reckless, as year after year of uneventful crossings of the Atlantic went by; while still others marvel at the fact that after the *Titanic* hit the iceberg and the certainty of her doom was made clear by Thomas Andrews, Smith, who had been portrayed time after time as being such an outstanding leader, should be so ineffective in his efforts to get the passengers into the lifeboats.

Had Captain Smith been given command of a vessel that, because of its immense size, demanded ship-handling and navigational skills he didn't possess? Had he grown complacent, even careless, because in his forty years at sea he had never been in a serious accident, let alone had a ship sink while he was serving on board? Why did Smith give the appearance of being controlled, decisive, and very much in command until Thomas Andrews informed him that the *Titanic* was going to sink and take half the people on board with her, then from that moment seemed to almost be reduced to being a mere spectator as the tragedy unfolded? Ultimately, was Captain Smith a seaman who had been lucky for forty years, and suddenly had no idea what to do when he realized his luck had run out?

To conclude that Captain Smith bore a considerable share of the responsibility for the collision itself is inescapable. By early evening on April 14, he was fully aware that the *Titanic* was proceeding at high speed into a section of the North Atlantic where ice was known to be about, and had already altered the *Titanic*'s course to take her some twelve to fifteen miles farther south of the normal shipping lane in order to avoid what he thought to be the worst concentration of ice. What he didn't know was that the icefield ahead of the *Titanic* was far larger than he believed. Had all of the six wireless messages concerning ice been properly posted on the bridge or in the chartroom, the extent of the ice floe the *Titanic* was steaming toward would have been much clearer, so that Captain Smith could have radically altered his course in order to avoid it. The problem was that there was no clear-cut procedure for handling wireless messages of this sort, so Phillips and Bride did with them what they thought best: at times sending the messages up to the bridge immediately, at others handing them to the nearest officer, at still others letting them sit in the wireless office while they worked on the passenger's traffic. Unfortunately this resulted in the six messages being scattered across the ship, one (from the *Baltic*) even winding up in Bruce Ismay's pocket.

Critics of Captain Smith have been quick to point out that this admittedly haphazard handling of wireless messages deprived the captain and his officers of vital information affecting the safe navigation of the ship. But the fault was not so much Captain Smith's as it was that of the prevailing attitude of captains and officers of passenger ships on the North Atlantic run in the early years of the twentieth century. The technology of wireless was still relatively new to many of these men, and as a consequence most of them hadn't thought out the implications of the increased communication capabilities wireless offered: very few had realized that wireless gave them the opportunity to virtually look over the horizon and anticipate danger before it hove into view. Even fewer had worked out set procedures for the wireless operators to follow when they received messages affecting the navigation of the ship. At the same time, the wireless industry itself had very few regulations or conventions to guide the operators in such a situation. Attempting to blame Captain Smith for the inept way in which the ice warnings were handled rings a little hollow, since the conditions that existed on the *Titanic* were the same as those on most of the ships on the North Atlantic. If Captain Smith failed to appreciate the potential that wireless communications had to improve the safe navigation of his ship, it was not due to willful ignorance, for it was a shortcoming shared by nearly all of his colleagues.

Nevertheless, because Captain Smith was aware from the one or two messages he had seen that ice lay across the *Titanic*'s course, there were some precautions he could have taken but didn't, and for that he was clearly responsible. While he did alter the *Titanic*'s course farther south to avoid the ice and issued orders for the lookouts to be alert for ice ahead, he failed to post extra lookouts. That this would have been a wise precaution was amply demonstrated by Captain Rostron aboard the *Carpathia*, when as she was beginning her frantic dash north to come to the *Titanic*'s aid, he posted no fewer than seven additional lookouts to watch for ice. Significantly, four of them were posted on the foredeck, rather than up in the crow's nest or on the bridge, since it was a well-known fact that it was easier to spot ice from deck level than from higher up. Smith's failure to post extra lookouts may have been the most serious mistake he ever made.

Another mistake was the decision to maintain a speed of 22 knots, the fastest the ship had ever gone. This though may have been an error committed out of ignorance: if Captain Smith, having already altered course to the south, wasn't aware of the full extent of the ice floe spreading across the *Titanic*'s course—and the evidence is that he wasn't—then he wouldn't have seen the necessity of reducing speed. To some degree, Bruce Ismay, with his obsession with bettering the *Olympic*'s time on her maiden voyage, may have contributed to this. Captain Smith, impending retirement or no, would have been less than human if he hadn't been susceptible to the urge to carry out his employer's wishes, and so was inclined to not reduce speed.

Of course, the speed the *Titanic* was making as she approached the iceberg had a direct effect on the time and distance it took her to respond to the movement of her rudder. No one will ever know for sure just how familiar Captain Smith was with the turning radius and response time of the *Titanic*, though there is little reason to believe that they would have differed significantly from those of the *Olympic*, which Smith had commanded for nearly a year. Smith had an outstanding reputation among professional seamen as an expert ship handler; but, the question persists as to whether or not Smith knew just how clumsy and heavy these new ships were. Yet asking the rhetorical question, "Had ships gotten too big for Captain Smith?" implies that there were other captains who had the ability to better handle ships the size of the *Olympic* and *Titanic*. In plain truth there weren't. The two White Star sisters were the largest ships in the world, fully a third larger than the next largest ships, the *Lusitania* and *Mauretania*, and no one had any more experience with them than Captain Smith. The handling characteristics of the *Olympic* class ships were uncharted territory, and if Smith overestimated the maneuverability of those vessels, there was nobody with the credentials to gainsay him.

Simply put, the decisions Captain Smith made about navigation and shipboard procedures on the *Titanic* right up to the moment of the collision, while in hindsight frighteningly casual in some respects, were in fact singularly unremarkable when put in perspective: his actions were very much in line with the standard practices on board most Atlantic liners of the day. To expect him to radically depart from those practices—and it should be kept in mind that for the forty years he had been at sea those same practices had never gotten him involved in serious accident or emergency—would be to demand a foresight, even a prescience, that is beyond the ability of most mortals.

It is after the collision occurs that Captain Smith's behavior and decision-making becomes far more questionable. For the first twenty or twenty-five minutes after the impact, the captain was very much the embodiment of command, instantly giving orders to ensure the safety of the ship, having the carpenter ascertain the damage, putting Ismay (who always seemed to be underfoot at the worst possible times) firmly in his place, conferring with Thomas Andrews about the effect the damage would have on the ship. But just about midnight, his powers of decision and command seemed to desert him. For the next two hours and twenty minutes, he would be only a shadow of his former self, isolating himself on the bridge, failing to pass on critical information to his officers and senior seamen, acting and reacting slowly to reports and rapidly changing circumstances, and giving half-hearted orders, some of which the crew would openly defy. Clearly something had happened; the question is what?

The answer lies in what passed between Thomas Andrews and Captain Smith when they had finished their inspection and returned to Andrews's cabin, A-36. The absolute certainty with which Andrews pronounced the *Titanic*'s doom must have been like a body blow to Smith, but worse was to come: when Andrews confirmed that the ship carried enough lifeboats to hold only half the people on board, it must have seemed like Smith's worst nightmare had come true. The safety of the ship and every person on board her, regardless of how many regulations were complied with, no matter how many Bruce Ismays were aboard, were the sole responsibility of the ship's captain, and now Captain Smith had failed that responsibility. All of Smith's superb seamanship, his forty years at sea without a serious accident, his twenty-seven years of command without ever having lost a single life entrusted to his care, his unqualified confidence in the capabilities of modern shipbuilding, had all been swept away in the ten seconds it took for the iceberg to open up the *Titanic*'s starboard side.

From that moment on, Smith would exhibit all the characteristics of someone suddenly overwhelmed by circumstances. What orders and instructions he would give would often be incomplete or impractical: after Smith had ordered the lifeboats uncovered, he had to be prodded by Second Officer Lightoller to have them swung out and begin loading the passengers; when he wanted to load the boats from the Promenade Deck, he completely forgot that the forward half of the deck was enclosed, making loading from there impossible; and his idea for filling the half-empty boats from the gangways on D Deck made no sense at all.

He also failed to make it clear to his officers and senior seamen—the quartermasters, bosun's mates, and able-bodied seamen—that the ship was in mortal danger, and so didn't impart any real sense of urgency to them. One of the most remarkable aspects of the *Titanic*'s sinking is that very few people on board regarded the situation as serious for more than an hour after the collision—in fact it was nearly 1:15 before Fourth Officer Boxhall was told the ship was going to sink. While no doubt Smith wanted to avoid a panic among the passengers, and quite possibly the crew as well, not letting his officers know just how serious the emergency was may well have contributed to a false sense of security among them, which in turn caused them to allow a number of the boats to leave the ship less than half full.

It is almost certain that only Bruce Ismay, Thomas Andrews, and Captain Smith knew for sure that there were far too few lifeboats on the *Titanic* to hold all the people aboard her. Again, by not informing the officers of this discrepancy, Smith may have unwittingly caused an even greater loss of life, because so many of the lifeboats left the ship only partially filled. Certainly, the knowledge that the number of boats was inadequate was not something to be shared with the passengers, but it isn't difficult to believe that the *Titanic*'s officers would have acted differently had they realized the truth. Nor did Smith give any instructions on how "Women and children first!" was to be interpreted. This led to Lightoller taking it to mean women and children only, while Murdoch was more flexible, allowing some married couples into the boats, and a few single men when there weren't any women immediately nearby.

Finally, Captain Smith isolated himself on the bridge, leaving it only occasionally to walk a few yards aft to the wireless office, to inquire of Bride and Phillips if there were any ships coming to the *Titanic*'s aid. He never made his way down the Boat Deck to observe how the loading and launching of the lifeboats was proceeding, never bothered to ascertain if his orders were being carried out, never inquired as to whether all the passengers and crew had been roused and were accounted for.

What had happened to Captain Smith? Dr. Dorothy Mihalyfi, a clinical psychologist from Boca Raton, Florida, who specializes in crisis counseling, reviewed Smith's actions and behavior at the author's request. In her opinion, Smith was in a state of mental shock, as she put it, "a temporary disfunctionality." Smith had believed that the ship was unsinkable, had believed in his abilities as a ship's captain, had believed that he had taken all the necessary precautions. Now the entire edifice around which his authority was built had come crashing down. Completely dumbfounded by the situation, he was in a blank state of immobility, a mental void similar to that of a boxer who has taken too many punches, and though he refuses to go down, can no longer defend himself or fight back. In such a case the referee would step in to stop the fight, but there was no referee on April 15, 1912.

Instead, Smith was confronted at every turn by the awful finality of what had occurred: every order he gave and every instruction he issued reminded him anew of the dreadful conclusion the night's events must lead to, and the knowledge inhibited his ability to make decisions. Dr. Mihalyfi observes that Smith's awareness of the terrible loss of life that was imminent would have loomed up like a wall before him every time he was called upon to choose a course of action. As a consequence indecision was easier, and isolation on the bridge made it easier still. It was quite possible that Smith couldn't bring himself to go out onto the Boat Deck and see the faces of so many people who were very shortly going to die.

It went deeper than that, as well. Dr. Mihalyfi points out that it is quite common for someone who has undergone a severe psychological trauma to enter a state where they become completely hopeless, resigning themselves to their fate. They develop a feeling that the circumstances are insurmountable, that nothing can affect the outcome of the situation, and that any further effort on the part of the afflicted individual is pointless. Apparently this too overtook Captain Smith, as it seems he made little if any effort to reach any of the lifeboats after the *Titanic* sank. Indeed there can be few more perfect statements of hopelessness as when Smith told Phillips, "You look out for yourself. I release you. That's the way of it at this kind of time. . . ."

It is important to note that Dr. Mihalyfi's observations do not imply that Captain Smith went mad or was mentally deranged (note that Dr. Mihalyfi is a psychologist, not a psychiatrist), nor are they intended to impute an undeserved portion of the blame for the *Titanic*'s disaster to Captain Smith. Instead they make it clear that Smith was confronted with a situation that he wasn't prepared by emotion, experience, or training to handle. That Captain Smith was overwhelmed by circumstances is something for which he should be pitied, but never condemned. It is highly doubtful that any of us could have done any better.[1]

THE STORY OF THE *TITANIC* IS IN MANY WAYS A MODERN EPIC, AND IT SEEMED at times that the research needed to retell it correctly would have to be of epic proportions—and it very nearly was. While not exactly a cast of thousands, there were scores of people, at dozens of institutions of every description, in five countries scattered across two continents who made some kind of genuine, material contribution to this work. I would like to thank them all, and in particular single out those persons and institutions whose assistance were particularly significant.

As any writer will readily acknowledge, good librarians and archivists are the people who make a writer's work possible. Consequently, I want to acknowledge my debt to the staffs of the following libraries, museums, and archives:

The U.S. Library of Congress, where not only are the complete transcripts of the U.S. Senate investigation to be found, but also hundreds of *Titanic*-related references. In all my visits the staff was always a model of courtesy; the staff at the Van Zoeren (now the Van Wylen) Library at Hope College in Holland, Michigan, as well as the librarians and student assistants at the Grand Valley State University libraries in Allendale, Michigan, who all those years ago so willingly aided me in locating old, out-of-print books and obscure periodicals through the Michigan University Library System; the Public Library of Grand Rapids, Michigan, and in particular the library's city historian, Gordon Olsen, who labored diligently to help me in my researches about Senator William Alden Smith, as did Jeannie Larsen of the Archive Section of the Grand Rapids Public Museum, as well as providing information about several of the *Titanic*'s survivors who either hailed from southern Michigan or later settled there; the Orange County Library System, Orange County, Florida, and especially Miss Candace Critchfield, of the Orlando branch's Genealogy Department, who bent her considerable familiarity with immigration records, steamship manifests, and the like to the task of showing me how sharply the reality of immigration into the United States in the first decade of this century differed from the popular images created by latter day sensation-mongers masquerading as journalists.

A number of museums deserve particular mention, among them the Mariners' Museum of Newport News, Virginia, which possesses an outstanding collection of photographs of the *Titanic* and her contemporaries; the National Maritime Museum in Philadelphia, which holds most of the handful of artifacts that were recovered from the area of the Atlantic immediately after the *Titanic* went down; and the Maritime Museum of the Atlantic in Halifax, Nova Scotia, with its own collection of artifacts and archives. Most importantly, these museums are staffed by men and women who know ships and the sea, and so can give insights and perspectives on a subject that might otherwise escape an ordinary historian. Halifax in particular has never left its seafaring roots behind it, and the city and its people have treated the memory of the *Titanic* with great respect.

The Ulster Folk and Transport Museum of Belfast, Northern Ireland, possesses one of the finest collections of photographs of the *Titanic* in the world. In addition, the staff have a unique knowledge of the men who designed and built her, of their times and their world, and as a result can make those lives very, very real to a researcher like myself. I will always be grateful to them, especially Mr. Michael McCaughan, curator of maritime history, for the help they gave me.

The city of Southampton has never entirely forgotten the grief caused by the terrible death toll among the crew, most of whom called that ancient seaport home. As a result, the Southampton City Museums have always had a special interest in the *Titanic* and especially her crew. Because of this, the Museums, administered by the Southampton Heritage Centre, are a veritable treasure trove of information and photographs that make it possible to reconstruct the lives of the *Titanic*'s crewmen, as well as of the dark, grieving days that followed the sinking. My particular thanks go to the Museums' staff, and especially to Donald Hyslop, the community history manager of the Centre.

Admittedly the great days of British shipbuilding have passed in Belfast, but Harland and Wolff still construct some of the finest ships in the world. Even today, though, the firm is immensely proud of the three sisters, *Olympic*, *Titanic*, and *Britannic*, and there are many at the yard who still maintain that the finest ship to ever leave their ways was the *Titanic*. It was more than ten years ago that Mr. Tommy McCluskey showed me the concrete apron that was all that remained of Slips No. 2 and 3 where the three ships were built, and guided me around the shipyard that, while it has changed tremendously, is still recognizable as the yard in the photographs from 1912.

The British Public Records Office is the repository of the transcript of the Board of Trade inquiry into the loss of the *Titanic*. It runs to something over 2,000 pages, and the transcript is, for the most part, an exercise in rather turgid "legalese," but there were moments when my modern "American English" was not up to the demands of a 1912 lawyer's "English English" and the members of the staff of the PRO were always willing to help out "the fellow from the colonies."

Simply put, the National Maritime Museum in Greenwich, England, has no equal anywhere in the world for the breadth and depth of its resources or the accumulated knowledge of ships and the sea. Of particular help to me were comments and observations on the text made by Dr. Stephen Deucher, the exhibitions director. Dr. Deucher was responsible for setting up the now-famous "Wreck of the *Titanic*" Exhibition, which ran for a year, from October 1994 to October 1995, displaying to the public for the first time many of the artifacts recovered and preserved from the *Titanic* in the late 1980s.

In each of these institutions I conducted some major or at least significant portion of my research and in each I was always received with consummate professionalism and courtesy. Over the course of several years and many visits, the faces and names would often change, so that now I can only dimly recall some them, but to each and every one, I extend my genuine and sincere gratitude.

A special mention is deserved of certain individuals whose contributions to this work were so unique or so specific that they merit singling out: Mr. Walter Lord gave graciously of his time as well as his resources to help me gain a better perspective of all that happened the night of April 14–15, 1912; his spirit of cooperation and openness deserves to be emulated by more historians. Alistair Lang, of East Kilbride, Scotland, lent his engineering training and experience so that I could better understand the stresses the *Titanic*'s hull underwent as she was sinking and as she broke up. James Krogan, naval architect and president of James S. Krogan & Co. of Miami, Florida, took the time to explain the finer points of the *Titanic*'s design and construction. David Norris, a private investigator and amateur radio enthusiast from Burton, Michigan, was kind enough to recount to me the story of how he uncovered the fate of Harold Bride, and was also willing to share his knowledge of the early days of shipboard wireless. Matthew McLean, a retired bosun of the British Merchant Marine who now lives in Hollywood, Florida, offered advice that helped me avoid technical errors, and provided insight into the life of a British merchant seaman that was invaluable. Harold Butler, of Swartz Creek, Michigan, a former Able-Bodied Seaman in the American Merchant Marine (and, incidentally, my father) provided advice on nautical usage, terminology, and equipment. Dr. Dorothy Mihalyfi, a clinical psychologist with a practice in Boca Raton, Florida, provided invaluable insights into the motives and mentalities of several of the individuals involved with the loss of the *Titanic*. J. Reginald Bunting, of Lyme Regis, in Dorsetshire, England, formerly of the *London Times Educational Supplement*, read this book while it was still in manuscript form, and offered his insights, comments, and criticisms about its content and readability. Linda Miller at the *Grand Rapids Press*, successor to the *Herald* once owned by Senator Smith, provided leads, which often added fascinating bits of detail to the story. Jon

Webb and Lisa Fuller-Webb gave moral and sometimes material support that allowed this work to be completed. Jon Eaton made comments, criticisms, and observations that helped me develop ideas to improve this book's immediacy and integrity—and also saved me from a monumental blunder that would have had terribly embarrassing consequences for me. And lastly, but never in the least, my wife Eleanor put up with years of frustration and aggravation while this book was being written and marketed, but never gave up and never stopped believing in either it or me, even though there were times, I'm sure, when she felt that she was the last widow of the *Titanic*.

In every case, the people and institutions mentioned provided me with information or support—or both—of some kind, which makes me responsible for how I used it. If I have done so erroneously, the fault is entirely mine.

aft: referring to the rear or toward the rear of a ship.

after: also used to refer to the rear of the ship.

after deck: the section of upper deck aft of the superstructure.

amidships (midships): refers to the general area of the center of the ship.

astern: in the direction of the rear of the ship, or if in reference to a ship's motion, going backward.

bosun: a contraction of boatswain (the term boatswain is never used, except by landlubbers); the bosun is the senior seaman on board a ship.

bow: the front of the ship.

bulkhead: a structural (i.e., load-bearing) wall in a ship. A nonstructural wall is called a partition.

collapsible: a now-obsolete form of lifeboat, which had a rigid wooden keel and collapsing (folding) canvas sides, which were held up by iron or steel stays. Collapsible boats were made redundant by the invention of inflatable life rafts.

condenser: a large machine that cools the steam that has passed through a ship's engines and condenses it back into water, so that live steam is not being vented from the ship. Alternatively the water can be fed into the boilers again.

davit: a curved arm that supports a lifeboat while it is being filled, raised, or lowered. The lifeboat's falls are connected to the davits by means of pulleys.

displacement: a measure of a ship's size, expressed by how many tons of water she displaces when she is afloat; in order for a ship to float, the amount of water she displaces must be greater than the actual weight of the ship.

double-ended boiler: a boiler having fireboxes (furnaces) at both ends.

fall: the lines by which lifeboats are raised and lowered.

fantail: an open area at the very stern of a ship.

fo'c's'le (forecastle): an ancient term used to denote the forward area of a ship in general, and often identifies the crew's quarters in that area.

fore: a shortened form of forward.

foredeck: a raised section of deck at the forward end of a ship.

forepeak: the forwardmost compartment of a ship.

forward: toward the front of a ship.

funnel: the nautical term for a smokestack—properly speaking, ships never have smokestacks, only funnels.

gangway: a large double-width doorway in the side of a ship's hull.

hawse pipe: an opening in the deck or hull of a ship through which mooring lines or anchor chains are passed.

keel: the very bottom of the ship; immensely strong, the keel is the main structural member of a ship's hull.

knot: a unit of speed and distance; a knot in speed is 1.15 land miles per hour; a knot in distance is 2,000 yards.

lead line: a length of manila rope attached to a lead weight and marked off in feet and fathoms, used to determine water depth either inside or outside a ship.

masthead light: a white light carried high up on a ship's mainmast, used along with sidelights to allow ships to determine each other's bearing, course, and speed at night.

poop deck: a raised deck structure at the very stern of a ship.

port: the left side of a ship.

reciprocating engine: a steam-driven engine which has large pistons that are driven up and down by high-pressure steam, moving much like the pistons in an automobile motor, which turn the propeller by means of a crankshaft.

screw: another term for a propeller.

sidelight: a running light located at the side of a ship's bridge; sidelights are red for port, green for starboard, and allow ships to determine each other's bearing, course, and speed at night.

single-ended boiler: a boiler having fireboxes (furnaces) at only one end.

starboard: the right side of a ship.

stay: a heavy cable used to support a funnel or mast.

steerage: a common term for Third Class, originally referring to the location of the Third Class accommodations, which were located in the most cramped and undesirable parts of the ship, often around the steering gear.

stern: the rear of a ship.

superstructure: that part of the ship that is built on top of the hull, which is the actual load-bearing structure of the ship.

turbine: a type of marine engine that consists of a large rotor covered with blades onto which steam is directed, causing the rotor to turn, which then turns the propeller by means of a shaft.

upper deck(s): the deck or decks that are exposed to the open air, i.e., there are no decks built above them.

well deck: a section of an upper deck that sits at a slightly lower level than the deck area fore and aft of it. Usually found between the superstructure and the fore or after decks.

NOTES

CHAPTER ONE

1. John Malcolm Brinnin, *The Sway of the Grand Saloon,* 361; Don Lynch, *Titanic, an Illustrated History,* 16, 19.

2. *The Shipbuilder,* Special Number, Midsummer 1911, 7–16; Brinnin, 362–63; John Eaton and Charles Haas, *Titanic: Triumph and Tragedy,* 17–18.

3. Michael Davie, *Titanic, the Life and Death of a Legend,* 32; *Triumph and Tragedy,* 18.

4. Brinnin, 242–44; Davie, 115–18; Walter Lord, *A Night to Remember,* 82; Wynn Craig Wade, *The Titanic, End of a Dream,* 32.

5. Brinnin, 316.

6. Humphrey Jordan, *Mauretania,* 18.

7. Brinnin, 325; Geoffrey Marcus, *The Maiden Voyage,* 31; Wilton J. Oldham, *The Ismay Line,* 365–88; Wade 34.

8. Colin Simpson, *The Lusitania,* 12–13; Wade, 33–34.

9. Brinnin, 322–23, 336–37; Simpson, 13–15.

10. A great deal of ruckus has been raised over the years about the name of the third ship. When launched she was given the name *Britannic,* an old and respected name in the White Star Fleet, and many historians have maintained that this was always intended to be the third sister's name. But authoritative contemporary accounts, including *New York Times, Scientific American,* and *Lloyd's Register* all identify the ship as the *Gigantic.* Moreover, at least one former manager at Harland and Wolff has gone on record saying that *Gigantic* was indeed the proposed name for the third sister. Most convincing of all though is that when taken together the three names, *Olympic, Titanic,* and *Gigantic,* all convey a sense of enormous power, size, and grandeur, something that *Britannic,* however dignified, does not—it just doesn't fit. After the loss of the *Titanic,* when sheer size was no longer a drawing card for passengers, the more subdued *Britannic* was substituted for the name of the third vessel. White Star felt it best not to tempt fate again.

11. *The Shipbuilder,* 17–43; Thomas Bonsall, *Titanic,* 10–11; Lynch, 19–22; *Triumph and Tragedy,* 20–21.

12. *The Engineer,* 3 March 1910, 209–15; *The Engineer,* 4 March 1911, 678–81; *Engineering,* 26 May 1911, 678–81; *The Shipbuilder,* 19–43; *Scientific American,* Supplement #1850, 17 June 1911; 380–83; *A Night to Remember,* 36; *The Night Lives On,* 29–33; *Triumph and Tragedy,* 20–29.

13. A legend persists to this day in some parts of Ireland that the ship sank because of a "secret message" contained in her hull number, 3909-04: when viewed in a mirror, the number spells out the words NO POPE—provided some liberty is taken with the 4. The liner was doomed, so the legend goes, because of the number the heathen Protestants in Ulster assigned to her. Unfortunately for this theory, which would make good copy for the *National Enquirer*, the only numbers ever officially assigned to the *Titanic* were Harland and Wolff's Hull No. 401, and her Board of Trade number, which was 131,428. The author wishes to thank Tommy McCluskey of Harland and Wolff and Bosun Matthew McLean of the British Merchant Marine (Ret.), for sharing this story.

14. Eighty years later, a popular myth would grow up around these plates, and the quality of the steel used to make them, when tests performed on samples of the plates would reveal that there were impurities in the steel. When compared with modern steels now required by shipping regulations, the *Titanic*'s hull plates were found to be brittle and subject to fracturing when struck. Some sources would imply that Harland and Wolff had used inferior-quality plating in order to save money, and that false economy would contribute to the loss of the *Titanic*. The truth, as is often the case, is far more mundane: metallurgy, though having made great strides in the half century since the mass production of steel had been developed, was still a far-from-precise science, and exactly how different impurities affected the molecular structure and physical properties of steel were imperfectly understood. In point of fact, the steel in the plates used to construct the *Olympic*, *Titanic*, and *Gigantic* was pretty much standard in the shipbuilding industry, and similarly impure steel could be found in the hull plates of almost every ship on the North Atlantic at the time.

15. Shan Bullock, *Thomas Andrews, Shipbuilder*, 17–21.

16. Bullock, 21–23.

17. Though the stories are today sometimes doubted by laymen, professional astronomers confirm that in the spring of 1910, when Halley's comet missed striking the earth by less than a half-million miles, the night skies were indeed brightly illuminated by the comet's tail. On some nights the light was almost bright enough to read by, and the weirdly glowing sky caused many people to believe that the end of the world was approaching.

18. *The Engineer*, 2 June 1911, 575; *The Shipbuilder*, 129–34; Bonsall, 12–13; Lynch, 22–23; *Triumph and Tragedy*, 20–29.

19. All technical details of the *Titanic*'s machinery are taken from *The Shipbuilder*, Special Number, Midsummer 1911.

20. *The Shipbuilder*, 68–69.

21. By way of contrast, the author questioned an agent for Cunard about the cost of a one-way passage in the finest suite available in the *Queen Elizabeth II*; the price was just over $15,000 for a four-day voyage.

22. All details of the *Titanic*'s accommodations are taken from *The Shipbuilder*, 69–107; John Maxtone-Graham, *The Only Way to Cross*, 121–28; Oldham, 238–45; *The Night Lives On*, 94–95.

23. Bonsall, 33; *Triumph and Tragedy*, 44–50; Wade, 38–39.

CHAPTER TWO

1. Lawrence Beesley, *The Loss of the SS Titanic*, 11; Marcus, 26.
2. *The Night Lives On*, 35.
3. John Keegan, *1914, Opening Moves*, 3.
4. Marcus, 21–23.
5. Richard O'Connor, *Down to Eternity*, 35.
6. Although Arthur Ryerson didn't know it, there was another Ryerson who would also be traveling on the *Titanic*: a dining saloon steward by the name of William E. Ryerson. The two men were distant cousins, though no one knows for sure if either man was aware the other was on board.
7. Marcus, 20; Wade, 141–42.
8. Walter Lord, *The Good Years*, 269; Lynch, 29–41; Marcus, 17–23, 35–36, 50–51; Tuchman, 245–47; Wade, 141–42.
9. Lynch, 29; Wade, 48.
10. There are few more enlightening experiences than visiting the coal mine at the Summerlea Industrial Park and Museum outside of Glasgow, Scotland. Located on the site of an old ironworks, there is a coal mine nearby, long abandoned but now restored as an educational exhibit. Here visitors are taken some forty feet underground and allowed to see firsthand the appalling conditions coal miners had to work under as late as the first quarter of the twentieth century. The author's guide during his visit happened to be his father-in-law, James Lang of East Kilbride, a retired electrical fitter and amateur historian who had worked for several years at Summerlea on various restoration projects.
11. *The Daily Mail, The Edinburgh Review, The Glasgow Herald, The Illustrated London News, The London Times, The Southhampton Times*: coverage of the Coal Strike was continuous in these newspapers from the beginning of the strike to its settlement, in the case of the London papers due to their extensive circulation, in the others due to the direct effect the strike was having on local economies. Walter Lord, *The Good Years*, 320–30; William Manchester, *The Last Lion, Vol. I, Visions of Glory*, 61–74; Marcus, 23–24; Tuchman, 351–69.
12. *Destination: Disaster*, 68–69.
13. *The Southhampton Times*, 9, 10, 11 April 1912; *Triumph and Tragedy*, 55, 72; Wade, 45–46.
14. Brinnin, 375; Marcus, 37; *Triumph and Tragedy*, 71–72.
15. Charles Lightoller, *The Titanic and Other Ships*, 218–19.
16. *The Shipbuilder*, 125–26; *A Night to Remember*, 106; *The Night Lives On*, 83–84.
17. British Inquiry (Br. Inq.), Nos. 21280, 21281; *The Night Lives On*, 87–88, 89–90.
18. David Hutchings, *R.M.S. Titanic, a Modern Legend*, 21; *A Night to Remember*, 50.
19. Marcus, 91–92; *Triumph and Tragedy*, 73.
20. Marcus, 37; *Triumph and Tragedy*, 73–74.
21. J. A. Fletcher, *Travelling Palaces*, 139–40.
22. Beesley, 15–16; Marcus, 42; *Triumph and Tragedy*, 76.

23. *Southampton Evening Echo*, 21 June 1967; *Southampton Times*, 11 April 1912; *Liberty Magazine*, April 23, 1932; Logan Marshall, ed. *The Sinking of the Titanic*, 32; Hutchings, 21; Lightoller, 220; Lynch, 33–35; *The Night Lives On*, 36–37; *Triumph and Tragedy*, 76–77; Wade, 242–44.

24. In his book, *The Loss of the SS Titanic*, Lawrence Beesley maintains that the whistle blasts were actually sounded to signal to an Isle of Wight paddle steamer to get out of the *Titanic*'s way. Despite being a careful and dedicated researcher, Beesley was an incurable "wet blanket," as well as something of a snob, to whom Captain Smith's acknowledgment of Beken would be unthinkable. Actually, Smith saluting the photographer with the *Titanic*'s whistle was entirely in keeping with the captain's nature.

25. *Southampton Evening Echo*, 21 June 1967; *Southampton Times*, 11 April 1912; Beesley, 22; *Destination: Disaster*, 84; Marcus, 46–47.

CHAPTER THREE

1. Br. Inq., No. 12326–12330; Marcus, 47–48; *The Night Lives On*, 43–44.
2. Bullock, 61–62; *A Night to Remember*, 33.
3. American Inquiry (Amer. Inq.), 72, 584–85.
4. Charles Pellegrino, *Her Name, Titanic*, 204–206; *Triumph and Tragedy*, 92–94.
5. Br. Inq., No. 12621–12623; Marcus, 51; *The Night Lives On*, 47–48.
6. Lightoller, 206.
7. Marcus, 81.
8. *A Night to Remember*, 37; Marcus, 39; Wade, 65.
9. Lightoller, 214; Brinnin, 364–65; Marcus, 39–41; *A Night to Remember*, 36–37; *The Night Lives On*, 38–41.
10. *Destination: Disaster*, 93–94; Marcus, 70–71; *A Night to Remember*, 52.
11. Estelle Stead, *My Father*, 342.
12. Lynch, 38; Marcus, 59–60.
13. *A Night to Remember*, 110; *Destination: Disaster*, 90–91; Lynch, 38; *Triumph and Tragedy*, 100–101.
14. Lynch, 39.
15. *Destination: Disaster*, 89–90; *Triumph and Tragedy*, 101.
16. *Destination: Disaster*, 89–90; Marcus, 60; *Triumph and Tragedy*, 101.
17. Marcus, 58.
18. Ibid., 58 and 81.
19. Amer. Inq., 220–21, 270–71, 369; Marcus, 83.
20. Hutchings, 28.
21. *A Night to Remember*, 110; Marcus, 30.
22. *The Night Lives On*, 48–49.
23. Col. Archibald Gracie, *The Truth About the Titanic*, 19–20.
24. *Colliers*, 4 May 1912, 10–14.
25. Gracie, 5–6, 10.
26. *Colliers*, 4 May 1912, 10–14.

27. Wade, 48.

28. Lynch, 40; Pellegrino, 181–82.

29. Lynch, 77; Marcus, 108.

30. *A Night to Remember*, 47; Lynch, 138.

31. Marcus, 105.

32. Gracie, 8–9; Marcus, 150; *Triumph and Tragedy*, 114.

33. Marcus, 106; *Triumph and Tragedy*, 114.

34. A legend that has persisted for decades about the *Titanic's* maiden voyage is that Ismay was pressuring Captain Smith to make a record-breaking crossing. This is not true. However high-handed and arrogant his behavior might be, Ismay could not alter the laws of physics. The Olympic-class ships, which displaced over 46,000 tons, had engines generating some 55,000 shaft horsepower (shp), which were capable of driving the *Olympic* and *Titanic* at a maximum of 24½ knots. In contrast, the *Lusitania* and *Mauretania*, which at the time were routinely trading speed records, displaced only 33,000 tons, but were driven by turbines which generated 68,000 shp. This gave the two ships a top speed of 26½ to 27 knots, clearly speeds the *Olympic* or *Titanic* could never attain. Additionally, the *Lusitania* and *Mauretania*, besides being lighter and having more powerful engines, had much superior hull forms, thanks to Admiralty assistance with their designs, a feature which may have added as much as a knot to their top speed.

35. Am. Inq., 963–64; Br. Inq., No. 18828–18840; *A Night to Remember*, 82; Marcus, 116; *The Night Lives On*, 60.

36. Transcribed from the original in the possession of the Southhampton City Museums.

37. *Marconigraph*, June 1911; Karl Baarslag, *SOS*, 20 and 30.

38. *A Night to Remember*, 37; Lynch, 71–72; Baarslag, 24–46.

39. Amer. Inq., 393, 825, 963–64; Br. Inq., No. 8943, 15689, 16099, 16122, 16176, 18828–18840.

40. Br. Inq., No. 16791.

CHAPTER FOUR

1. Br. Inq., No. 17704–17709.

2. Amer. Inq., 963–64.

3. Br. Inq., No. 13611–13635; Lynch, 79–80; *Triumph and Tragedy*, 115.

4. Marcus, 109.

5. *A Night to Remember*, 178.

6. Beesley, 46–48; Lynch, 77–79; Marcus, 108; *Triumph and Tragedy*, 115.

7. Amer. Inq., 937; Br. Inq., No. 13707–13724, 16918–16922; Lightoller, 222–23; *Triumph and Tragedy*, 115.

8. Amer. Inq., 902; Br. Inq., No. 2401–2408, 13656–13671, 17250–17280.

9. Br. Inq., No. 8988–9020; Marcus, 120–21; *A Night to Remember*, 37–38; Wade, 352.

10. Am. Inq., 357–63; Br. Inq., No. 1027, 13734, 15353, 15355, 17275–17280, 17299–17326; *A Night to Remember*, 14; Lynch, 84–85; Marcus, 128.

11. In 1912, helm orders were still given according to the tradition of the earliest days of sail; that is, by the direction the tiller bar was pushed in order to turn the ship, not the direction the rudder was turned. Murdoch's order of "Hard a starboard!" meant that Hitchens turned the wheel to the right, which caused the big steam-powered rudder motor in the stern to turn to the right, making the rudder pivot left. Helm orders on British merchant ships weren't rationalized until the mid-1930s when it was finally decided to set the helm controls up so that the wheel and the rudder moved the same direction.

12. Amer. Inq., 359–61; Br. Inq., No. 17299–17326; *A Night to Remember*, 14–15; Marcus, 128–29; *The Night Lives On*, 77–79.

13. Amer. Inq., 533–34, 600–602, 671; *A Night to Remember*, 15–16.

14. Amer. Inq., 512–15; *A Night to Remember*, 14–15; Lynch, 91; Wade, 241–42.

15. Amer. Inq., 111, 332–33, 986–99; *A Night to Remember*, 16, 26; Wade, 241.

16. Amer. Inq., 884; *A Night to Remember*, 18–19.

17. Amer. Inq., 966, 1002, 10096; Wade, 242–43.

18. Amer. Inq., 42, 1142; *A Night to Remember*, 16; Pellegrino, 21–22.

19. Amer. Inq., 235–36; Br. Inq., No. 15358–15385; *A Night to Remember*, 19 and 32.

20. *A Night to Remember*, 33.

21. Report to the Mersey Commission (Br. Rpt.), 32–34; *Marine Review*, May 1912, 154–60; *A Night to Remember*, 35–36; Marcus, 132; *The Night Lives On*, 74. For many years it was believed that the iceberg had torn a 300-foot-long continuous gash in the *Titanic*'s side, apparently a belief formed by a spate of speculative illustrations in the popular press, which showed the liner being sliced open like a giant tin can. It was with some shock, then, that Dr. Robert Ballard reported in 1986, when he was able to closely examine the wreck, that there was no evidence of such a gash. Yet, that such a gash was highly unlikely had been established as far back as May 1912. Edward Wilding, a marine architect for Harland and Wolff, in a brilliant piece of theoretical engineering, concluded from the reports of the rate at which the breached compartments flooded that the total area in those compartments open to the sea was approximately 12 square feet. This would have meant that a continuous cut in the *Titanic*'s hull 300 feet long would have been only a half-inch wide for it's entire length—a difficult feat for a cutting torch, let alone an iceberg. It wasn't until 1996 that ultrasonic probes conducted by Paul Mathias were able to conclusively establish that there was no gash: the damage done was indeed a seires of bent plates, split seams, and small holes—the total area open to the sea being just a little over 12 square feet.

22. Br. Inq., No. 664–668, 1860–1867, 3997–4002, 3715–3729, 3736; *Engineering*, 14 June 1912, 847–50; *Marine Review*, May 1912, 154–60.

23. Amer. Inq., 27–41; Br. Rpt. 32–34; *Marine Review*, May 1912, 154–160; *Syren and Shipping*, 24 April 1912; Marcus, 295; *The Night Lives On*, 85.

24. *Parliamentary Debates (Commons)*, 15 April–25 October 1912; *Engineering*, 14 June 1912, 847–50; *Marine Review*, May 1912, 154–60; Brinnin, 250–51, 267–69, 347–51; Marcus, 37; Wade, 75.

CHAPTER FIVE

1. Amer. Inq., 69; Br. Inq., No. 13734; Lightoller, 227.

2. Amer. Inq., 260.

3. Ibid., 436.

4. Ibid., 1103; *New York Times*, 19 April 1912; Beesley, 80–82; Gracie, 14–16.

5. Amer. Inq., 1024; *Colliers*, 4 May 1912, 10–14; Beesley, 50–53.

6. Amer. Inq., 1147; *Semi-Monthly Magazine (Washington Post)*, 26 May 1912, 3–4; *A Night to Remember*, 25.

7. Marcus, 137.

8. *A Night to Remember*, 25.

9. Amer. Inq. 995–96.

10. Ibid., 332.

11. Ibid., 794 and 808; Beesley, 52; Gracie, 17.

12. *A Night to Remember*, 25; Wade, 248.

13. Lynch, 73; Wade, 247.

14. Amer. Inq., 228–29, 1032–36.

15. Br. Inq., No. 1917–1932.

16. Ibid., No. 708–827, 1940–1957.

17. *Harper's Weekly*, 29 April 1912; Elizabeth Shutes quoted in Gracie, 251–52; Marshall, 67.

18. Amer. Inq., 333; Beesley, 78; Lynch, 96.

19. The bulk of the recounting of what transpired in the wireless shack comes from Bride's interview in the *New York Times*, April 20, 1912; additional information comes from his testimony before the Senate Committee, 103–61, 1045–55, as well as from the author's conversations with private investigator David Norris in April 1992.

20. *A Night to Remember*, 40–41; Wade, 244–45.

21. Amer. Inq., 1114; Br. Inq., No. 933–936.

22. Amer. Inq., 885.

23. Amer. Inq., 1105; Dr. Dodge quoted in Gracie, 292; *A Night to Remember*, 42.

24. *A Night to Remember*, 45.

25. Amer. Inq., 109 and 808.

26. Amer. Inq., 1148–49.

27. This incident would provide generations of gossip mongers with a source of endless speculation. It is usually maintained, and under the circumstances reasonably so, that an illicit liaison was taking place in C-78. Given the social and moral tone of the period, public revelation of the affair would have been disastrous for all involved, hence the reluctance of the couple inside to open the door. If such was the case, their secret stayed safe with them that night, most likely all the way to the bottom of the Atlantic.

28. Amer. Inq., 807–8; *A Night to Remember*, 43; Lynch, 98.

29. *A Night to Remember*, 44 and 45.

30. Br. Inq., No. 9963–9997.

31. *The Shipbuilder*, 125–26; Lynch, 101.

32. Amer. Inq., 331; Molly Brown quoted in Gracie, 127–28.
33. Amer. Inq., 1040–41; *Semi-Monthly Magazine (Washington Post)*, 26 May 1912, 3–4; *A Night to Remember*, 44; Edith Russell quoted in Pellegrino, 211–212.
34. *Colliers*, 4 May 1912, 10–14.
35. Lynch, 94–95.
36. Amer. Inq., 1121.
37. Gracie, 7; *A Night to Remember*, 47–48.
38. Amer. Inq., 72–73.
39. Ibid., 72–88; Lightoller, 229–31.
40. Beesley, 83–84.
41. Amer. Inq., 227.
42. Ibid., 988–1000; Gracie, 228–33.
43. Amer. Inq., 577, 810, 988–1000; Gracie, 228–35.
44. Amer. Inq., 105–10.
45. Ibid., 235–37.
46. Wade, 280.
47. Amer. Inq., 111–12.
48. Br. Inq., No. 11337–11409; *The Night Lives On*, 90.
49. Amer. Inq., 332; *Harper's Weekly*, April 29, 1912; *A Night to Remember*, 54.
50. Amer. Inq., 519.

CHAPTER SIX
1. Bullock, 69–72; Marcus, 139–40.
2. Amer. Inq., 796; Br. Inq., No. 2792–2801.
3. Br. Inq., No. 2008–2096; *A Night to Remember*, 57–58; *Triumph and Tragedy*, 149.
4. It's worth keeping in mind that a red sidelight or running light is always shown from the port (left) side of a ship's bridge and a green sidelight is shown from the starboard (right) side, then taking the time to compare the movements of the unknown ship seen from the *Titanic* with those of the drifting *Californian* relative to the unknown ship she spotted, as described in Chapter 10.

This and all subsequent passages concerning the *Titanic*'s rockets and the unknown ship on the horizon are primarily derived from the transcripts of the American and British inquiries, where the two subjects are inextricably linked. The most significant sections are cited here.

The Rockets: Amer. Inq., 237–239, 289–307, 294, 328, 401, 519, 832, 1145; Br. Inq., 1195–1207, 1199, 2582–2583, 4997–5006, 10103, 12496, 14150–14155, 14168–14127, 15066, 15494–15400, 17684, 17972.

The Unknown Ship: Amer. Inq., 114, 235–236, 295, 307, 328, 346, 358, 359, 448–449, 520, 520–524, 544, 564, 565, 570, 611–612, 648, 827–828, 909, 990; Br. Inq., 2419–2420, 10264–10274, 10268, 14149, 15385–15409, 17669–17674, 17854–17869, 18001–18017, 18002, 18069.

Also: Beesley, 79–80; Gracie, 21–24; Wade 338–61; Leslie Reade, *The Ship That Stood Still*, 143–49.

5. Bride's Interview, *New York Times*, 20 April 1912.

6. Amer. Inq., 1100, 1109, 1149–50, 1162; *A Night to Remember*, 62 and 63; *Semi-Monthly Magazine (Washington Post)*, 26 May 1912, 3–4; Lightoller, 238; Marcus, 149–50.

7. Lynch, 112.

8. *New York Times*, 19 April 1912; Marshall, 61.

9. Lynch, 112 and 117.

10. Gracie, 19, 32, 124; *A Night to Remember*, 74.

11. Lightoller, 233–34.

12. Amer. Inq., 595, 602, 755; Bullock, 71; *A Night to Remember*, 67; Wade, 291 and 293.

13. Amer. Inq., 79, 334–35; *Colliers*, 4 May 1912, 10–14; Molly Brown quoted by Gracie, 128.

14. Lightoller, 233–34; *A Night to Remember*, 66.

15. *Harper's Weekly*, 20 April 1912; Elizabeth Shutes quoted by Gracie, 254.

16. Amer. Inq., 1166; Lynch 94 and 115.

17. Br. Inq., No. 9885–9907, 11289–11322; *New York Sun*, 22 April 1912.

18. Amer. Inq., 1210–45; *New York Sun*, 22 April 1912; *A Night to Remember* 112–14; Marcus, 160–61; *The Night Lives On*, 113–25; Wade, 380–83.

19. Richard Harding Davis, *Our English Cousins*, 149–50.

20. *Journal of Commerce: Report of the Titanic Inquiry* (1912), 267; Lightoller, 243; *A Night to Remember*, 75; Marcus, 161.

21. Gracie, 25.

22. Lightoller, 240.

23. Amer. Inq., 240.

24. Ibid., 273–75, 526, 798, 810–12, 971–72, 1041; Br. Inq., No. 5141–5153, 11501–11730, 12647–12668.

CHAPTER SEVEN

1. In years to come armchair navigators would frequently suggest that Captain Smith should have had the *Titanic* steam over to this other ship. While certainly a plausible idea, given the benefit of hindsight, it had certain drawbacks at the time that certainly would have caused the captain to reject the idea even if it had been brought up. Most significantly, Captain Smith knew his ship had been badly damaged, but just how extensively was uncertain—at one point Andrews had used the phrase "torn to bits below." There was the distinct possibility that if the ship's structure was affected, trying to make headway in a sinking condition might actually make the damage worse and drive the bow right under, sinking the ship in a matter of minutes. Three years later, the *Lusitania* would sink less than twenty minutes after she was struck by a German torpedo, and her speed of eighteen knots contributed heavily to the rapidity of her sinking: her forward momentum literally drove her bow down under the water.

2. Later a great deal of fuss was raised by Germany over Phillips's treatment of the *Frankfort*'s wireless operator, including a formal protest by the German ambassador to

Great Britain. The Germans said that Phillips didn't treat the *Frankfort*'s operator
with the same courtesy that he did the operator of, say, the *Olympic*. They maintained, with a great show of wounded Teutonic dignity, that this was because the
Frankfort's wireless was operated by German Telefunken and not British Marconi, or
simpler still, because the *Frankfort* was a German ship and the *Olympic* was British.
Obviously, the German's weren't about to admit that the *Frankfort*'s operator might
have been, based on the nature of his queries, rather dense. The Germans were
extremely touchy about any slight, real or imagined, in those last few years before the
Great War.

3. *New York Times*, 20 April 1912.

4. Br. Inq., No. 17090–17109; *New York Times*, 21 April 1912.

5. Amer. Inq. 19–21; Rostron, 63.

6. *The Night Lives On*, 159.

7. Amer. Inq., 19–21; *Scribner's Monthly*, March 1913, 354–64; Captain Sir
James Bisset, *Ladies and Tramps*, 276–80; Captain Sir Arthur Rostron, *Home From
the Sea*, 57–63; *A Night to Remember*, 138–41.

8. *A Night to Remember*, 59; Wade, 60.

9. Pellegrino, 212.

10. Amer. Inq., 605, 648, 674, 822, 1146; Wade, 292–93.

11. Lynch, 117.

12. Amer. Inq., 798–800; Beesley, 316–20; Dr. Dodge quoted in Gracie, 294–
95; Wade, 293–94.

13. Marcus, 158.

14. *New York Times*, 15 April 1912.

15. O'Connor, 154–56; Wade, 54–57.

16. During his testimony before the U.S. Senate inquiry, Lowe described every
man who tried to stow away in one of the lifeboats or force his way into one as an
"Italian." The imputation of cowardice was so inflammatory that the Italian ambassador to the United States, Signor Cusani, demanded—and received—a written
apology from Lowe. Amer. Inq., 116–28, 605, 615–16, 1109–12; *Semi-Monthly
Magazine (Washington Post)*, 26 May 1912, 3–4.

17. Amer. Inq., 800–802; Beesley, 72–80; Wade, 298–99.

18. Amer. Inq., 645; Wade, 299.

19. Beesley, 83–84; *Destination: Disaster*, 31–32; *The Night Lives On*, 137–38.

20. Marshall, 96–97.

21. Gracie, 4–5, 27; *A Night to Remember*, 82; Marcus, 314; Marshall, 75–76;
Wade, 89–90.

CHAPTER EIGHT

1. *New York Times,* 20 April 1912.

2. Amer. Inq., 887–88; *A Night to Remember*, 80.

3. Amer. Inq., 8, 519–20, 960; Br. Inq., No. 18611–18635; Br. Rpt., 38; Lynch,
132; Wade, 299–300.

4. Amer. Inq., 990–92; Gracie, 27, 42, 44.

5. Amer. Inq., 240, 548, 1100; Wade, 301.

6. Gracie, 32.

7. Amer. Inq., 81, 581–83, 1107; Gracie, 30–32; *A Night to Remember*, 84–85; *Triumph and Tragedy*, 156; Wade, 301–3.

8. Amer. Inq., 587.

9. Lightoller, 243.

10. Amer. Inq., 587, 831; Gracie, 37–39; *A Night to Remember*, 86; Wade, 307–8.

11. Amer. Inq., 80–81, 587, 588, 831–33, 887; Gracie, 37–39; Mrs. Walter Stephenson quoted in Gracie, 193–94; Lynch, 133; Wade, 307–9.

12. *New York Times*, 20 April 1912.

13. Amer. Inq., 794; *A Night to Remember*, 89.

14. Lightoller, 243–44.

15. Gracie, 44–46; Lightoller, 245–46.

16. Amer. Inq., 161; *New York Times*, 20 April 1912; Lynch 135–37; Marcus, 155–56; author's conversations with private investigator David Norris in July 1995.

17. For years it has been commonly believed that the last music played by the *Titanic*'s band was either the Episcopalian hymn "Autumn" or the popular waltz "Songe d'Automne." The evidence for this has rested solely on the uncorroborated testimony of Harold Bride, who told a reporter for the *New York Times* that the last song he remembered the band playing was called "Autumn." Bride, though, was the only person with that recollection, and he never specified if he meant the hymn or the waltz. Neither piece of music is listed in the White Star Line's music book for 1912. Significant as well is that the hymn is not called "Autumn," only the melody is (much like the melody of the hymn "O God, Our Help in Ages Past" is known as "St. Anne's"), and usually only a professional musician will refer to a piece of music that way. A very strong case can be made for the hymn legend has always said was the last music played aboard the *Titanic*. There are a number of accounts of survivors who recalled hearing "Nearer, My God, to Thee," and the American melody, called "Bethany," was well known to most Americans, and was sometimes heard in British churches as well, so it is understandable for both British and American survivors to recall hearing the hymn. (It should be pointed out that if Bride did mean that hymn, parts of the two hymns sound remarkably similar, so that someone hearing only snatches of the melody, as was undoubtedly the case in Bride's circumstances, might mistake one hymn for the other.) "Nearer, My God, to Thee" was known to be a favorite of Bandmaster Hartley's, and was the hymn played at the graveside of all deceased members of the Musician's Union. Perhaps most convincing of all is a report in the *Daily Sketch* on April 22, 1912, in which a colleague of Hartley's recalled how some years earlier, while still aboard the *Mauretania*, that he asked Hartley what he would do if he found himself on the deck of a sinking ship. Hartley replied that he would assemble the ship's orchestra and play "O God, Our Help in Ages Past" or "Nearer, My God, to Thee." Somehow, that seems definitive enough.

18. Gracie, 27, 51–56; Bullock, 73.

19. Author's conversation with naval architect James Krogan.

20. Marshall, 51.

21. Br. Inq., No. 10544–10551; Gracie, 312–13; Wade, 310–11.

22. Amer. Inq., 67–69, 87, 91; *Christian Science Journal*, October 1912; Lightoller, 247–50.

23. Amer. Inq., 91–92, 120; Gracie, 59–60; Lightoller, 249; author's conversation with naval architect James Krogan in June 1995.

24. Gracie, 49, 67–68.

25. Jack Thayer quoted by Gracie, 221–22.

26. Amer. Inq., 628.

27. Ibid., 1156.

28. Coroner's records, Public Archives of Nova Scotia; *A Night to Remember*, 100.

29. Gracie, 89–90; *A Night to Remember*, 101; Lynch 145; Marcus, 159; Wade, 90–91, 310.

30. *The Night Lives On*, 129–33.

31. Gracie, 27; Wade, 90.

32. *A Night to Remember*, 101–2.

33. Amer. Inq., 69, 280, 339, 530–31, 563, 609–10, 620, 818, 1108; Br. Inq., No. 3858–3869, 3883–3885, 5673–5681, 6251–6266, 11512–11525, 15078–15081; Gracie, 51–56; Lightoller, 247–52; Wade, 311–21; author's conversations with naval architects James Krogan, William Gartzke, Jr., and David K. Brown, Royal Corps of Naval Constructors, June 1995.

CHAPTER NINE

1. Gracie, 70–72; Lightoller, 250–51.

2. The exact nature of the break-up of the wreck will never be known for certain. This passage is based on conversations with American naval architects James Krogan, William Gartzke, Jr., and British Naval Constructor David K. Brown, RCNC, along with discussions with Allistair Lang, E-M.E., of East Kilbride, Scotland.

3. Gracie, 73–76; *Outlook*, 27 April 1912, 898–905; *A Night to Remember*, 89.

4. Survivors tales recounted by Gracie, 313–20; Wade, 326–27.

5. Amer. Inq., 87, 91, 110, 161, 628, 786, 1053; Br. Inq., No. 6261–6299, 14122–14138; Jack Thayer quoted by Gracie, 223–24; Wade, 191–93.

6. Amer. Inq., 227; *Colliers*, 4 May 1912, 3–4; Lightoller, 252; Wade, 326.

7. Amer. Inq., 111, 242–44, 277–78, 526, 538, 570, 811–12, 827, 842, 1010–12, 1100; Lynch, 144; Wade, 328–29.

8. Amer. Inq., 573, 971; Br. Inq., No. 5141–5153, 11501–11730, 12647–12668, 12875–12895; Gracie, 269–79; *Coronet*, June 1931, 94–97.

9. Amer. Inq., 116–30, 605–7, 615–19, 677–82, 1109; *Semi-Monthly Magazine (Washington Post)*, 26 May 1912, 3–4; Mrs. Alexander Compton quoted in Gracie, 168–70; *A Night to Remember* 119–20; Wade, 331–33.

10. Amer. Inq., 19–21; *Scribner's Monthly*, March 1913, 354–64; Bisset, 279–84; Rostron, 63.

11. Amer. Inq., 583, 1109; Mrs. Stephenson and Miss Eustis quoted in Gracie, 194–97.

12. The nickname, which appears to have originated in Molly's hometown of Denver, Colorado, would forever identify her with the *Titanic*. In the early 1960s a Broadway musical loosely based on Molly's life (and later a movie starring Debbie Reynolds as Molly) would be produced bearing Molly's nickname as its title. Amer. Inq., 333–36, 363, 451; *Colliers*, 4 May 1912, 10–14; Molly Brown quoted in Gracie, 134–39; *Coronet*, October 1949, 116–21; *A Night to Remember*, 121, 128–29; Lynch, 144, 146, 149; Wade, 329.

13. Amer. Inq., 87–93, 110, 161, 628–30, 785–90; Gracie, 87–103; Jack Thayer quoted in Gracie, 223; *New York Times*, 20 April 1912; Wade, 334.

14. Lord, 122–23; Lynch, 148; Marshall, 70 and 116.

15. Amer. Inq., 528, 800, 1144; Beesley, 135–36; Mrs. Stephenson quoted in Gracie, 195; *A Night to Remember*, 123–25.

16. *A Night to Remember*, 125.

17. Marshall, 114.

18. Amer. Inq., 143–44, 570; Lynch, 144; Marshall, 113–14; *A Night to Remember*, 125.

19. Amer. Inq., 138, 145, 174; Elizabeth Shutes quoted in Gracie, 258–59.

20. Amer. Inq., 22, 243, 1104; Elisabeth Allen quoted in Gracie, 180; Beesley, 196–202; *Scribner's Monthly*, March 1913, 354–64; *A Night to Remember*, 144–45; Lynch, 150.

21. *A Night to Remember*, 141 and 145.

22. Bisset, 292; Marshall, 187; Rostron, 72.

23. Beesley, 135–36; *A Night to Remember*, 149; Wade, 327.

24. Amer. Inq., 88–92, 112, 166, 632–33; *New York Times*, 20 April 1912; Gracie, 107–9; Marcus, 173; Wade, 334.

25. Amer. Inq., 122–28, 590, 615, 677, 832, 891; Gracie, 315–20; Elisabeth Compton quoted in Gracie, 169–70; Lynch, 154.

26. *A Night to Remember*, 152 and 154.

27. *Harper's Weely*, 29 April 1912; Elizabeth Shutes quoted in Gracie, 259–60.

28. Amer. Inq., 22–28; Br. Inq., No. 18896–19055; Lynch 154–56.

29. *A Night to Remember*, 153.

30. Ibid., 154, 155–56.

31. Gracie, 110–13; Lynch, 156; Marcus, 193–94.

32. *Scribner's Monthly*, March 1913, 354–64; Rostron, 75–77; *Triumph and Tragedy*, 179–80.

33. *A Night to Remember*, 166–67.

34. Marcus, 310; *Coronet*, May 1953, 30; *United States Naval Institute Proceedings*, March 1968.

CHAPTER TEN

1. The contents of this chapter were drawn primarily from the transcripts of the American and British investigations, along with Leslie Reade's *The Ship that Stood Still*, as well as from specific contemporary newspaper articles. For an overview of the

Californian incident, see the references listed below. For specific details see the notes for the rest of the chapter.

Amer Inq., 289–307, 359, 544, 570–73, 708–12, 720–22, 827–28, 903, 1118–20.

Br. Inq., No. 6897–6954, 6999–7000, 7090–7094, 7280–7294, 7476–7533, 7552–7572, 7829–7866, 7880–7896, 7948–7956, 7971, 8022–8037, 8503– 8064, 8988–9020, 13682–13695.

Br. Rpt., 45–46.

2. Br. Inq., 6766, 7426–7429, 7455; Reade, 43–44.

3. Br. Inq., 8272, 8275, 8282, 8289.

4. Ibid., 7439, 7469, 7472, 7475, 7552–7553, 7838, 7870, 8042; Reade, 62– 77. Again, it is worth the reader remembering that a ship's port sidelight is red and the starboard on is always green. With this in mind a comparison of the movement of the "mystery ship" seen from the *Titanic* and the movements of the *Californian* are quite revealing.

5. Br. Inq., No. 7483–7510, 7515, 7522, 7552–7572, 7650–7651, 7829–7856; Reade, 78–94; *Daily Mirror*, 15 May 1912.

6. Amer. Inq., 745; Br. Inq., No. 7971.

7. Br. Inq., No. 8017, 8022–2037.

8. Br. Inq., No. 13682–13695; Mersey Report, 45–46.

9. Br. Inq., No. 6970–6973, 8768, 9058–9059.

10. Br. Inq., No. 87031–87038.

11. Br. Inq., No. 7061, 7336–7337.

CHAPTER ELEVEN

1. Lynch, 159–63; Marcus, 196–200.

2. Sir Cosmo and Lady Duff Gordon really were having a bad time of it. They were not unkind people, as Sir Cosmo demonstrated when he offered to help the crewmen in Lifeboat 1 "start new kits," i.e., purchase new personal belongings. Though some of their actions demonstrated a real lack of sympathy for the sensibilities of others, they never set out to deliberately offend anyone. *Liberty Magazine*, 23 April 1912; Marcus, 198–99; *Triumph and Tragedy*, 192.

3. Amer. Inq., 11; *New York Herald*, 16–18 April 1912; *New York Evening Sun*, 16 April 1912; *New York Times*, 15–19 April 1912; *New York World*, 16–20 April 1912; Wade, 76–77.

4. *New York Evening Sun*, 17–18 April 1912; *New York Herald*, 18 April 1912; *New York Times*, 18–19 April 1912; *New York World*, 18 April 1912; *A Night to Remember*, 161–62; Marcus, 197–98; Wade, 79–80, 366–68.

5. Wade, 82.

6. See the following newspapers for 19–20 April 1912: *New York American*, *New York Evening Mail*, *New York Evening Post*, *New York Herald*, *New York Sun*, *New York Times*, *New York World*, *Philadelphia North American*, *Philadelphia Press*, *Wall Street Journal*; *Scribner's Monthly*, March 1913, 354–64; Rostron, 67–71; *A Night to Remember*, 163; Lynch, 166; Wade, 81–87.

7. *London Daily Mail*, 23 April 1912.

8. *London Daily Mail*, 23 April 1912.

9. *London Daily Mail*, 22–23 April 1912; *Southampton Times*, 21–27 April 1912; *Triumph and Tragedy*, 205.

10. Conversation with Terry Wise, former third purser on the *Yarmouth Castle*, February 27, 1997.

CHAPTER TWELVE

1. Marcus, 121; *The Night Lives On*, 193–94; Wade, 115–23; for details of Smith's career in Congress and the Senate, see nearly any issue of the *Detroit Free Press, Detroit News, Flint Journal, Grand Rapids Evening Press, Grand Rapids Herald*, or *Grand Rapids News* (today the last three all have merged into the *Grand Rapids Press*) for the years of 1895–1919.

2. Wade, 146–54.

3. Marcus, 210; Wade, 156.

4. Letter to Senator Francis G. Newlands, quoted in Wade, 375.

5. Amer. Inq., 29, 81, 1108; *New York American*, 21 April 1912; *New York Tribune,* 19–21 April 1912; *New York Herald*, 20 April 1912; *San Francisco Chronicle*, 19 April 1912; Marcus 208–11; Wade, 160–65.

6. Amer. Inq., 110–75; Wade, 201–7, 366–70.

7. Interestingly enough, Lightoller was to lead a minor mutiny of sorts among the *Titanic*'s officers. The officers were billeted in the same hotel as the rest of the crew, the Continental, all of them living on the same floor and eating together in the hotel's dining room. This was a totally unacceptable situation for Lightoller: as far as he was concerned, the accommodations were adequate for the crew's needs, but it was unthinkable that the officers should be expected to stay in the same hotel, let alone mess with the men. Lightoller expected that the same kind of separation between officers and crew that existed at sea should be preserved on land, going so far that at one point he told Bill McKinstry, Senator Smith's private secretary and unofficial intermediary, "As an officer, I am not going to be quartered with the crew." Aghast, McKinstry replied, "My God, your Captain sleeps quartered with the crew beneath the waves!" But Lightoller was obstinate, and finally the manager of the Continental offered a compromise—the officers would be given better rooms on a different floor than the crewmen and would be served their meals separately—and Lightoller accepted. Amer. Inq., 85–97, 772–89; Marcus, 216; Wade, 215.

8. Amer. Inq. 92, 120, 790.

9. *London Daily Telegraph*, 26 April 1912.

10. *Illustrated London News*, 25–26 April 1912; *London Daily Express,* 23, 24, 27 April 1912; *London Daily Mail*, 22–25, 28 April 1912; *London Globe*, 27–30 April 1912; *London Morning Post*, 27 April 1912; *London Standard*, 25, 26 April 1912; *London Times*, 21–29 April 1912.

11. *Illustrated London News*, 24 April 1912.

12. *John Bull*, April 27, 1912.

13. *Illustrated London News*, 29 April 1912; *John Bull*, April 27, 1912; *Review of Reviews*, Vol, 46, 168.

14. Wade, 385–86.

15. Amer. Inq., 328, 346, 358–59, 448–49, 524.

16. *New York World*, 24 April 1912; Wade, 341–42.

17. Amer. Inq., 709–15; *Boston American*, 26 April 1912; Wade, 354–56.

18. Amer. Inq., 772–846; *Boston Journal*, 27 April 1912.

19. Wade, 346–352.

20. Amer. Inq. 19–30.

21. *Report of the Senate Committee on Commerce pursuant to S. Res. 283, Directing the Committee to Investigate the Causes of the Sinking of the "Titanic"* with speeches by *William Alden Smith and Isidor Rayner*, 62nd Congress, 2nd session, May 28, 1912, S. Report 806 (#6127).

22. *Report of the Senate Committee on Commerce pursuant to S. Res. 283, Directing the Committee to Investigate the Causes of the Sinking of the 'Titanic'* with speeches by *William Alden Smith and Isador Rayner*, May 28, 1912, Senate Document #476, Library of Congress #6594, 92.

23. Hutchings, 32–36.

24. Lynch, 182; Marcus, 223–24; *The Night Lives On*, 198–99; *Triumph and Tragedy*, 260–61.

25. Lightoller, 257; Lynch, 182–85; Marcus, 262–63, 264; *Triumph and Tragedy*, 260–61.

26. Marcus, 264; Wade, 387.

27. Br. Inq., No. 7483–7510, 7552–7572, 7829–7896, 8988–9020; Reade, 226–37.

28. Br. Inq., No. 13682–13695; Br. Rpt., 46–49; Reade, 105–6, 114–39, 141–42, 300–10.

29. Br. Inq., No. 11501–11730, 14197–14209, 14414–14425, 12647–12668, 12875–12895.

30. *Report on the Loss of the Titanic (S.S.)*; H.M.S.O., 1912.

31. Reade, 268–72.

32. Br. Rpt., 30–56.

CHAPTER THIRTEEN

1. The descriptions of the cemeteries in Halifax, as well as of the inscriptions on the headstones, come from the author's visits to Halifax in August 1986 and September 1997.

2. Davie, 224–25; Lynch, 174; Wade, 110–11.

3. *Destination: Disaster*, 98–99.

4. Wade, 110–111.

5. *Coroner's Records of the City of Halifax and the Province of Nova Scotia*, Public Archives of Nova Scotia. Attempts to identify unknown victims would continue for years, some identifications being made as recently as 1991, when *Titanic* International, a group of *Titanic* enthusiasts led by Charles Haas and John Eaton, identified No. 23 as Wendla Maria Heininen, a twenty-three-year-old woman from Helsinki,

Finland. Her name was subsequently carved into the face of her headstone at Fairview Cemetery, as were those of five other victims who had been identified after their interment.

6. Conversation with Dan Conlin, The Maritime Museum of the Atlantic, Halifax, Nova Scotia, Canada, on September 2, 1997.

7. Conversation with Dan Conlin, September 2, 1997; Davie, 229; *Destination: Disaster*, 103; *Triumph and Tragedy*, 232–33.

8. Author's visit; *Destination: Disaster*, 103–4.

9. Author's visit; *Destination: Disaster*, 105.

CHAPTER FOURTEEN

1. Dr. Robert Ballard, *The Discovery of the Titanic*, 75–83; Pellegrino, 105–6.

2. Davie.

3. Ballard, 101.

4. Information supplied by Dr. Stephen Deucher, exhibitions director, National Maritime Museum, in conversation with author in October 1995. Dr. Deucher was responsible for creating the highly successful "Wreck of the *Titanic* Exhibition."

5. *The Titanic in a New Light*, 67–75.

6. There has always been an element of "sour grapes" to Bob Ballard's continued protests against the salvage and recovery of artifacts from shipwrecks, especially the *Titanic*, but then he has had a string of particularly bad luck in the salvage sweepstakes. First, the two expeditions to the *Titanic* were partially funded by the U.S. Navy, which forbade any recovery of artifacts from the wreck. Next came his discovery of the German battleship *Bismarck* and the exploration of the Japanese and American warships of Guadalcanal. Warships always remain the property of their country of origin, and the United States, Germany, and Japan all have laws prohibiting any salvage by civilians from sunken vessels belonging to their navies. Finally, his dives on the wreck of the *Lusitania* in 1994 came six years after the salvage firm Oceanics, Inc., had recovered most of the retrievable artifacts from that great liner.

7. *Triumph and Tragedy*, 309–11, 313–15.

8. Advertisement for RMS *Titanic*, Inc., in *The Miami Herald*, 15 June 1996.

9. Marketing letter sent to this writer by RMS *Titanic*, Inc., dated May 12, 1996. The author indicated in the text was Walter Lord. That Mr. Lord had neither been formally asked by RMS *Titanic*, Inc., to participate nor indicated his willingness to do so, was confirmed by this writer in a telephone conversation with Mr. Lord on July 9, 1996.

10. *New York Times*, 26–31 August 1996; Alexandra Foley, director of information, RMS *Titanic*, Inc., in conversations with author in June and July 1996; Charles Haas, historical advisor to RMS *Titanic*, Inc., in conversations with author, June 1996.

11. A&E Home Video, *Titanic*, Vol 3.

CHAPTER FIFTEEN

1. *Wall Street Journal*, April 16, 1912.

2. Marcus, 298.

3. Brinnin, 380–81.

4. Wade, 382.

5. *The Good Years*, 272–73.

6. Wade, 430–34.

7. A&E Home Video, *Titanic*, Vol. 4.

8. "The Convergence of the Twain" by Thomas Hardy, from *Collected Poems*, The Macmillan Company. Used by permission.

EPILOGUE

1. *The Night Lives On*, 222.

2. Interview with David Norris, P.I., July 8, 1996.

APPENDIX II

1. Br. Rpt., 46.

APPENDIX III

1. Interview with Dorothy Mihalify, Ph.D., August 26, 1996.

BOOKS

Ballard, Robert D. *The Discovery of the Titanic*. New York: Warner, 1987.

Beesley, Lawrence. *The Loss of the SS Titanic*. Boston: Houghton Mifflin, 1912.

Bisset, Captain Sir James. *Ladies and Tramps*. Glasgow: Brown and Ferguson, 1955.

Brinnin, John Malcolm. *The Sway of the Grand Saloon*. New York: Delacorte, 1971.

Bullock, Shan F. *A Titanic Hero: Thomas Andrews, Shipbuilder*. Baltimore: Norman, Remington, 1913.

Davie, Michael. *Titanic: the Death and Life of a Legend*. London: Bodley Head, 1986.

Eaton, John P. and Charles Haas. *Titanic: Destination Disaster*. New York: W. W. Norton, 1987.

Eaton, John P. and Charles Haas. *Titanic: Triumph and Tragedy*. New York: W. W. Norton, 1988.

Fletcher, R. A. *Travelling Palaces*. London: Boothby, 1913.

Gracie, Archibald. *The Truth About the Titanic*. New York: Kennerly, 1913.

Hoffman, William and Jack Grimm. *Beyond Reach: The Search for the Titanic*. New York: Beaufort, 1982.

Hyslop, Donald, Alistair Forsyth, and Sheila Jemima. *Titanic Voices: Memories of the Fatal Voyage*. New York: St. Martin's Press, 1997.

Jordan, Humphrey. *Mauretania*. London: Hodder and Stoughton, 1937.

Keegan, John. *August 1914: Opening Moves*. New York: Ballantine, 1971.

Lightoller, Charles H. *The Titanic and Other Ships*. London: Ivor Nicholson and Watson, 1935.

Lord, Walter. *The Good Years*. New York: Harper, 1960.

———. *The Miracle of Dunkirk*. New York: William Morrow, 1976.

———. *The Night Lives On*. New York: William Morrow, 1986.

———. *A Night to Remember*. New York: Hold, Rinehart and Winston, 1955.

Marcus, Geoffrey. *The Maiden Voyage*. New York: Viking Press, 1969.

Marshall, Logan, ed. *The Sinking of the Titanic*. No locale or publisher listed, 1912.

Maxtone-Graham, John. *The Only Way to Cross*. New York: Macmillan, 1972.

Padfield, Peter. *The Titanic and the Californian*. New York: John Day, 1965.

Pellegrino, Charles. *Her Name, Titanic*. New York: Avon Books, 1988.

O'Connor, Richard. *Down to Eternity*. New York: William Morrow, 1957.

Oldham, Wilton J. *The Ismay Line*. Liverpool: The Journal of Commerce, 1961.

Reade, Leslie. *The Ship That Stood Still*. New York: Ingraham Book Company, 1994.

Rostron, Capt. Sir Arthur. *Home From the Sea*. London: Hodder and Stoughton, 1937.

Simpson, Colin. *The Lusitania*. Boston: Little, Brown and Company, 1972.

Thayer, John B. [Jack]. *The Sinking of the S.S. Titanic*. Riverside, Conn.: 7 C's Press, 1974.

Tuchman, Barbara. *The Proud Tower*. New York: Macmillan, 1966.

Wade, Wynn Craig. *The Titanic: the End of a Dream*. New York: Penguin, 1979.

TECHNICAL JOURNALS

"The Launch of the *Titanic*." *The Engineer* 111 (2 June 1911).

"Loss of the Steamship *Titanic*." *Marine Review* 42 (May 1912) 156–60.

"The *Olympic* and *Titanic*—Two Giant Ocean Steamships." *Scientific American*, Supplement #1850 (17 June 1911) 380–83.

"The *Olympic* and *Titanic*." *The Engineer* 111 (3 March 1911) 209–15.

"*Olympic* and *Titanic*." *The Shipbuilder* 6, Special Number (Midsummer 1911).

"The Senate Committee's Report on the *Titanic*" and "The Shortcomings of Wireless at Sea." *Scientific American* 106 (8 July 1912) 510.

"The *Titanic* and *Lusitania*: A Final Forensic Analysis." *Marine Technology* 33:4 (October 1996) 241–89.

"The *Titanic* Inquiry." *Engineering* 93 (14 June 1912): 802–806, Continued (21 June 1912) 847–50.

"The White Star Line." *The Engineer* 109, Supplement (24 June 1910).

"The White Star Liner *Olympic*." *Engineering* 90 (21 October 1910) 564–72, Continued (4 November 1910) 620–21, Continued (18 November 1910) 693–95.

"The White Star Liner *Titanic*." *Engineering* 91 (26 May 1911) 678–81.

"White Star Liners *Olympic* and *Titanic*." *The Engineer* 109 (4 March 1911) 678–81.

PERIODICALS

Ballard, Robert D. "How We Found *Titanic*." *National Geographic*, (December, 1985).

————. "A Long, Last Look at *Titanic*." *National Geographic*, (December, 1986).

Bellairs, Carlyon. "The *Titanic* Disaster." *Contemporary Review*, (1912) 788–97.

Candee, Helen Churchill. "Sealed Orders." *Colliers*, (4 May 1912) 10–14.

Carrothers, John C. "Lord of the *Californian*." *United States Naval Institute Proceedings* (March 1968).

Collyer, Charlotte. "How I Was Saved from the *Titanic*." *Semi-Monthly Magazine* (Washington Post) (26 May 1912) 3–4.

Duff Gordon, Lady Cosmo. "I Was Saved From the *Titanic*." *Coronet* (June 1951) 94–97.

Fowler, Gene. "The Unsinkable Mrs. Brown." *Coronet* (October 1949) 116–21.

Greenspan, Bud. "Deaf to Disaster." *Coronet*, (May 1953) 31.

Griffin, Henry F. "Sixteen Boats and a Quiet Sea." *Outlook* (27 April 1912) 898–905.

Kamuda, Edward S. "Reflections of a Disaster." *The Titanic Commutator*, (April 1974).

Lightoller, Charles H. "Testimonies from the Field." *Christian Science Journal* (October 1912).

Rostron, Arthur H. "The Rescue of the *Titanic* Survivors." *Scribners Monthly* (March 1913) 354–64.

Weeks, Jack. "*Titanic*." *Holiday* (June 1953) 91–94.

Young, Filson. "God and Titan." *Saturday Review* (20 April 1912) 490.

————. "A Sea Birth." *Saturday Review* (27 April 1912) 520–21.

NEWSPAPERS
Boston American
Boston Globe
Boston Post
Chicago Tribune
Detroit Free Press
Detroit News
Edinburgh Review
Flint (MI) Journal
Glasgow Herald
Grand Rapids Evening Press
Grand Rapids Herald
Grand Rapids News
Illustrated London News
London Daily Express
London Daily Mail
London Globe
London Morning Post

London Standard
London Times
New York American
New York Evening Mail
New York Evening Post
New York Herald
New York Sun
New York Times
New York World
Philadelphia North American
Philadelphia Press
Providence Evening Bulletin
Toronto Globe
Wall Street Journal
Washington Evening Star
Washington Post

GOVERNMENT DOCUMENTS

Great Britain, *Parliamentary Debates* (Commons), 5th series, 37–42, April
    15–October 25, 1912.
Great Britain, *Report on the Loss of the "Titanic" (S.S.)*, HMSO, 1912.
U.S. Congress, Senate, *Hearings of a Subcommittee of the Senate Commerce
    Committee pursuant to S. Res. 283, to Investigate the Causes leading to the
    Wreck of the White Star liner "Titanic."* 62nd Congress, 2nd session, 1912,
    S. Doc. 726 (#6167).
U.S. Congress, Senate, *International Conference on Safety of Life at Sea*, 63rd
    Congress, 2nd session, 1914, S. Doc 463 (#6594).
U.S. Congress, Senate, *Report of the Senate Committee of Commerce pursuant to
    S. Res. 283, Directing the Committee to Investigate the Causes of the Sinking
    of the "Titanic," with speeches by William Alden Smith and Isidor Rayner*,
    62nd Congress, 2nd session, May 28, 1912, S. Rept. 806 (#6127).
U.S. Navy Department, "Report of the Hydrographer." *Annual Reports of the
    Navy Department*, Appendix 3, 193–208. Washington, D.C.: Govern-
    ment Printing Office, 1913.

ARCHIVES

United Kingdom
    Harland and Wolff Shipyards, Belfast, Northern Ireland. Historical Sec-
        tion, *Titanic* Collection (now in the possession of the Ulster Folk and
        Transport Museum).
    National Maritime Museum, Greenwich, London, England: *Titanic* Col-
        lection and Wreck of the *Titanic* Exhibition.
    Public Records Office, London, England. Documents #BT100/259
        (Cargo Manifests); #BT100/260 (Ship's Articles); #M12266/12

(Order for Formal Investigation); #MT9/920/4 M23780 (Sailing Clearances); #MT9/ 920/5 M23448 (Request for Hearing by Captain Stanley Lord); #MT15/142 M13505 (Crew Muster).

Southampton Maritime Museum (Wool House), Southampton, Surrey, England. William Burroughs Hill Collection, Stuart Collection, *Titanic* Archive.

Ulster Folk and Transport Museum, Belfast, Northern Ireland. Department of Archival Collections. R. C. W. Courtney Collection.

Republic of Ireland

Provincialate of the Society of Jesus, Dublin. Father Francis Brown Collection.

Public Records Office of the County of Cork, Cobh. Emigration Records, April 1912.

United States

Grand Rapids Public Museum, Grand Rapids, Michigan. William Alden Smith Collection.

Library of Congress, Washington, D.C. Manuscript Division: The Presidential Papers of William Howard Taft: Case Files #303 (Major Archibald Butt) and #3175 (*Titanic*).

Mariner's Museum, Newport News, Virginia.

Port Authority of New York, New York City. Collector of Customs Office, Immigration Records, April 1912.

Titanic Historical Society, Indian Orchard, Massachusetts. THS Archives, including "Remember the *Titanic*," a series of recorded interviews with survivors, made for the tenth anniversary of the founding of the THS (1972).

Canada

Public Archives of Nova Scotia, Halifax, Nova Scotia. Records of the Coroner's Office, April 22–May 15, 1912.

INDEX

Note: All officers and crew, unless otherwise identified, are from the Titanic.

A Night to Remember (book), 137, 209
"A Night to Remember" (film), 210
Abbott, Rosa, 141, 154
Abelseth, Olaus, 89–90, 135, 141
Adams, Brooke, 182
Adriatic, 47, 72
Allison, Hudson, 80, 100, 101
Allison, Mrs. (Bessie), 100
Allison, Lorraine (daughter), 100
Allison, Trevor (son), 100
Alvin, 213–215
America, 50
Amerika, 62
Anderson, Rev. Roger, 156
Andrea Doria, x
Andrews, Thomas, 21, 43, 77, 94, 95, 103, 248
  assesses damage to *Titanic*, 71–72, 72–73; career, 12–14; last seen, 132; oversees construction of *Titanic*, 13–15; urgency in loading lifeboats, 102
Andrews, Mrs. (Helen), 14
ANGUS, 211–12, 213
Appleton, Charlotte, 55, 69, 101
Argo, 207, 212, 213
Arizona, 73
Astor, Col. John Jacob, 27–28, 51, 78, 83, 90, 94, 97, 127, 128
  body recovered, 200–201; eccentricities of, 28; eulogized, 224; fate of, 135–36, 223; scandal over divorce and remarriage, 28
Astor, Mrs. (Madeline), 28, 78, 83–84, 90, 94, 127, 149
Atlantic, 73
Atlantis II, 213, 215

Ballard, Robert, 208, 210–12, 213, 275.n6
Baltic, 59, 60, 62, 63, 120, 149

Backworth, Algernon, 142
Baron de Hirsch Cemetery, 202, 203, 204
Barrett, Fireman James, 71–72, 81, 97, 153, 186
Baxter, Storekeeper Thomas, 204
Beattie, Thomson, 141
Beauchamp, Fireman George, 150
Becker, Mrs. Allen (Nellie), 32–33, 118, 233
Becker, Marion (daughter), 33, 118, 233
Becker, Richard (son), 33, 118, 233
Becker, Ruth (daughter), 33, 118, 119, 234
Beesley, Lawrence, 65, 76, 77, 82, 88, 119, 146, 231, 262.n24
Beken, Frank, 42, 262.n24
Belfast, Northern Ireland, 3, 21, 177
Belford, Chief Night Baker Walter, 68, 140
Bell, Chief Engineer Joseph, 68, 96, 109, 130, 175, 226
Bentham, Lillian, 149–50
Biles, J. H., 192
Binns, Jack, 37–38
binoculars, 44, 66, 183
Birma, 98, 120
Bishop, Dickinson, 56, 69, 78, 88, 226, 231
Bishop, Mrs. (Helen), 56, 69, 78, 88, 231
Bishop, Steward W., 76
Bisset, 2nd Officer James (*Carpathia*), 152
Blair, David, 44
Blue Ribband, 7–8
Board of Trade, 38, 72, 182, 185, 193, 196, 260.n13
Board of Trade Inquiry, 192–97
  and *Californian*, 194, 196; and Captain Lord, 194, 196; and Sir Cosmo Duff Gordon, 194–95, 196; class hostilities expressed during, 195; composition of, 192; conclusions and findings, 195–97; and Lord Mersey, 192; purpose of, 193; *Titanic* crewmen quarantined during, 192

Boat Drill, 57–58
Boat Train, 27, 33, 36
Boat 1, 110, 138, 143–44, 167
Boat 2, 94, 126–27, 143, 146, 151, 152, 153, 175
Boat 3, 93, 103, 111, 123, 147, 150, 154
Boat 4, 91, 94, 99, 127–28, 138, 147, 149, 150, 153–54
Boat 5, 91, 92, 93, 97, 103, 110, 111, 138, 146, 149, 150
Boat 6, 91, 100, 101, 102, 146, 147–48, 149, 150, 175
Boat 7, 91, 92, 110, 111, 132, 146, 153, 154
Boat 8, 100, 101, 105, 109, 143, 150, 151
Boat 9, 102, 118, 150, 151
Boat 10, 117–18, 144, 153
Boat 11, 102, 118, 146
Boat 12, 144, 149, 153–54, 156
Boat 13, 101, 110, 113, 118–19, 121, 138, 150, 153, 154
Boat 14, 99, 121, 138, 144–45, 146, 149, 154, 155, 218, 226
Boat 15, 105, 119, 122, 150
Boat 16, 121, 122, 146
Boston American, 187
Bowyer, Pilot George, 40–51
Boxhall, 4th Officer Joseph, 41, 53, 62, 70–71, 73, 74, 75, 79, 80, 94, 98, 110, 113, 152, 210
    attempts to contact "mystery ship," 113; appears at Senate investigation, 186; career of, 53, 234; in charge of Boat 2, 126–27, 143, 152
Bradley, George, 54
Brailey, Pianist Theodore, 49
Bremen, 200
Brice, Seaman W., 68, 118
Bricoux, Cellist Roger, 49
Bride, Junior Wireless Operator Harold, 60–62, 66, 82, 97, 98–99, 125, 169, 175, 269.n17
    fate of, 234; fight with stoker, 131; sells story to *New York Times*, 170, 183; testifies before the Senate, 183; trapped under Collapsible B, 133, 142; works *Carpathia*'s wireless, 167–68
Britannic, 235.
Brown, Purser E. G. (*Carpathia*), 116, 152
Brown, Steward Edward, 133, 136, 141
Brown, Mrs. J. J. (Molly), 27, 29, 101, 102, 147–48, 226, 232, 271.n12
Brown, Mrs. J. Murray, 55, 101, 129–30, 208
Brown, Thomas William, 33, 99, 218

Brown, Mrs. (Elizabeth), 33, 99
Brown, Edith (daughter), 33, 218
Browne, Frances M., 50
Buckley, Daniel, 80, 86, 96, 106–7, 121, 226
Buley, Seaman Edward, 68
Burgess, Asst. Baker Charles, 83
Buss, Kate, 65, 89, 118, 150, 231
Butler, Reginald, 200
Butt, Maj. Archibald, 30–31, 69, 94, 100, 122, 126, 135, 136, 170, 177
Byles, Father Thomas, 78, 135

Caldwell, Mrs. Albert, 39
Caldwell, Alden (son), 119, 146
Californian, 66, 157, 164–65, 186, 189, 194, 240–44
    fate of, 237; missing entries in log of, 65, 188, 194; missing scrap log of, 188, 194; position of, 244; position of bow to unidentified ship, 160, 162, 163; rockets seen from, 162–63, 164, 186; stopped by icefield, 159, unknown ship appearance, 160, 163; wireless watch aboard, 160–61
Candee, Mrs. Helen Churchill, 55, 56, 89, 101, 142, 148, 200, 232
Captain's Inspection, 57
Carlisle, Alexander, 39, 94
Caronia, 62, 63
Carpathia, 98, 113–14, 120, 149, 164–65, 168, 169, 189, 194
    arrives in New York, 170–72; fate of 235; picks up survivors, 151–57; respond's to distress call, 116–17, 145–46; return voyage to New York, 167
Carter, Rev. Earnest, 57, 65, 150
Carter, Mrs. (Lillian), 57, 65, 150
Carter, William, 69, 127, 155, 226, 231
Carter, Mrs. (Lucile), 127, 128
Carter, William, Jr. (son), 128, 154
Case, Howard, 55, 77, 101
"Cavalcade," 209
Cave, Steward Herbert, 205
Cavell, Trimmer George, 109, 175
Cavendish, Turrell, 99
Cavendish, Mrs. (Julia), 88, 99
Cedric, 168, 181, 182
Chambers, Norman, 80, 88
Chambers, Mrs. (Bertha), 80
Chandowson, Victorine, 30, 84, 103
Chaston, Edward, 192
Cherbourg, 27, 43, 44, 48
Cherry, Gladys, 84, 143, 226
Chester, USS, 170
Chevre, Paul, 110

Clark, Mrs. Ada, 138
Clark, Bass-violinist Fred, 49, 204
Clarke, Capt. A. W., 192
Clarke, Capt. Maurice H., 38, 196
Cleaver, Alice, 100
Clench, Seaman Fred, 67, 87
Clinch, Seaman Frederick, 153
Coffey, Fireman John, 51
Cohen, Gus, 101, 107
Collapsible A, 126, 131, 141–42, 154
Collapsible B, 126, 131, 133, 134, 138, 142, 148–49, 151, 153
Collapsible C, 125, 130, 138, 146
Collapsible D, 128–30, 153, 154
Collett, Stewart, 88
Colley, E. P., 55
Collins, Chef John, 134
Collyer, Harvey, 77–78, 88, 121
Collyer, Mrs. (Charlotte), 77–78, 88, 121, 149
Collyer, Marjory (daughter), 77, 88
Compton, Mrs. Alexander (Mary), 100
Compton, Alexander, Jr. (son), 100
Compton, Sara (daughter), 100
Cork Harbour (Queenstown), 50
Cornell, Mrs. R. C. (Malvina), 55, 101
Cottam, Wireless Operator Harold (*Carpathia*), 146, 167, 169
   receives *Titanic*'s distress signal, 114; story sold to *New York Times*, 170, 183
Coutts, Minnie, 104
Coutts, Leslie (son), 104
Coutts, William (son), 104
Coward, Noel, 210
Crawford, Steward Alfred, 68–69, 85
Crosby, Capt. Edward Gifford, 84, 92
Crosby, Mrs. (Catherine), 84, 92, 149
Crosby, Harriet (daughter), 84, 92
Cunard, 7, 9–10, 16, 123, 205
Cunningham, Steward Andrew, 85

Daily Mail (London), 173–74
Daily Mirror (London), 184
Daily Telegraph (London), 184
Daly, Eugene, 52, 57
Daly, Peter, 78, 133, 141
Daniel, Robert, 88
Daniels, Sarah, 80, 100
Davidson, Mrs. Thornton (Orian), 151
Dean, 1st Officer H. (*Carpathia*), 114, 115, 117
Dean, Steward George H., 205
de Villiers, Madam Bertha, 150
Diamond, Seaman Frank, 150

Dick, Albert, 95
Dick, Mrs. (Vera), 95, 150
Dillon, Trimmer Thomas, 109, 150
Divine Services, 58
Dobbins, James, 16
Dodd, Steward George, 83
Dodge, Washington, 84, 110, 119, 135, 154
Dodge, Mrs. (Ruth), 84, 88, 154
Dodge, Washington, Jr. (son), 154
Douglas, Walter, 69, 99, 126, 224
Douglas, Mrs. (Mahala), 69, 99, 152
Drew, James, 84
Drew, Mrs. (Lulu), 84
Drew, Marshall (nephew), 84
Duff Gordon, Sir Cosmo, 45–46, 110, 143–44, 167, 222, 231, 272.n2
Duff Gordon, Lady (Lucile), 45–46, 110, 143–44, 167, 232, 272.n2
Dyker, Adolf, 86, 99

Elizabeth II, 233
Elliot, Trimmer Everett Edward, 205
Etches, Steward Henry, 79, 85, 92, 143
"Eternal Father, Strong to Save," 65
Evans, Wireless Operator Cyril (*Californian*), 160, 161, 164, 190
Evans, Edith, 55, 101, 129–30, 208
Evans, Seaman Frank, 68, 118

Fairview Cemetery, 201–2, 204–5
Farrell, Jim, 106
Firearms, 93, 110, 121, 122, 125
Fleet, Lookout Frederick, 66–67, 98, 147
Florida, 38, 73
Fortune, Mark, 99
Fortune, Mrs. (Mary), 99
Fortune, Charles (son), 99
Francatelli, Laura, 143–44, 167
Frankfort, 98, 114, 117, 265.n2
Franklin, Phillip A. S., 168, 169, 186
Frauenthal, Henry, 93, 223
Freeman, Ernest Edward Samuel, 204
Frolicher, Marguerite, 69, 88–89

Gallagher, Martin, 101
Gatti, Louis (Luigi), 49, 94
Geller, Arne, 215, 216
George V, 27, 226
Gibson, Dorothy, 92
Gibson, Apprentice Officer James (*Californian*), 161, 162–63
Gigantic, 10, 93, 235, 259.n1
Gill, Engineer Ernest (*Californian*), 187
Gilnagh, Kathy, 57, 106

Glynn, Mary, 101
Goldsmith, Franklin, 52, 129
Goldsmith, Mrs., 52, 129, 138, 234
Goldsmith, Franklin, Jr. (son), 52, 129, 138, 143
Gough–Calthorpe, R. Adm. Sommerset, RN (Ret.), 192
Gracie, Col. Archibald, 31, 55, 77, 79, 82, 90, 101, 109, 123, 127, 128, 131, 134, 139, 142, 148, 154, 232
Graham, Mrs. William (Edith), 55, 101, 103
Graham, Margaret (daughter), 55, 101
Great Coal Strike, 35–36, 37, 173, 261.n11
Groves, 3rd Officer Charles Victor (*Californian*), 159, 160, 161
Guggenheim, Benjamin, 27, 28–29, 85, 123, 223

Haddock, Capt. H. J. (*Olympic*), 186
Haines, Seaman Albert, 118
Halifax, Nova Scotia, 169, 199, 200, 203
Hamburg-Amerika Shipping Line, 7–8, 9, 123
Hamilton, Engineer Frederick (*Mackay-Bennett*), 199
Harbinson, W. D., 195
Harder, George, 77
Hardy, Steward John, 129–30
Hardy, Thomas, 229
Harland, Edward, 4–5
Harland and Wolff, 3, 4–6, 9, 14, 15, 16, 20, 53, 93, 103, 194
Harper, Henry Sleeper, 81, 103, 154
Harper, Mrs. (Renee), 30, 64, 76, 129, 232
Harris, Stuart, 208
Harper, Rev. John, 56
Harper, Nina (daughter), 56
Hart, Benjamin, 56
Hart, Mrs. (Esther), 56, 138, 232
Hart, Eva (daughter), 56, 138, 232–33
Hart, Steward John, 87, 89, 104–5, 109, 122
Hartley, Bandmaster Wallace, 49, 91, 122, 131, 175, 177, 204, 226, 269.n17
Harvey Asst. Engineer Herbert G., 81, 97
Hawke, HMS, 20, 48
Hays, Charles, 27, 29, 78–79, 82, 94, 123
Hays, Mrs. (Clara), 32
Hemming, Trimmer Samuel, 63, 76, 83, 131, 136, 175
Hendrickson, Fireman Charles, 143
Hesketh, Asst. 2nd Engineer James, 71–72, 81
Hippach, Jean Gertrude, 147

Hitchen, Quartermaster Robert, 65, 67, 102, 147–48
Hoffman, Louis. *See* Navatril, Michel, Sr.
Hogeboom, Mrs. John (Anna), 88
Hogg, Lookout G. A., 92, 153
Homer, Harry, 54
Hoyt, W. H., 145
Hubbard, Elbert, 225
Hughes, Chief Steward Harry (*Carpathia*), 116
Hume, 2nd Violinist John Law "Jock," 49, 204
Hurd, Charles, 153
Hurley, Rev. William G., 23
Hurst, Greaser Walter, 79, 111, 136, 142, 148
Hutchinson, Ship's Carpenter James, 63, 70, 83

ice, iceberg(s), ix, 1, 59, 63–64, 65, 66, 67, 68, 69, 70, 78, 82, 97, 137, 153, 159, 161, 235, 246
IFREMER, 212, 214
Illustrated London News, 185
International Mercantile Marine (IMM), 8–9, 14, 16, 181, 182, 190, 233
Ireland, 50
Ismay, J. Bruce, 3–4, 9–10, 14, 16, 58–59, 60, 62, 88, 97–98, 103, 138, 154, 191, 223, 247
    assists in loading lifeboats, 93, 126; at U.S. Senate investigation, 181–82; blamed for disaster, 182; dictates speeds to Captain Smith, 59; early life and career, 6–7; escape, 126; interferes in loading lifeboats, 91, 93; reaction to collison, 70, 72; sells White Star Line, 9; subsequent career, 233
Ismay, Thomas, 4, 6–9
Isaccs, Sir Rufus, 194, 195, 244

Janson, Carl, 136
Jason, Jr. (*JJ*), 213
Jewell, Lookout Archie, 66
John Bull (periodical), 185
Johnson, Steward James, 67, 123
Johnstone, Chief Engineer (*Carpathia*), 115
Jones, Seaman Thomas, 143, 151
Jonnson, Carl, 79, 86
Joughin, Baker Charles, 87
Julian, Henry Forbes, 32

Kemish, Fireman George, 71, 97
Kent, Edward A., 55, 101, 200

Knorr, 207

Krins, Violist George, 49

Lange, Robert, 207

Lardner, Capt. F. H. (*Mackay–Bennett*), 199, 203

Le Suroit, 212

"Lead Kindly Light," 65

Leader, Alice, 109

Lee, Lookout Reginald, 66–67, 98

Leitch, Jessie, 56

Lightoller, 2nd Officer Charles Herbert, ix, 41, 44, 63–64, 65, 73, 74, 99, 110, 131, 138, 141, 193

at U.S. Senate investigation, 183; assigned to lifeboats, 91, 102–3, 126–30; early career of, 46–47; escapes *Titanic*, 133; in charge of Collapsible B, 142, 148; subsequent career of, 233–34; threatens passengers with revolver, 126–27; uneasiness, 47

Lindell, Edvard, 141–42

Lindell, Mrs. (Elin), 141–42

London Scottish Drill Hall, 192

Long, Milton, 126, 134

Lord, Capt. Stanley (*Californian*), 159, 164–65, 187, 240–44

and the Board of Trade, 194, 196, 197; at U.S. Senate investigation, 188; character of, 194; informed of rockets, 162, 163, 187, 188; instructions to officers on watch, 162; observes unknown ship, 161, 188; subsequent career of, 234.

Lord, Walter, 71, 137, 140, 197, 209, 275.n9

Lowe, 5th Officer Harold, 40, 53, 92–93, 97–98, 121, 146

at U.S. Senate investigation, 184; defies Bruce Ismay, 93; fires revolver, 121, 122; in charge of Boat 14, 122, 154, 155; prejudices of, 118, 121, 144, 145, 268.n16; returns to pick up swimmers, 144–45; stops rush on Boat 14, 121–22; subsequent career of, 234; supervises loading Boats 11 and 13, 117–19

Lucas, Seaman William, 130

Lusitania, 9–10, 16, 38, 61, 159, 263.n34

Lyon, Cdr. Fitzhugh, RNR, 192

McCawley, T. W., 56

McElroy, Purser Hugh, 39–40, 86, 125–26, 224

McGee, Frank, 116 146, 154, 167

McGough, James R., 70, 92, 97

McGough, Seaman Paddy, 151

Mackay–Bennett, 199, 200–201, 203

Marconi, Gugliemo, 170, 183

Marconi Marine, 60–61

Marechal, Pierre, 110, 132

Martin, Nicholas, 45

Marvin, Daniel, 99

Marvin, Mrs. (Mary), 99, 150

Mauretania, 9–10, 16, 49, 61, 159, 263.n34

May, Arthur, 173

May, Mrs., 173

May, Arthur, Jr. (son), 173

Memorial to *Titanic* victims, 176–77, 204

Mersey, Lord John Charles Bigham, 192–94, 195, 196

Mesaba, 63, 64

Meyer, Mrs. Edgar (Leila), 148

Mihalyfi, Dorothy, 249–50

Milling, Jacob, 51

Millet, Frank, 31, 78, 94, 122

Minahan, W. T., 99

Minahan, Mrs., 99

Minahan, Daisy (daughter), 144

Morawik, Earnest, 89

Morgan, J. P., 8–9, 14, 16, 168, 181

Morning Post (London), 184

Moody, 6th Officer James, 41, 53, 63, 66–67, 75, 98, 121

Moore, Clarence, 69, 94, 122, 126, 224

Moss, Steward William, 83

Mount Olivet Cemetery, 202, 204

Mount Temple, 98, 120, 149, 156–57, 164

Muller, Interpreter L., 87, 104

Mullins, Kate, 106

Murdoch, 1st Officer William, 41, 44, 65, 73, 74, 86, 99, 110, 111

assigned to starboard lifeboats, 90–91, 92–93, 105, 110, 126; early career of, 46; last seen, 133; stops rush on Boat 15, 122; stops rush on Collapsible C, 125; tries to avoid collison, 67, 70, 263.n11

Murphy, Kate, 106

"Mystery ship" seen from *Titanic*, 98, 113, 119, 129

sidelights on, 98, 113, 129

Nadir, 217

Nautile, 216, 217

Navatril, Michel, Sr., 129, 201, 203

Navatril, Edmond (son), 129

Navatril, Michel, Jr., (son), 129, 146

"Nearer, My God, To Thee," 131, 132, 136, 269.n17

New York, 41–42

New York Evening Mail, 170
New York Evening Sun, 170
New York Herald, 168, 170
New York Times, 119–21, 168
New York World, 170
Nichols, Bosun Alfred "Big Neck," 39, 103
Nomadic, 44
Noordam, 62, 63
Norddeutscher-Lloyd Shipping Line, 7–8, 9
Norman, Douglas, 65, 89, 118, 150

"O God, Our Help in Ages Past," 58, 269.n17
Ocean Dock (Southampton), 23, 36
Oceanic, 41, 42
Odell, Kate, 50
Odell, Mrs. Lillie, 50
Ogden, Louis, 153, 154–55
Ogden, Mrs., 153, 156
O'Laughlin, F. W. N., 39–40, 81, 95
Olliver, Quartermaster Alfred, 65, 150
Olympic, 10, 20, 48, 93, 98, 114, 117, 120, 148, 186, 208, 235
Osman, Seaman Frank, 68
Otsby, Helen, 92

Pain, Alfred, 118, 150
Paintin, Captain's Steward Arthur, 53
Parisian, 169
Parks, Seaman Samuel, 127
Paulson, Gosta Leonard, 203
Penasco, Victor de Satode, 100, 150
Penasco, Mrs. (Josefina), 100, 150, 151
Perkis, Quartermaster Walter, 150, 153
Peuchen, Maj. Arthur Godfrey, 69, 78–79, 82, 85, 88, 94, 102, 147–48
Phillips, Sr. Wireless Operator John "Jack," 60–62, 66, 92, 97, 98, 113, 114, 117, 125, 175, 177
    cuts off *Californian*'s ice warning, 66, 160; death of, 49; fights with stoker, 131; sends "CQD," 82–83, 98–99; sends first "SOS" in history, 99; sends last signals, 131
Pirrie, Lord William James, 3, 6, 9–10, 14–15, 16
Pitman, 3rd Officer Herbert, 41, 73, 87, 92, 138, 142, 209, 210
    defies Bruce Ismay, 91; career of, 53, 234; in charge of Boat 5, 92–93; reaction to collision, 75–76
Pitt, Barry, 24
Poingdestre, Able Seaman John, 79, 96
Pusey, Fireman R., 144

Queenstown (Cobh), Ireland, 50

RMS *Titanic*, Inc., 215–18
    accused of graverobbing, 217, 233; attempt to raise hull of *Titanic*, 217–18
"Raise the *Titanic!*" (film), 210
Ranger, Greaser Thomas, 96, 109
Ray, Steward F. Dent, 79, 88, 96, 110, 118–19, 150, 154
Rees, 3rd Officer (*Carpathia*), 171
Republic, 37–38, 73
Review of Reviews, 185
Reynolds, Harold, 204
rockets, 94, 97–98, 113, 119, 162–63, 187, 188, 240–42
Robinson, Stewardess Annie, 95
Roebling, Col. Washington Augustus, 30, 55
Romaine, C. H., 54
Roosevelt, Theodore, 31, 227
Rosenshine, George, 45
Rostron, Capt. Arthur H. (*Carpathia*), 114, 145–46, 170–71, 247
    at U.S. Senate investigation, 188–89; early career of, 115; oversees recovery of survivors, 151–52; prepares for rescue, 115–16; respond's to *Titanic*'s distress signal, 115; subsequent career of, 235
Rothes, Countess of, 84, 100, 143, 151, 225
Rowe, Quartermaster George, 68, 94, 175
    attempts to contact "mytery ship," 113; fires distress rockets, 98, 110, 113, 119, 125; takes command of Collapsible C, 126
Rush, Alfred, 129
Russell, Edith, 44–45, 88, 118, 146, 233
Ryerson, Arthur, 30, 59, 76, 84, 94, 99, 122, 126, 127–28, 224
Ryerson, Mrs. (Emily), 30, 59, 76, 84, 99, 127–28, 150
Ryerson, Emily (daughter), 84
Ryerson, Jack, (son), 128

Sarnoff, David, 117
Scanlon, Thomas, 195
Scarrott, Seaman Joseph, 121
Schwabe, Gustavus, 4, 6
Scorpion, USS, 212
"Scotland Road," 86, 87, 96
Scott, Greaser Fred, 109
Sealby, Capt. Inman (Ret.), 189
Senior, Fireman Harry, 136
Seward, Fred, 77, 92
Shepherd, Asst. Engineer, 97

Ship's orchestra, 41, 43, 49, 91, 122, 131, 136–37. *See also individual members*
Shipbuilder (periodical), 1, 18
Shutes, Exlizabeth, 55, 81–82, 154
Siverthorne, Spencer, 76, 84
Simpson, Asst. Surgeon J. Edward, 64, 128
Sjoblom, Anna, 106
Slayter, Hilda, 146
Sloan, Stewardess Mary, 95
Slocombe, Masseuse Maud, 44, 147
Sloper, William, 82, 92, 226
Smith, Clinch, 55, 79, 82, 90, 101, 127
Smith, Capt. Edward J., 21, 41–42, 43, 57, 58, 59, 62, 64, 74, 77, 80, 83, 90, 91–92, 94, 98–99, 100, 105, 109, 110, 113, 126, 132, 189, 190
alleged suicide of, 136; early career of, 47–48; failed attempts to load lifeboats, 91, 146; ice precautions taken by, 64, 65, 246; inspects ship after collision, 71–73; last seen, 136; on modern shipbuilding, 48; orders "Abandon Ship," 130; orders distress signal sent, 82; orders passengers mustered, 73; orders rockets fired, 98; puts officers in charge of lifeboats, 91; reaction to collision, 70–73, 245–50
Smith, Postal Clerk Iago, 70
Smith, Lucien P., 69, 83, 85, 94, 99–100
Smith, Mrs. (Mary), 83, 85, 94, 99–100
Smith, Sen. William Alden, 172, 183, 196, 197, 228
and Bruce Ismay, 181–82; and Captain Lord, 188, 191–92; and *Californian*, 187–88, 191–92; early career of, 179–80; conducts U.S. Senate investigation, 183–84, 185–86; defense of, 185; gaffes of, 184; lampooned by British press, 184–85; methods of cross–examination, 185–86; on Captain Smith, 189, 190; presents finds, 190
Snyder, John, 92
Snyder, Mrs., 92
Solomon, Abraham, 110
Southampton, 21, 23, 172–74, 176–77
Stanwyck, Barbara, 209
Stead, William T., 32, 78, 85, 122–23
steerage passengers. *See* Third Class passengers
Steffanson, Lt. Bjorn, 55, 69, 76, 84, 101, 125, 130, 224
Stengel, C. E., 69–70, 110, 138
Stengel, Mrs. (Annie), 69–70
Stephenson, Mrs. Walter (Martha), 70
Stewart, Albert, 78, 85

Stewart, Chief Officer George (*Californian*), 163, 164
Stewart, Steward John, 132, 145
Stockholm, x
Stone, 2nd Officer Herbert (*Californian*), 161, 162–63, 164
Straus, Isidor, 30, 109, 177, 209, 223
Straus, Mrs. (Ida), 109, 177, 208, 209
Stunke, Johana, 200
Symons, Lookout George, 44, 66, 111, 143
Syren and Shipping (periodical), 184

Taft, William Howard, 30, 31, 170, 177
Taylor, Pianist P. C., 49
Teutonic, 61
Thayer, John B., Sr., 30, 95, 126, 225
Thayer, Mrs. (Marion), 30, 95, 127, 150, 154, 155
Thayer, John, Jr., "Jack" (son), 30, 76, 77, 88, 126, 134, 138, 142, 154, 155, 227–28, 231
"The Convergence of the Twain," 230–31
The Night Lives On, 210
Third Class passengers, 78, 103–4, 104–8, 122, 209, 224–25
boarding procedures, 40; immigration laws concerning, 40, 106; obstacles to Boat Deck encountered by, 40, 104, 106–7; overlooked by ship's officers and crew, 105; participate in U.S. Senate investigation, 183; roused after collision, 86–87, 103; social life aboard ship, 57, 65–67
Thompson, Fireman John, 67, 87, 141
Thorne, Maybelle, 45
Titanic, ix, 41, 42, 43, 51–52, 54, 56, 62, 63, 64, 65, 97, 102, 114, 117, 120, 125, 139, 145–46, 147, 152, 188, 189, 194, 199, 212, 218–19, 235
appearance of, 10; in popular culture, 209–10; artifacts recovered from, 215–16, 218; boilers and engines of, 16–17, 239; boiler rooms, 1, 4, 6, 71–72, 79, 81, 96, 97, 109, 140, 207; breaks up, 138, 140; collision with iceberg, 67–72; conception of, 3–4, 9–10; condition of the wreck, 213–14; considered "unsinkable," 11; construction of, 11–13; crew lost on, 172, 226; damage done by iceberg to, 72, 213–14, 264.n21; dimensions and specifications of, 10, 237–39; effect of loss in technology, 222–23; effect of loss on social attitudes, 223–27; firing of distress

Titanic (continued)
 rockets, 97–98, 113, 119; First Class accommodations, 17–19; ice warnings received by, 59, 60, 62; launch of, 3, 14–16; lifeboats carried by, 38–39, 72, 93–94, 171–72, 195 *See also individual Boats*; maiden voyage of, 20, 48; modifications to, 20; number of lives lost on, 156, 169, 239; number of survivors, 156, 239; official announcement of sinking, 169; provisions carried, 36–37; proximity of *Californian* to, 240–44; recovery, identification, and burial of victims, 199–203; restaurant staff locked in quarters, 107, 139; salvage, 215–18; sea trials of, 21; Second Class accommodations of, 19; sees unidentified ship nearby, 98; sinking, 137–38; steel used in construction of, xi, 260.n14; stops at Cherbourg, 43–45, stops in Queenstown, 50–51; Third Class accommodations, 19–20; top speed of, 17, 237, 263.n34; watertight construction of, x, 11; wreck found, 209
"*Titanic*" (American film), 209
"*Titanic*" (German film), 209
Titanic Historical Society, 210
"*Titanica*" (IMAX film), 215
Traffic, 44
Troutt, Winnie, 51, 118, 129, 233
Tulloch, George, 216, 217, 218. *See also* RMS *Titanic*, Inc.

U.S. Coast Guard, 209
U.S. Hydrographic Office, 62, 188, 190
U.S. Senate investigation, 79, 181–92
 and Bruce Ismay, 181–82; and Captain Lord, 187–88; and Captain Rostron, 188–89; and 5th Officer Lowe, 184, 186; and 2nd Officer Lightoller, 183–84; competence and legality of questioned by British press, 184–85; conclusions and recommendations of, 190–92

Van Anda, Carr, 120–21

Victims, 199, 200, 202
 recovery of, 199–201; identification of, 200, 202; burial of, 202–4; graves of, 199, 204, 205–6
Virginian, 120, 169
Vulcan, 41–42

Wade, Wynn Craig, 224
Wall Street Jounal, 222
Walter, Rabbi Jacob, 202
Warren, Mrs. Helen, 92
Wennerstrom, August, 107, 122, 141–42, 225
Wheat, Steward Joseph, 80, 96
White, Electrician Alfred, 96
White, Mrs. J. Stuart (Ella), 69, 109, 147, 151
White Star Line, 4, 5, 6, 9, 10, 14, 23, 45, 123, 129, 168–69, 183, 184, 190, 194
Whitely, Steward Thomas, 142
Widener, George, 30, 64, 126, 224
Widener, Harry, 30, 69
Wilde, Chief Officer Henry Tighe, 41, 44, 63, 70–71, 73, 76, 90–91, 110, 125
 early career of, 52; misgivings about *Titanic*, 52; possible suicide of, 136
Willard, Constance, 101
Williams, Norris, 86, 141
Wilson, Asst. Engineer Bertie, 81
Wireless, 60–62, 117, 131, 161–62, 190
Witter, Steward James, 76, 102
Wolff, Gustav, 4
"Women and children first," ix, 92, 100, 105, 110, 115, 227
Woolner, Hugh, 55, 69, 101, 109, 125, 130, 146, 154, 223
Wright, Fred, 56, 90
Wright, Marion, 57, 65, 89, 118, 150, 232

Yarmouth Castle, 175
Yasbeck, Antoni, 79
Yasbeck, Mrs. (Celini), 79, 102, 151
Yates, Jay (alias "J. H. Rogers"), 54, 123
Young, Capt. A. H. F., 196
Young, Marie, 100

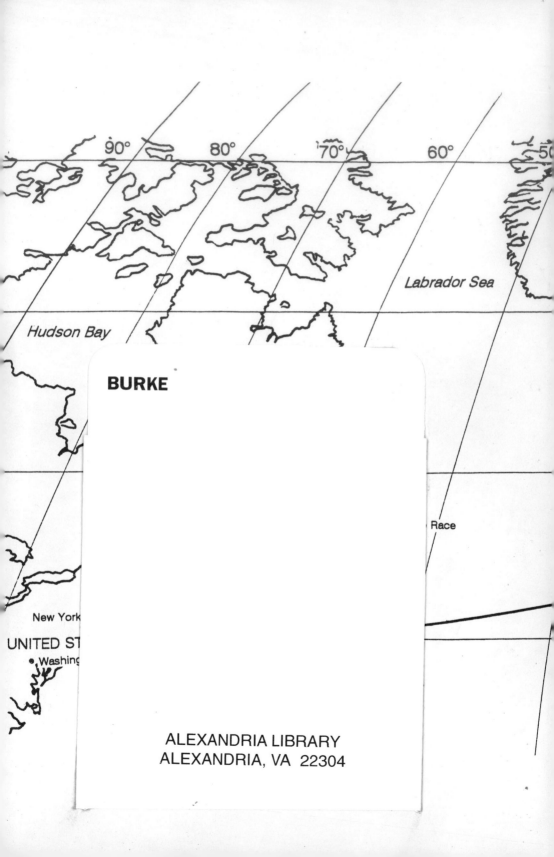

90° 80° 70° 60° 50°

Labrador Sea

Hudson Bay

BURKE

Race

New York

UNITED ST

• Washing